Expert Psychological Testimony for the Courts

THE CLAREMONT BOOK SERIES ON APPLIED SOCIAL PSYCHOLOGY

This series of volumes highlights important new developments on the leading edge of applied social psychology. Each volume focuses on one area in which social psychological knowledge is being applied to the resolution of social problems. Within that area, a distinguished group of authorities present chapters summarizing recent theoretical views and empirical findings, including the results of their own research and applied activities. An introductory chapter frames the material, and points out common themes and varied areas of practical applications. Thus, each volume brings trenchant new social psychological ideas, research results, and fruitful applications to bear on an area of current social interest. The volumes will be of value not only to practitioners and researchers, but also to students and lay people interested in this vital and expanding area of psychology.

Series books published by Lawrence Erlbaum Associates:

- *Reducing Prejudice and Discrimination*, edited by Stuart Oskamp (2000).
- *Mass Media and Drug Prevention: Classic and Contemporary Theories and Research*, edited by William D. Crano and Michael Burgoon (2002).
- *Evaluating Social Programs and Problems: Visions for the New Millennium*, edited by Stewart I. Donaldson and Michael Scriven (2003).
- *Processes of Community Change and Social Action*, edited by Allen M. Omoto (2005).
- *Applications of Nonverbal Communication*, edited by Ronald E. Riggio and Robert S. Feldman (2005).
- *Stigma and Group Inequality: Social Psychological Perspectives*, edited by Shana Levin and Colette van Laar (2006).
- *Expert Psychological Testimony for the Courts*, edited by Mark Costanzo, Daniel Krauss, and Kathy Pezdek (2007).

Expert Psychological Testimony for the Courts

Edited by

Mark Costanzo
Daniel Krauss
Claremont McKenna College

Kathy Pezdek
Claremont Graduate University

Routledge
Taylor & Francis Group
LONDON AND NEW YORK

First published 2007 by Lawrence Erlbaum Associates, Inc.

Published 2019 by Routledge
2 Park Square, Milton Park, Abingdon, Oxon OX14 4RN
52 Vanderbilt Avenue, New York, NY 10017

Routledge is an imprint of the Taylor & Francis Group, an informa business

Cover design by Kathryn Houghtaling Lacey

Library of Congress Cataloging-in-Publication Data

Expert psychological testimony for the courts / Mark Costanzo, Daniel Krauss, Kathy Pezdek, editors.
p. cm.
Includes bibliographical references and index.
ISBN 0-8058-5647-1 (cloth : alk. paper)
ISBN 0-8058-5648-X (pbk. : alk. paper)
ISBN 1-4106-1439-5 (e book)
1. Forensic psychology—United States. 2. Evidence, Expert—United States. 3. Forensic psychiatry—United States. 4. Criminal psychology—United States. I. Costanzo, Mark. II. Krauss, Daniel (Daniel A.) III. Pezdek, Kathy.
KF8922.E97 2006
347.73'67—dc22 2005037886
CIP

ISBN 13: 9780805856477 (hbk)
ISBN 13: 9780805856484 (pbk)

Contents

1

Varieties and Vagaries of Expert Psychological Testimony: An Introduction

Mark Costanzo
Daniel Krauss
Claremont McKenna College
Kathy Pezdek
Claremont Graduate University

During the past two decades, the frequency and range of expert testimony by psychologists have increased dramatically. Twenty years ago, nearly all such testimony involved clinical psychologists offering their assessments of particular defendants, especially in such areas as competence to stand trial and insanity. Although these traditional clinical areas remain important, courts now routinely hear expert testimony from cognitive, developmental, and social psychologists. The increasing prominence of expert psychological testimony appears to be the result of two factors: the rapidly expanding research base in areas of interest to the courts, and changes in the legal standards governing the admissibility of scientific evidence.

This book brings together leading scholars who have contributed to the scientific foundation of expert testimony and who have also served as expert witnesses. Chapter 2 provides an overview of issues surrounding the admissibility of expert testimony, and chapter 12 explores the ethical and practical dilemmas faced by psychological experts who testify in court. Each of the nine intervening chapters focuses on a different area of expert testimony. These areas include forensic identification evidence, interrogations and potentially false confessions, eyewitness memory and identification, sexual harassment, mitigation testimony in death penalty cases, the insanity defense, battered woman syndrome, prediction of future dangerousness, and child custody evaluations. For all but chapters 2 and 12, the authors were asked to address the following four questions:

1. What is typically the content of expert testimony on ______?
2. How strong is the scientific foundation for expert testimony on ________?
3. Is there research on how jurors respond to expert testimony on ________?
4. How might the legal system (e.g., procedures, standards, instructions) be modified in light of psychological research on ______?

The chapters that follow show the broad range and varied content of expert testimony offered by psychologists. In addition to reviewing the research evidence that serves as the basis for testimony, each chapter also explores how the courts have responded and should respond to research and expert testimony.

In chapter 2, Bruce Sales and Daniel Shuman examine how the courts decide whether expert testimony by psychologists will be admitted into evidence. Until the late 20th century, trial court evidentiary decisions had rarely been the basis for an appeal, let alone the grounds for a successful appeal. However, beginning in 1993, in a series of decisions addressing the admissibility of experts in federal court under the law of evidence, in *Daubert v. Dow Pharmaceutical, Inc.* (1993) and two subsequent cases, *General Electric v. Joiner* (1997) and *Kumho Tire Co. v. Carmichael* (1999), the Supreme Court precipitated more attention to the admissibility of expert testimony than had occurred in the preceding 250 years. Sales and Shuman consider the reasons for this change in emphasis and concern, the problems that the law revision has encountered and is likely to encounter in judicial administration, and potential solutions to these conceptual and practicable dilemmas.

In chapter 3, William Thompson and Simon Cole consider how psychological processes influence the interpretation of physical evidence such as fingerprints and DNA. Forensic identification evidence seeks to identify the source of a physical trace, such as biological material or the impression of a body or object. Forensic scientists often make source attributions—that is, determinations that items of physical evidence have (or might have) a common source. Expert testimony about source attributions is a common feature of modern criminal trials. Thompson and Cole examine the judgment and decision-making process experts use to make source attributions in various forensic disciplines, and identify four common ways experts characterize those determinations: simple match (no statistics), match plus statistics, qualitative assessment of certainty, and individualization. Their chapter discusses the strength of the scientific foundation for such testimony, comparing the relatively strong validation for DNA evidence with the weaker (or nonexistent) validation for other forensic disciplines. Thompson and Cole review research on jurors' reactions to forensic testimony and discuss possible legal reforms that could strengthen the quality of expert forensic testimony and reduce the likelihood that it will be presented in a misleading manner.

Chapter 4 explores research and testimony on police interrogation and false confessions. Recent exonerations of prisoners because of DNA evidence have revealed that the number of convictions based on false confessions is much higher than previously supposed. Mark Costanzo and Richard Leo explore why a false confession might appear credible to judges and jurors, and describe the types and dynamics of false confessions. They propose a person–situation analysis that describes how suspect risk factors (youth, mental retardation, mental illness, temporary impairments, and vulnerable personality) can interact with factors in the interrogation process (control, social isolation, certainty of guilt, minimization of culpability, and faulty interpretation of suspect behavior) to produce false confessions. Finally, Costanzo and Leo discuss the admissibility and content of expert testimony on interrogations and confessions and describe several ways of reducing both the occurrence and impact of false confessions.

Expert testimony on eyewitness memory and identification is the subject of chapter 5. During the past decade, it has become clear that faulty eyewitness evidence has been the major source of evidence used to convict innocent people who were later exonerated based on forensic DNA. Yet, ironically, jurors tend to find eyewitness testimony especially compelling. Kathy Pezdek argues that one way to assist jurors in evaluating eyewitness evidence more accurately is to present the testimony of an expert witness on the fallibility of eyewitness memory and identification. The role of the eyewitness expert witness is described, the scientific foundation for eyewitness expert testimony is summarized, and the response of typical jurors to such testimony is presented. Given the fertile nature of scientific research on the psychological factors that influence eyewitness memory, eyewitness expert witnesses are increasingly likely to be called on to consult with legal professionals and to testify in court. The chapter ends with several suggestions for modifying the legal system in light of the psychological research on eyewitness memory and identification.

Psychologists have played a role in many sexual harassment cases, testifying on such issues as the mental health consequences of sexual harassment, the social and organizational climate in which sexual harassment is most likely to occur, and the reasons why a target of such behavior might or might not complain about harassing behavior. In chapter 6, Maureen O'Connor examines this testimony and the research that supports it. Given the nature of the adversary system, psychologists testify on both sides of sexual harassment cases, often leading to a battle of the experts that can call into question the utility of the psychological information for those tasked with deciding the case. Some of these battles have been quite heated and raise interesting questions about the role of expert witnesses in the legal system. O'Connor examines the scope of the psychological knowledge that experts have brought to bear in sexual harassment cases, the limits of that knowledge, some of the important battles that have occurred in sexual harassment cases, and the extent to which such testimony affects juror decision making.

The presentation of mitigating evidence in the penalty phase of a capital trial is not meant to justify or diminish the significance of a murder, but to explain criminal behavior in a way that is useful to capital jurors making a sentencing decision. In chapter 7, Karen Salekin explains how mitigation evaluations are conducted and what information might be useful to jurors. The basic procedure consists of conducting a thorough investigation of the defendant's life in an effort to reveal influential factors in the developmental process. Despite robust findings regarding the viability of risk factors and protective factors, research has indicated that this information may not be conveyed very effectively to capital jurors. Jurors are not equipped to use this information, are confused by their legal charge in these proceedings, and lack effective guidance about how to weigh mitigating circumstances against aggravating circumstances. Other problems may also interfere with jurors' understanding of mitigation evidence. For example, the very process of death qualification may preclude a juror from considering mitigating circumstances, and jurors may view psychological testimony presented in these hearings as biased and therefore give it little weight. Salekin suggests ways that psychologists can inform courts of the research basis for psychological testimony and discusses potential ways that research in psychology can contribute to mitigation evidence in capital cases.

Expert testimony on the insanity defense is the subject of chapter 8. Norman Finkel examines the expert psychological testimony proffered in two recent high-profile insanity cases: those of Andrea Pia Yates and of Lee Boyd Malvo. In both cases, multiple experts testified, reaching not only divergent but highly suspect conclusions about each defendant's state of mind and whether he or she knew right from wrong. Finkel argues that expert psychological conclusions occur within a legal context that places constraints—some new ("the law's madness") and some quite old ("insanity's disconnect")—on the telling of the story. Thus, what may appear to be "the irresistible impulses of experts" to exceed scientific and legal constraints may not be the whole story. When expert testimony is examined within these larger contexts, certain types of "mistaken opinions" take on a new psychological and legal significance. In the end, the disciplines of psychology and law may be further apart with regard to the essence of insanity than they were in 1800. Consequently, creating a test for insanity that is consistent, coherent, valid, and worthy of respect seems to be a fading dream.

Because jurors often harbor misinformation about battered women and the battering context, expert testimony pertaining to battered woman syndrome is often admitted in trials of battered women who have killed their abusers. Regina Schuller and Gwen Jenkins explore this topic in chapter 9. Since its first entry into the courtroom in the late 1970s, battered woman syndrome testimony has been used with some frequency in the United States, Canada, Australia, and New Zealand. Although the admissibility of the testimony was heralded as a landmark victory for battered women (indeed, the impetus it provided for the courts' eventual acknowledgment of the obstacles confronting a battered woman's claim of self-defense represents a significant legal achievement), concerns regarding its use were quickly voiced. In particular, the testimony, which describes the common patterns found in battering relationships and its impact on a woman, has been criticized on the grounds that it focuses on the woman's passivity and portrays a singular profile of battered women. This view is at variance with the varied reactions and responses of battered women. Schuller and Jenkins first outline the content of the testimony, with particular attention given to its scientific validity. Following this, they review research on the impact of such testimony, and conclude with a reformulation of expert testimony that focuses on the social reality of the battered woman's situation as opposed to her psychological reactions to the abuse.

The U.S. legal system relies heavily on experts' ability to differentiate between individuals who will and will not commit future crimes. This occurs in a variety of legal settings including: capital sentencing, civil commitment of sexual offenders and the mentally ill, and pretrial detention of criminal defendants. In chapter 10, Daniel Krauss and Joel Lieberman explore testimony on future dangerousness. Expert predictions may be based on "unstructured clinical judgments" in which experts intuitively combine information that they believe will be predictive of future dangerousness, or on "actuarial" instruments that indicate exactly how specific empirically verified risk factors should be combined. Krauss and Lieberman discuss the scientific basis for both clinical and actuarial assessments and describe a more recent approach known as "guided professional judgments" that combines the benefits of clinical and actuarial approaches. Using expert testimony in capital murder trials as an exemplar, they discuss the legal basis for admitting future dangerousness testimony (under the *Frye* and *Daubert* standards) and the predictive limitations of such testimony. They also present a theoretical explanation for why jurors tend to inappropriately give greater weight to clinical testimony over actuarial testimony. They conclude with a discussion of policy implications and recommendations for procedural changes that courts could adopt to reduce problems associated with future dangerousness testimony.

When separating or divorcing parents are unable to reach an agreement regarding custody of their children, such decisions must be made by the court, in consideration of "the best interests of the children." In chapter 11, Randy Otto and David Martindale explore how this important decision is made. In many contested custody cases, judges and attorneys ask psychologists (as well as other mental health professionals) to assess members of the dissolving family. These requests are predicated on assumptions that: (a) such decisions involve consideration of a number of factors that are psychological in nature; (b) psychologists and other mental health professionals, as a function of their specialized knowledge, training, and experience, are able to offer information and insights about the parties and their children that the court might not otherwise have or consider; and (c) provision of this information will result in more accurate legal decisions and better outcomes for children and their parents. Otto and Martindale critique existing legal standards for child custody decision making, and propose more workable alternatives. Next, evaluation practices of mental health professionals who conduct such evaluations are discussed. Finally, the scientific basis for expert testimony offered by psychologists and other mental health professionals is reviewed, and recommendations for defensible practice are offered.

In chapter 12, Michael Saks and Richard Lanyon explore the dilemmas and ethical conflicts that often arise when experts testify in court. The task of being a competent and ethical expert witness is difficult for a variety of reasons. The most challenging dilemma is presented by the structure of the role of the expert, which confronts such witnesses with an inherent role conflict. This role evolved into its contemporary form as the legal process grew adversarial in the latter part of the 18th century, resulting in a shift of control over witness selection, preparation, and presentation from judges to advocates. First, Saks and Lanyon explore the ethical implications of this role structure. Next, they discuss the most serious and common pitfalls of being an expert witness—as a matter of both ethics and competence—and how to avoid them.

Together these chapters illuminate most of the areas in which psychologists serve as expert witnesses, highlight areas where there are gaps in our knowledge base, and suggest ways of enhancing the application of psychological research to important legal issues. The increased prominence of expert psychological testimony in the courts and the reduction of barriers between the disciplines of psychology and law are welcome opportunities that can benefit both fields and the vast number of people they serve.

REFERENCES

Daubert v. Dow Pharmaceutical, Inc., 509 U.S. 579 (1993).
Frye v. United States, 293 F. 1013 (D.C. Cir. 1923).
General Electric v. Joiner, 522 U.S. 136 (1997).
Kumho Tire Co. v. Carmichael, 526 U.S. 137 (1999).

2

Science, Experts, and Law: Reflections on the Past and the Future*

Bruce D. Sales
University of Arizona
Daniel W. Shuman
Southern Methodist University

The admissibility of expert testimony in court is an issue assigned to trial court judges. When their admissibility decisions are appealed, the traditional rules that govern the scope of appellate review of trial court evidentiary decisions has resulted in appellate court deference to trial court decisions about the admissibility of expert testimony. This is done for at least two reasons. First, it avoids destabilizing trial court decisions. A trial judge may make dozens of evidentiary decisions in a trial lasting a couple of days, and hundreds of decisions in trials that last for a week or more. If perfection in evidentiary rulings was demanded of trial judges, few trials would survive appellate scrutiny. Second, it recognizes that the dry trial transcript reviewed by the appellate court will not capture the full flavor of the circumstances to which the trial court's ruling responded. The

*Professor Shuman's work on the chapter was supported by a summer research grant from the Dedman School of Law.

consequence of this deference was that evidentiary decisions were rarely the basis for a successful appeal.

Indeed, the U.S. Supreme Court had only infrequently agreed to weigh in on expert evidence admissibility decisions from the time of its inception to the late 20th century. Although the Court's decisions have occasionally addressed the admissibility of expert testimony under the law of evidence, these decisions broke no new ground and manifested deference to the trial court's decision:

> Whether a witness is shown to be qualified or not as an expert is a preliminary question to be determined in the first place by the court; and the rule is, that if the court admits the testimony, then it is for the jury to decide whether any, and if any what, weight is to be given to the testimony. Cases arise where it is very much a matter of discretion with the court whether to receive or exclude the evidence; but the appellate court will not reverse in such a case, unless the ruling is manifestly erroneous. (*Spring Co. v. Edgar*, 1879, p. 658)

More recent Supreme Court decisions involving expert testimony concern the constitutional dimensions of criminal prosecution. *Barefoot v. Estelle* (1983) concluded that the U.S. Constitution does not prevent the state from offering a psychiatric prediction of the defendant's future dangerousness in a capital sentencing proceeding even if that testimony is challenged as unreliable. *Ake v. Oklahoma* (1985) concluded that when defendants have made a preliminary showing that their sanity at the time of the offense is likely to be a significant factor at trial and defendants lack financial resources to obtain expert psychiatric assistance, the constitution requires that access to an expert be provided by the state. And *Rock v. Arkansas* (1987) concluded that the exclusion of hypnotically refreshed testimony is an unconstitutional limit on defendants' rights to testify on their own behalf. Save for instances in which the U.S. Constitution was implicated, until the late 20th century, the Supreme Court left the matter of expert witness admissibility to the discretion of the trial courts. Then beginning in 1993, in a series of decisions addressing the admissibility of experts in federal court under the Federal Rules of Evidence (*Daubert v. Merrell Dow Pharmaceutical, Inc.*, 1993; *General Electric v. Joiner*, 1997; *Kumho Tire Co. v. Carmichael*, 1999), the Supreme Court paid more attention to the standards for the admissibility of expert testimony than it had in the preceding 250 years.

The purpose of this chapter is to address and evaluate the efficacy in this recent surge in legal activity. We accomplish our goals by first briefly introducing the way in which the rules for the admissibility developed.

We then consider the factors that drove the changing admissibility standards, and follow it with a critique of whether these standards accomplish their goal. Finally, we consider the potential role of psychology in aiding in the administration of this law and improving its implementation.

A BRIEF INTRODUCTION TO THE DEVELOPMENT OF THE RULES FOR ADMISSIBILITY

In both the state and federal courts, the rules that governed the admissibility of evidence at trial developed through a patchwork of judge-made, common law decision making. In an effort to modernize as well as clarify these rules, on January 2, 1975, Congress enacted the Federal Rules of Evidence, which codified the rules that govern the admissibility of evidence in the federal courts. Many states chose to adopt a version of the codified federal rules either verbatim or with minor variations (Bernstein & Jackson, 2004; Rossi, 1995).[1] Federal Rule of Evidence 702 governs the admissibility of expert testimony in the federal courts. Rule 702, as originally codified, provided: "If scientific, technical, or other specialized knowledge will assist the trier of fact to understand the evidence or to determine a fact in issue, a witness qualified as an expert by knowledge, skill, experience, training, or education, may testify thereto in the form of an opinion or otherwise."

One of the issues that was not clearly resolved by the codification of the federal rules was the threshold scrutiny that should be applied to expert testimony under 702 and related rules. In *Frye v. United States* (1923) the D.C. Court of Appeals articulated a test that directed the federal courts to ascertain whether disputed novel scientific methods had been generally accepted in the field to which they belonged. *Frye*'s test assumed that science evolved in a linear process: Reliable scientific theories would come to be generally accepted by experts in the field who could be counted on to provide expert testimony, and unreliable scientific theories would be discarded by the relevant community of experts and thus lack the general acceptance needed for admissibility. As *Frye* came to be more widely applied, the meaning of general acceptance more sharply questioned, and the wisdom of popularity as a proxy for validity

[1]The Supreme Court has limited authority to tell the states how to run their court systems in matters constitutionally allocated to the states. Thus, in the main, the states are free to develop their own rules for the admissibility of evidence unencumbered by U.S. Supreme Court's decisions.

and reliability more widely debated, the newly codified Federal Rules of Evidence made no reference to it, leaving some federal courts to infer that *Frye* remained good law and others to infer that it had been overruled (Giannelli, 1980).

Nearly 20 years later, in *Daubert v. Merrell Dow Pharmaceuticals* (1993), the U.S. Supreme Court first interpreted Federal Rules of Evidence 702 and addressed whether *Frye* (1923), which was not mentioned in the text or advisory committee notes to 702, survived codification of the federal rules. The Supreme Court held that the Federal Rules of Evidence governing the admissibility of expert evidence did not rest on the *Frye* test, but instead demanded independent assessment of the relevance and reliability of challenged expert evidence.[2] Having rejected *Frye*, the Supreme Court was left to fashion a standard to guide the trial court's implementation of the relevance and reliability requirements. Relying on Karl Popper's (1989) approach to science grounded in falsifiability, the Supreme Court articulated a number of considerations to assist trial courts in assessing the proffered evidence's evidentiary reliability, including its falsifiability, peer review, error rate, and general acceptance.

As an interpretation of the Federal Rules of Evidence, the decision bound only federal courts. Although a number of state courts that had adopted versions of the Federal Rules of Evidence chose to follow *Daubert* (1993) or their interpretation of it, they were not constitutionally mandated to do so. Therefore, admissibility of the same evidence may differ from jurisdiction to jurisdiction, with specific expert evidence admissible in one court but not another. Despite this, there is one overarching consistency that is self-evident. The last 20 years has witnessed more attention to the admissibility of expert evidence than the preceding 250 years. Why did this occur?

FACTORS DRIVING THE CHANGING STANDARDS IN THE ADMISSION OF EXPERT TESTIMONY

Although it is not possible to ascertain cause and effect with any scientific precision, it is likely that at least three factors have contributed to

[2]Federal Rule of Evidence 103 provides that objections to the admissibility of evidence that are not timely and specifically raised are waived. In practice, this means that only offers of expert evidence that are objected to will be considered by the trial judge. If opposing counsel fails to identify a potential objection or chooses not to raise it for tactical reasons, the testimony is admitted and the issue of believability or credibility for the fact finder is all that remains.

the rethinking of the admissibility of expert testimony in the law of evidence: the changing perceptions by scientists of what is expertise, the changing externalities affecting experts, and the changing externalities affecting the law. The order in which we address these factors should not be understood to imply our belief about the relative importance of each factor.

Changing Scientific Expertise

One likely reason for changing legal standards for expert evidence admissibility is to respond to the exponential growth in the amount and quality of scientific information. Scientists are keenly aware of this growth, particularly as it is manifested in the growth of scientific journals. There was an estimated 250% increase in the number of scientific journals between 1960 and 1995. There are now between 80,000 and 100,000 scientific journals globally (Tenopir & King, 2000). "Overall journal growth characteristics clearly show the predominance of 3.3% [or more] compound annual growth" (Mabe & Amin, 2001, p. 147). This annualized increase reflects the growth and specialization of scholarly information and its availability. Although not all newly published research is excellent or even good, there can be no question that this growth reflects the fact that more detailed scientific knowledge has developed, and there is more to master in any subfield of science, than ever before. In addition, over time new research methods, statistical methods, and research technologies have evolved, making the corpus of expert knowledge more sophisticated. Thus, the acquisition of a doctoral degree does not automatically qualify one as an expert on any particular topic.

Frustrated by their perception of the lack of scientific expertise on the part of some expert witnesses (Loftus, 1993); the legal system's failure to draw careful distinctions about the quality and the relevance of available research (e.g., Krauss & Sales, 2000); and the impact on resulting legal decisions; many scientists and scientific organization have sought to raise the quality of science relied on in the courts. Their efforts have taken multiple tacks: writing in legal journals (Anderson, Parsons, & Rennie, 2001); offers of independent expertise from scientific associations to the courts (American Association for the Advancement of Sciences, 2005); and filing of amicus briefs with the courts (Bruck & Ceci, 1995). These efforts have not fallen on deaf ears. Recent case law contains numerous examples of judges (*In re Corning, Inc. Securities Litigation*, 2004) and lawyers taking a more aggressive approach to the application of science in the courtroom (e.g., *DeLuca by DeLuca v. Merrell Dow Pharmaceuticals, Inc.*, 1990).

Changing Externalities Affecting Experts

Notwithstanding the rising scientific tide, another set of factors has contributed to the perception of expert witnesses providing less reliable evidence and a consequential call to raise the threshold for the admissibility of their testimony. Those factors are the financial and the nonfinancial stakes of courtroom battles.

A panoply of legal developments have resulted in a high demand for expert testimony. Courts have recognized a host of new claims (e.g., products liability claims). For example, psychologists are now asked to testify on the effectiveness of product labels and warnings (*Milanese v. Rust-Oleum Corp.*, 2001). Courts have also recognized new damages. For example, whereas earlier case law disallowed damages for mental and emotional harm as the result of a negligently caused psychological injury, courts now increasingly allow such damages, increasing the need for testimony by psychologists (*Dillon v. Legg*, 1968). Finally, courts have recognized new procedural devices (e.g., multidistrict and class action joinder rules) that vastly expand the number of cases and their value (*Jenson v. Eveleth Taconite Co.*, 1997). One result of these developments is an increased demand for experts who are offered lucrative compensation, often vastly in excess of what they could make in their chosen profession. For mental health professionals, this disparity is exacerbated by managed care's cost-control efforts. Because most experts are selected by attorneys whose job it is to present the strongest case for their client, and experts who disappoint their attorney or employer are unlikely to be retained again or develop a favorable reputation, the financial threats to the reliability of the expert testimony are profound.

Moreover, as the Fifth Circuit Court of Appeals noted in *In re Air Crash Disaster at New Orleans, La.* (1986): "Many experts are members of the academic community who supplement their teaching salaries with consulting work. We know from our judicial experience that many such able persons present studies and express opinions that they might not be willing to express in an article submitted to a refereed journal of their discipline or in other contexts subject to peer review" (p. 1234). The perceptions of judges about the evidentiary reliability of the information presented by experts have been negatively affected by financial pressures that compromise the accuracy of some expert testimony and experts who advocate for a cause rather than present expert information. This has resulted in calls for changes in the admissibility standard for expert testimony to protect jurors from junk science in the courtroom.

In addition to these financial tensions that threaten the reliability of expert testimony, other nonfinancial factors pose a substantial threat to reliability. Our courtrooms have become battlefields for important social and political issues including school prayer, abortion, and homosexual marriage. Although the appropriate role of the courts in deciding these battles is a matter for constitutional law scholars (Cox, 1987), the reliability of the expert information on which courts rely when they entertain cases presenting such issues is appropriate for examination here. One nonfinancial factor that can affect the reliability of expert testimony is the extent to which experts perceive their role as an advocate for the retaining party rather than purely an advocate for their expert knowledge. The extent to which an expert adopts the former role (e.g., because of passion for a cause) threatens the reliability of the expert information on which courts rely. A prime example of this issue is information provided to the courts regarding battered woman's syndrome. Faigman and Wright (1997) showed how a morally driven quest to help women who have been abused by their partners can corrupt the judicial fact-finding process. Even when an expert chooses to be an advocate for expert knowledge, the selectivity of an attorney's use of expert testimony may result in the fact finder not receiving a complete representation of what the science teaches.

Changing Externalities Affecting the Law

A number of influences on the standard for expert admissibility are not the result of factors directly addressed to experts, but rather are the result of factors affecting the way we view the role of the legal system in our society. For example, expert witness admissibility has found itself caught up in the battle over tort reform, in which the advocates' goals are decreasing or increasing the availability of tort damage claim awards for untoward events. Berger (2001) argued that the admissibility decisions judges make are influenced in some cases by the preferences they have for certain values. When a judge values most highly the right of injured victims to have their day in court, then the judge will be more liberal in admitting plaintiffs' experts than if the judge values the accuracy of proffered information most highly. When a judge evinces the latter predilection, some plaintiffs will be prevented from pursuing their grievance because they lack expert testimony necessary to prove their case (Huber, 1988). Value choices also permeate the decisions that state drafters of evidence rules make when crafting the admissibility rules.

Integral to this debate is the assumption made about the behavior of juries. Tort reform proponents who support raising the threshold for the admissibility of experts posit, or assume, that juries are beguiled by unreliable but persuasive experts (Huber, 1988). Commentators (e.g., Gottesman, 1998) and courts (e.g., *Logerquist v. McVey*, 2000) less sympathetic to this goal of tort reform evince greater faith in the common sense of juries: "Reduction or obliteration of the jury function may be seen by some as the ultimate tort reform, but it is one prohibited by our organic law" (*Logerquist*, p. 130).

Another example of a substantive debate about the law that is principally not about experts, but has spilled over into expert admissibility, arises from the insanity defense. Unlike the prior example on tort reform, which addresses the reliability threshold for the admission of expert testimony, this example uses a threshold based on the form of the opinion, which is addressed in an amendment to the Federal Rules of Evidence.[3] In the criminal prosecution for an attempt on the life of then-President Reagan, John W. Hinckley, Jr., the defendant, was acquitted on the basis of insanity. In response to a trial marked by contradictory conclusions from eminent forensic experts, and to oft-repeated calls over time for the elimination or narrowing of the insanity defense, Congress narrowed the defense but did not eliminate it in the federal courts.

> (b) No expert witness testifying with respect to the mental state or condition of a defendant in a criminal case may state an opinion or inference as to whether the defendant did or did not have the mental state or condition constituting an element of the crime charged or of a defense thereto. Such ultimate issues are matters for the trier of fact alone.

These requirements are in addition to the requirements imposed by Rule 702 (qualifications and reliability) and Rule 703 (permissible bases):

> The facts or data in the particular case upon which an expert bases an opinion or inference may be those perceived by or made known to the expert at or before the hearing. If of a type reasonably relied upon by experts in the particular field in forming opinions or inferences upon the subject, the facts or data need not be admissible in evidence in order for the opinion or inference to be

[3]The requirements of Federal Rule of Evidence 704(b) addressing the form of the testimony:

> admitted. Facts or data that are otherwise inadmissible shall not be disclosed to the jury by the proponent of the opinion or inference unless the court determines that their probative value in assisting the jury to evaluate the expert's opinion substantially outweighs their prejudicial effect. (Rule 703)

One aspect of this revision was a revival of the much assailed ultimate issue rule. This common law rule of evidence, which once prohibited the admissibility of expert opinions that embraced the ultimate issue in the case the jury was asked to decide, was premised on a fear that allowing experts to testify on the ultimate issue would usurp the function of the jury. The Federal Rules of Evidence rejected the common law rule and allowed ultimate issue testimony,[4] when the rules were originally codified. The drafters of the Federal Rules relied on modern evidence law scholars who decried the confusion created over what actually was the ultimate issue in the case and championed the ability of the jury to reject unsupported conclusory testimony. In 1984, when Congress narrowed the insanity defense in response to Hinckley's insanity acquittal, it added a new ultimate issue rule to the Federal Rules of Evidence (Rule 704(b)) that applied only to mental health experts testifying about mental responsibility issues in criminal cases (i.e., the insanity defense), although the repeal of the common law ultimate issue rule was left intact in all other cases.[5]

DAUBERT'S FUTURE

Despite these factors driving the changing standards in the admission of expert testimony, and *Daubert*'s (1993) response to many of the questions posed by the text of the Federal Rules of Evidence, the response found in *Daubert* and its progeny has left much to be desired and poses numerous challenges for *Daubert*'s future. *Daubert* interpreted Federal Rule of

[4]"Testimony in the form of an opinion or inference otherwise admissible is not objectionable because it embraces an ultimate issue to be decided by the trier of fact." (Fed. R. Evid. 704 as originally promulgated)

[5](a) Except as provided in subdivision (b), testimony in the form of an opinion or inference otherwise admissible is not objectionable because it embraces an ultimate issue to be decided by the trier of fact.

(b) No expert witness testifying with respect to the mental state or condition of a defendant in a criminal case may state an opinion or inference as to whether the defendant did or did not have the mental state or condition constituting an element of the crime charged or of a defense thereto. Such ultimate issues are matters for the trier of fact alone. (Fed. R. Evid. 704 as amended)

Evidence 702 that governs the admissibility of expert evidence, and provided "general observations" (p. 593) that may be more appropriately described as pragmatic considerations about the rule to aid in its implementation. We know that these decisions apply with equal force to the admissibility of all proffered experts in the federal courts, and have been adopted in whole or in part by most of the state courts (Bernstein & Jackson, 2004; Rossi, 1995). And we know that the appellate courts have been instructed to give deference to trial court admissibility decisions. One might expect that only the details of application of these standards remain to be fleshed out. However, where this process will or should lead is less clear. Often courts and commentators view the new law as monolithic (i.e., the bar for admissibility is raised or lowered), but that does not encourage thoughtful debate or analysis (Cole, 2004; La Morte, 2003). Rather there are a host of pending and nascent issues that will determine the next decade of expert admissibility decisions (Sales & Shuman, 2005).

Guiding the Trial Courts

As noted earlier, the current articulation and application of standards leave trial courts with little guidance about when and how to apply *Daubert* (1993) factors:

> A trial judge determining the admissibility of an ... expert's testimony may consider one or more of the specific *Daubert* factors. The emphasis on the word "may" reflects *Daubert's* description of the *Rule 702* inquiry as "a flexible one." *509 U.S., at 594, 113 S.Ct. 2786.* The *Daubert* factors do *not* constitute a definitive checklist or test, *id., at 593, 113 S.Ct. 2786*, and the gatekeeping inquiry must be tied to the particular facts, *id., at 591, 113 S.Ct. 2786.* Those factors may or may not be pertinent in assessing reliability, depending on the nature of the issue, the expert's particular expertise, and the subject of his testimony. (*Kumho Tire Co. v. Carmichael, 1999, p. 138*)

This absence of guidance presents a host of problems for trial courts.

If the *Daubert* (1993) factors may be applied optionally by trial courts, and if these courts can also apply any other factors that they think appropriate consistent with Federal Rule of Evidence 702, then there is the potential for a substantial disparity in outcomes in cases presenting similar types of expert evidence. By way of example, this is exactly what occurred in two cases relying on the *Daubert* factors dealing with expert testimony about recovered repressed memories: *State v. Hungerford* (1997) and *Shahzade v. Gregory* (1996). One might expect that the same criteria applied to the same science would yield the same result. But although *Hungerford* and *Shahzade* both applied *Daubert*, they reached different outcomes on the admissibility of recovered repressed memories based on significant differences in the rigor in which they reviewed the underlying science. Providing crucial guidance to the trial courts while still preserving their discretion is a formidable problem. Apart from the legalistic reasons that encourage us to treat like cases alike, asking non-scientifically trained judges facing crowded dockets to sort through a mass of competing information to evaluate validity and reliability thresholds without detailed guidance from appellate courts invites difficulties.

Another challenge to uniformity in the judicial implementation of the rules is that they are tools to implement a larger agenda. In their implementation of rules for the admissibility of expert evidence, trial courts are guided by Federal Rule of Evidence 102, which articulates the overarching goals for all of the rules of evidence:[6] fairness, efficiency, truth, and justice. Yet, a careful review of the post-*Daubert* (1993) case law reveals that these goals are not applied consistently by the courts in its implementation (Sales & Shuman, 2005).

Consider, for example, the first goal, fairness. One requirement of fairness is that courts, when reaching an admissibility judgment about expert information, proceed consistently from case to case. Yet in practice this does not always occur. Courts look to three very different sources of expert information with potentially vastly different levels of validity: primary, secondary, and tertiary. Primary sources refer to the actual reports of the science and are what scientists rely on when judging the validity of a particular piece of information. Secondary sources are reviews conducted by other experts and, although they are used by scientists, run the risk of introducing reviewer bias into the presentation of the science. It is axiomatic that scientists would prefer to read the primary source rather than the secondary source in reaching their judgments. Tertiary sources are those that are authored by lawyers (e.g., reviews of science in law reviews) and judges (e.g., prior court opinions) and provide the least assurance of accuracy, at least to scientist observers. Because courts considering the same admissibility issue (e.g., should expert testimony about repressed memories be admitted) rely on different sources of information,

[6]"These rules shall be construed to secure fairness in the administration, elimination of unjustifiable expense and delay, and promotion of growth and development of the law of evidence to the end that the truth may be ascertained and proceedings justly determined" (Federal Rule of Evidence 102).

the result is inconsistent decisions that violate the goal of fairness (Sales & Shuman, 2005).

Just as the case law is strewn with examples of inconsistent approaches to sources of scientific information (i.e., unfairness), so it is also littered with examples of inconsistent application among courts favoring one goal over another. Any decision to permit a case premised on a complex scientific issue about which there is some disagreement to proceed to trial creates inefficiencies, no matter how just it may be to do so. The breast implant litigation (*In re Breast Implant Cases*, 1996) presented complex questions of causation that were costly and time consuming to resolve, yet necessary for a just resolution of the plaintiffs' claims against the defendants. What level of doubt or scientific disagreement justifies what level of time and expense to address these issues? The cases simply do not address such issues, even though courts do issue summary judgment decisions and ration the time the lawyers receive during the trial (e.g., to present their case in chief). The challenge for appellate courts is to provide guidance about how to balance the goals (e.g., understanding what time and expense can be justified to reach a just result).

The guidance dilemma is made more complex than is apparent because the goals of fairness, efficiency, truth, and justice each have multiple meanings. Truth in Federal Rule of Evidence 102 can be interpreted to refer to accuracy, the result of the adversarial battle, or a system-wide goal (Sales & Shuman, 2005). Truth as accuracy refers to the ascertainment of a fact that is demonstrably accurate. Truth as the result of an adversarial battle refers to the process for fact finding embedded in the adversary system, which places the responsibility for discovering and presenting evidence on those with the greatest stake in the outcome. And, truth as a system-wide goal refers to a concern with accuracy in fact finding across cases. There are cases that support the courts' use of each of these different definitions of truth even though they may result in different outcomes. For example, consider truth as the result of an adversarial battle:

> From this perspective, "when a trial court … rules that an expert's testimony is reliable, this does not necessarily mean that contradictory expert testimony is unreliable." A judge who embraces this approach may "think that an expert has good grounds to hold the opinion that he or she does even though the judge thinks that the opinion is incorrect." This approach is in opposition to viewing truth as an absolute discernable state of knowledge on which the judge has a monopoly. (Sales & Shuman, p. 85)

Under this definition of truth, judges will be more likely to let the tactical decisions of the trial attorneys dictate the admissibility of the expert testimony. This bias in favor of deferring to the litigants' tactical decisions is found in the words of a federal judge addressing an expert's admissibility: "Absent affidavit or other evidence to suggest that the methodology underlying Dr. Goldstein's diagnosis is scientifically invalid in this case—and there has been absolutely no such evidence proffered by the Government—the court concludes that Dr. Goldstein's testimony is admissible" *United States v. Sturman*, 1998, p. *6). The challenge for providing effective guidance for the courts then is to understand the multiple meanings of each of the Federal Rule of Evidence 102 goals and how each of those definitions should be prioritized within and across goals.

Principled Application of the Admissibility Standard

Some of the most damning criticism of the application of *Daubert* (1993) is that the rigor of its application has been unprincipled and colored by partisan goals:

> Some [judges] endorse science's strict standard because they doubt that [toxic tort] ... litigation serves a useful social purpose. Others point to the need to deter future risks and to compensate those exposed to excessive risk through no fault of their own.... The point is that whatever standard of proof is chosen—whether by the scientific or legal community—reflects and furthers the policy objectives that the particular discipline is seeking to achieve. When judges exclude scientific evidence in some of the particular circumstances ... their decisions reflect a policy choice; they are not making value-free determinations that are the inevitable consequence of a system of rational proof. (Berger, 2001, pp. 301–302)

Whether it has been the result of tactical choices made by lawyers about the cases in which to challenge the scientific reliability of evidence under *Daubert* and its progeny, the failure of lawyers to identify an appropriate challenge, or the biases of trial judges ruling on these challenges, *Daubert* has been differentially applied.

Daubert (1993) has been raised and most rigorously applied in toxic tort and products liability cases (Shuman, 2003), but less so in other types of litigation (Shuman & Sales, 1999). The abuse of discretion standard for appellate review allows the problem to perpetuate because of the absence of effective appellate review. When courts apply rigorous threshold scrutiny in some classes of cases but not others, it implies that science is being used to achieve certain political ends. This undercuts the value and perception of science as it is applied in society's most visible institution—the law. It also implies that some cases are simply more important than others. Why do courts allow, for example, clinical opinion to be admitted in child custody litigation but would exclude such opinion in toxic tort cases? Whatever one may think about a ranking of case importance, custody and visitation cases involving the future of our children, in which *Daubert* and its progeny are rarely applied, would seem to deserve a higher ranking than cases that are merely about money (e.g., personal injury cases) in which *Daubert* and its progeny are more often applied. For the legitimacy of the law and science, it is important to respond to this challenge.

Is *Daubert* Practicable?

Unlike *Frye* (1923), which deferred to the relevant profession, *Daubert* (1993) demanded that federal trial courts ruling on a challenge to an expert's admissibility independently determine evidentiary reliability. No better explanation of the fear that this would impose an unreasonable burden on the federal trial court judiciary exists than that contained in Chief Justice Rehnquist's concurring and dissenting opinion in *Daubert:*

> The Court speaks of its confidence that federal judges can make a "preliminary assessment of whether the reasoning or methodology underlying the testimony is scientifically valid and of whether that reasoning or methodology properly can be applied to the facts in issue." Ante, at 12. The Court then states that a "key question" to be answered in deciding whether something is "scientific knowledge" "will be whether it can be (and has been) tested." Ante, at 12. Following this sentence are three quotations from treatises, which speak not only of empirical testing, but one of which states that "the criterion of the scientific status of a theory is its falsifiability, or refutability, or testability," ante, pp. 12–13.
>
> I defer to no one in my confidence in federal judges; but I am at a loss to know what is meant when it is said that the scientific status of a theory depends on its "falsifiability," and I suspect some of them will be, too.
>
> I do not doubt that Rule 702 confides to the judge some gatekeeping responsibility in deciding questions of the admissibility of proffered expert testimony. But I do not think it imposes on them either the obligation or the authority to become amateur scientists in order to perform that role. I think the Court would be far better advised in this case to decide only the questions presented, and to leave the further development of this important area of the law to future cases. (*Daubert*, pp. 600–601)

Was Chief Justice Rehnquist's prediction accurate? Have *Daubert* (1993) and its progeny resulted in an impracticable test given its demands and the lack of scientific and technical background of the federal and state judiciaries? One way to measure judicial capacity to implement *Daubert* is to ask whether trial judges understand scientific methods and data-analytic techniques sufficiently well to engage competently in a *Daubert* analysis. Attempts to test the ability of judges to define the scientific terminology at the heart of *Daubert* (e.g., falsifiability) provide evidence that reinforces Chief Justice Rehnquist's pessimism about *Daubert*'s practicability. For example, Dobbin et al. (2002), in a survey of state trial judges, found that only 6% understand the scientific meaning of one of the *Daubert* criteria—falsifiability.

There are also numerous decisions in which judges make fundamental scientific errors in evaluating evidentiary reliability. For example, in *State v. Anderson* (1994), the New Mexico Supreme Court was faced with an offer of DNA evidence from the Federal Bureau of Investigation. Although the court applied *Daubert* (1993), it focused its attention on whether the DNA analysis performed by the government agency was peer reviewed, rather than directly judging the validity of the technique. Unfortunately, there are numerous reasons why peer review is not equivalent to validation (Sales & Shuman, 2005). Peer review may be a vehicle to assist in collegial scrutiny of validation, but without knowing what the review comprised, it provides no assurance of validation. To compound the error in the court's logic, it concluded that presentations at "scientific conferences, workshops and other forums for the exchange of ideas and through the dissemination of unpublished and non-peer- reviewed writings" (*State v. Anderson*, p. 44) constituted peer review. Although conferences are excellent fora for sharing one's research with others, they are not intended to substitute for a rigorous analysis of the validity of one's work, nor is time typically allotted to conference participants to allow such a review to occur.

But this negative picture of *Daubert*'s (1993) practicability is not uniform. There are numerous instances of thoughtful scientific analysis by trial judges. In *Valentine v. Pioneer Chlor Alkali Co.* (1996), for example, the plaintiffs brought suit for the neurotoxic effects of breathing in chlorine produced by the defendant. The trial court was faced with a defense challenge to the plaintiff's expert's opinion that relied on an article that had not been published in a peer-reviewed scientific journal. Rather than summarily rejecting the opinion, the trial judge engaged in a thoughtful critique of the methodology that formed the basis for the article:

> In summary, Dr. Kilburn's study suffers from very serious flaws. He took no steps to eliminate selection bias in the study group, he failed to identify the background rate for the observed disorders in the Henderson community, he

> failed to control for potential recall bias, he simply ignored the lack of reliable dosage data, he chose a tiny sample size, and he did not attempt to eliminate so-called confounding factors which might have been responsible for the incidence of neurological disorders in the subject group. As a result, his conclusions that the plaintiffs exposure to atmospheric chlorine caused their neurological disorders cannot be said to be derived from acceptable scientific methodology. (*Valentine*, p. 678)

Although the evidence on *Daubert*'s (1993) practicability is mixed, what is clear is that *Daubert*'s implementation will require assistance if it is to be effective, both in the form of appellate guidance and judicial scientific education (Sales & Shuman, 2005). How that should be accomplished and what it should contain are issues that require future attention. *Daubert*, *General Electric* (1997), and *Kumho* (1999) are only the beginning of the answer to the question of how federal judges (or state courts that follow them) should address the relevance and reliability of expert testimony, not the final answer.

What Does the *Daubert* Trilogy Mean for Clinical Information?

Daubert (1993) spoke to the admissibility of scientific expert testimony. It did not address the offer of clinical opinion as that issue was not before the Supreme Court. In *Kumho* (1999), the Supreme Court was faced with the question of how trial courts should assess the admissibility of nonscientific information, and held that *Daubert* should be applied to proffers of all expert testimony. Although courts have flexibility in deciding which if any of the *Daubert* factors should be applied, they also have the option of applying any other factors that they think will help them determine the evidentiary reliability of the expert information. The question for psychology and a host of other professions is what criteria should be applied to assess the evidentiary reliability of clinical opinions. Although the accuracy of scientific information can be evaluated by assessing the validity of the scientific research from which the results or information were derived, it is difficult to determine the validity of clinical opinion because it was derived from professional experience and not subjected to scientific testing to determine the validity of the resulting opinion.

This distinction poses a dilemma for the courts. If they apply *Daubert* (1993) and its progeny rigorously, clinical opinion testimony as a class will be denied admissibility because of problems demonstrating falsifiability, error rates, and so on. This would leave the courts without expert guidance in deciding many kinds of cases (e.g., custody and visitation) that to date have relied on clinical opinion experts. If courts seek to admit the best of this class of expert testimony, they are left to rely on an assessment of the scientific reliability (consistency) of the approach used to reach the opinion with that of like experts. If the admissibility of clinical opinion testimony is to be based on the practitioner's professional experience, all the court can ask is whether like practitioners would use the same approach when reaching an opinion and if they would reach a similar conclusion. This is remarkably similar to the rejected *Frye* (1923) general acceptance test.

This approach describes the prevailing current trial court practice to clinical opinion testimony. In an attempt to make the comparison to like experts more rigorous, some recent decisions, particularly those dealing with differential diagnosis, have looked at the specific steps that clinical experts use to derive their opinions. For example, the Fifth Circuit Court of Appeals in *Moore v. Ashland Chemical, Inc.* (1997) listed the following steps that required consideration: whether the physician (a) personally examined the plaintiff; (b) personally took a detailed medical history from the plaintiff; (c) used differential diagnosis and etiology in reaching his or her conclusion; (d) reviewed the tests, reports and opinions of other doctors; (e) reviewed other facts or data reasonably relied on by medical experts in forming opinions or inferences as to medical causation; (f) referred to medical literature; and (g) utilized the doctor's training and experience in reaching his or her judgment. Unfortunately, these steps do not address the validity of the clinical opinions (Sales & Shuman, 2005). Personal examinations, history taking, reviewing other records, reading clinical literature, and using one's professional experience are subjective efforts that do not guarantee an accurate representation of a patients' medical or psychological problems. Even reviewing the results of prior medical tests is suspect because practitioners rarely spend the time to assess the validity of those tests or the conclusions drawn from those results by other practitioners. Moreover, the accuracy of the conclusion that results from combining such information is not empirically tested so there is no way to know its validity. Not surprisingly, the accuracy of differential diagnosis has been vigorously questioned in the courts (compare *Westberry v. Gislaved Gummi AB*, 1999, with *Glastetter v. Novartis Pharms. Corp.*, 2001).

The concern over the criteria that ought to govern the admissibility of clinical opinion testimony is not one that will disappear easily or quickly. With a greater focus on science and its validity, courts cannot help but ask what justifies admitting unvalidated expert opinions. But the judge who excludes opinion testimony risks leaving the jury without factual guidance when rendering its decision.

PSYCHOLOGY'S ROLE IN *DAUBERT'S* FUTURE

Finally, responding to the issues noted in the prior section should not just be the concern of the courts. Psychology also can play a positive role in shaping the implementation of the law of admissibility for expert evidence.

Guiding the Trial Courts

As we discussed earlier, the *Daubert* (1993) trilogy does not encourage appellate courts to provide specific guidance to trial courts both as a consequence of the abuse of discretion standard for appellate review and the discretion afforded trial courts to choose which factors to apply to scrutinize the evidentiary reliability of a challenged expert. This judicial gap invites professional organizations to provide guidance to the trial courts. Although professional organizations cannot dictate to courts what evidence should be admitted, they are uniquely situated to inform courts regarding professional gold standards. For example, although the science underlying psychological custody evaluations is an issue that has generated much debate (Shuman, 1997), the American Psychological Association's *Guidelines for Child Custody and Divorce Proceedings* (1994) make clear that if psychologists have anything worth hearing comparing the ability of competing parents, the evaluation requires the examining psychologist to evaluate both parents. This guideline provides practicable guidance to trial courts about psychology's perception of threshold reliability requirements (*District of Columbia v. Wilson*, 1998).

This is but one example where psychology might exert effort in developing consensus guidelines about the state of the science and practice. Although such guidelines reflect secondary interpretations (as opposed to the primary literature) of the state of the field, if the consensus is from an appropriate representation of people truly expert in the field, then its advice arguably is worthy of serious consideration by the courts. These documents will need to be periodically updated for them to remain authoritative because of the evolving state of scientific research.

Given the logistical demands in mounting such efforts, we suggest that organizations such as the American Psychological Association and the American Psychological Society are in an excellent position to oversee them (Sales & Shuman, 2005).

Principled Application of the Admissibility Standard

As we noted before, whatever the merits of the *Daubert* (1993) approach to admissibility, there has been harsh criticism leveled arguing that it has been implemented in an unprincipled manner favoring certain classes of litigants. Psychology has no control over when the behavior of judges and lawyers might result in unprincipled application of *Daubert*, but it does have control over the behavior of psychologists. To the extent that psychologists as experts are willing to provide only competent expert testimony for either side, they go a long way toward ensuring that one class of litigants is not favored over another. Psychologists whose conduct as experts violates professional norms for competence should be subject to professional disciplinary action that is as aggressive as that applied to unethical behavior with patients or research subjects (*Budwin v. American Psychological Association*, 1994).

One way to increase the likelihood of competent testimony is to create a mechanism whereby psychologists know that their expert testimony will be scrutinized. Peer review of expert testimony lets psychologists know that their testimonial behavior will be scrutinized by other experts, and offers a unique opportunity for constructive criticism of expert behavior on the witness stand. Such review could occur through publication in existing journals or through creation of a new journal devoted to expert evidence in litigation (Lempert, 2001; Sales & Shuman, 2005; Sales & Simon, 1993).

Is *Daubert* Practicable?

As we noted previously, *Daubert* (1993) demands of trial judges an independent determination of evidentiary reliability. Pointing to empirical surveys of the lack of scientific acumen of the trial courts and anecdotal examples of courts misunderstanding basic scientific concepts, critics challenge *Daubert*'s practicability. But practicability is a moving target. Even if the critics of judges' knowledge of scientific concepts are correct, that is not an excuse for psychology and other fields of science from teaching, writing, and testifying with an eye to raising the scientific knowledge of the trial court judiciary.

Psychologists should become involved as presenters in federal and state continuing education meetings for judges and lawyers. Their presentations offer the potential to educate the judiciary and the lawyers who practice before them about what constitutes science and what are accepted methods and data analytic techniques in science, as well as provide broad surveys of the current state of knowledge in various substantive areas of psychology and the limitations of that knowledge. Psychologists also should present this information in some of their writings that are directed toward the bench and the bar (e.g., Faigman, Kaye, Saks, & Sanders, 2002). Where these writings are not the result of a consensus conference, the individual authors bear a heavy responsibility to represent accurately and explain fully any ongoing debates within the scientific community. Finally, psychologists should recognize that in their capacity as expert witnesses, from their initial contact with an attorney to their in-court presentation on the witness stand, they have an important responsibility to play a role as educators of judges and lawyers about the methodology of science and scientific knowledge.

What Does the *Daubert* Trilogy Mean for Clinical Information?

Although some scientists disapprove (e.g., Grove & Barden, 1999), courts applying *Daubert* (1993) and its progeny have not barred the admissibility of clinical information even though it is typically impossible to accurately assess its validity. And, there is nothing in the case law to suggest that this state of affairs is likely to change. What can psychologists do to increase the evidentiary reliability of this category of testimony? Forensic clinical psychologists are aware of the methods and procedures they employ to respond to issues raised in legal proceedings. Where these techniques lack demonstrable relevance or reliability, they are best situated to frame issues for research and strongly encourage the conduct of that research.

REFERENCES

Ake v. Oklahoma, 470 U.S. 68 (1985).

American Association for the Advancement of Sciences. (n.d.). *Court appointed scientific experts: A demonstration project*. Retrieved February 10, 2005 from http://www.aaas.org/spp/case/case.ht

American Psychological Association. (1994). Guidelines for child custody and divorce proceedings. *American Psychologist*, *49*, 677–680.

Anderson, W. L., Parsons, B. M., & Rennie, D. (2001). *Daubert*'s backwash: Litigation-generated science. *University of Michigan Journal of Law Reform*, *34*, 619–682.

Barefoot v. Estelle, 463 U.S. 880 (1983).

Berger, M. A. (2001). Upsetting the balance between adverse interests: The impact of the Supreme Court's trilogy on expert testimony in toxic tort litigation. *Law and Contemporary Problems*, *64*, 289–326.

Bernstein, D. E., & Jackson, J. D. (2004). The *Daubert* trilogy in the states. *Jurimetrics Journal*, *44*, 351–366.

Bruck, M., & Ceci, S. J. (1995). Amicus Brief for the case of State of New Jersey v. Margaret Kelly Michaels presented by the Committee of Concerned Social Scientists. *Psychology, Public Policy, and Law*, *1*, 272–322.

Budwin v. American Psychological Association, 29 Cal.2d 453 (Cal. Ct. App. 1994).

Cole, S. A. (2004). Grandfathering evidence: Fingerprint admissibility rulings from *Jennings* to *Llera Plaza* and back again. *American Criminal Law Review*, *41*, 1189–1276.

Cox, A. (1987). The role of the Supreme Court: Judicial activism or self-restraint? *Maryland Law Review*, *47*, 118–138.

Daubert v. Dow Pharmaceutical, Inc., 509 U.S. 579 (1993).

DeLuca by DeLuca v. Merrell Dow Pharmaceuticals, Inc., 911 F.2d 941 (3rd Cir. 1990).

Dillon v. Legg, 441 P.2d 912 (Cal. 1968).

District of Columbia v. Wilson, 721 A.2d 591 (D.C. App. Ct. 1998).

Dobbin, S. A., Gatowski, S. I., Richardson, J. T., Ginsburg, G. P., Merlino, M. L., & Dahir, V. (2002). Applying *Daubert*: How well do judges understand science and scientific method? *Judicature*, *85*, 244–247.

Faigman, D. L., Kaye, D. H., Saks, M. J., & Sanders, J. (Eds.). (2002). *Modern scientific evidence: The law and science of expert testimony* (2nd ed.). St. Paul, MN: West Group.

Faigman, D. L., & Wright, A. J. (1997). The battered woman syndrome in the age of science. *Arizona Law Review*, *39*, 67–115.

Frye v. United States, 293 F. 1013 (D.C. Cir. 1923).

General Electric v. Joiner, 522 U.S. 136 (1997).

Giannelli, P. C. (1980). The admissibility of novel scientific evidence: Frye v. United States, a half-century later. *Columbia Law Review*, *80*, 1197–1250.

Glastetter v. Novartis Pharms. Corp., 252 F.3d 986 (8th Cir. 2001).

Gottesman, M. H. (1998). From *Barefoot* to *Daubert* to *Joiner*: Triple play or double error? *Arizona Law Review*, *40*, 753–780.

Grove, W. M., & Barden, R. C. (1999). Protecting the integrity of the legal system: The admissibility of testimony from mental health experts under *Daubert/Kumho* analyses. *Psychology, Public Policy, and Law*, *5*, 224–242.

Huber, P. W. (1988). *Liability: The legal revolution and its consequences*. New York: Basic Books.

In re Air Crash Disaster at New Orleans, La., 795 F.2d 1230 (5th Cir. 1986).

In re Breast Implant Cases, 942 F. Supp. 958 (E.D.N.Y. & S.D.N.Y. 1996).

In re Corning, Inc. Securities Litigation, 349 F.Supp.2d 698 (S.D.N.Y. 2004).

Jenson v. Eveleth Taconite Co., 13 F.3d 1287 (8th Cir. 1997).

Krauss, D., & Sales, B. (2000). Legal standards, expertise, and experts in child custody decision-making. *Psychology, Public Policy, and Law*, 6, 843–879.

Kumho Tire Co. v. Carmichael, 526 U.S. 137 (1999).

La Morte, T. M. (2003). Sleeping gatekeepers: *United States v. Llera Plaza* and the unreliability of forensic fingerprinting evidence under *Daubert*. *Albany Law Journal of Science and Technology*, *14*, 171–214.

Lempert, R. (2001). The economic analysis of evidence law: Common sense on stilts. *Virginia Law Review, 87*, 1619–1712.

Loftus, E. (1993). The reality of repressed memories. *American Psychologist, 48*, 518–537.

Logerquist v. McVey, 1 P.3d 113 (Ariz. 2000).

Mabe, M., & Amin, M. (2001). Growth dynamics of scholarly and scientific journals. *Scientometrics, 51*, 147–162.

Milanese v. Rust-Oleum Corp., 244 F.3d 104 (2d Cir. 2001).

Moore v. Ashland Chemical, Inc., 126 F.3d 679 (5th Cir. 1997).

Popper, K. (1989). *Conjectures and refutations: The growth of scientific knowledge* (5th ed.). New York: HarperCollins.

Rock v. Arkansas, 483 U.S. 44 (1987).

Rossi, F. F. (1995). The federal rules of evidence: Past, present, and future. A twenty-year perspective. *Loyola Los Angeles Law Review, 28*, 1271–1281.

Sales, B. D., & Shuman, D. W. (2005). *Experts in court*. Washington, DC: American Psychologyical Association.

Sales, B. D., & Simon, L. (1993). Institutional constraints on the ethics of expert testimony. *Ethics and Behavior, 3*, 231–249.

Shahzade v. Gregory, 923 F. Supp. 286 (D. Mass. 1996).

Shuman, D. W. (1997). What should we permit mental health professionals to say about the "best interests of the child": An essay on common sense, *Daubert*, and the rules of evidence. *Family Law Quarterly, 31*, 551–569.

Shuman, D. W. (2003). Science, law, and mental health policy. *Ohio Northern University Law Review, 29*, 587–605.

Shuman, D. W., & Sales, B. D. (1999). The impact of *Daubert* and its progeny on the admissibility of behavioral and social science evidence. *Psychology, Public Policy, and Law, 5*, 3–15.

Spring Co. v. Edgar, 99 U.S. 645 (1879).

State v. Anderson, 881 P.2d 29 (N.M. 1994).

State v. Hungerford, 697 A.2d 916 (N.H. 1997).

Tenopir, C., & King, D. W. (2000). Towards electronic journals: Realities for scientists, librarians, and publishers, Psycoloquy: 11, #84 Electronic Journals (1), available at http://psycprints.ecs.soton.ac.uk/archive/00000084/#html, visited January 4, 2005.

United States v. Sturman, WL 126066 (S.D.N.Y. 1998).

Valentine v. Pioneer Chlor Alkali Co., 921 F. Supp. 666 (D. Nev. 1996).

Westberry v. Gislaved Gummi AB, 178 F.3d 257 (4th Cir. 1999).

3

Psychological Aspects of Forensic Identification Evidence

William C. Thompson
Simon A. Cole
University of California, Irvine

Forensic scientists are often asked to compare two items of evidence (e.g., blood stains, hairs, bullets, glass fragments, toolmarks, fingerprints) to determine whether they have (or might have) a common source (Inman & Rudin, 2001). Testimony about such comparisons is called *forensic identification evidence.* This type of evidence frequently plays a crucial role in criminal trials by helping to link the defendant to the crime. For example, the defendant could be associated with an item of evidence, often called a trace, recovered from an incriminating location. Or the victim of the crime could be associated with a trace found on the defendant's body, property, or vehicle. There are a variety of types of forensic identification evidence, including DNA profiles (e.g., Imwinkelried & Kaye, 2001; National Research Council [NRC], 1992, 1996; Thompson & Krane, 2003), latent prints (i.e., finger, palm, or sole prints taken from a crime scene; Benedict, 2004; Cole, 2004; Epstein, 2002; La Morte, 2003; Mnookin, 2001; Sombat, 2002), bitemarks (Saks, 1998), toolmarks (Schwartz, 2004; Springer, 1995), hair and fiber analysis, handwriting analysis, footprints, shoe prints, and comparative bullet lead analysis (Imwinkelried & Tobin, 2003; NRC, 2004).

Forensic identification evidence raises important psychological issues. One set of issues concerns forensic experts themselves: The manner in which experts make comparisons between items of evidence, the process of judgment and decision making that underlies their determinations that items match or do not match, and the susceptibility of their methods to bias and error are all important potential areas for psychological study. A second set of issues concerns jurors. Among the key psychological issues are jurors' ability to comprehend testimony on complex and often arcane technical issues, their ability to draw appropriate conclusions from the probabilistic and statistical data that sometimes accompany forensic evidence, the manner in which jurors evaluate forensic evidence and integrate it with other evidence in the trial, and the susceptibility of their judgments to bias and inappropriate influence.

THE CONTENT OF EXPERT TESTIMONY

Our focus in this chapter is on expert testimony that purports to make what we call a "source attribution"—that is, a determination that two physical items have (or might have) a common source. In order to make an "inference of common source" (Inman & Rudin, 2001; p. 137) a forensic scientist will examine the two items and will often test or analyze the items in various ways. If the comparison reveals inconsistent features, the analyst will report an "exclusion." If the comparison reveals some amount of consistent information and no significant or unexplainable differences, the analyst will report a "match" or "inclusion" (Inman & Rudin, p. 137). If the evidence is too limited or ambiguous to make a determination, the analyst will report that the comparison is inconclusive.

Determining Whether Items Match: Objective Standards and Subjective Judgment

In some forensic disciplines, such as DNA analysis, there are objective standards for what constitutes a match between two samples. DNA analysts use sophisticated, computer-controlled instruments that produce output showing the genetic characteristics (called *alleles*) that the instrument detects at various locations (called *loci*) on the genomic DNA found in each sample (Thompson, Ford, Doom, Raymer, & Krane, 2003). Figure 3.1 shows DNA test results of five samples: blood from a crime scene and reference samples of four suspects. This analysis includes three loci, labeled "D3S1358," "vWA," and "FGA." Each person has two alleles (shown as peaks on the graphs) at each locus, one from the maternal portion and the other from the paternal portion of the chromosome (in some instances there is a single peak because the same allele was inherited

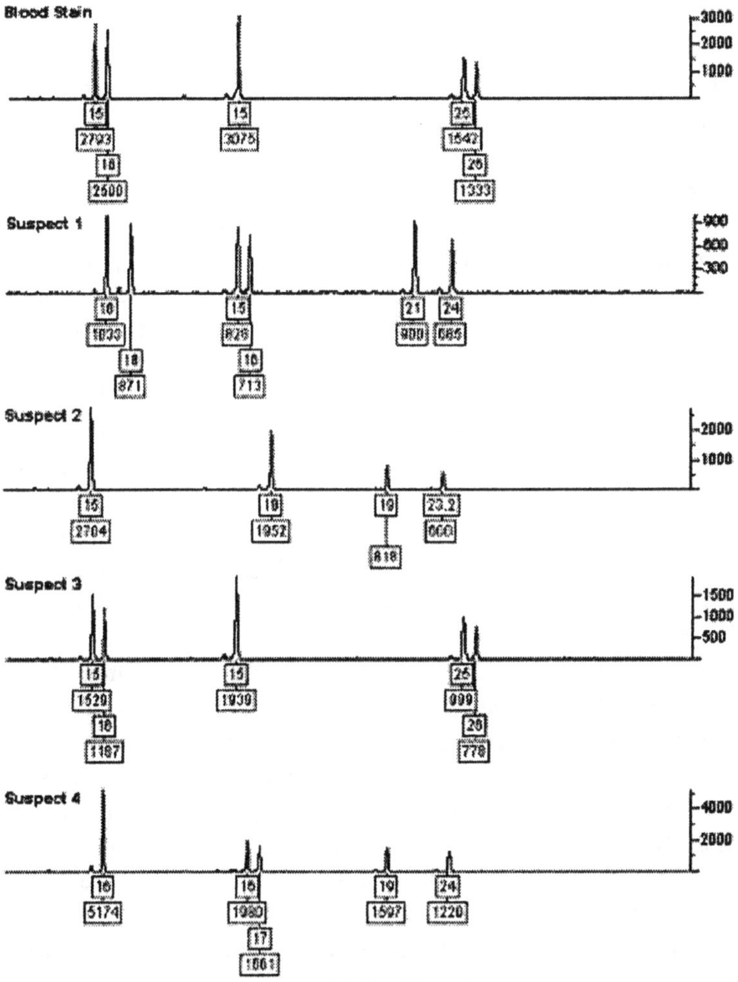

FIG. 3.1. DNA test results for five samples at three genetic loci; boxes immediately below each peak identify the allele it represents and the peak height (signal strength).

from both parents). The position of the peaks on each graph (known as an electropherogram) indicates the length of a small fragment of the DNA molecule at a specific location (*locus*) on the human genome. Forensic DNA tests examine areas of the genome where there tends to be variation among people in the length of these fragments, allowing samples from different people to be distinguished. The height of the peaks corresponds roughly to the quantity of DNA present.

The basic standard for a DNA match requires complete, one-to-one correspondence between the alleles in the two samples. As can be seen, the profile of Suspect 3 corresponds completely to that of the crime scene sample, hence it is a match that indicates Suspect 3 is a possible source of the blood at the crime scene. Suspects 1, 2, and 4 are eliminated as possible sources because one or more of their alleles differs from the crime sample.

For clear-cut test results like those shown in Fig. 3.1, interpretation is straightforward: All experts would agree that the DNA profile of Suspect 3 matches the DNA profile of the evidence, whereas the profiles of the other suspects do not match. However, DNA tests sometimes produce ambiguous results that are subject to multiple interpretations (Thompson, 1995, 1997a). Figure 3.2 shows a comparison between the DNA profile of a saliva sample from the skin of a sexual assault victim and the profile of a suspect. Experts differed over whether these two profiles match. For example, some experts thought the peak labeled "12" at locus "D3S1358" was a true allele, others thought it was merely noise in the system. The experts also differed over whether the peak labeled "OL allele" at locus "FGA" was a spurious anomaly that could be safely ignored, or whether it might be hiding another allele. When interpreting ambiguous results like those shown in Fig. 3.2, human analysts rely heavily on subjective judgments to distinguish signal from noise, explain anomalies, and account for discrepancies (Thompson, 1995, 1997a). Consequently, even though there is an objective standard for what constitutes a DNA match, analysts' interpretation of the test results in some cases still entails an element of subjective judgment (Risinger, Saks, Thompson, & Rosenthal, 2002; Thompson, Ford, et al., 2003).

Once a DNA analyst determines that two profiles match, the next step is to estimate the probability that the match could have occurred by coincidence. This is typically done by consulting databases to determine the frequency of the matching alleles in various reference populations. These frequency estimates, often called *random match probabilities* (RMPs), are then presented to the jury along with the DNA evidence.

In many forensic disciplines, standards for what constitutes a match are vague, poorly defined, or even nonexistent, and consequently the match determination rests even more heavily on subjective judgment. When asked to determine whether two bullets could have been fired from the same gun, for example, firearms examiners will typically examine the bullets under a comparison microscope to see if the striations (markings) on the bullet are similar (Schwartz, 2004, 2005). However, no standards exist to specify how many or what kind of striations must correspond before the analyst may declare the two bullets to match. According to

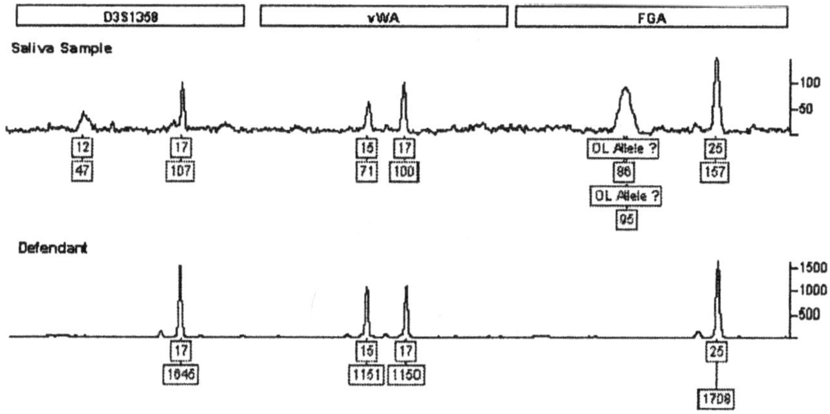

FIG. 3.2. DNA test results for saliva sample and suspect at three genetic loci.

Schwartz, analysts often declare a match notwithstanding some discrepancies between striation patterns, so long as the analyst concludes that the discrepancies are not significant. Whether a discrepancy is significant is itself a subjective determination for which no standards exist. Hence, the match determination is entirely subjective. The process leading to the determination occurs entirely within the minds of the examiners (while they look at a magnified image of the bullets). Often the only record of the determination is a written conclusion that the two bullets match or do not match.

Latent print examiners try to identify impressions of "friction ridge skin" (skin from the fingers, palms, and soles). They compare impressions of unknown origin (which, following Champod, Egli, & Margot, 2004, we call *marks*) with exemplars of known origin (prints). Marks are typically faintly visible latent prints that must be developed using methods such as powders, chemical fumes, or alternative light sources. Although computers now assist human examiners in searching fingerprint databases for candidate matches, computers never make a final determination of source attribution. That determination, contrary to popular television depictions, is always made by a human examiner.

Because of pressure distortion, printing artefacts, and various other effects, no two imprints even of the same finger are exactly alike. Therefore, latent print examiners (LPEs) may conclude that two impressions were made by the same finger despite evident differences between them. In general, LPEs look at ridge characteristics (Fig. 3.3), which are locations where the friction ridges end abruptly or bifurcate.

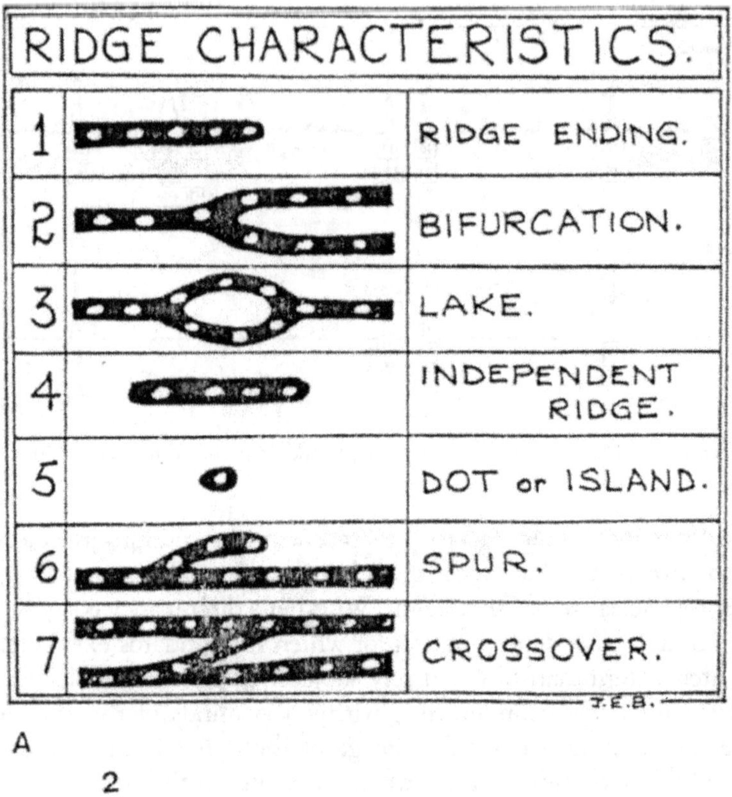

FIG. 3.3. Ridge characteristics.

There is some debate within the profession over whether examiners should look only at such ridge characteristics or whether even finer friction ridge detail, such as the shapes of ridges themselves, the attributes of the characteristics (as opposed to merely their relative location), and the location of pores, should also be utilized (Ashbaugh, 1999). The *one-dissimilarity rule* states that a single unexplainable dissimilarity necessitates a conclusion of exclusion (Thornton, 1977). However, LPEs must constantly make decisions about whether differences should count as unexplainable dissimilarities (or differences or discrepancies) or explainable dissimilarities (or distortions; Leo, 1998; Scientific Working Group on Friction Ridge Analysis Study and Technology, 2003a).

Assuming that the examiner believes all the ridge detail is consistent, the examiner must then decide whether there is sufficient consistent

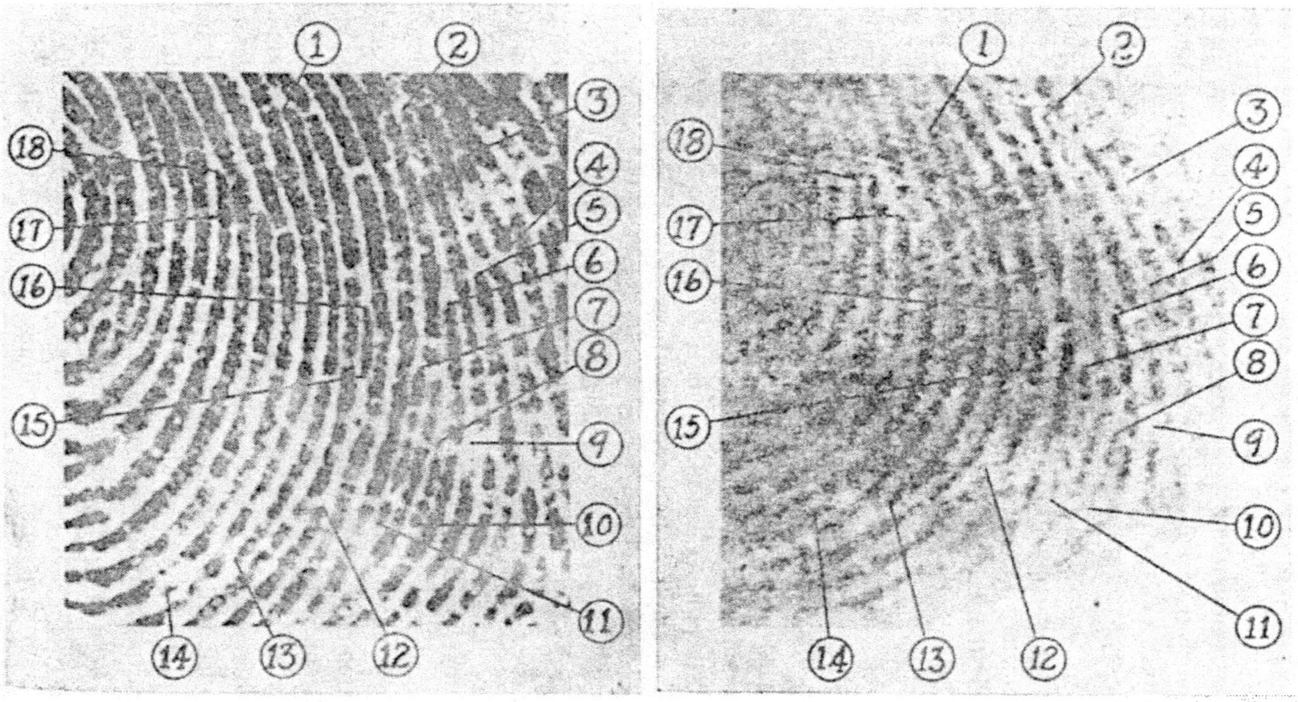

FIG. 3.4 A known-to-unknown fingerprint comparison.

ridge detail to warrant a conclusion of individualization. In contrast to the situation for DNA, no data estimating the rarity of particular ridge details or combinations of details exists (Zabell, 2005, pp. 155–156). Consequently, LPEs have no scientific basis on which to estimate the probability of a random match between two impressions, and they present no statistics in connection with their testimony. If they find sufficient consistent ridge detail they simply declare a positive identification or individualization, claiming that the potential donor pool for the mark has been reduced to one and only one area of friction ridge skin to the exclusion of all other friction ridge skin in the world.

How do they determine whether there is sufficient consistent ridge detail to warrant such a strong conclusion? LPEs follow one of two approaches (Champod, 1995; Cole, 1999). One school of thought, strongest in the continental European countries, is to set a threshold specifying the minimum number of corresponding ridge characteristics necessary to make a conclusion of individualization. (Fig. 3.4) The threshold varies from country to country but is generally between 8 and 16 matching points ("European Fingerprint Standards," 2002). There is, however, no empirical basis for these thresholds, which are simply agency or national norms. There is no way to know whether any particular threshold is high enough to justify the claim of individualization (i.e., the claim that the RMP is 0). Moreover, misidentifications have been known to occur even under the highest point thresholds (Cole, 2005, p. 1024).

A second school of thought, which is most prevalent in the Anglo-American countries, rejects arbitrary point thresholds as unscientific. Instead, it advocates that the LPE intuit when the amount and rarity of the corresponding ridge detail is sufficient to warrant a conclusion of individualization (Ashbaugh, 1999). The necessary amount and rarity of consistent friction ridge detail is not defined, other than—tautologically—by reference to the examiner's own judgment: "Individualization occurs when a latent print examiner, trained to competency, determines that two friction ridge impressions originated from the same source, to the exclusion of all others" (Scientific Working Group on Friction Ridge Analysis Study and Technology, 2002, §3.3.1).

Little is known about the manner in which examiners make these intuitive judgments, although studies have found variability among examiners in their analysis of features contained in marks (Evett & Williams, 1996; Langenburg, 2004). There have been no studies of the amount or type of ridge detail necessary to convince examiners that the detail is rare enough to reduce the random match probability to zero. This is an unexplored psychometric question of considerable potential importance to the legal system.

It should now be clear that forensic scientists in all disciplines rely partly on subjective judgment to reach conclusions, and that conclusions in some areas are almost entirely subjective. Commentators have argued that forensic scientists' reliance on subjective judgment to make match determinations is problematic because such judgments are subject to observer effects and other forms of bias (Risinger et al., 2002; Thompson, Ford, et al., 2003). For example, these judgments may (consciously or unconsciously) be affected by "domain-irrelevant" information derived from the investigative process (Risinger et al.). One recent study showed that, in cases in which the fingerprint evidence was ambiguous, naive subjects comparing fingerprints were more likely to reach conclusions of identification if they had been exposed to emotionally stimulating materials, such as graphic crime-scene photographs and descriptions of violent crimes (Dror, Péron, Hind, & Charlton, 2005). Another study found that professional LPEs could be influenced to reach different conclusions when given misleading contextual information (Dror, Charlton, & Péron, 2006). A recent FBI report (Stacey, 2004) took the position that even professional LPEs are more susceptible to observer effects in high-profile cases (though we regard this conclusion as unsupported by evidence, as yet; Cole, 2005; Thompson & Cole, 2005). Clearly this is an important area for further study.

The Meaning of a Match: Class and Individual Characteristics

Forensic scientists distinguish two types of matches: those in which the items share class characteristics—features that place them in the same category or class (categories or classes populated by more than one person or thing); and those in which the items share individual characteristics—a unique combination of features. Matching blood types and DNA profiles are class characteristics to the extent that more than one person would have them.

Matching fingerprints and some matching toolmarks are said to be individual characteristics (although the claims that these disciplines can actually know when they have narrowed the potential donor pool to one have been greeted with skepticism in the scholarly literature and are sometimes challenged in court; Bunch, 2000; Cole, 2004; Nichols, 2003).

When testifying about matches between items, most experts use one of the four general approaches summarized and illustrated in Table 3.1.

TABLE 3.1
Four Approaches to Expert Testimony About Source Attributions

Type of Testimony	*Simple Match*	*Match Plus Statistic*	*Qualitative Statement*	*Individualization*
Typical statements in expert testimony	The samples "match" or "are consistent" and therefore "could have a common source"	The samples "match" or "are consistent" and the frequency of the matching characteristics in [a reference population]is 1 in "X"	The samples "probably have a common source" or the comparison provides "very strong evidence" that the samples have a common source	The samples have been "positively identified" as being from the same source "to the exclusion of [all other such items in the world]"

When testifying about matches on class characteristics, experts typically use one of the approaches we label "simple match," "match plus statistic," or "qualitative statement." When testifying about matches on what they believe to be individual characteristics, experts typically use the approach we call "individualization."

Simple Match (No Statistics). In some instances, analysts simply testify that two items share certain class characteristics without providing a numerical characterization of the rarity of the characteristics or the strength of the match for showing the items have a common source. We call such testimony simple match testimony. For example, the analyst may state that two fibers are both composed of blue rayon of the same diameter and are not otherwise distinguishable, but the analyst will present no statistics on the frequency or rarity of blue rayon or on the probability that fibers from a different source would share the matching characteristics. In some cases, as when an analyst testifies that a footprint was made by a size 10 Nike shoe of a certain type, a juror might reasonably be expected to make a rough commonsense-based estimate of the rarity of the class characteristic. (Or, industry data could theoretically be presented to the jury.)

When reporting a match that involves class characteristics, forensic analysts typically testify that the matching items could have a common source. For example, an analyst might say that two fragments of glass could have come from the same broken window or that two bullets with similar metal composition could have come from the same box. During cross-examination, analysts typically concede that the samples could also have come from different sources that happen to be indistinguishable. However, anecdotal evidence suggests that expert witnesses sometimes overstate the value of a match on class characteristics, as when a hair analyst gives an opinion "that there was a transfer of hair from the Defendant to the body of" the victim even though experts accept that human hair cannot be uniquely identified (Stafford Smith & Goodman, 1996, p. 273; see also Yardley, 2001).

Match Plus Statistics. Obviously, the preceding testimony presents difficulties for a jury. The probative value of a match for proving two items have the same source may vary greatly depending on the commonality of the matching characteristics within a relevant population of persons or things. In addition, there is the potentially prejudicial nature of the word *match* itself. Jurors might infer that *match* implies something more akin to individualization (see later discussion), rather than merely the consistency between certain (perhaps quite common) attributes (American Board of Forensic Odontology, 1999). One way of aiding jurors is to accompany the testimony about a match with a statistical estimate of the rarity of the matching characteristics within a relevant population of people or things. For most types of forensic evidence, however, statistical data on the frequency of class characteristics are limited or nonexistent. The major exceptions have been serology and DNA testing. In connection with DNA and serology matches, forensic analysts nearly always present statistics on the frequency of the matching characteristics (in some reference population or populations). Indeed, courts in many jurisdictions refuse to admit evidence of a DNA match unless it is accompanied by valid statistical estimates of the frequency of the matching characteristics (Kaye & Sensabaugh, 2000; Thompson, 1997b). A DNA analyst might testify, for example, that the matching DNA profile would be found in approximately 1 person in 8 million among Caucasians, 1 person in 10 million among African Americans, and 1 person in 5 million among Hispanics (Thompson, Taroni, & Aitkin, 2003).

Analysts compute the frequency of DNA profiles based on studies of the frequency of the various genetic alleles that make up the profile in various populations. Because the alleles are assumed to be statistically independent of one another, the frequencies of the various matching alleles are multiplied together to determine the frequency of the entire profile.

Data on the frequency of matching DNA characteristics can be presented in a variety of ways. If the frequency of the matching DNA profile is 1 in 1 million in a particular reference population, for example, jurors might be told that 1 person in 1 million would have the profile or that the random match probability (RMP) is 1 in 1 million (Koehler, Chia, & Lindsey, 1995). In the United Kingdom, the Forensic Science Service typically reports, in such a case, that the "chance of observing the DNA profile if it originated from another individual unrelated to [defendant]" is 1 in 1 million. Some laboratories in the United States convert the frequency into a likelihood ratio and report, for example, that the DNA profile found in the evidentiary sample is 1 million times more likely if the evidentiary sample came from the defendant than if it came from an another unrelated individual (Butler, 2005).

Because likelihood ratios are the most precise way to characterize the results of paternity tests and DNA comparisons involving mixed samples (Evett & Weir, 1998), juries often hear likelihood ratios in connection with such evidence. For example, a jury might be told that the results of a paternity test are X times more likely if the accused man is the father of a child than if a man chosen randomly (from some reference population) is the father. Or a jury might be told that the mixed DNA profile found in a bloodstain is X times more likely to have occurred if the stain consists of a mixture of blood from the victim and the defendant than if the stain is a mixture of blood from the victim and a randomly chosen man who is unrelated to the defendant (see Thompson, 1996, 1997b, for discussion of problematic aspects of likelihood ratio computations).

Estimates of the error rate or false-positive rate of forensic comparisons are rarely presented in criminal trials. In theory, data on false-positive rates would be highly relevant. When evaluating the strength of a match for proving that two items have a common source, the jury must consider two factors. One factor, as already discussed, is the probability of a *coincidental match*. The second factor is the probability of a *false positive*. A false positive, as we use that term here, occurs when a forensic expert erroneously reports a match between two samples that in fact do not match on the characteristics being compared. A false positive might occur due to error in the collection and handling of the samples (e.g., mislabeling), incorrect reading or misinterpretation of test results, or incorrect reporting of test results (Thompson, Taroni, & Aitkin, 2003). Although experience has shown that false positives can occur (Koehler, 1995, 1997; Peterson & Markham,

1995a, 1995b; Thompson, Taroni, & Aitkin, 2003), the rate at which they occur is difficult to estimate based on existing data, and even if the overall rate of error for a particular type of comparison were known, the relevance of the overall statistic to the probability of error in a particular case would be debatable (see, e.g., NRC, 1996: arguing that general error rates for DNA testing have little relevance to particular cases; see Koehler, 1997; Thompson, 1997a, for alternative views). Forensic experts rarely testify about error rates. When opposing counsel try to introduce such data (e.g., data on error rates in proficiency tests) courts often exclude it on grounds that its relevance to the case at hand is too tenuous. Thompson, Taroni, and Aitkin discussed the paradoxical nature of the situation with regard to DNA testing, where courts require statistics on the frequency of matching DNA profiles, but not on the probability of a false positive: "It is considered essential to know, with a high degree of scientific certainty, whether the frequency of random matches is 1 in 1000, 1 in 10,000, or one in one million, but unnecessary to have comparable estimates of the frequency of false positives" (p. 47). Thompson, Taroni, and Aitkin suggested the two types of data are treated differently in part due to a fallacious belief that data on false positives are less important.

In some disciplines, expert witnesses have testified to probabilities using numbers based on unrepresentative databases, faulty statistical inferences, or both. Expert witnesses on microscopic hair comparison, for example, have made probabilistic statements to juries based on inappropriately applying the product rule to situations in which the requirement of statistical independence is not met (Bisbing et al, 2002; Stafford Smith & Goodman, 1996, pp. 267–271).

Qualitative Assessments Of Certainty. Some disciplines, recognizing both the need to convey to the juror an assessment of the certainty of the source attribution and the lack of any statistical data on which to base any such assessment, offer qualitative guidelines for calibrating the certainty of source attributions. For example, the American Board of Forensic Odontology promulgated the following "degrees of certainty" for bitemark testimony:

1. Source attribution to reasonable medical certainty
2. Probable source attribution
3. Possible source attribution
4. Improbable that suspect is source
5. Suspect is not source
6. Inconclusive (1999)

Although this scale brings greater clarity to the phrasing of bitemark testimony, it is unclear whether it renders such testimony more valid. According to some commentators, the analyst's decision as to where any given comparison sits along the scale rests entirely on a subjective evaluation of bitemarks (Saks, 1998).

Individualization. Thus far, we have discussed testimony about matches between items that share class characteristics. In some forensic disciplines, experts believe that when comparing two items they can identify characteristics, or sets of characteristics, that are unique. These supposedly unique features are individual characteristics. When such characteristics are found, forensic experts say they have individualized the source of the items—that the potential sources have been reduced to one and therefore that the two items being compared necessarily have a common source.

In at least one discipline, latent print identification, expert witnesses are mandated by professional guidelines to only give testimony of individualization. Current guidelines mandate that LPEs may offer only three conclusions in their reports or their testimony:

1. Individualization
2. Exclusion
3. Inconclusive (Scientific Working Group on Friction Ridge Analysis Study and Technology, 2003b, pp. 358–359)

Individualization is defined as "the determination that corresponding areas of friction ridge impressions originated from the same source to the exclusion of all others (identification)" (Scientific Working Group on Friction Ridge Analysis Study and Technology, 2003a, p. 12).

The Association of Firearms and Toolmark Examiners (AFTE) "encourages" expert witnesses to phrase their conclusions as follows:

1. IDENTIFICATION—Agreement of a combination of individual characteristics and all discernible class characteristics where the extent of agreement exceeds that which can occur in the comparison of toolmarks made by different tools and is consistent with the agreement demonstrated by toolmarks known to have been produced by the same tool.
2. INCONCLUSIVE—A. Some agreement of individual characteristics and all discernible class characteristics, but insufficient for an identification.

   B. Agreement of all discernible class characteristics without agreement or disagreement of individual characteristics due to an absence, insufficiency, or lack of reproducibility.

C. Agreement of all discernible class characteristics and disagreement of individual characteristics, but insufficient for elimination.

3. ELIMINATION—Significant disagreement of all discernible class characteristics and/or individual characteristics.
4. UNSUITABLE—Unsuitable for microscopic comparison. (AFTE, 1998, p. 86)

Whether the AFTE's conception of identification is tantamount to individualization, whether the professional organization's encouragement amounts to a mandate, and to what extent these guidelines are adhered to in practice are topics of spirited debate (Nichols, 2006; Schwartz, 2005, p. 13).

Other disciplines may occasionally give evidence in terms of individualization. Indeed, even DNA analyses, which, as we have seen, are usually accompanied by statistics, may sometimes be given as individualizations. When the estimated frequency of the matching DNA profile is very low, some labs simply state "to a scientific certainty" that the samples sharing that profile are from the same person. For example, the FBI laboratory claims two samples are from the same person if the estimated frequency of the shared profile among unrelated individuals is below 1 in 260 billion. Other labs use different cutoff values for making identity claims. All of the cutoff values are arbitrary: There is no scientific reason for setting the cutoff at any particular level.[1] Moreover, these identity claims can be misleading because they imply that there could be no alternative explanation for the match, such as laboratory error or accidental cross-contamination of samples, and they ignore the fact that close relatives are far more likely to have matching profiles than unrelated individuals.

One curious aspect of the tradition of phrasing latent print evidence as individualizations is that expert witnesses are banned from using probabilities in their testimony. A 1979 Resolution of the International Association for Identification (IAI), the main professional organization for LPEs in North America, stated, "Any member, officer or certified latent print examiner who provides oral or written reports, or gives

[1]The rationale for the FBI's threshold is that the probability of finding a duplicate profile among unrelated individuals in a population the size of the United States' drops below 0.05 when the frequency of the profile is below 1 in 260 billion (Budowle, Chakraborty, Carmody, & Monson, 2000). Budowle et al. acknowledged that the choice of 0.05 as a cutoff is a "policy decision." When the FBI's policy was first announced, it was touted as a "scientific breakthrough." (FBI, 1989) It would be more accurate, in our view, to call it a semantic breakthrough.

testimony of possible, probable, or likely friction ridge identification shall be deemed to be engaged in conduct unbecoming such member, officer, or certified latent print examiner" (p. 1).[2]

Typically, latent print testimony is given in one of two ways. In some cases, LPEs testify that they have "identified" the mark as belonging to the defendant or that the mark "matched" the defendant. In other cases, LPEs will testify that the defendant "made" the mark. In either of these scenarios, LPEs often buttress the conclusion by testifying that they are positive, that the match is a "positive identification" or a "positive match", or that the identification of the defendant is to the exclusion of every other individual in the world. One laboratory's protocol suggests the following testimony for a garden variety latent print comparison: "The latent impression developed on exhibit ____ has been identified as the fingerprint impression of ________" (New Hampshire State Police Forensic Laboratory, 2005, p. 4).

In many cases, LPEs quantify the certainty of their conclusions as 100%. Although probabilistic conclusions are purportedly banned, this rule apparently refers only to probabilities less than 1. The absurdity of this situation was highlighted in a recent case, *Michigan v. Ballard* (2003). An LPE testified "that she was '99 percent' certain that defendant's fingerprint was found in the stolen car." A majority of a Michigan Court of Appeals panel found that this testimony had "no scientific foundation" and "no demonstrated basis in an established scientific discipline and rested solely upon Ms. Dyke's [the LPE's] personal opinion" (*Michigan v. Ballard*, p. 9).[3] The irony, of course, is that the probability Dyke offered in her testimony was not too high, but rather too low. Had Dyke testified, like many of her colleagues, that the match was 100% certain, her conclusions would likely not have garnered the court's attention.

STRENGTH OF THE SCIENTIFIC FOUNDATION

There is great variability in the scientific foundation underlying different types of forensic science testimony. Whereas DNA testing is relatively well validated through extensive programs of research on the reliability

[2]This odd mandate originated in noble intentions. Historically, the aim appears to have been to discipline LPEs to give testimony only when they were absolutely certain. This was supposed to inculcate an ethic of conservatism in the practice (Cole, 1998). The danger, of course, is that the same policy may have the effect of inducing examiners to exaggerate the probative value of their findings. In addition, it creates the false impression that latent print evidence is somehow nonprobabilistic (Champod et al., 2004; Champod & Evett, 2001).

[3]This finding was subsequently reversed on appeal.

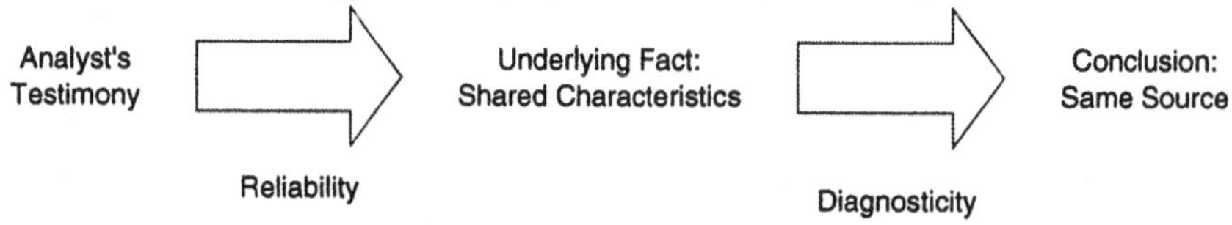

FIG. 3.5. Reliability and diagnosticity.

of the laboratory methods and the rarity of DNA profiles (NRC, 1992, 1996), many types of forensic evidence have little or no validation—leaving uncertainty about both the reliability of the procedures for determining matches and the value of a match for proving the matching items have a common source (Saks & Koehler, 2005).

When discussing the scientific foundation for forensic evidence, it is helpful to distinguish two elements that Schum and his colleagues labeled *reliability* and *diagnosticity* (Schum, 1994; Schum & DuCharme, 1971). The reliability of forensic testimony is its value for proving an underlying fact: typically that two items share class or individual characteristics. The diagnosticity of forensic testimony is the value of the underlying fact (the shared characteristics) for establishing that two items have a common source. Figure 3.5 presents this relationship.

Although many areas of forensic science are so poorly validated that no reliable data are available on either reliability or diagnosticity, that situation should improve in the near future as forensic scientists come under increasing pressure to improve their validation (e.g., Kennedy, 2003; Saks & Koehler, 2005).

Validation of DNA Tests

When DNA evidence was first introduced in U.S. courts in the late 1980s it was heralded as "the greatest advance in crime fighting technology since fingerprints" (*People v. Wesley*, 1988). After a brief honeymoon period in which DNA testimony was accepted without challenge, however, a number of scientific critics emerged who questioned both the reliability and the diagnosticity of forensic DNA (Thompson, 1993). The most heated debate concerned the rarity of DNA profiles. The methods that forensic laboratories were using to compute random match probabilities assumed the statistical independence of a number of distinct genetic markers identified by the tests. After several prominent scientists and an NRC (1992) report questioned the independence assumptions, a number of courts held DNA evidence inadmissible on grounds that the underlying method for statistical estimation was not generally accepted in the scientific community.[4] These courts reasoned that DNA evidence is meaningless in the absence of valid statistical estimates of the random match probability. Hence, by their analysis, the scientific dispute over the methods for estimating the frequency of DNA profiles precluded admissibility of DNA evidence altogether. Interestingly, courts have never applied this analysis to other types of forensic evidence. Courts may have treated DNA differently because it appeared to be such powerful evidence or because of its novelty.

In any event, these court rulings had a positive effect on the science underlying forensic DNA testing: The prospect of negative admissibility rulings spurred much-needed research on the distribution of genetic markers in human populations (Thompson, 1997a). It also prompted forensic scientists to develop validation standards designed to ensure the reliability of DNA evidence (Butler, 2005). This population research made it possible to assess the independence assumptions underlying the statistical methods. After some tweaking of the methods (NRC, 1996) the balance of scientific opinion tipped strongly in their favor and the admissibility of DNA testing was assured.

Although current DNA technology is capable of producing highly reliable results, questions are sometimes raised about the quality of laboratory work. Key issues include the potential for biased or mistaken interpretation of laboratory results and the possibility for error due to mishandling of samples. Acknowledging problems with the quality of early DNA testing procedures, a 1992 report of the NRC called for broader scrutiny of forensic DNA testing by a scientific body from outside the law enforcement community.

In response, the FBI created its own advisory body that was initially called the Technical Working Group for DNA Analysis Methods (TWGDAM) and more recently called the Scientific Working Group for DNA Analysis Methods (SWGDAM). The FBI director appoints its members. Although it has not satisfied all critics of forensic laboratory practices, this body has been credited with issuing guidelines that have improved the quality of forensic DNA work. For example, SWGDAM guidelines call for each analyst to take two proficiency tests each year.

---

[4]At that time, most states applied the Frye standard (*Frye v. United States*, 1923), which requires that a novel form of scientific evidence be generally accepted in the relevant scientific community before the evidence can be admitted in court.

Another quality assurance mechanism is laboratory accreditation. The American Society of Crime Laboratory Directors Laboratory Accreditation Board (ASCLAD-LAB) is a nonprofit organization that reviews the protocols and procedures of forensic DNA laboratories and issues a certificate of accreditation to those meeting its standards. To help ensure the competence of laboratory workers, a professional organization called the American Board of Criminology has developed a certification program for DNA analysts.

Despite these efforts, problems occasionally come to light. Errors have occurred in proficiency tests, although they are infrequent. Occasional errors arising from accidental switching and mislabeling of samples or misinterpretation of results have come to light in court cases. In several cases, misinterpretation of a DNA test contributed to wrongful convictions that were later overturned when more extensive DNA tests, by other laboratories, proved the inmates' innocence (Thompson, Ford, et al., 2003).

A 1996 report of the NRC suggested that retesting of samples is the best way to address remaining concerns about the quality of laboratory work. The great sensitivity of PCR-based DNA tests makes it possible to split samples for duplicate analysis in most cases.

Latent Prints

In 1997, Stoney wrote, "From a statistical viewpoint, the scientific foundation for fingerprint individuality is incredibly weak" (p. 67). Nothing has occurred in the interim that would lead us to revise this assessment, but we would add that the scientific foundation for the *accuracy* of latent print identification (in our opinion, the more crucial question) is also weak, from any viewpoint. Given the extraordinary certainty of latent print testimony detailed earlier, this weakness is especially glaring. After nearly a century of courtroom use, no validation studies have been performed to assess LPEs' fundamental claim: that they can make correct source attributions (Haber & Haber, 2003). Preliminary studies have measured the accuracy of naive subjects, not LPEs (Boychuk & Vokey, 2004; Tangen, Vokey, & Allan, 2000; Torry & Vokey, 2005; Vokey, Tangen, & Boychuk, 2004).

Part of the problem is that no metric has been devised to measure the amount of information contained in a mark or the amount of corresponding information between two impressions. Although it certainly seems possible to develop systems for classifying features of marks and to do studies on the frequency of those features in various populations, no one has yet published such studies. So there is no scientific basis for estimating the probability of a random match to a given configuration of friction ridge detail. Nevertheless, examiners assume that certain patterns are so rare as to be unique, and that they have the ability to identify such patterns.

A key psychological (and epistemological) question is whether LPEs can really make such determinations accurately. Consider for a moment the mental process required to determine that a known area of friction ridge skin (e.g., a defendant's fingertip) is the only possible source of a mark found at a crime scene, to the exclusion of all other friction ridge skin in the universe. One obvious approach would be to estimate the rarity of the configuration of ridge characteristics and then to judge the likelihood that a configuration of characteristics this rare would be duplicated in any other area of friction ridge skin anywhere in the world.[5] However, this would require examiners to make accurate estimates of extremely small random match probabilities, a daunting prospect given the difficulties people have with probability estimation (Lichtenstein, Fischhoff, & Phillips, 1982; Plous, 1993, chap. 12). It seems unlikely that examiners, relying entirely on intuitive judgment and without computational formulas or other forms of guidance, would be able to accurately determine whether, for example, the random match probability for a specific configuration of ridge characteristics is 1 in 1 million, 1 in 1 billion, or 1 in 1 trillion. Yet the differences among these estimates will have a huge impact on the likelihood of there being a duplication in the world's population of friction ridge skin, which is estimated to range from 50 to 60 billion fingers (taking into account only fingers of individuals currently living, and excluding the dead, the not yet conceived, nonhuman primates, palms, and soles). Moreover, even if examiners could determine with precision the random match probability, it would be difficult for them, without computational aids, to estimate the probability of a duplication in such a large population of fingers. (Suppose the examiner knew, for example, that a particular set of features would be found on 1 finger in 1 trillion. What is the likelihood of there being a second such finger in a population of 60 billion?) People's general tendency to underestimate the probability of disjunctive events (Bar-Hillel, 1973) is likely to produce

[5]The examiner would also need to consider how low the probability of a duplication would need to be to justify the claim that the probability of a duplication is (effectively) zero. As noted earlier in connection with DNA evidence, the threshold for declaring uniqueness is ultimately a policy judgment rather than a scientific question. Yet this is a question examiners must implicitly answer every time they make an intuitive judgment of individualization.

underestimates of the probability of a duplication, and hence may lead examiners too readily to judgments of individualization. In light of these problems, LPEs' claim that they can accurately determine through intuitive judgment when the random match probability has effectively been reduced to zero seems implausible.

Of course it is not clear that analysts actually make their determinations of individualization in the manner posited here: that is, by first estimating the rarity of the matching ridge detail and next estimating the likelihood of a duplication among the world population of fingers. They may rely on a simpler heuristic strategy. The Interpol European Expert Group on Fingerprint Identification (IEEGFI, 2004, §8.12.7) noted that, if the task is individualization, "The scientific problem that the fingerprint examiner is facing is to single out the donor of the print out of a potential of over 60 billion fingerprints." And yet, presented with a print pair, the examiner faces a potentially overwhelming temptation to simply ask, "Do I *think* it's him or not?" (original emphasis; IEEGFI, 2004, §8.12.7). Although IEEGFI claims examiners can resist this temptation through training and sheer self-discipline, LPEs have offered no proof whatsoever that they can. Nor is there any evidence that analysts who adopt the approach recommended by the IEEGFI perform fingerprint identifications more accurately than those who do not.

What foundation, then, does latent print identification have? First, there are statistical models that suggest that friction ridge skin patterns are highly variable and that exact duplication is unlikely (Pankanti, Prabhakar, & Jain, 2002; Stoney, 2001). This is useful—if duplication could be demonstrated, then the value of latent print evidence would be greatly reduced—but it is of limited utility. The principal problem is that little is known beyond the broad-brush statement that exact duplication is unlikely. The further question, of how different the most similar friction ridge patterns within a given population are, remains unanswered and, without a metric for similarity, unanswerable.

Second, there is anatomical research on the development of friction ridge skin (Babler, 1975, 1978, 1983, 1987, 1990, 1991; Bonnevie, 1924; Cummins & Midlo, 1943; Wertheim & Maceo, 2002; Whipple, 1904). This literature establishes that embryonic temperature and pressure are significant variables in the development of friction ridge skin. The further conclusion "that the process of prenatal development causes an *infinite variation* [italics added] of individual friction ridge details" (Moenssens, 2003, p. 32), does not seem, to us, to be warranted by the research. In any case, understanding the development of friction ridge skin is of limited value in establishing whether an expert community can make correct source attributions from trace impressions of that skin.

Third, after nearly a century of courtroom use, latent print identification has produced a relatively small number of exposed false-positive errors (Cole, 2005). The value of this datum is of course undermined by the unlikelihood of latent print false-positive errors being exposed. Although the "test of time" remains a primary resource for courts' and LPEs' continued confidence in latent print identification, it makes for a weak foundation for any knowledge claim, let alone claims as strong as those made by LPEs (Cole, 2004, 2006).

Indeed, although it might be said that the practice of latent print identification has some scientific foundation in the variability of friction ridge skin, latent print expert *testimony* might be said to have no scientific foundation at all. If we assume, for example, that a LPE has evaluated a mark and a print and concluded that all the friction ridge detail in the mark is consistent with the print, the LPE has no scientific data with which to assess the probative value of that conclusion and convey it to the jury. The latent print profession's historical solution of simply rounding the probative value up to 1 cannot be sustained.

Other Disciplines

With the notable exception of forensic DNA analysis, most forensic identification disciplines can offer only startlingly weak scientific foundations for their testimony. Although most areas boast substantial scientific literatures concerning the detection, recovery, and classification of crime scene traces, it is the scientific foundation for source attribution testimony that is typically lacking. Toolmark identification, like latent prints, lacks a scientific foundation to support the inordinately strong expert testimony that is mandated within the profession. As Schwartz (2005) observed, "Firearms and toolmark examiners have taken only the most minimal steps towards developing the necessary statistical empirical foundations for their identity claims" (p. 4).

Other forensic identification techniques, such as bitemark analysis, handwriting identification, and microscopic hair comparison, have similar problems. Like latent prints and toolmarks, bitemark identification has a solid scientific foundation that establishes that bitemarks can provide probative information, but little research that establishes the validity, or measures the accuracy, of bitemark identification in practice. Bowers

(2002) concluded, "Reliability of dental opinion historically is based on intuition derived from the expert's 'experience,' not scientific data" (p. 259). In addition, proficiency test data have revealed disappointing accuracy rates among practicing forensic odontologists (Bowers). Bitemark identification distinguishes itself from latent prints and toolmarks primarily by its more modest testimonial claims.

Handwriting identification has shown poor results on proficiency tests (Risinger, 2002). Many other areas of forensic analysis have generated poor results on (nonblind) proficiency tests (Peterson & Markham, 1995a, 1995b). No controlled empirical studies of microscopic hair comparison have been performed (Stafford Smith & Goodman, 1996, p. 234). However, a study in which hair comparison conclusions were compared to results of mitochondrial DNA tests on the same evidence showed high rates of disagreement (Houck & Budowle, 2002; Risinger & Saks, 2003; for a dissenting interpretation, see Houck, 2004).

JURY RESEARCH

A number of studies have examined mock jurors' reactions to forensic evidence (for reviews see Kaye & Koehler, 1991; Koehler, 2001; Thompson, 1989). One line of research examined how statistics on the RMP affect the weight that jurors give to a forensic match (Faigman & Baglioni, 1988; Goodman, 1992; Smith, Penrod, Otto, & Park, 1996; Thompson & Schumann, 1987). These studies asked jurors to revise an initial (prior) estimate of a suspect's probability of guilt after receiving forensic evidence implicating the suspect. The studies compared jurors' posterior judgments to the posteriors specified by Bayesian models. In general, jurors' judgments of the posterior probability of guilt were lower than Bayesian posteriors. This finding was taken as evidence that jurors are more conservative than they should be when revising judgments in light of a forensic match or, in other words, that people give less weight to forensic evidence than they should.

Although this finding is consistent with a large body of research showing that people tend to be conservative in Bayesian updating tasks (Griffin & Tversky, 1992; Kraemer & Weber, 2004; Slovic, Fishhoff, & Lichtenstein, 1977; Slovic & Lichtenstein, 1971), there are several important caveats. First, subjects' apparent conservatism in these early studies may have been due, in part, to the inadequacy of the Bayesian models. In these models the likelihood ratio depended on a single variable—the random match probability. Although these likelihood ratios may have reflected the diagnostic value of the forensic match, they failed to capture any uncertainty about its reliability. In other words, the Bayesian models against which subjects' judgments were compared implicitly assumed the forensic tests were error-free. This is a big assumption and one that subjects probably did not share (Navon, 1978; Schklar & Diamond, 1999). Second, many of the studies may have had scaling problems in their dependent measures. The studies generally asked jurors to estimate the likelihood of the suspect's guilt on a scale of probability (0–1.00) or as a percentage (0–100%). It is possible that the apparent conservatism arose simply from a reluctance to use the endpoints of these scales.

Two more recent studies (Nance & Morris, 2002; Schklar & Diamond, 1999) employed better Bayesian models that incorporated both the probability of a coincidental match and the probability of a false positive due to laboratory error. These studies found that judgments were still, on average, somewhat more conservative than Bayesian norms, thereby bolstering the evidence that conservatism is a valid phenomenon.

However, not all subjects in the early studies made conservative judgments. The pattern of responses suggested that some subjects were responding inappropriately to the forensic evidence due to what some researchers labeled fallacious interpretation of the statistical data (Thompson, 1989; Thompson & Schumann, 1987) and other researchers called "semantic confusion" (Koehler, 1996). Thompson and Schumann labeled one error the "prosecutor's fallacy." Victims of this fallacy equate the random match probability with the probability the matching items have a different source. If the defendant matches the perpetrator of a crime on a characteristic found in 2% of the population, for example, victims of the fallacy assume there is only a 2% chance the defendant is not the perpetrator and therefore a 98% chance defendant is guilty. This reasoning is erroneous, of course, because it fails to consider the prior probability that the defendant is the perpetrator. Erroneous inference of this type might well lead people to give more weight to evidence of a forensic match than they should, particularly if the prior probability of the suspect's guilt is low (Thompson).

Some jurors also made judgments consistent with a second error that Thompson and Schumann (1987) called the "defense attorney's fallacy." When the suspect and perpetrator matched on a characteristic found in 2% of the population, for example, they apparently reasoned that 2% of the population comprises thousands of people and concluded that there is little or no relevance in the defendant's membership in such a large group. What this reasoning misses, of course, is that the forensic evidence drastically narrows the range of people who might be guilty without eliminating the defendant.

Nance and Morris (2002) reported that some of their subjects committed a third type of error. They equated the conditional probability that a suspect would match if he was not the source with the probability of the suspect's guilt. When told that the defendant and perpetrator matched on a characteristic found in 4% of the population, for example, they concluded irrationally that this meant there was a 4% chance the defendant was the perpetrator. The Nance and Morris study did not include deliberation, so it is unclear whether this misunderstanding, which was observed in 5% of jurors, would survive exposure to other points of view during deliberation.

Jurors also appear to have difficulty aggregating or combining information about random match probabilities with information about the probability of a false positive. In most cases, the probability of an erroneous match being reported if the suspect is not the source can be estimated with fairly good accuracy by simply adding together the random match probability (RMP) and the false positive probability (FPP). However, research suggests that jurors do not combine the RMP and FPP in an additive manner. In a provocative study, Koehler et al. (1995) found that jurors gave far more weight to DNA evidence when they were told the FPP was .02 and the RMP was 0.000000001 (1 in 1 billion) than when they were told the FPP was .02 and they were given no information about the RMP. This finding is counternormative. The low RMP should have made little difference to the jurors because it was dwarfed by the high FPP[6] and hence the low RMP should not significantly change the value of the DNA evidence. Koehler et al. suggested that jurors might have been unduly influenced by the flashy one-in-a-billion statistic or that they might have averaged rather than summed the RMP and FPP when assigning weight to the DNA evidence. Schklar and Diamond (1999) also found evidence of misaggregation. In their study, jurors gave significantly more weight to DNA evidence when they were told the RMP was 0.000000001 and the FPP was 0.02 (or vice versa) than when told the combined probability that the laboratory would report an incorrect match due to either a random match or a false positive was 0.02.

Studies have examined jurors' reactions to a number of variations in the way statistical evidence is presented and have found that logically inconsequential differences in the format of the evidence can have significant effects. For example, several studies found that jurors give more weight to

[6]The sum of .02 and .00000001 is very close to .02.

forensic evidence when the RMP is presented as a conditional probability (Thompson & Schumann, 1987) or likelihood ratio (Nance & Morris, 2002) than when it is presented as a frequency (Hoffrage, Lindsey, Hertwig, & Gigerenzer, 2000; Lindsey, Hertwig, & Gigerenzer, 2003).

This finding may arise in part because conditional probabilities and likelihood ratios induce more judgments consistent with fallacious reasoning (Nance & Morris, 2002; Thompson & Schumann, 1987). But it is probably also due to a phenomenon that Koehler labeled exemplar cueing (Koehler, 2001; Koehler & Macchi, 2004). In a clever series of studies, Koehler demonstrated that people give less weight to evidence of a forensic match when the match statistics are presented in a manner that cues or suggests the possibility of a coincidence. For example, Koehler and Maachi found that people gave less weight to matching evidence when the frequencies were presented in a manner that suggested multiple people matching (2 in 1,000) than when the frequencies were presented in a mathematically equivalent manner that did not (0.2 in 100). According to exemplar cueing theory, people assign weight to the evidence of a match according to how readily they can imagine others matching, rather than by any more formal process, and hence can be influenced by variations in presentation format that are logically inconsequential.

Overall, the studies suggest that people are not intuitive Bayesians and that their judgments of forensic evidence may be influenced by variables that would be given no weight in a Bayesian model. Moreover, the research suggests that people sometimes use suboptimal strategies for combining different types of statistical evidence, and for combining forensic evidence with other evidence in a case, that may cause them to undervalue or overvalue forensic evidence.

Latent Prints

As explained previously, latent print evidence is typically given in very strong terms. What impact this has on a jury is not clear. Most commentators would probably agree that fingerprint evidence enjoys a strong presumption of accuracy among jurors. As a Utah Court of Appeals judge put it, "In essence, we have adopted a cultural assumption that a government representative's assertion that a defendant's fingerprint was found at a crime scene is an infallible fact, and not merely the examiner's opinion" (*State v. Quintana*, 2004, Thorne, J., concurring).

Illsley (1987) conducted the most comprehensive jury research on fingerprint evidence so far. Illsley surveyed 1,000 potential jurors who were serving jury duty at four different courts in Utah (one federal, three state). Not surprisingly, Illsley found that jurors think very highly of fingerprint evidence. Ninety-three percent agreed with the statement "Fingerprint identification is a science," and only 2% disagreed. Eight-five percent agreed with the statement "Fingerprints are the most reliable means of identifying a person," and only 8% disagreed. These responses suggest that jurors bring very favorable preconceptions to the evaluation of latent print evidence. At the same time, Illsley's study suggests that this favorable predisposition does not necessarily translate to "infallibility"[7]; three quarters of respondents agreed with the statement "It is possible for a fingerprint expert to make a mistake when comparing two fingerprints."

LEGAL REFORMS

A major problem with forensic identification evidence, at present, is the willingness of experts to present conclusions with unwarranted certainty. As discussed, experts frequently make assertions about the accuracy of their methods and results that are unsupported, or inadequately supported, by scientific research. This mismatch between expert testimony and underlying science might be addressed in two ways. First, experts might be encouraged, or required, to moderate the strength of their conclusions so that their testimony stays within scientifically supportable bounds. Second, the scientific foundations of the field might be improved to that point that more confident assertions are justified. In this section we discuss several possible ways to bring about these reforms.

Professional Standards

Self-regulation by forensic scientists has not been particularly successful at addressing the problems discussed here. Although professional societies have promulgated standards for a number of forensic science disciplines, the

[7]Many LPEs claim that the technique is "infallible" (Cole, 2005, p. 987). Laboratory studies of juror perception of latent print evidence are just getting underway (Dahl, Brimacombe, & MacLean, 2005). Reardon, Danielsen, and Meissner (2005) found that fingerprint evidence was the most important form of evidence in simulated cases, outweighing eyewitness and alibi evidence. They found that jurors were sensitive to the number of corresponding ridge characteristics and to the quality of marks. Curiously they found that the expert's declaration of a match had no influence on the jurors' evaluation of the evidence. This would suggest that Judge Pollak's proposed remedy (*United States vs. Llera plaza I*, 2002) of allowing LPEs to attest to similarities but not to matches would not have made a difference.

standards generally focus more on assuring uniformity in procedures and testimony than assuring that testimony is well grounded in science. The standards promulgated by latent print and toolmark examiners, which require experts to express conclusions with absolute certainty, are excellent examples of the disconnect that can arise between standards and science.

The limitations of professional self-regulation may arise, in part, from the institutional and social context in which forensic science is practiced. Thompson (1997a, p. 408) offered an analysis of the context of forensic DNA testing that may also apply to other forensic disciplines:

> The tests are developed by individuals and organizations that have a professional, and in some instances, a financial stake in their rapid acceptance in the courtroom. Those who develop and promote the tests also design and perform the bulk of the research to validate them. The test procedures, validation and casework generally receive outside scrutiny only from scientists who are themselves involved in the adversary process as consultants and expert witnesses for litigants. Thus, forensic ... testing is not an independent area of academic science; it is a technical field in which procedures are designed, shaped and performed specifically to play a role in litigation.
>
> Moreover, the field is dominated by experts and laboratories whose primary clients are law enforcement agencies and whose typical role in litigation is to provide evidence supporting criminal prosecutions. In this context, pressures exist to distort science to serve law enforcement goals.... The desire to be helpful to law enforcement leads forensic scientists to design, validate and perform ... tests in ways that strike a compromise between scientific rigor and other goals, such as maintaining the analysts' discretion to resolve ambiguities in accordance with other information about a case.

The limitations of self-regulation are also apparent in the frequent failure of forensic scientists to detect and expose fraudulent conduct by their colleagues. Cases in which forensic scientists were proven to have engaged in scientific fraud, such as fabrication of test results, are surprisingly common (Giannelli, 1997; Kelly & Wearne, 1998; see also cases compiled at http://www.corpus-delicti.com/forensic_fraud.html). A striking feature of these fraud cases is how few were exposed by forensic scientists. Most of the cases were exposed only after extraordinary circumstances, such as postconviction DNA exonerations, revealed the innocence of a person convicted by the fraudulent evidence (Scheck, Neufeld, & Dwyer, 2000). If self-regulation is inadequate for policing outright scientific fraud, it is unlikely to be effective for controlling testimony that, though not intentionally dishonest, is exaggerated and misleading.

In recent years there has been a trend toward accreditation of forensic laboratories. ASCLD-LAB is the leading accrediting body. It sends outside experts to review the protocols and procedures of laboratories seeking accreditation. Accreditation is undoubtedly helpful in assuring that laboratories meet minimal standards for training, equipment, documentation, and reporting. However, the expert panels that perform the reviews consist almost exclusively of forensic scientists from other, similar laboratories. Thus, for example, personnel from Laboratory A evaluate the latent print procedures of Laboratory B, and vice versa. Consequently, the accreditation process may be more helpful for assuring consistency with established practices in the field than for evaluating the validity and appropriateness of those practices. A better approach might be to create independent review panels that include academic scientists as well as forensic practitioners.

Legislation

A variety of bills have been proposed, and some passed into law, for regulating forensic science at the state and federal levels. New York established a state forensic science commission with the power to oversee the operation of state crime laboratories. Following a major scandal involving the Houston Police Crime Lab (Bromwich, 2005), Texas recently passed similar legislation (McVicker, 2005). Several states require state-operated laboratories to be accredited by ASCLD-LAB. Congress has required DNA laboratories to meet certain standards to be eligible for federal funding. Although this legislation is helpful, it has not yet touched the issues we focus on here—that is, the mismatch in many forensic disciplines between courtroom assertions and scientific foundation. These issues may be too technical, too specific, and too dependent on the evolving state of science to be appropriate subjects for legislation.

Admissibility Standards

Perhaps the most likely pathway to reform is more active involvement of trial court judges in policing forensic testimony. The power of judges, in their role as gatekeepers, to exclude invalid testimony is widely acknowledged and was made explicit, for federal courts, by the U.S. Supreme Court's ruling in *Daubert v. Merrell Dow Pharmaceuticals* (1993). Before *Daubert*, most courts applied some version of the general acceptance test (also called the *Frye* [1923] standard) under which scientific evidence was admissible if it was "generally accepted" in the relevant scientific community. Under the *Frye* standard, it was difficult to exclude problematic testimony, such as the certainty claims of latent print and toolmark examiners, because those claims were (and are) "generally accepted" by forensic practitioners (notwithstanding the absence of scientific proof).[8]

Many scholars expected that forensic science would face more exacting judicial scrutiny under the *Daubert* (1993) standard (Faigman, Saks, & Porter, 1994; Jonakait, 1994; Saks, 2000). After *Daubert*, challenges were indeed raised to several types of forensic testimony that had long been established as admissible evidence (Fradella, O'Neill, & Fogarty, 2004), including handwriting analysis (Hartfield, 2002) and latent print identifications (Cole, 2004). However, the judicial gatekeepers have, to date, been surprisingly lenient in what they will let pass—admitting forensic testimony even when its scientific foundation is clearly flimsy (Cole; Risinger, 2000). This judicial leniency may arise in part from ignorance of science. Based on a survey of 400 state court judges, one research group concluded that "many of the judges surveyed lacked the scientific literacy seemingly necessitated by *Daubert*" (Gatowski et al., 2001, p. 433). Another study found that judges performed poorly when evaluating the merits of scientific experiments, often failing to appreciate serious threats to validity (Kovera & McAuliff, 2000). Improving judicial education in scientific methods, and particularly the requirements of scientific validation, would clearly be helpful.

But ignorance of science is not the only problem. The judicial leniency in admitting forensic identification evidence may arise in part from sympathy for prosecutors, who are the major proponents of forensic evidence (Risinger, 2000). It may also arise in part because courts themselves, rather than the scientific community or scientific institutions, have become the principal sources of legitimation for many forensic identification techniques (Cole, 2004). Another factor may be judges' concerns that excluding such testimony will deny to law enforcement the vital benefits of whole categories of forensic evidence (Fradella et al., 2004).

To the extent such concerns exist, we believe they are misplaced. In the long run, stricter standards for admissibility will do more to strengthen than to harm forensic science. The experience with DNA evidence is

[8]When applying the *Frye* (1923) standard courts occasionally looked beyond practitioners of a particular discipline to the broader scientific community. Hence, astrology is inadmissible even though it might be generally accepted by practicing astrologers. But courts have rarely looked beyond forensic scientists when evaluating the admissibility of forensic identification evidence. The exceptions (*People v. Kelly*, 1976; *Williamson v. Reynolds*, 1995) involve forms of evidence (voice spectrography or microscopic hair comparison) that lack a strong presumption of belief.

instructive. The rulings in the early 1990s that excluded DNA evidence because the underlying statistics were poorly validated did not spell the doom of DNA evidence. To the contrary, these rulings had important positive effects: "It was the prospect of negative admissibility rulings that spurred much-needed research on the problem of population structure, research that otherwise might not have been done" (Thompson, 1997a, p. 423). We believe similar positive benefits would arise from rulings excluding other poorly validated forms of forensic identification evidence. Although such rulings might hinder prosecution in a few cases, they would force forensic practitioners to either moderate their testimony or strengthen their scientific validation so that their testimony rests on a stronger scientific footing. Because courts are the primary users of forensic identification evidence, they retain the greatest amount of leverage to effect reform. We believe stricter judicial standards for the admissibility of forensic identification evidence are the surest and fastest pathway to reform of the field of forensic identification science.

ACKNOWLEDGMENT

This project was funded in part by the National Science Foundation (Award #SES-0347305). The views expressed, and responsibility for any errors, are the authors'.

REFERENCES

American Board of Forensic Odontology. (1999). *Bitemark methodology guidelines*. Retrieved from http://www.abfo.org/bitemark.htm

Ashbaugh, D. R. (1999). *Quantitative-qualitative friction ridge analysis: An introduction to basic and advanced ridgeology*. Boca Raton, FL: CRC Press.

Association of Firearms and Toolmark Examiners. (1998). Theory of identification as it relates to Toolmarks. *AFTE Journal, 30*(1), 86.

Babler, W. J. (1975). Early prenatal attainment of adult metacarpal-phalangeal rankings and proportions. *American Journal of Physical Anthropology, 43*, 327–332.

Babler, W. J. (1978). Prenatal selection and dermatoglyphic patterns. *American Journal of Physical Anthropology, 48*, 21–28.

Babler, W. J. (1983, Spring). How is epidermal ridge configuration determined. *Newsletter of the American Dermatoglyphics Association, 2*, 3–4.

Babler, W. J. (1987). Prenatal development of dermatoglyphic patterns: Associations with epidermal ridge, volar pad and bone morphology. *Collegium Antropologicum, 11*, 297–304.

Babler, W. J. (1990). Prenatal communalities in epidermal ridge development. In N. M. Durham & C. C. Plato (Eds.), *Trends in dermatoglyphic research* (pp. 54–68). Dordrecht, The Netherlands: Kluwer.

Babler, W. J. (1991). Embryological development of epidermal ridges and their configurations. *Birth Defects Original Article Series*, *27*(2), 95–112.

Bar-Hillel, M. (1973). On the subjective probability of compound events. *Organizational Behavior and Human Performance*, 9, 396–406.

Benedict, N. (2004). Fingerprints and the Daubert standard for admission of scientific evidence: Why fingerprints fail and a proposed remedy. *Arizona Law Review*, 46, 519–549.

Bisbing, R. E., Deadman, H., Houck, M. M., Palenick, S., & Rowe, W. F. *Peer review report: State v. Bromgard*. (2002).

Bonnevie, K. (1924). Studies on papillary patterns of human fingers. *Journal of Genetics*, *15*, 1–112.

Bowers, C. M. (2002). Identification from bitemarks: Scientific issues. In D. L. Faigman, D. H. Kaye, M. J. Saks, & J. Sanders (Eds.), *Science in the law: Forensic science issues* (pp. 244–293). St. Paul, MN: West Group.

Boychuk, J., & Vokey, J. R. (2004, April). *On the psychophysics of fingerprint identification*. Paper presented at the Banff Annual Seminar in Cognitive Science, Banff, Alberta, Canada.

Bromwich, M. (2005). *Third report of the independent investigator for the Houston Police Department crime laboratory and property room*. Houston, TX: Fried, Frank, Harris, Shriver, & Jacobson, LLP.

Budowle, B., Chakraborty, R., Carmody, G., & Monson, K. L. (2000). Source attribution of a forensic DNA profile [Electronic version]. *Forensic Science Communications*, *2*(3).

Bunch, S. G. (2000). Consecutive matching criteria: A general critique. *Journal of Forensic Sciences*, *45*, 955–962.

Butler, J. M. (2005). *Forensic DNA typing: Biology and technology behind str markers* (2nd ed.). San Diego, CA: Academic Press.

Champod, C. (1995). Edmond Locard: Numerical standards and "probable" identifications. *Journal of Forensic Identification*, *45*, 136–163.

Champod, C., Egli, N., & Margot, P. A. (2004, October). *Fingermarks, shoesole and footprint impressions, tire impressions, ear impressions, toolmarks, lipmarks, bitemarks: A review*. Paper presented at the 14th Interpol Forensic Science Symposium, Lyon, France.

Champod, C., & Evett, I. W. (2001). A probabilistic approach to fingerprint evidence. *Journal of Forensic Identification*, *51*, 101–122.

Cole, S. (1999). What counts for identity? The historical origins of the methodology of latent fingerprint identification. *Science in Context*, *12*, 139–172.

Cole, S. A. (1998). Witnessing identification: Latent fingerprint evidence and expert knowledge. *Social Studies of Science*, *28*, 687–712.

Cole, S. A. (2004). Grandfathering evidence: Fingerprint admissibility ruling from *Jennings* to *Llera Plaza* and back again. *American Criminal Law Review*, *41*, 1189–1276.

Cole, S. A. (2005). More than zero: Accounting for error in latent fingerprint identification. *Journal of Criminal Law and Criminology*, 95, 985–1078.

Cole, S. A. (2006). Is fingerprint identification valid? Rhetorics of reliability in fingerprint proponents' discourse. *Law and Policy*, *28*, 109–135.

Cummins, H., & Midlo, C. (1943). *Finger prints, palms and soles: An introduction to dermatoglyphics*. Philadelphia: Blakiston.

Dahl, L. C., Brimacombe, C. A. E., & MacLean, C. (2005, March). *Fingerprint versus eyewitness evidence: Equally important in the forensic drama?* Paper presented at the American Psychology Law Society, La Jolla, CA.

Daubert v. Merrell Dow Pharmaceuticals, 509 U.S. 579 (1993).

Dror, I. E., Charlton, D., & Péron, A. E. (2006). Contextual information renders experts vulnerable to make erroneous identifications. *Forensic Science International, 156*, 74–78.

Dror, I. E., Péron, A. E., Hind, S.-L., & Charlton, D. (2005). When emotions get the better of us: The effect of contextual top-down processing on matching fingerprints. *Applied Cognitive Psychology, 19*, 799–809.

Epstein, R. (2002). Fingerprints meet *Daubert:* The myth of fingerprint "science" is revealed. *Southern California Law Review, 75*, 605–657.

European Fingerprint Standards. (2002). *Fingerprint Whorld, 28*(107), 19.

Evett, I. W., & Weir, B. S. (1998). *Interpreting DNA evidence: Statistical genetics for forensic scientists*. Sunderland, MA: Sinauer.

Evett, I. W., & Williams, R. L. (1996). A review of the sixteen points fingerprint standard in England and Wales. *Journal of Forensic Identification, 46*, 49–73.

Faigman, D., & Baglioni, A. (1988). Bayes' theorem in the trial process. *Law and Human Behavior, 12*, 1–17.

Faigman, D., Saks, M. J., & Porter, E. (1994). Check your crystal ball at the courthouse door, please: Exploring the present, worrying about the future of scientific evidence. *Cardozo Law Review, 15*, 1799.

Federal Bureau of Investigation. (1998, February). DNA profiling advancement. *FBI Law Enforcement Bulletin, 67*(2), 24.

Fradella, H. F., O'Neill, L., & Fogarty, A. (2004). The impact of Daubert on forensic science. *Pepperdine Law Review, 31*, 323–361.

Frye v. United States, 293 F. 1013 (D.C. Ct. App. 1923).

Gatowski, S. I., Dobbin, S. A., Richardson, J. T., Ginsburg, G. P., Merlino, M. L., & Dahir, V. (2001). Asking the gatekeepers: A national survey of judges on judging expert evidence in a post-*Daubert* World. *Law and Human Behavior, 25*, 433–458.

Giannelli, P. (1997). The abuse of scientific evidence in criminal cases: The need for independent crime laboratories. *Virginia Journal of Social Policy and the Law, 4*, 439–478.

Goodman, J. (1992). Jurors' comprehension and assessment of probabilistic evidence. *American Journal of Trial Advocacy, 16*, 361–389.

Griffin, D., & Tversky, A. (1992). The weighing of evidence and the determinants of confidence. *Cognitive Psychology, 24*, 411–435.

Haber, L., & Haber, R. N. (2003). Error rates for human fingerprint examiners. In N. K. Ratha & R. Bolle (Eds.), *Automatic fingerprint recognition systems* (pp. 339–360). New York: Springer.

Hartfield, L. C. (2002, November). Daubert/Kumho challenges to handwriting analysis. *The Champion, 26*, 24–36.

Hoffrage, U., Lindsey, S., Hertwig, R., & Gigerenzer, G. (2000). Communicating statistical information. *Science, 290*, 2261–2262.

Houck, M. M. (2004). Forensic science, no consensus. *Issues in Science and Technology, 20*(2), 6–8.

Houck, M. M., & Budowle, B. (2002). Correlation of microscopic and mitochondrial DNA hair comparisons. *Journal of Forensic Sciences, 47*(5), 1–4.

Illsley, C. (1987, July). *Juries, fingerprints, and the expert fingerprint witness*. Paper presented at the International Symposium on Latent Prints, Quantico, VA.

Imwinkelried, E. J., & Kaye, D. H. (2001). DNA typing: Emerging or neglected issues. *Washington Law Review, 76*, 413–474.

Imwinkelried, E. J., & Tobin, W. A. (2003). Comparative bullet lead analysis (CBLA) evidence: Valid inference or ipse dixit? *Oklahoma City University Law Review, 28*, 43–72.

Inman, K., & Rudin, N. (2001). *Principles and practice of criminalistics: The profession of forensic science*. Boca Raton, FL: CRC Press.

International Association for Identification. (1979). Resolution VII. *Identification News, 29*, 1.

Interpol European Expert Group on Fingerprint Identification II. (2004). *Method for fingerprint identification*. Retrieved from http://www.interpol.int/Public/Forensic/fingerprints/Working Parties/IEEGFI2/default.arp

Jonakait, R. N. (1994). The meaning of Daubert and what that means for forensic science. *Cardozo Law Review, 15*, 2103–2116.

Kaye, D. H., & Koehler, J. J. (1991). Can jurors understand probabilistic evidence? *Journal of the Royal Statistical Society, Series A, 154*, 75–81.

Kaye, D. H., & Sensabaugh, G. F., Jr. (2000). Reference guide on DNA evidence. In J. Cecil (Ed.), *Reference manual on scientific evidence* (Vol. 2, pp. 485–576). Washington, DC: Federal Judicial Center.

Kelly, J. F., & Wearne, P. K. (1998). *Tainting evidence: Inside the scandals at the FBI crime lab*. New York: Free Press.

Kennedy, D. (2003). Forensic science: Oxymoron? *Science, 302*, 1625.

Koehler, J. J. (1995). The random match probability in DNA evidence: Irrelevant and prejudicial? *Jurimetrics, 35*, 201–219.

Koehler, J. J. (1996). On conveying the probative value of DNA evidence: Frequencies, likelihood ratios, and error rates. *University of Colorado Law Review, 67*, 859–886.

Koehler, J. J. (1997). Why DNA likelihood ratios should account for error (even when a National Research Council report says they should not). *Jurimetrics, 37*, 425–437.

Koehler, J. J. (2001). When are people persuaded by DNA match statistics? *Law and Human Behavior, 25*, 493–513.

Koehler, J. J., Chia, A., & Lindsey, J. S. (1995). The random match probability (RMP) in DNA evidence: Irrelevant and prejudicial? *Jurimetrics, 35*, 201–219.

Koehler, J. J., & Macchi, L. (2004). Thinking about low-probability events. *Psychological Science, 15*, 540–546.

Kovera, M. B., & McAuliff, B. D. (2000). The effects of peer review and evidence quality on judge evaluations of psychological science: Are judges effective gatekeepers? *Journal of Applied Psychology, 85*, 574–586.

Kraemer, C., & Weber, M. (2004). How do people take into account weight, strength and quality of segregated vs. aggregated data? Experimental evidence. *Journal of Risk and Uncertainty, 29*(2), 113–142.

La Morte, T. M. (2003). Sleeping gatekeepers: *United States v. Llera Plaza* and the unreliability of forensic fingerprinting evidence under *Daubert*. *Albany Law Journal of Science and Technology, 14*, 171–214.

Langenburg, G. M. (2004). Pilot study: A statistical analysis of the ACE-V methodology—analysis stage. *Journal of Forensic Identification, 54*(1), 64–79.

Leo, W. F. (1998). Distortion versus dissimilarity in friction skin identification. *Journal of Forensic Identification, 48*(2), 125–129.

Lichtenstein, S., Fischhoff, B., & Phillips, L. D. (1982). Calibration of probabilities: The state of the art to 1980. In D. Kahneman, P. Slovic & A. Tversky (Eds.), *Judgment under uncertainty: Heuristics and biases* (pp. 306–334). Cambridge, England: Cambridge University Press.

Lindsey, S., Hertwig, R., & Gigerenzer, G. (2003). Communicating statistical DNA evidence. *Jurimetrics, 43*, 147–163.

McVicker, S. (2005, June 20). Commission created to look into crime labs. *The Houston Chronicle, Section B*, p. 5.

Michigan v. Ballard, 2003 Mich. App. LEXIS 547 (Mich. Ct. App. 2003).

Mnookin, J. L. (2001). Fingerprint evidence in an age of DNA profiling. *Brooklyn Law Review, 67*(1), 13–70.

Moenssens, A. (2003). Fingerprint identification: A valid reliable "forensic science?" *Criminal Justice, 18*(2), 31–37.

Nance, D. A., & Morris, S. B. (2002). An empirical assessment of presentation formats for trace evidence with a relatively large and quantifiable random match probability. *Jurimetrics, 42*, 403–448.

National Research Council. (1992). *DNA technology in forensic science*. Washington, DC: National Academy Press.

National Research Council. (1996). *The evaluation of forensic DNA evidence*. Washington, DC: National Academy Press.

National Research Council. (2004). *Forensic analysis: Weighing bullet lead evidence*. Washington, DC: National Academy Press.

Navon, D. (1978). Statistical and metastatistical considerations in analyzing the desirability of human Bayesian conservatism. *British Journal of Mathematical and Statistical Psychology, 304*, 205–212.

New Hampshire State Police Forensic Laboratory. (2005). *Latent print examination: Interpretation and reporting of conclusions* (3rd ed., Vol. IDU-001-03).

Nichols, R. G. (2003). Firearm and toolmark identification criteria: A review of the literature, Part II. *Journal of Forensic Sciences, 48*, 318–327.

Nichols, R. (2006). The scientific foundations of firearms and tool mark identification: A response to recent challenges. *California Association of Criminalists News*, 8–27.

Pankanti, S., Prabhakar, S., & Jain, A. K. (2002). On the individuality of fingerprints. *IEEE Transactions on PAMI, 24*, 1010–1025.

People v. Kelly, 549 P.2d 1240 (Cal. 1976).

People v. Wesley, 553 N.Y.S.2d 643 (N.Y. Sup. Ct. 1988).

Peterson, J. L., & Markham, P. N. (1995a). Crime laboratory proficiency testing results, 1978–1991, I: Identification and classification of physical evidence. *Journal of Forensic Sciences, 40*, 994–1009.

Peterson, J. L., & Markham, P. N. (1995b). Crime laboratory proficiency testing results, 1978–1991, II: Resolving questions of common origin. *Journal of Forensic Sciences, 40*, 1009–1029.

Plous, S. (1993). *The psychology of judgment and decision making.* New York: McGraw-Hill.

Reardon, M., Danielsen, E., & Meissner, C. A. (2005, March). *Investigating juror perceptions of fingerprint evidence in criminal cases.* Paper presented at the American Psychology-Law Society, La Jolla, CA.

Risinger, D. M. (2000). Navigating expert reliability: Are criminal standards of certainty being left on the dock? *Albany Law Review, 64,* 99–152.

Risinger, D. M. (2002). Handwriting identification. In D. L. Faigman, D. H. Kaye, M. J. Saks, & J. Sanders (Eds.), *Science in the law: Forensic science issues* (pp. 113–193). St. Paul, MN.: West Group.

Risinger, D. M., & Saks, M. J. (2003). A house with no foundation. *Issues in Science and Technology, 20,* 35–39.

Risinger, D. M., Saks, M. J., Thompson, W. C., & Rosenthal, R. (2002). The *Daubert/Kumho* implications of observer effects in forensic science: Hidden problems of expectation and suggestion. *California Law Review, 90,* 1–56.

Saks, M. J. (1998). Merlin and Solomon: Lessons from the law's formative encounters with forensic identification science. *Hastings Law Journal, 49,* 1069–1141.

Saks, M. J. (2000). Banishing *ipse dixit:* The impact of *Kumho Tire* on forensic identification science. *Washington and Lee Law Review, 57,* 879–900.

Saks, M. J., & Koehler, J. J. (2005). The coming paradigm shift in forensic identification science. *Science, 309,* 892–895.

Scheck, B., Neufeld, P., & Dwyer, F. (2000). *Actual innocence.* New York: Doubleday.

Schklar, J., & Diamond, S. S. (1999). Juror reactions to DNA evidence: Errors and expectancies. *Law and Human Behavior, 23*(2), 159–184.

Schum, D. A. (1994). *Evidential foundations of probabilistic reasoning.* New York: Wiley.

Schum, D. A., & DuCharme, W. M. (1971). Comments on the relationship between the impact and the reliability of evidence. *Organizational Behavior and Human Performance, 6,* 111–131.

Schwartz, A. (2004). A challenge to the admissibility of firearms and toolmark identifications: Amicus brief prepared on behalf of the defendant in *United States v. Kain,* Crim. No. 03-573-1 (E.D. Pa.). *Journal of Philosophy, Science and Law, 4,* 1–32.

Schwartz, A. (2005). A systemic challenge to the reliability and admissibility of firearms and toolmark identification. *Columbia Science and Technology Law Review, 6,* 1–42.

Scientific Working Group on Friction Ridge Analysis Study and Technology. (2002). *Friction ridge examination methodology for latent print examiners* (ver. 1.01 ed.). Retrieved from http://www.swgfast.org

Scientific Working Group on Friction Ridge Analysis Study and Technology. (2003a). *Glossary—consolidated* (ver. 1.0 ed.). Retrieved from http://www.swgfast.org/Glossary-consolidated_ver_1.pdf

Scientific Working Group on Friction Ridge Analysis Study and Technology. (2003b). Standards for conclusions (ver. 1.0 ed.). *Journal of Forensic Identification, 54,* 358–359.

Slovic, P., Fishhoff, B., & Lichtenstein, S. (1977). Behavioral decision theory. *Annual Review of Psychology, 28,* 1–39.

Slovic, P., & Lichtenstein, S. (1971). Comparison of Bayesian and regression approaches to the study of information processing in judgment. *Organizational Behavior and Human Performance, 6,* 649–744.

Smith, B. C., Penrod, S. D., Otto, A. L., & Park, R. C. (1996). Jurors' use of probabilistic evidence. *Law and Human Behavior, 20*, 49–82.

Sombat, J. M. (2002). Note, latent justice: Daubert's impact on the evaluation of fingerprint identification testimony. *Fordham Law Review, 70*, 2819.

Springer, E. (1995). Toolmark examinations: A review of its development in the literature. *Journal of Forensic Sciences, 40*, 964–968.

Stacey, R. B. (2004). A report on the erroneous fingerprint individualization in the Madrid train bombing case. *Journal of Forensic Identification, 54*, 706–718.

Stafford Smith, C. A., & Goodman, P. D. (1996). Forensic hair comparison analysis: Nineteenth century science or twentieth century snake oil? *Columbia Human Rights Law Review, 27*, 227–291.

State v. Quintana, 103 P.3d 168 (Utah Ct. App. 2004).

Stoney, D. A. (1997). Fingerprint identification: Scientific status. In D. L. Faigman, D. H. Kaye, M. J. Saks, & J. Sanders (Eds.), *Modern scientific evidence* 2 (pp. 55–78). St. Paul, MN: West Group.

Stoney, D. A. (2001). Measurement of fingerprint individuality. In H. C. Lee & R. E. Gaensslen (Eds.), *Advances in fingerprint technology* (pp. 327–387). Boca Raton, FL: CRC Press.

Tangen, J. M., Vokey, J. R., & Allan, L. G. (2000, July). *What's in a fingerprint? A PCA approach to fingerprint identification and categorisation.* Paper presented at the Joint Meeting of the Experimental Psychology Society and the Canadian Society for Brain, Behaviour, and Cognitive Science, Cambridge, England.

Thompson, W. C. (1989). Are juries competent to evaluate statistical evidence? *Law and Contemporary Problems, 52*, 9–41.

Thompson, W. C. (1993). Evaluating the admissibility of new genetic identification tests: Lessons from the "DNA war." *Journal of Criminal Law and Criminology, 84*, 22–104.

Thompson, W. C. (1995). Subjective interpretation, laboratory error and the value of forensic DNA evidence: Three case studies. *Genetica, 96*, 153–168.

Thompson, W. C. (1996). DNA evidence in the O. J. Simpson trial. *University of Colorado Law Review, 67*, 827–857.

Thompson, W. C. (1997a). Accepting lower standards: The National Research Council's second report on forensic DNA evidence. *Jurimetrics, 37*, 405–424.

Thompson, W. C. (1997b). Forensic DNA evidence. In B. Black & P. Lee (Eds.), *Expert evidence: A practitioner's guide to law, science and the FJC manual* (pp. 195–266). St. Paul, MN: West Group.

Thompson, W. C., & Cole, S. A. (2005). Lessons from the Brandon Mayfield case. *The Champion, 29*, 42–44.

Thompson, W. C., Ford, S., Doom, T., Raymer, M., & Krane, D. (2003). Evaluating forensic DNA evidence: Elements of a competent defense review. *The Champion, 27*, 16–25.

Thompson, W. C., & Krane, D. E. (2003). DNA in the courtroom. In J. Moriarty (Ed.), *Psychological and scientific evidence in criminal trials* (pp. 11-1–11-75). St. Paul, MN: West Group.

Thompson, W. C., & Schumann, E. L. (1987). Interpretation of statistical evidence in criminal trials: The prosecutor's fallacy and the defense attorney's fallacy. *Law and Human Behavior, 11*, 167–187.

Thompson, W. C., Taroni, F., & Aitkin, C. G. G. (2003). How the probability of a false positive affects the value of DNA evidence. *Journal of Forensic Sciences, 48*, 1–8.

Thornton, J. (1977). The one-dissimilarity doctrine in fingerprint identification. *International Criminal Police Review, 32*, 89–95.

Torry, M. E., & Vokey, J. R. (2005, May). *Fingerprint matching and naive observers*. Paper presented at the Banff Annual Seminar in Cognitive Science, Banff, Alberta, Canada.

United States v. Llera Plaza, 179 F. Supp. 2d 492 (E.D. Pa. 2002), *vacated*, 188 F. Supp. 2d 549.

Vokey, J. R., Tangen, J. M., & Boychuk, J. (2004, June). *On the identification of latent fingerprints*. Paper presented at the Annual Meeting of the Canadian Society for Brain, Behaviour and Cognitive Science, St. John's, Newfoundland and Labrador, Canada.

Wertheim, K., & Maceo, A. (2002). The critical stage of friction ridge pattern formation. *Journal of Forensic Identification, 52*, 35–85.

Whipple, I. L. (1904). The ventral surface of mammalian chiridium with special reference to the conditions found in man. *Zeitschrift für Morphologie und Anthropologie, 7*, 261–368.

Williamson v. Reynolds, 904 F. Supp. 1529 (E.D. Okla. 1995).

Yardley, J. (2001, May 8). Flaws in chemist's findings free man at center of inquiry. *The New York Times*, p. A1.

Zabell, S. L. (2005). Fingerprint evidence. *Journal of Law and Policy, 13*, 143–170.

4

Research and Expert Testimony on Interrogations and Confessions

Mark Costanzo
Claremont McKenna College
Richard A. Leo
University of San Francisco School of Law

On a spring evening in 1989, a 28-year-old investment banker was jogging in New York's Central Park when she was pulled from the jogging path into a nearby ravine. She was raped and brutally beaten. She was found unconscious, having lost more than 70% of the blood in her body. Miraculously, she survived. And, mercifully, she has no memory of the attack. Because of the savage assault she suffered more than 17 years ago, she still suffers from balance, hearing, vision, and memory problems (Meili, 2003).

In the hours and days following the assault, police quickly focused their investigation on a group of boys—ages 14 to 16—who had harassed several other people in Central Park earlier in the evening. Six boys were interrogated over the course of a day and half, and five of them finally confessed to the rape and beating of the jogger. Although a hair found on one of the boys appeared to match the hair of the victim, the main incriminating evidence was the confessions. All five were convicted of participating in the assault. Their sentences ranged from 5 to 15 years in prison (Sullivan, 1992).

In 2002, a prison inmate named Mathias Reyes underwent a religious conversion, contacted authorities, and informed them that he alone had raped the Central Park jogger. He was serving time for four rapes and a murder committed in the summer of 1989. A DNA sample from Reyes was compared to DNA from a semen stain on the jogger's sock. It was a match. The five boys were eventually exonerated. All five confessions had been false.

Although the psychological study of interrogation and confession dates back to Hugo Munsterberg's 1908 classic *On the Witness Stand*, a substantial scientific literature on false confessions did not begin to accumulate until the 1980s. Scholars have long pointed out the importance of interrogation and the potential for false confessions (see Kassin & Wrightsman, 1985; Ofshe, 1989; Zimbardo, 1967), but there have been at least two significant obstacles to empirical research in this important area. First, it is often difficult to know for certain whether a contested confession is truly false. Consequently, the development of DNA identification technology in the 1990s, and the resulting exoneration of innocent prisoners, provided a major boost to research on this topic by helping scholars identify scores of proven false confessions to serious crimes (see Drizin & Leo, 2004; Leo & Ofshe, 1998; Scheck, Neufeld, & Dwyer, 2000). A second obstacle has been the difficulty of studying false confessions in the psychological laboratory. A realistic, convincing laboratory simulation of a police interrogation would require that the experimenter induce levels of stress in research participants that would violate ethical standards. Moreover, the crushing potential consequences of a false confession—a trial and possible prison sentence—cannot be fully simulated in the laboratory. Although experimental research in this area remains difficult, recent laboratory studies have contributed to our understanding of the psychology of interrogation, including the diagnosticity of particular approaches (Russano, Meissner, Kassin, & Narchet, 2005) as well as the perceptual biases that sometimes contribute to wrongful convictions based on false confessions (Kassin, Meissner, & Norwick, 2005).

Over the past 15 years, social scientists have drawn on multiple methodologies (observational studies, case studies, archival research, and laboratory studies) to advance our understanding of the social influence processes and biases that lead to false confessions and wrongful convictions (Davis & O'Donahue, 2003; Kassin & Gudjonsson, 2004). In addition, our ability to meaningfully study these processes has been greatly aided by the mandatory practice of recording interrogations in England (since 1984) and in several American states (for example, Alaska since

1985 and Minnesota since 1994). Voluntary videotaping of interrogations is now spreading to police agencies across the United States (Drizin & Reich, 2004; Ofshe & Leo, 1997a; Sullivan, 2004).

We do not know—and it may be impossible to know—how many false confessions occur each year or what percentage of confessions are false (Leo & Ofshe, 1998). However, based on aggregated case studies by the Innocence Project and others, we do know that approximately 14% to 25% of known wrongful convictions appear to involve false confessions—that is, a false confession was the primary or sole evidence against the defendant. Recently, in the most comprehensive study of false confessions to date, Drizin and Leo (2004) examined 125 proven false confessions. They found that 80% of these false confessions occurred in murder cases, another 9% involved rape, and 3% involved arson. Some have argued that this overrepresentation of serious cases is a result of the strong pressure on police to solve cases involving violent crime (Gross, 1996; Warden, 2003).

We also know that a confession has a powerful impact on the outcome of a case. In 1986, Supreme Court Justice William Brennan observed, "Triers of fact accord confessions such heavy weight ... that the introduction of a confession makes other aspects of a trial in court superfluous, and the real trial, for all purposes, occurs when the confession is obtained" (*Colorado v. Connelly*, 1986, p. 182). There is much research to suggest that Brennan's observation is correct. In the Drizin and Leo (2004) sample, when suspects falsely confessed then pled *not guilty* and proceeded to trial, the conviction rate was 81%. A series of mock trial experiments by Saul Kassin and his colleagues also show the power of confessions. When Kassin and Neumann (1997) systematically compared eyewitness, character, and confession evidence, they found that confessions produced the highest conviction rate. Kassin and Sukel (1997) found that even when mock jurors recognized that a confession was coerced, they were not able to discount it when reaching a verdict. In sum, all the available evidence indicates that a confession is extremely difficult for jurors to discount or ignore, even if that confession is false, even if it is coerced, and even when there is little corroborating evidence.

WHY A FALSE CONFESSION MIGHT LOOK TRUE

We might hope that judges and jurors could easily tell the difference between true and false confessions. Unfortunately, false confessions often *look and sound* true. There appear to be several factors that lend authenticity to a bogus confession.

Confessor Effects

One important factor that contributes to the judgment that a confession is likely true is the level of detail provided by the confessor. Surprisingly, false confessors often provide highly detailed accounts of the crimes they did not commit.[1] For example, the videotaped portions of the five false confessions in the Central Park jogger case offer a chilling account of an assault and gang rape. The false confessors described how the crime happened step by step, who assaulted the victim, and the victim's injuries. They recounted what the accomplices said to one another during the assault and, in some instances, they physically acted out parts of the crime, showing how the victim was pulled from the jogging path, how they touched her, and how they ripped the clothes from her body (Sullivan, 1992).

Even in cases where the details provided by the false confessor are inconsistent with the available physical evidence or the accounts of accomplices to the crime (there were many such inconsistencies and inaccuracies in the Central Park jogger confessions), details appear to make the confession more convincing. The particulars provided by false confessors may come from several sources: They may simply be a product of how the confessor imagines that the crime might have transpired, the specifics may have been gleaned from news accounts of the crime and repeated by the suspect, or the details may have been provided to the suspect by police—intentionally or unintentionally—over the course of the interrogation process. We will have more to say later in this chapter about using the details provided by the confessor to assess the veracity of the confession. For now, the important point is that, compared to a general admission, a confession that includes vivid, specific details about a crime is more likely to be seen as authentic.

A second factor that lends credence to a confession is motive. If, in addition to providing a detailed account of the crime, the false confessor provides a convincing reason *why* he or she committed the crime, the account is likely to be more believable. Motive is an essential element of a convincing story (McKee, 2001). Evidence in support of this proposition comes from research on the "story model" of juror decision making

[1]The issue of whether true confessions actually contain more detail than false confessions awaits empirical investigation. Research using criterion-based content analysis (CBCA) suggests that in some areas (e.g., accounts of alleged sexual abuse), true accounts may be significantly more detailed than false accounts (Blandon-Gitlin, Pezdek, Rogers, Brodie, in press).

(Pennington & Hastie, 1993). According to this model, jurors evaluate whether a story is plausible on the basis of its coverage and coherence. Research indicates that for a variety of case types, including capital murder (Costanzo & Peterson, 1994), rape (Olsen-Fulero & Fulero, 1997), and sexual harassment (Huntley & Costanzo, 2003), attorneys present motives for crimes and jurors seek out motives for crimes. A motive—such as greed, lust, jealousy, revenge, betrayal—completes the story of the crime. Even after hearing all of the evidence at trial, jurors in many cases are left to speculate about a defendant's motive. In contrast, hearing defendants explain, in their own words, the motivation for their crime is likely to have far more impact.

A confession that contains details of how the crime occurred and a clear statement of motive is more likely to result in a conviction. But a final element that may increase the believability of a confession is some expression of remorse. Remorse may be especially compelling because it may intuitively appear not to be a response to coercion, but a spontaneous emotional response. Details and motive rest on memory—recalling why and how the crime happened. An apology or expression of regret may appear to be a sincere and voluntary expression. Like details and motive, remorse may lend a tone of realism and plausibility to a false confession.

Observer Effects

It is helpful to look at confessions in social-psychological context. Research on attributional biases suggests that people are likely to infer that a confession is valid. There is a huge literature in social psychology demonstrating that when analyzing another person's behavior, we tend to underestimate the power of situational forces (Aronson, 2004). In the case of confession evidence, we tend to discount the pressures of interrogation. There is even evidence that a camera angle showing only the confessor leads to more dispositional attributions than an angle showing both the interrogator and the suspect (Lassiter & Geers, 2004).

A second observer effect is that when we analyze the behavior of others, we usually begin with an assumption of rationality. That is, we assume that people we observe are probably behaving in their own self-interest, in a way that leads to benefits and avoids costs. Confessing to a crime we did not commit is clearly contrary to self-interest. Unless a suspect is mentally impaired or has been subjected to torture, observers who have not experienced a coercive interrogation are likely to have great difficulty imagining why anyone might offer a false confession (Leo, 2001).

Finally, jurors often do not see confessions in their entirety. Instead, they may see a recap—a preselected portion of a videotaped confession. In some cases, interrogators do not even turn on the video camera until after the suspect has confessed and the confession is clear and well rehearsed. Consequently, what a jury might see is only the end product of a long, grueling process of interrogation. What is seen on videotape may have been orchestrated, shaped, and rehearsed. The details and motives given by the confessor may have been fed to the suspect over time, and the coercive process that culminated in a confession may not be salient to jurors.

TYPES OF FALSE CONFESSIONS

Several classification schemes have been proposed to differentiate between types of false confessions. For a fuller discussion of these taxonomies, we refer the reader to Ofshe and Leo (1997a) and Kassin and Gudjonsson (2004). For our purposes, it is useful to distinguish between four types of false confessions by looking across two dimensions: Instrumental or Authentic, and Voluntary or Coerced. Instrumental confessions are those offered as a means to an end, to achieve some goal. Often the goal is simply to bring an end to a highly aversive interrogation. In contrast, authentic false confessions are the result of confessors' genuine but false belief that they may have actually committed the crime. Coerced false confessions are produced by intense psychological pressures (and occasionally physical pressure) from interrogators while voluntary false confessions are given freely by the confessor.

Four Types of False Confessions

	Coerced	Voluntary
Instrumental	End interrogation by acquiescence	Protect Someone Else Gain Notoriety
Authentic	Confessor becomes persuaded that he or she is guilty	Confessor is delusional or mentally ill

FIG. 4.1. Four types of false confessions.

Instrumental-Coerced false confessions occur when, as a result of a long or intense interrogation, suspects confess to crimes they know they did not commit. In this type of false confession, suspects become convinced that the only way to end the interrogation or to receive more lenient treatment is to agree that they committed the crime in question. This is the most common type of false confession.

Instrumental-Voluntary false confessions occur when suspects implicate themselves in crimes they did not commit in an effort to achieve some goal. For example, a member of a criminal gang or organization may falsely confess to a crime to protect someone higher up in the organization. Or, parents may intentionally offer a false confession to protect their child from being convicted of a crime. The goal might even be to achieve fame or notoriety. After he was captured, the serial killer Henry Lee Lucas falsely confessed to scores of unsolved murders in an apparent attempt to gain notoriety as the most prolific serial murder in history. People have voluntarily confessed for a variety of peculiar reasons—to impress a girlfriend, to provide an alibi for one's whereabouts while having an affair, to get revenge on police by making them look incompetent (Gudjonsson, 2003).

An *Authentic-Coerced* false confession occurs when, as a product of a long or intense interrogation, suspects become convinced—at least temporarily—that they may have actually committed the crime. In most authentic-coerced confessions, the confessors typically do not develop false memories but, instead, come to believe that they may have committed the crime despite having no memory of doing so. At the suggestion of the interrogators, the suspects may come to temporarily believe that they "blacked out" or "repressed" their memories of the crime. In some cases, interrogators have suggested (and innocent suspects have come to believe) that the suspects suffer from multiple personality disorder and that a separate personality—unrecognized by the confessors—temporarily emerged to commit the crime. In a few exceptional cases, intensely coercive interrogations have caused innocent suspects to create false but vivid memories of crimes they did not commit (Ofshe, 1992; Wright, 1994).

Finally, an *Authentic-Voluntary* false confession occurs when someone who may or may not be a serious suspect confesses to a crime with little or no pressure from interrogators. In high-profile, well-publicized cases police investigators sometimes receive multiple, unsolicited confessions from delusional or mentally ill people who appear to believe they have committed the crime.

A PERSON–SITUATION ANALYSIS OF FALSE CONFESSIONS: SUSPECT AND INTERROGATION RISK FACTORS

Social psychologists conceptualize behavior as an interaction between the person and the situation. That is, individual characteristics and situational forces combine to produce human behavior. If situational forces are extremely powerful, they are likely to overwhelm individual differences (Ross & Nisbett, 1991). In the area of false confessions, prolonged physical torture (a powerful situation) would likely induce nearly all of us to confess to crimes we did not commit. However, a less aversive form of interrogation (a less powerful situation) would allow individual strengths and vulnerabilities to have an effect. For example, a significant minority of suspects might falsely confess if subjected to a psychologically coercive interrogation that lasted several hours. When the situational pressures are weak—for example, when there is little coercion—only the most psychologically vulnerable people are likely to falsely confess. The most dangerous person-situation combination occurs when a psychologically vulnerable suspect is subjected to a highly coercive interrogation.

The Person: Factors Internal to the Suspect

There are several types of suspect vulnerabilities that raise the risk of false confessions. Risk factors internal to the suspect include youth, mental retardation or cognitive impairment, mental illness, vulnerable personality, as well as various forms of temporary impairment:

1. Youth: Many of the best-known examples of false confessions (including the Central Park jogger case) have involved a juvenile or young suspect. In the Drizin and Leo (2004) sample of proven false confessions, 32% were under the age of 18, and 63% were under the age of 25. The finding that juvenile suspects waive their Miranda rights at a rate about 12% higher than adult suspects also makes juveniles more vulnerable to false confessions (Grisso, 1999).
2. Mental retardation or cognitive impairment: Various forms of cognitive impairment including low intelligence or mental retardation appear to put suspects at risk for false confessions. In the Drizin and Leo (2004) sample, 22% of the false confessors could be classified as mentally retarded. Mentally retarded individuals tend to be more acquiescent and more likely to agree with illogical

questions, and are probably more easily confused by the tactics of interrogators (Finlay & Lyons, 2002).

3. Mental illness: We know that 10% of the Drizin and Leo (2004) sample were diagnosed with some form of mental illness. We do not know how many false confessors have undiagnosed impairment of some kind. Like mentally retarded suspects, mentally ill suspects may suffer from an inability to foresee the long-term consequences of admissions made in the interrogation room.
4. Vulnerable personality: People differ in their ability to resist coercion and persuasion. Although there may be several aspects of personality that make people vulnerable to false admissions (e.g., need for approval and social anxiety), two traits—high suggestibility and compliance to authority—have been specifically investigated because of their relationship to false confessions. Gisli Gudjonsson developed and tested two measures for use in this area: the Gudjonsson Compliance scale and the Gudjonsson Suggestibility scales (Gudjonsson, 2003).
5. Temporary impairments: In addition to stable personality vulnerabilities, a variety of transitory states may increase the risk of false confessions. Sleep deprivation lowers our resistance to coercion, and drugs or alcohol make us less able to evaluate the consequences of our actions. Grief has also been implicated in false confessions. Several false confessions have involved a husband or son who, in a state of grief, confessed to killing a wife, mother, or sister. All of these temporary states of impairment create mental confusion and appear to weaken resistance to coercion.

One final point: Although innocence is a logical precondition for making a false confession rather than a risk factor, Kassin (2005) noted that innocence itself may contribute to false confessions. People with no prior criminal records are more likely to waive their Miranda rights (Leo, 1996b), perhaps because they feel that they have nothing to hide, or because they do not want to look guilty. Once in the interrogation room, they may admit to involvement in a crime, thinking that the misunderstanding can be cleared up later.

The Situation: Factors in the Interrogation Process

Crime investigators draw a clear distinction between "interviews" and "interrogations" (Inbau, Reid, Buckley, & Jayne, 2001). Interviews are nonaccusatory conversations designed to gather information about a crime or to identify the likely perpetrator. In contrast, the goal of interrogation is to get a confession. An interrogation begins with an accusation, for example, "The evidence shows that you definitely committed this crime." Interrogations vary in length, intensity, and the number and type of techniques used, but all are designed to induce the suspect to confess. Because the interrogator has already reached the conclusion that the suspect is guilty of the crime, interrogations tend to be confrontational and emotionally intense.

By far, the most influential of all modern interrogation methods is the Reid technique (Inbau et al., 2001). According to the Reid and Associates, Inc. website (2005), more than 300,000 interrogators have been trained to use the technique since 1974. The Reid approach is divided into nine steps beginning with direct confrontation and ending with a written confession. Underlying the nine steps are at least five basic elements. These situational elements include control, social isolation, certainty of guilt, minimization or elimination of culpability, and interpretation of suspect behavior:

1. Control: Suspects are interrogated in a small, sparse, room where every aspect of the situation—lighting, type of chairs, furniture arrangement, the direction of the conversation, and the length of the interrogation—is controlled by the interrogator. A key goal is to remove the psychological comfort of familiar surroundings, and to communicate—in large and small ways—that the suspect has lost control of the situation. It is worth noting that interrogation manuals and training include recommendations on even the smallest aspects of the interrogation environment (size of room, type of chair to be used) as well as behavioral scripts (when to stand and when to sit, when to move closer, key phrases to use).
2. Social isolation: Suspects are almost always interrogated alone. This is done to deprive the suspect of emotional support and to minimize contradictory information. The presence of a friend or ally might bolster the suspect's resistance to persuasion and might lead to additional challenges to the interrogator's version of events. The combination of control and social isolation frees up interrogators to create the social reality of the situation. Alone in a carefully constructed, alien environment, it is impossible for a suspect to independently assess the interrogator's claims about the crime and the evidence. These conditions have the psychological effect of disorienting and creating anxiety in the suspect.

3. Certainty of guilt: The interrogation begins with a direct accusation that the suspect committed the crime. An innocent suspect will respond to this accusation with denials, but interrogators are trained to challenge, cut off, and dismiss all denials. The message to suspects is: "You did it, we know you did it, the evidence against you is irrefutable." To bolster the claim that denial is futile, police may use a variety of evidence ploys. That is, they cite real or fabricated evidence that clearly establishes guilt. Examples of such ploys may include claims that others have implicated the suspect (eyewitnesses saw you do it, or others have told us you did it) or various forms of physical evidence (fingerprints, DNA, videotape from a security camera). Ofshe and Leo (1997a) described a variety of creative lies told by interrogators to convince suspects that they are caught. These accusations and claims of incriminating evidence occasionally convince innocent suspects that their only option is to falsely agree to or admit guilt.
4. Minimization or elimination of culpability: To clear the path for an admission of guilt, interrogators offer face-saving justifications or excuses for the crime. For example, it might be suggested that someone suspected of murder killed the victim by accident or in self-defense. It might be suggested to someone suspected of theft that the money was stolen to pay for an important family expense, or suggested to someone suspected of rape that he engaged only in consensual sex. The purpose of supplying a minimizing or exculpatory reason for committing the underlying act is to imply—but never explicitly state—that anyone making a judgment about the act (e.g., a judge, jury, or employer) would likely recommend more lenient treatment.
5. Interpretation of suspect behavior: Interrogators are trained to read verbal and nonverbal behavior as a means of determining whether a suspect is lying. Unfortunately, the behavioral cues interrogators are taught to interpret are flawed indicators of deception (DePaulo et al., 2003). Scores of studies have examined whether people can detect when others are lying or telling the truth. The general finding is that both untrained observers and people with relevant professional training (police, psychiatrists, polygraph examiners) perform only slightly better than chance. Where chance accuracy is 50%, average accuracy is about 54%. Interestingly, training to improve accuracy does not reliably improve the ability to detect lies, but it does have effects: After

> training, people are more confident about their judgments, and they list more reasons for their judgments (Costanzo, 1992; Kassin & Fong, 1999).

"Confirmation bias" refers to the finding that once people form an impression or belief about someone, that belief is resistant to change because people seek out information that confirms the belief. During interrogation, police are prone to interpret suspect behavior in light of a belief that the suspect is guilty. In the interrogation room, the behavior of the suspect as well as further denials can be interpreted as evidence of guilt. For example, Kassin et al. (2005) had prison inmates give true and false videotaped confessions to crimes they did or did not commit. Next, police detectives and college students judged the truthfulness of these statements. College students performed better than chance at distinguishing true from false confessions, but police detectives did not. However, detectives were significantly more confident about the accuracy of their judgments, and showed a bias toward judging false confessions as true. The tendency to infer guilt increased with job experience and interrogation training.

FALSE CONFESSIONS AS DECISIONS

It is obviously difficult to imagine how suspects could reasonably weigh alternatives and come to the conclusion that offering a false confession is in their own self-interest. A key factor that should figure into suspects' decision-making process is the strongly negative potential outcome of confessing: a conviction and possibly a prison sentence. How is it, then, that someone who is innocent might decide that it makes sense to offer a false confession?

Most models of decision making rely on a modified rational model (March, 1994), that is, people weigh the value of alternatives and the subjective probabilities of various consequences that may arise from choosing each alternative. However, several elements of the interrogation process are likely to make the decision less than fully rational. Because the suspect is presumed to be guilty, the interrogation process is designed to make continued denials untenable. Once the suspect is convinced that his denials are implausible and ineffective, the objective is to make a confession appear to be the best available alternative. An analysis of false confessions as decisions must take into account the unusual characteristics of the interrogation process, including stress, lack of social support, constrained alternatives, manipulation of subjective probabilities, and the perceived costs and benefits of confessing.

First, the highly stressful, emotionally taxing process of interrogation is likely to impair our capacity to think clearly and dispassionately evaluate alternatives (Costanzo, 2004; Davis & O'Donahue, 2003). Second, as discussed earlier, the suspect is intentionally deprived of support from others—the suspect is alone in the room with an interrogator and without any friends or allies who could bolster his or her resistance. In contrast, for most important decisions, we weigh the alternatives, take our time, and talk with people we trust. In the context of an interrogation, it is impossible to independently assess whether the claims about the evidence (e.g., about fingerprints or eyewitnesses) against you are true. Third, by manipulating the subjective probabilities, the clear message is that evidence is overwhelming and that a judge or jury will have no difficulty finding you guilty. The probability of negative consequences is apparently very high—even if you are innocent, you will be convicted. Fourth, as noted earlier, in the rarified world of the interrogation room, the option of denying involvement in the crime seems to make things worse. The alternative of admitting involvement (for a justifiable reason) may appear to be your only course of action. And the consequences of making an admission may seem less serious—perhaps if you just admit you did it, you can escape the interrogation room and, because you are innocent, you will be able to straighten out everything later. Or, at least you may be able to receive a reduced charge, sentence, or punishment. Finally, as a result of all these factors, the short-term benefit of ending the interrogation may become so salient that it outweighs the potential long-term costs. In short, the suspect may come to believe that it is in his self-interest to confess.

Several researchers discussed the factors that may influence the decision to confess (Kassin, 2005; Ofshe & Leo, 1997a). The most elaborate clinical analysis of interrogation and the decision to confess was provided by Gudjonsson (2003). He discussed how the decision to confess is facilitated by internal pressure to confess (the desire to relieve feelings of guilt), external pressures (police intimidation and fear), and perception of proof (the belief that the incriminating evidence is strong). In addition, he discussed cognitive, emotional, social, and physiological factors that may enter into the decision to confess.

Ofshe and Leo (1997a, 1997b) proposed a two-step process of psychological manipulation and influence through which the techniques of modern police interrogation are structured to move (presumed guilty) suspects from denial to admission. The first stage culminates in a state of hopelessness and despair produced by the realization that denying involvement in the crime is futile. This state of hopelessness is achieved through the tactics of attacking all denials, challenging the veracity of the suspects' memory and alibi, and using real or fabricated evidence to demonstrate the suspects' guilt. During the second stage, the interrogator suggests inducements to motivate the suspect to perceive that it is in his self-interest to comply with the interrogator's wishes and confess. Interrogators guide suspects to this conclusion by implying that the crime may be understandable or excusable and by implying that a full admission will cause the case to be treated more leniently by the legal system. Taken together, these two steps of interrogation are designed to manipulate a suspect's perceptions of his available choices and the consequences that attach to each set of choices. Through this sequential two-step process of influence, modern interrogation leads to the decision to confess falsely either by leading the suspect to believe that his situation, though unjust, is hopeless and will only be improved by confessing; or by persuading him that he probably committed a crime about which he has no memory and that confessing is the appropriate and optimal course of action.

THE ADMISSIBILITY AND CONTENT OF EXPERT TESTIMONY ON INTERROGATIONS AND CONFESSIONS

Like other forms of expert testimony, the admissibility of expert testimony on potentially false confessions is governed by the *Frye* standard, the *Daubert* standard, and Rule 702 of the Federal Rules of Evidence. Because these general standards are fully discussed and evaluated in other chapters of this book (see Sales & Shuman, chap. 2, this volume), we describe only a few of the leading cases on the admissibility and content of expert testimony on interrogation and confessions (for a fuller discussion of this topic, see Fulero, 2004).

Three Important Cases Involving Expert Testimony on Interrogation and Confessions

In *Crane v. Kentucky* (1986), the U.S. Supreme Court reviewed a case involving the murder of a liquor store clerk in Louisville, Kentucky. Investigators were initially frustrated in their efforts by the lack of physical evidence linking anyone to the crime. However, a week after the murder,

Mr. Crane was arrested in connection with the robbery of a local service station. He was 16 years old at the time of arrest. During the course of a long interrogation, Crane confessed to several robberies and the shooting of a police officer. When asked about the liquor store murder, he initially denied involvement, but eventually confessed to that crime as well. Many of the details offered by Crane were at odds with other evidence in the case. For example, although the murder occurred at approximately 10:40 p.m., Crane said it happened during the day. Although no money was missing from the cash register, Crane described taking the money from the cash register. He later recanted his confession and claimed that it had been the result of coercion.

The defense attorney sought to introduce evidence about the coercive circumstances surrounding the confession. Mr. Crane had been held in a small, windowless room, interrogators denied his repeated requests to telephone his mother, he was interrogated for several hours, as many as six police officers were in the interrogation room at the same time, and the police interrogators behaved in an intimidating manner. Having already ruled that the confession was "voluntary," the trial judge ruled that information challenging the credibility of the confession could not be "developed in front of the jury." Crane was found guilty and sentenced to 40 years in prison.

Although the Kentucky Supreme Court affirmed the conviction and ruled that the trial judge did not err by excluding testimony about the circumstances surrounding the confession, the U.S. Supreme Court later reversed and remanded the case. The Supreme Court held that "certain interrogation techniques, either in isolation, or as applied to the unique characteristics of a particular suspect, are so offensive to a civilized system of justice that they must be condemned under the Due Process Clause of the Fourteenth Amendment." (p. 684) Furthermore, the Court held:

> A defendant's case may stand or fall on his ability to convince the jury that the manner in which the confession was obtained casts doubt on its credibility ... stripped of the power to describe to the jury the circumstances that prompted his confession, the defendant is effectively disabled from answering the one question every rational juror needs answered: If the defendant is Innocent, why did he previously admit his guilt? (p. 688)

In 1991, the California Court of Appeals reviewed a case involving expert psychological testimony on interrogation and confessions (*California v. Page*, 1991). In that case, Bradley Page had been convicted of killing his girlfriend, Bibi Lee (for a fuller analysis of the Page case, see Leo & Ofshe,

2001; Pratkanis & Aronson, 1991; Wrightsman & Kassin, 1993). In November of 1984, three undergraduates at the University of California, Berkeley—Bradley Page, Bibi Lee, and Robin Shaw—went for a run in the Oakland Hills. Lee became separated from her friends and went missing. Her body was found in the Oakland Hills about 5 weeks later. The main evidence against Page was his "confession" (Leo & Ofshe, 1998, 2001). He admitted to "going off on her," hitting and kicking her, leaving her unconscious, later returning to have sex with her dead body, and then burying her in a shallow grave he had dug with the hubcap of his car.

By about 10:00 a.m. on the day after the discovery of Lee's body, Page was in an interrogation room at the Oakland police department. He was "interviewed" for 1½ hours and then gave a tape-recorded statement denying any involvement in Lee's death. Page then agreed to take a polygraph test to prove his innocence. In response to the polygraph examiner's questions, he denied knowing anything about the murder. However, the polygraph examiner falsely informed him that the machine indicated that he was lying about his lack of involvement in the crime (Leo & Ofshe, 2001). Following the polygraph test, he was taken back to the interrogation room where the interrogation process continued until sometime after 1:00 a.m. the following day. During the course of more than 15 hours of interrogation, the police emphasized that they knew Page was lying because he failed the polygraph test, he behaved suspiciously, and he had not searched seriously enough for Lee after her disappearance. Page was asked to close his eyes and imagine how it might have happened. When he was unable to recall specific details, interrogators suggested that he might have "blacked it out." An officer told him he would sit in jail and "rot from the inside out" if he could not remember what happened. To escalate the pressure on Page, the officers then told him two lies about the evidence in the case: that they found his fingerprints at the scene, and that an eyewitness had identified his car near the crime scene. They also suggested that he probably killed her by accident, in the midst of a heated lover's quarrel. In addition to the taped statement mentioned earlier, Page made three more taped statements (though in total only 3 hours of Page's 16-hour interrogation was recorded by the Oakland police). In the second statement, he agreed to a scenario in which he killed Lee and had sex with her corpse. In the third and fourth statements, he retracted his confession and said that it was the result of fear, isolation, confusion, threats, and police requests to imagine the crime (see Leo & Ofshe for a fuller analysis of the interrogation techniques that led to Page's confession and retraction).

The expert retained to testify about Page's confession was Elliot Aronson, an eminent social psychologist and professor at the University of California, Santa Cruz. During expert testimony, Aronson discussed the process of persuasion under conditions of stress and the psychological factors that might cause a suspect to falsely confess. Aronson's testimony also relied on general research findings in the area of social influence, including such classic studies as Asch's (1956) studies on conformity, and Milgram's (1983) studies of obedience. Aronson's general analysis of the Page confession was that the lengthy, coercive interrogation combined with social isolation weakened Page's resistance to influence. When the authority figures then confronted him with false—but seemingly incontrovertible—incriminating evidence (fingerprints and an eyewitness) he began to doubt his own memory and struggled to make sense of these discrepancies. Aronson also noted that police officers exploited Page's continuing guilt about leaving the park without Lee, and threatened that he would rot in prison unless he confessed to the crime.

During expert testimony, Aronson was also permitted to make specific reference to excerpts from the audiotaped statements, pointing out, for example, the tentative and vague character of Page's descriptions ("I envision a slope, little bit of a slope ... underneath the branches of a tree"). The judge did impose restrictions on the expert testimony—no opinion could be offered about whether Page's confession was false (such forbidding of "ultimate issue" testimony is typical for most forms of expert psychological testimony). Although Page was acquitted of first-degree murder at his first trial and the jury hung on the lesser included offense of voluntary manslaughter, at the retrial Page was convicted of voluntary manslaughter. After the defense appealed the conviction on the grounds that the trial court had placed too many restrictions on the expert testimony, the appeals court found that the restrictions were proper and consistent with the U.S. Supreme Court's reasoning in *Crane* (1986).

The third and final case we believe is worth mentioning here is *United States v. Hall* (1996, 1997), in which the Seventh Circuit Court of Appeals vacated the kidnapping and murder conviction of Larry Hall because the trial court had improperly excluded the testimony of two defense experts. The first, Dr. Richard Ofshe, was a professor of sociology at the University of California, Berkeley and a nationally recognized expert on coercive persuasion and false confessions. Dr. Ofshe "would have testified about the fact that experts in his field agree that false confessions exist, that individuals can be coerced into giving false confessions, and that certain indicia can be identified to show when they are likely to occur" (*United States v. Hall*, 1996, pp. 8–9). The second expert, a psychiatrist (Arthur Traugott), "would have testified about Hall's susceptibility to various interrogation techniques and his propensity to give a false confession." The trial judge had ruled that such testimony would "invade the prerogative of the jury" and "add nothing to what the jury would know from common experience." In vacating the conviction and remanding the case, the Seventh Circuit found that expert testimony may have been critical for Hall's defense and should have been allowed (*United States v. Hall*, 1996). The federal district court subsequently held a *Daubert* hearing and held that "the science of social psychology, and specifically the field involving the use of coercion in interrogations, is sufficiently developed in its methods to constitute a reliable body of specialized knowledge under Rule 702" (*United States v. Hall*, 1997, pp. 22–23).

The Content of Expert Testimony

The general role of the expert witness in cases involving a potentially false confession is to educate the jury or judge about the process and tactics of interrogation, and the psychological factors that might lead a suspect to falsely confess. When an objective record of the interrogation exists—an audiotape or videotape—the expert reviews that record and is generally permitted to offer an analysis of which factors may be present in the specific confession being considered by the court. Generally, it is the job of the expert witness to assist the fact finder by pointing out what factors should be considered in evaluating the reliability of a confession so that the jury can decide how much weight should be assigned to the confession. As in other areas, no "ultimate opinion" testimony on whether a particular confession is true or false is admissible. This prohibition is consistent with ethical standards for psychologists (Roesch, Hart, & Ogloff, 1999). Although there is little specific research on how jurors respond to expert testimony in this domain, research from other domains indicates that jurors use such testimony responsibly and are not likely to overweight expert testimony on interrogations and confessions (Cutler, Penrod, & Dexter, 1990; Vidmar et. al., 2000).

Except when the account of the crime given by the confessor directly contradicts the physical evidence in the case or it can be shown that it was physically impossible for the confessor to have committed the crime, it is usually not possible for an expert to determine with absolute certainty whether a confession is true or false. However, the following characteristics should increase skepticism about the veracity of a confession:

1. Lack of independent knowledge or corroborating evidence: In cases of false confessions, close examination of the postadmission narrative (the account of the crime given to investigators after the suspect says, "I did it") typically reveals substantial discrepancies between the postadmission narrative and the known facts of the crime. A true postadmission narrative should provide accurate crime details, lead to the discovery of new evidence, and reveal facts and information only the true perpetrator would know. Absent contamination by police or outside sources, the postadmission narrative of an innocent false confessor will not fit the facts of the crime, will be replete with errors, and will not lead police to new, missing or derivative evidence (Leo & Ofshe, 1998; Ofshe & Leo, 1997a).
2. A highly coercive interrogation: Coerciveness can be defined in a variety of ways. Some possible elements of coercion include sleep deprivation, food deprivation, threats, promises, long duration, and the use of multiple interrogators. Psychologically coercive interrogation is usually the primary cause of police-induced false confessions in the modern era (Ofshe & Leo, 1997a). Excessively long interrogations are inherently coercive, and raise the risk of false confessions. In the Drizin and Leo (2004) study of proven false confessions, the average length of a confession was 16.3 hours. Lengthy interrogations lead to increased pressure from interrogators, extended social isolation, and fatigue that reduces a suspect's ability to resist police pressure. Long interrogations are frequently accompanied by sleep and food deprivation.
3. A vulnerable confessor: The presence of one or more of the suspect risk factors described earlier (youth, mental retardation, mental illness, vulnerable personality, temporary impairment) may raise doubts about the reliability of the confession (see Gudjonsson, 2003). The mentally impaired and juveniles are especially vulnerable to giving false confessions in response to high-pressure police interrogations (Drizin & Leo, 2004).

Many false confessions produced by coercion appear to follow a pattern where suspects repeatedly deny involvement in a crime, then, after a long, coercive interrogation, reluctantly capitulate and make a tentative admission of guilt. In many known false confessions, confessors quickly recanted soon after they left the interrogation room. Therefore, an additional hypothesis that needs further exploration is whether a pattern of repeated denials, capitulation, and quick retraction also distinguishes false from true confessions.

Of course, these are *potential* indicators of false confessions. Some suspicious confessions turn out to be true, and the truthfulness of other suspicious confessions cannot always be verified. Often, people who confess are convicted and sent to prison. These people may continue to proclaim their innocence for years but, unless clearly exonerating evidence is later uncovered or it turns out that it was physically impossible for the confessor to have committed the crime, we cannot be absolutely certain that an individual is truly innocent.

CHANGING THE LEGAL SYSTEM IN LIGHT OF PSYCHOLOGICAL RESEARCH: POSSIBLE SOLUTIONS TO THE PROBLEM OF FALSE CONFESSIONS

Jurors, judges, lawyers, police officers, and the public share the common goal of increasing the probability of inducing guilty people to confess while simultaneously reducing the probability of false confessions by innocent suspects. As research in this area continues to advance, we will eventually be able to specify the best interrogation practices—those that increase the probability of inducing guilty suspects to confess *without* causing innocent suspects to falsely confess. Some of these practices are already evident and current research findings suggest several ways of moving us closer to our common goal.

Reform Interrogation Training

During the training of police interrogators, there needs to be far more emphasis on the problems, causes, and consequences of false confessions. When asked about the possibility of false confessions, a common response of those who train interrogators is, "We don't interrogate innocent people" (Kassin, 2005). The theory is that police screen out innocent suspects through initial interviews or preliminary evidence gathering, and that only the guilty proceed to the interrogation stage of the investigation. However, actual police work does not appear to conform to this idealized model of crime investigation. Documented false confessions reveal that many innocent suspects are subjected to highly coercive interrogation techniques based on little more than a hunch or a misreading of a suspect's behavior as suspicious or deceptive. In addition, interrogation training needs to make far more modest claims about behavioral cues to deception. Research shows that it is extremely difficult for observers to make reliable judgments about whether someone is lying. Furthermore, research indicates that many of the behavioral cues identified by interrogation trainers do not differentiate liars from truth tellers. When faulty cues to deception are combined with the confirmation bias, police may put enormous pressure on innocent suspects. Some will falsely confess.

Impose Time Limits on Interrogations

One of the striking features of the false confession cases described earlier is the length of the interrogations. All lasted more than 10 hours. According to an empirical study by Leo (1996b), most interrogations last, on average, under 2 hours. However, in the Drizin and Leo (2004) study of 125 proven false confessions, the average length of interrogation was 16.3 hours. Clearly, longer interrogations appear to increase the risk of false confessions by fatiguing the suspect and thus impairing his ability and motivation to resist police pressures. As Davis and O'Donahue (2003) pointed out, exhaustion "may lead to greater interrogative suggestibility via deficits in speed of thinking, concentration, motivation, confidence, ability to control attention, and ability to ignore irrelevant or misleading information" (p. 957). An obvious potential reform would be to specify a time limit, such as no more than 4 hours (more than twice the amount of the typical interrogation).

Although some in law enforcement may object to a specified time limit, we believe that reasonable police would agree with it because it will only rarely undermine their ability to elicit true confessions. As Inbau et al. (2001) argued, "Rarely will a competent interrogator require more than approximately four hours to obtain a confession from an offender, even in cases of a very serious nature.... Most cases require considerably fewer than four hours" (p. 597). One complication may be when to start the clock. If an information-gathering interview transitions into a high-pressure interrogation, does every minute of contact count? If a frightened suspect is held overnight or for several hours in an isolated cell, do those hours count as part of the interrogation process? Would two 3-hour interrogations separated by several hours in a jail cell exceed the time limit? We believe that clear rules can be established, but we should expect resistance from those who believe that we should not give suspects the ability to wait out the time limit.

Videotape the Entire Interrogation Process

Numerous scholars in the last decade have called for the mandatory electronic recording of interrogations (Drizin & Colgan, 2001; Johnson, 1997; Kassin & Gudjonsson, 2004; Leo, 1996a; Slobogin, 2003; Westling, 2001; White, 1997). Videotaping the interrogation creates a permanent, reviewable record that can later be fully evaluated by judges, lawyers, jurors, and experts. Six states—Alaska (1985), Minnesota (1994), Illinois (2005), Maine (2004), New Mexico (2005), and Wisconsin (2005)—and the District of Columbia (2005) already require the videotaping of interrogations in some or all felony cases. The Supreme Court of Massachusetts recently ruled that confessions produced by unrecorded interrogations entitle the defendant to a special cautionary instruction to jurors (*Commonwealth of Massachusetts v. DiGiambattista*, 2004).

In addition to the creation of an enduring record of the interrogation, videotaping should have other salutary effects: It would reduce extreme and aggressive forms of coercion and have a civilizing effect on the behavior of interrogators; it would help to prevent false or unsubstantiated claims of police coercion; and it would allow for an assessment of the verbal, paralinguistic, and nonverbal behavior of both the suspect and the interrogator (Drizin & Reich, 2004; Sullivan, 2004). There is even research on *how* interrogations should be videotaped. In a series of studies by Daniel Lassiter and his colleagues (e.g., Lassiter & Geers, 2004; Lassiter & Irvine, 1986), it was shown that a neutral "equal focus camera perspective" showing both the suspect and the interrogator best enables jurors to assess the voluntariness of the confession and the coerciveness of the interrogation.

There appears to be relatively little resistance to this proposed reform. In a recent survey of 238 police departments in 38 states, Sullivan (2004) found strong support for videotaping interrogations. Reasons for police support of videotaping included: reduces the necessity for note taking, frees up the interrogators to focus on the suspect, enables officers to replay portions of the interrogation to check information, reduces the number of defense claims of coercion, and reduces the amount of time interrogators spend in court defending their interrogation practices. Routine videotaping would also create a large data archive that would enable researchers to determine with much greater precision how interrogations go wrong to produce false confessions. Such an archive would greatly enhance our ability to specify the best interrogation practices.

Police departments could also make use of these videotapes to improve the training of interrogators. For all these reasons, videotaping ought to be a national standard.

Limit Lying About Evidence and Psychological Trickery

Some scholars have argued for limiting police use of deception and trickery in the interrogation process (McMullen, 2005; White, 1979; Young, 1996). We believe that policymakers should reconsider the role of police deceit and trickery in eliciting false confessions and whether more effective limits should be placed on deceptive interrogation. Police training manuals (Inbau et al., 2001) continue to insist that police deception short of explicit promises and threats does not produce false confessions. Yet many false confessions are the product of interrogations in which police used false-evidence ploys and pretended to possess damning physical evidence against the suspect even though, in reality, none existed (Drizin & Leo, 2004; Ofshe & Leo, 1997b). As more American police electronically record interrogations, deception during interrogation will become more visible to judges, juries, and the public. The issue of the limits of deceptive interrogation deserves more attention than it has received in American law and policy.

In 1986, enactment of the Police and Criminal Evidence Act (PACE) made it illegal in England and Wales to trick suspects or to lie about evidence for the purpose of inducing a confession. The available evidence suggests that this prohibition against lying has not impaired the ability of police to extract confessions. Irving and McKenzie (1989) found that the number of admissions of guilt during police interrogations is not significantly lower than it was before the PACE reforms. However, a study by McConville (1992) found, at least in some cases, that the use of prohibited tactics such as lies and threats has been moved outside of the interrogation room (e.g., to questioning conducted in homes or police cars). Here, as in the United Kingdom, some police officers will be reluctant to abandon the use of lies and evidence ploys because they believe that lying is one of the most powerful weapons in their interrogation arsenal.

A special category of trickery does not involve claims of tangible evidence against a suspect (fingerprints, DNA, eyewitnesses) but the use of dubious psychological ploys. Suggestive psychological techniques that have led to false confessions from vulnerable suspects include asking suspects to close their eyes and imagine how a crime might have happened, using a polygraph test (or a voice stress analyzer) to convince suspects that the interrogator knows they are lying, suggesting that the suspects may have "blacked out" or repressed all memories of committing the crime, or suggesting that the suspects may suffer from a multiple personality disorder and that an evil, submerged personality of the suspects may have briefly surfaced to commit the crime.

Require an Appropriate Adult When Interrogating a Vulnerable Suspect

This proposed requirement is one of the reforms put in place by PACE (1986) and there appears to be little reason not to adopt such a requirement in the United States. In the great majority of cases, *vulnerable* would be defined as being a juvenile, although suspects known to be mentally ill or mentally retarded would also be considered vulnerable. Under current standards, interrogators exploit suspect vulnerabilities in ways that too often lead to false confessions. The person designated as an appropriate adult might be a lawyer, or a person (independent of police interrogators) specially trained to fill this role. We would suggest that parents should not play this role because parents do not necessarily provide a safeguard against false confessions. For example, in the Central Park jogger case, four of the five boys who confessed had a parent present for most or all of the interrogation. And, the father of one of the boys put additional pressure on his son to confess, apparently believing the son would only be released if he admitted guilt.

Provide Expert Testimony on Interrogations and Confessions

It will come as no surprise that we endorse the use of responsible expert testimony on interrogation practices and the psychology of false confessions. But we are not alone: In recent years a number of scholars have called for the use of expert testimony in this area (Davis & O'Donahue, 2003; Kassin & Gudjonsson, 2004; White, 2003). There is now a substantial and well-accepted body of scientific research on this topic, and the use of social science expert testimony in cases involving a disputed interrogation or confession has become increasingly common. As Kassin and Gudjonsson noted, "In this new era of DNA exonerations, however, it is now clear that such testimony is amply supported not only by anecdotes and case studies of wrongful convictions, but also by a long history of basic psychology and an extensive forensic science literature" (p. 59).

As we have seen, the vast majority of American case law supports the admissibility of such expert testimony (see Fulero, 2004, for a review). Although there have been a few cases in which courts have not permitted expert testimony, they are exceptional; social psychologists have testified in hundreds of criminal and civil trials that have generated no written opinions (Kassin & Gudjonsson, 2004). We conclude this chapter by pointing out that it often serves the interest of justice to present the social science research on the psychology of police interrogation, coercion, and false confession to jurors and judges. Without the educational and sensitizing effect of expert testimony, judges and jurors may simply accept a confession at face value even though it may be coerced and false (as occurred in all DNA exonerations based on false-confession evidence). Failure to allow expert testimony may contribute to the erroneous conviction and incarceration of an innocent person.

Expert testimony in disputed cases may be necessary because the traditional procedures of the adversarial system (e.g., opening and closing arguments, cross-examination of witnesses, cautionary instructions to juries) are not sufficient to safeguard innocent individuals against the likelihood of wrongful conviction based on unreliable confession evidence. The purpose of expert testimony is to educate triers of fact about the findings of scientific research on interrogation and confessions. Such testimony helps judges and jurors understand the psychological principles, practices, and processes of modern interrogation so that they can better discriminate between reliable and unreliable confessions.

Expert testimony may reduce the number of police-induced false confessions that lead to wrongful convictions in three ways: (a) its direct effect on the decision making of the judge at pretrial suppression hearings (at which time the judge decides which evidence to allow at trial and which to exclude), (b) its direct effect on the decision making of jurors at trial, and (c) its indirect effect on the behavior of police and prosecutors. The use of social science expert testimony at pretrial suppression hearings will make judges more likely to exclude from evidence coerced confessions, some percentage of which are likely to be false. As a result, the use of pretrial expert testimony will result in the admission of fewer police-induced false confessions into evidence at trial, which in turn will result in fewer wrongful convictions.

If a factually disputed confession is introduced at trial, the obvious question in the mind of jurors (as noted in *Crane*, 1986) is likely to be, "If the defendant is innocent, why did he previously admit his guilt?" Although the question is obvious, the answer is not. A confession is a powerful piece of evidence, and many defendants have been convicted and sent to prison based solely or primarily on their confession. At trial, social science expert testimony can aid the jury by: (a) discussing the scientific research literature documenting the phenomenon of police-induced false confessions, (b) explaining how and why particular interrogation methods and strategies can cause the innocent to confess, (c) identifying the conditions that increase the risk of false confession, and (d) explaining how experts generally analyze the postadmission narrative and its fit (or lack of fit) with objectively knowable crime facts for clues about a confession's reliability (or lack of reliability). By educating the jury about the existence, psychology, causes, and indicia of police-induced false confession, social science expert testimony at trial should reduce the number of confession-based wrongful convictions.

Finally, the use of expert testimony in pretrial suppression hearings and at jury trials should exert an educative and corrective effect on the future behavior of police and prosecutors. When interrogation experts testify, police and prosecutors take notice—especially in high-profile cases that rest entirely on disputed confession evidence (like the Central Park jogger case). Like all of us, police and prosecutors do not like to have their mistakes exposed or their conclusions challenged. Police do not like to be criticized for using inappropriate or coercive methods, or to be shown to have elicited demonstrably false confessions. Prosecutors do not like to be criticized for indicting defendants based solely on coerced or false confessions, to be forced to dismiss charges after a judge suppresses the defendant's confession, or to have a defendant acquitted because of an unreliable confession. By exposing flaws, social science expert testimony in disputed confession cases may deter misbehavior and improve police and prosecutorial screening practices. It should lead to a decline in the use of psychologically coercive interrogation methods and a reduction in the number of false confessions elicited and introduced into evidence at trial. As a consequence, fewer innocent men and women will be wrongfully convicted because of false confessions.

REFERENCES

Aronson, E. (2004). *The social animal* (9th ed.). New York: Worth.

Asch, S. E. (1965). Opinions and social pressure. *Scientific American, 193*, 31–35.

Blandon-Gitlin, I., Pezdek, K., Rogers, M., & Brodie, L. (in press). Detecting deception in children: An experimental study of the effect of event familiarity on CBCA ratings. *Law and Human Behavior.*

California v. Page, 2 Cal. App. 4th 161 (1991).

Colorado v. Connelly, 497 U.S. 157 (1986).

Commonwealth of Massachusetts v. DiGiambattista, No. SJC = 09155 (August 16, 2004).

Costanzo, M. (1992). Training students to decode verbal and nonverbal cues: Effects on confidence and performance. *Journal of Educational Psychology, 84*, 308–313.

Costanzo, M. (2004). *Psychology applied to law*. Belmont, CA: Thompson/Wadsworth.

Costanzo, M., & Peterson, J. (1994). Attorney persuasion in the capital penalty phase: A content analysis of closing arguments. *Journal of Social Issues, 50*, 125–147.

Crane v. Kentucky, 476 U.S. 683 (1986).

Cutler, B., Penrod, S., & Dexter, H. (1990). Nonadversarial methods for sensitizing jurors to eyewitness evidence. *Journal of Applied Social Psychology, 20*, 1197–1207.

Davis, D., & O'Donahue, W. (2003). The road to perdition: Extreme influence tactics in the interrogation room. In W. O'Donahue (Ed.), *Handbook of forensic psychology* (pp. 897–996). New York: Basic Books.

Daubert v. Dow Pharmaceutical, Inc., 509 U.S. 579 (1993).

DePaulo, B., Lindsay, J., Malone, B., Muhlenbruck, L., Charlton, K., & Cooper, H. (2003). Cues to deception. *Psychological Bulletin, 129*, 74–112.

Drizin, S., & Colgan, B. (2001). Let the cameras roll: Mandatory videotaping of interrogations is the solution to Illinois' problem of false confessions. *Loyola University Chicago Law Journal, 32*, 337–424.

Drizin, S., & Leo, R. (2004). The problem of false confessions in the post-DNA world. *North Carolina Law Review, 82*, 891–1007.

Drizin, S., & Reich, M. (2004). Heeding the lessons of history: The need for mandatory recording of police interrogations to accurately assess the reliability and voluntariness of confessions. *Drake Law Review, 52*, 619–646.

Finlay, W., & Lyons, E. (2002). Acquiescence in interviews with people who have mental retardation. *Mental Retardation, 40*, 14–29.

Frye v. United States, 293 F. 1013 (D.C. Cir. 1923).

Fulero, S. (2004). Expert psychological testimony on the psychology of interrogations and confessions. In G. D. Lassiter (Ed.), *Interrogations, confessions, and entrapment* (pp. 247–263). New York: Kluwer.

Grisso, T. (1999). Juvenile offenders and mental illness. *Psychiatry, Psychology, and Law, 6*, 143–151.

Gross, S. (1996). The risks of death: Why erroneous convictions are common in capital cases. *Buffalo Law Review, 44*, 469–500.

Gudjonsson, G. (2003). *The psychology of interrogations and confessions*. New York: Wiley.

Huntley, J., & Costanzo, M. (2003). Sexual harassment stories: Testing a story-mediated model of juror decision-making in civil litigation. *Law and Human Behavior, 27*, 29–51.

Inbau, F. E., Reid, J. E., Buckley, J., & Jayne, B. (2001). *Criminal interrogation and confessions*. Gaithersburg, MD: Aspen.

Irving, B., & McKenzie, I. K. (1989). Police interrogation: The effects of the PACE Act. London: Police Foundation.

Johnson, G. (1997). False confessions and fundamental fairness: The need for electronic recording of custodial interrogations. *Boston University Public Interest Law Journal, 6*, 719–751.

Kassin, S. (2005). On the psychology of confessions: Does innocence put innocents at risk? *American Psychologist, 60,* 215–228.

Kassin, S., & Fong, C. T. (1999). I'm innocent! Effects of training on judgments of truth and deception in the interrogation room. *Law and Human Behavior, 23,* 499–516.

Kassin, S., & Gudjonsson, G. H. (2004). The psychology of confessions: A review of the literature and issues. *Psychological Science in the Public Interest, 5,* 33–67.

Kassin, S., Meissner, C., & Norwick, R. J. (2005). I'd know a false confession if I saw one: A comparative study of college students and police investigators. *Law and Human Behavior, 29,* 211–228.

Kassin, S., & Neumann, K. (1997). On the power of confessions: An experimental test of the fundamental difference hypothesis. *Law and Human Behavior, 21,* 469–484.

Kassin, S., & Sukel, H. (1997). Coerced confessions and the jury: An experimental test of the harmless error rule. *Law and Human Behavior, 21,* 27–46.

Kassin, S., & Wrightsman, L. (1985). Confession evidence. In S. Kassin & L. Wrightsman (Eds.), *The psychology of evidence and trial procedure* (pp. 67–81). Beverly Hills, CA: Sage.

Lassiter, G. D., & Geers, A. L. (2004). Evaluation of confession evidence: Effects of presentation format. In G. D. Lassiter (Ed.), *Interrogations, confessions, and entrapment* (pp. 197–214). New York: Kluwer.

Lassiter, G. D., & Irvine, A. A. (1986). Videotaped confessions: The impact of a point of view on judgments of coercion. *Journal of Applied Social Psychology, 16,* 268–276.

Leo, R. A. (1996a). The impact of Miranda revisited. *Journal of Criminal Law and Criminology, 86,* 621–692.

Leo, R. A. (1996b). Inside the interrogation room. *Journal of Criminal Law and Criminology, 86,* 266–303.

Leo, R. A. (2001). False confessions: Causes, consequences and solutions. In S. Westervelt & J. Humphreys (Eds.), *Wrongly convicted: Perspectives on failed justice* (pp. 36–54). New Brunswick, NJ: Rutgers University Press.

Leo, R. A., & Ofshe, R. J. (1998). The consequences of false confession: Deprivations of liberty and miscarriages of justice in the age of psychological interrogation. *Journal of Criminal Law and Criminology, 88,* 429–496.

Leo, R. A., & Ofshe, R. J. (2001). The truth about false confessions and advocacy scholarship. *Criminal Law Bulletin, 37,* 293–370.

March, J. G. (1994). *A primer on decision-making.* New York: Free Press.

McConville, M. (1992). Videotaping interrogations. *New Law Journal, 10,* 960–962.

McKee, R. (2001). *Story.* New York: HarperCollins.

McMullen, P. (2005). Questioning the questions: The impermissibility of police deception in interrogations of juveniles. *Northwestern University Law Review, 99,* 971–1006.

Meili, T. (2003). *I am the Central Park jogger.* New York: Scribner.

Milgram, S. (1983). *Obedience to authority.* New York: HarperCollins.

Munsterberg, H. (1908). *On the witness stand.* New York: Doubleday.

Ofshe, R. J. (1989). Coerced confessions: The logic of seemingly rational action. *Cultic Studies Journal, 6,* 1–15.

Ofshe, R. J. (1992). Inadvertent hypnosis during interrogation: False confessions due to dissociative state: Misidentified multiple personality disorder and the satanic cult hypothesis. *Journal of Clinical and Experimental Hypnosis*, *40*, 125–156.

Ofshe, R. J., & Leo, R. A. (1997a). The decision to confess falsely: Rational choice and Irrational action. *Denver University Law Review*, *74*, 979–1122.

Ofshe, R. J., & Leo, R. A. (1997b). The social psychology of police interrogation: The theory and classification of true and false confessions. *Studies in Law, Politics, and Society*, *16*, 189–251.

Olsen-Fulero, L., & Fulero, S. (1997). Commonsense rape judgments: An empathy-complexity theory of rape juror story making. *Psychology, Public Policy, and Law*, *3*, 402–427.

Pennington, N., & Hastie, R. (1993). The story model for juror decision-making. In R. Hastie (Ed.), *Inside the juror* (pp. 84–115). Cambridge, England: Cambridge University Press.

Police and Criminal Evidence Act. (1986). London: HMSO.

Pratkanis, A., & Aronson, E. (1991). *Age of propaganda: The everyday use and abuse of persuasion*. New York: Freeman.

Reid & Associates, Inc. (2005). *The Reid technique of interviewing and interrogation.* Retrieved from www.reid.comm

Roesch, R., Hart, S., & Ogloff, J. (1999). Specialty guidelines for forensic psychologists: Committee on ethical guidelines. *Law and Human Behavior*, *15*, 655–665.

Ross, L., & Nisbett, R. (1991). *The person and the situation*. New York: McGraw-Hill.

Russano, M. B., Meissner, C. A., Kassin, S. M., & Narchet, F. M. (2005). Investigating true and false confessions within a novel experimental paradigm. *Psychological Science*, *16*, 481–486.

Scheck, B., Neufeld, P., & Dwyer, J. (2000). *Actual innocence*. Garden City, NJ: Doubleday.

Slobogin, C. (2003). Towards taping. *Ohio State Journal of Criminal Law*, *1*, 309–322.

Sullivan, T. (1992). *Unequal verdicts: The Central Park jogger trials*. New York: Simon & Schuster.

Sullivan, T. P. (2004). *Police experience with conducting custodial interrogations*. Unpublished manuscript, Northwestern University School of Law, Center on Wrongful Convictions, Chicago, Illinois.

United States v. Hall, 93 F.3d 1337 (7th Cir. 1996).

United States v. Hall, 974 F. Supp. 1198 (1997).

Vidmar, N., Lempert, R., Diamond, S., Hans, V., Landsman, S., MacCoun, R., et al. (2000). Amicus brief: Kumho Tire v. Carmichael*Law and Human Behavior*, *24*, 383–400.

Warden, R. (2003). *The role of false confessions in Illinois wrongful murder convictions since 1970* (Center on Wrongful Convictions Research Report). Retrieved July 15, 2005, from www.law.northwestern.edu/depts/clinic/wrongful/FalseConfessions.htm (last accessed on July 15, 2005).

Westling, W. (2001). Something is rotten in the interrogation room: Let's try video oversight. *John Marshall Law Review*, *34*, 537–555.

White, W. (1979). Police trickery in inducing confessions. *University of Pennsylvania Law Review*, *127*, 581–629.

White, W. (1997). False confessions and the constitution: Safeguards against untrustworthy evidence. *Harvard Civil Rights-Civil Liberties Law Review, 32*, 105–157.

White, W. (2003). Confessions in capital cases. *University of Illinois Law Review, 2003*, 979–1036.

Wright, L. (1994). *Remembering Satan: A case of recovered memory and the shattering of an American family*. New York: Knopf.

Wrightsman, L., & Kassin, S. (1993). *Confessions in the courtroom*. Thousand Oaks, CA: Sage.

Young, D. (1996). Unnecessary evil: Police lying in interrogations. *Connecticut Law Review, 28*, 425–478.

Zimbardo, P. (1967). The psychology of police confessions. *Psychology Today, 1*, 17–20, 25–27.

5

Expert Testimony on Eyewitness Memory and Identification

Kathy Pezdek
Claremont Graduate University

Eyewitness evidence is critical for solving crimes, and it is often the sole source of evidence for determining who the perpetrator is. However, it has been estimated that each year in the United States, approximately 4,500 wrongful convictions occur based on mistaken eyewitness identifications (Penrod & Cutler, 1999). Studies consistently report that eyewitness misidentifications are the leading cause of erroneous convictions (Huff, 1987; Huff, Rattner, & Sagarin, 1996), and eyewitness evidence has been the major source of evidence used to convict innocent people who were later exonerated based on forensic DNA (Scheck, Neufeld, & Dwyer, 2000; Wells et al., 1998). Yet ironically, jurors tend to find eyewitness testimony especially compelling, despite the fact that: (a) the conditions under which most eyewitnesses observe a perpetrator are strongly associated with low subsequent identification accuracy; (b) mock jurors typically cannot accurately discriminate between accurate and inaccurate eyewitness identification testimony (Lindsay, Wells, & O'Connor, 1989); and (c) typical jurors misunderstand how memory works in general, and how specific factors affect the reliability of eyewitness identification (O'Toole, Cox, Easterly, & Schmechel, 2005). Psychologists who research eyewitness memory are aware of the factors associated with accurate versus inaccurate identification, and some of these psychologists testify in courts of law as eyewitness expert witnesses, to inform juries about these factors. The purpose of this chapter is to summarize the role that these eyewitness experts play in the courts.

The legal community today has a relatively favorable view of psychological research on eyewitness identification, but this has not always been the case. In his book, *On the Witness Stand*, Munsterberg (1908) presented research demonstrating the unreliability of eyewitness perception and memory, and argued that scientific psychology had much to offer the legal community on this topic. Attorneys and legal scholars were outraged with Munsterberg's suggestion that legal decisions should in any way be influenced by psychological research. For example, Moore (1907) wrote, "Among the legal profession it is familiar learning that experiments are valuable only when the conditions are fairly identical with those attending the occurrence under investigation.... Imagine him [Munsterberg] butting in with his so-called scientific experiments to appraise the testimony of a witness" (p. 127).

For most of the 20th century, there was a deep-rooted tension between legal procedures and scientific methods, and attorneys and judges were not keen on changing this. In fact, the records of American courts indicate that psychological research was not cited, nor did psychologists provide expert witness testimony, until the 1950s (Loh, 1981), and even then it was on topics of mental disorders, pretrial publicity, and civil rights, not on eyewitness memory. Fulero (1993) identified several early cases in which attempts to admit eyewitness expert testimony were rejected by the courts. In the cases of *Criglow v. State* (1931) and *People v. Collier* (1952), it was the trial courts' opinion that eyewitness expert testimony would "invade the province of the jury."

Since the mid-1980s, appellate courts have been more receptive to admitting eyewitness expert testimony (e.g., *People v. McDonald*, 1984; *State v. Chapple*, 1983; *State v. Moon*, 1986), and consequently, there has been a sharp increase in the number of trials in which eyewitness expert witnesses have testified. There are several reasons why the courts have become more open to eyewitness expert testimony. Some of the changes have been rooted in transitions in the legal field. First, there has been a shift in the legal criteria for admitting expert testimony from earlier requirements that the testimony must provide the jury with "appreciable help" (Ninth Circuit Federal Court of Appeals in *United States v. Amaral*, 1973) to more recently requiring that the expert testimony simply "assist" the jury (Rule 702 of the *Federal Rules of Evidence*, 1975). Second, it is now well established that errors in eyewitness identification are responsible for more cases of wrongful conviction than all other causes combined (Wells et al., 2000). In particular, more than 100 convictions have been overturned based on postconviction DNA evidence, and more than 75% of these are cases in which the initial convictions were based on eyewitness evidence (Scheck et al., 2000; Wells, 2001; Wells et al., 1998).

Some changes within the field of psychology have also aided in the admissibility of eyewitness expert testimony in courts. First, it is now clear that the information on eyewitness memory provided in expert testimony has "general acceptance" among psychologists (Kassin, Tubb, Hosch, & Memon, 2001). The "general acceptance" of the explanatory theory presented by an expert has been one of the criteria for admitting expert testimony since the classic case of *Frye v. United States* (1923), commonly called the *Frye* test. The acceptance of psychological research in legal contexts has been aided by the fact that there is a clear consensus within the field of psychology regarding what the acceptable standards of scientific proof are. Second, sufficient reliable evidence has accumulated over the past 30 years that we now have a much clearer understanding of how the personal and situation-specific variables operate with respect to crime (Cutler & Penrod, 1995). Finally, researchers have determined that some methods of assessing eyewitness memory are likely to promote incomplete or inaccurate recall or false identifications of innocent suspects (Wells et al., 2000). The high quality and the quantity of this research has been such that the U.S. Department of Justice has issued a set of national guidelines for the collection of eyewitness evidence in criminal cases (Technical Working Group for Eyewitness Evidence, 1999).

THE ROLE OF THE EXPERT WITNESS IN CASES INVOLVING EYEWITNESS MEMORY AND IDENTIFICATION

At the most general level, all expert witnesses attempt to educate the jury about a specific domain that is sufficiently beyond common experience that expert opinion could at least assist the trier of fact. There are numerous evidence codes that define and limit the scope of expert testimony in general, and eyewitness expert witnesses more specifically. In this chapter, I do not review these evidence codes, but rather focus on giving a general sense of typical eyewitness expert testimony. As a caveat, I need to say up front that no one really knows how many individuals testify as eyewitness expert witnesses, what the span of their qualifications is, or what the range is in the content of eyewitness expert testimony. I know about 10 psychologists who regularly testify as eyewitness expert witnesses, and I am familiar with the thrust of their testimony. These are academics with impressive publication track records in the field of eyewitness memory and identification. In this section of the chapter, I rely on what I know to be the content of the testimony of these individuals in discussing typical eyewitness expert testimony.

It is useful to begin this discussion by mentioning three things that eyewitness expert witnesses do not do. First, eyewitness expert witnesses rarely testify for the prosecution. This is not because they are prodefense; it simply reflects the way the courts work. If the prosecution considers their eyewitness case to be a strong one, they do not think that they need an eyewitness expert witness to tell the jury this, and if they have an eyewitness case without strong eyewitness evidence, they do not prosecute it. Thus, eyewitness expert witnesses are typically retained by the defense. Second, eyewitness expert witnesses, like all expert witnesses, cannot "speak to the ultimate issue." In other words, they cannot be asked about or comment on whether they think that the defendant is the real perpetrator; doing so would "invade the province of the jury." An eyewitness expert witness can address factors that were present in the case at hand and address how these factors affect eyewitness accuracy, but, it is up to the attorney—typically during closing argument—to make the links between these general factors and specific eyewitnesses.

Third, eyewitness expert witnesses do not test or interview eyewitnesses to determine whether they are reliable witnesses. In fact, an eyewitness expert witness is not permitted in court to comment directly on the circumstances or reliability of any eyewitness. The closest they can get to this is to respond to questions about a hypothetical situation that (of course) approximates the facts of the case at hand. This type of expert testimony is what Monahan and Walker (1988) called "social framework testimony" to distinguish it from other types of social science expert testimony that involve presenting the jury with data that were collected on the litigating parties.

Eyewitness Expert Pretrial Consultation

There are two aspects of the work done by an eyewitness expert witness: pretrial consultation and testimony. Ideally, an eyewitness expert witness gets involved in a case at the early stages, to assist the attorney in seeking relevant information prior to the trial, specifically at the preliminary hearing. However, the reality is that attorneys, especially public defenders, are constantly overworked and often do not get assigned a case until after the preliminary hearing. As a result, they give their eyewitness expert about as much time as they have to prepare for trial—frequently, only a couple of weeks. At this point, attorneys and the experts typically discuss the case on the phone so that: (a) the attorneys can determine whether eyewitness expert testimony is likely to work with their defense strategy and (b) the experts can determine whether there is a basis in the psychological research literature to question the reliability of the eyewitnesses in the case.

Once expert witnesses are retained on a case, they conduct the pretrial consultation. As part of the pretrial consultation, the experts review the relevant case materials—the police reports, investigators' reports, preliminary hearing transcript, and all lineup materials. The experts then prepare the attorney to present the eyewitness evidence to the jury. This involves, for example, consulting with the attorney to discern where there may be critical gaps in the information available about each eyewitness. In reviewing the case materials, the expert also assesses: (a) the conditions under which each eyewitness observed the perpetrator and (b) each eyewitness' identification history. The identification history is the timeline that maps out what types of identification tests were presented to each eyewitness and what the eyewitness' response was to each. From these data the eyewitness expert determines whether there may have been suggestive or biasing influences on the identification of the defendant.

After pretrial consultation, the attorneys decide whether to retain the eyewitness expert to testify in the trial, based on whether they think that the expert can advance their strategy for the case. The eyewitness expert then works with the attorney to prepare for testimony. Courtroom testimony is necessarily in a question-and-answer format; it is not an open-ended lecture. Thus, the attorney needs to be informed regarding the areas about which to question the expert. The pretrial work of an expert witness can be very effective preparing an attorney to present eyewitness evidence to the jury. Less than half of all cases on which I am retained as an eyewitness expert actually go to trial, and this appears typical from my conversations with other eyewitness experts. The majority of these cases are settled prior to trial, and a written declaration by an eyewitness expert frequently plays a role in the pretrial resolution of these cases.

Eyewitness Expert Trial Testimony

When a case does go to trial, most of the substance of the eyewitness expert testimony pertains to psychological factors that affect the accuracy of eyewitness memory. A brief summary of the research on these factors is discussed in the next section of this chapter. However, an effective expert witness does not just discuss each of these factors and present the relevant research. Rather, a successful expert witness tries to persuade the jurors and actually get them to think more accurately about eyewitness evidence. Jurors tend to overrely on eyewitness evidence; they find it overly compelling to hear an eyewitness say, for example, "That's the guy. I'll never forget his face!" The task of an eyewitness expert is to persuade the jury to evaluate the eyewitness evidence more analytically, so they can more accurately evaluate its reliability in light of the eyewitness circumstances in the case at hand.

This is done first by dispelling the myth that memory functions like a video camera. Eyewitnesses typically talk about memory as if they are just playing back a mental video-tape that has a picture of the perpetrator etched on it, and this fosters jurors' belief that memory works this way. Although this metaphor may be a useful one for talking about memory recall, it does not reflect how memory really works and, in fact, leads to many misconceptions about eyewitness memory. An important part of getting jurors to evaluate eyewitness evidence more accurately is dissuading them from using this mental model of eyewitness memory. One way of achieving this is by providing them with some everyday memory examples. It is useful, for instance, to ask jurors to think about the appearance of a U.S. penny, the vitamin pill that they take every day, the front of their house, the waitress who waited on them most recently in a restaurant, or, for a more salient event, the minister who married them or their delivery room nurse. When jurors attempt any of these memory tasks, they quickly realize that what they remember is not just a mental photograph of what they viewed. Expert testimony, like good teaching, involves not just dishing out information, but actually transforming the way people think about a domain.

Another challenge for an eyewitness expert is to convince the jury that eyewitnesses can make a misidentification even if they are extremely confident. Jurors have a difficult time reconciling a not-guilty verdict with a victim or witness who exclaimed, "That's the guy. I'll never forget his face!" Jurors also often think that casting a not-guilty vote invalidates the victim's terrifying experience, and no juror wants to be in that position.

A common way for the expert witness to deal with this challenge is to present the research indicating that there is only a modest correlation between eyewitness confidence and eyewitness accuracy (Sporer, Penrod, Read, & Cutler, 1995). Most eyewitness experts are scientists and as good scientists we usually try to convince people by presenting them with good data. However, it is useful for expert witnesses to remember that, for good or for bad, jurors do not typically think like scientists. For most people, a good example is more persuasive than a library full of good data. Fortunately, the postconviction DNA exoneration cases now avail to us more than a hundred good examples of cases in which confident eyewitnesses have been dead wrong.

THE SCIENTIFIC FOUNDATION FOR EXPERT TESTIMONY ON EYEWITNESS MEMORY AND IDENTIFICATION

As mentioned earlier, the bulk of the testimony by an eyewitness expert witness is focused on psychological factors that affect the accuracy of eyewitness memory and the research support for these effects. A great deal of research in the past several decades has focused on this topic. Excellent reviews of the research on eyewitness memory factors are available in a meta-analysis of facial identification studies by Shapiro and Penrod (1986), and more recently in the *Annual Review of Psychology* chapter by Wells and Olson (2003). Here I simply summarize these findings and discuss how eyewitness expert witnesses present this research to jurors.

The factors that affect the accuracy of eyewitness memory and identification have been categorized as either estimator variables or systems variables. Estimator variables, on which there is a great deal of research, are factors that effect eyewitness memory and identification and are not under the control of the criminal justice system. Systems variables, examined relatively more recently, are factors related to eyewitness identification that can be under the control of the criminal justice system.

The Confidence–Accuracy Relationship

When eyewitnesses testify in court, they usually express a high level of confidence in their identification of the defendant. After all, most eyewitnesses have selected the defendant from at least one, and usually multiple, prior lineups. Before presenting testimony about the estimator variables and systems variables that are relevant in a specific case, it is important to open jurors to the possibility that even a highly confident eyewitness can still be inaccurate. It makes sense that people would be more likely to trust the identification of a highly confident eyewitness than one expressing low confidence, but is confidence a useful indicator of accuracy?

There have been a sufficient number of studies on the accuracy-confidence relationship that conclusions about this relationship are now based on meta-analyses of these studies. The most recent of these meta-analyses was reported by Sporer et al. (1995). Across the 30 studies included in their meta-analysis (total sample size = 4,036), the accuracy-confidence relationship was $r = .29$, which, although statistically significant, accounts for only 8% of the variance. This means that if you think of the pie chart representing all factors that affect eyewitness identification accuracy, eyewitness confidence alone can account for 8% of this pie. This is typical of the low accuracy-confidence relationship reported in a number of other meta-analyses.

However, a stronger accuracy-confidence relationship was reported by Sporer et al. (1995) when they limited their analysis only to those individuals who chose to make an identification, $r = .41$. This finding is relevant to the courtroom situation because the eyewitnesses who testify in court are those who have chosen someone from a prior lineup, showup, or some other type of identification test. But how can an eyewitness expert help jurors understand what a .41 correlation between accuracy and confidence means? Wells, Olson, and Charman (2002) suggested that one way to think about this correlation is to draw the comparison to a similar relationship for which the correlation is in this same range. Using U.S. Department of Health and Human Services data, they reported that the correlation between a person's height and gender is .43. Thus, if we assume that eyewitnesses make accurate identifications about 50% of the time, encountering a highly confident mistaken identification would be about as common as encountering a tall female or a short male. Presenting the accuracy-confidence relationship to a jury in these terms would help diminish the sanctity of a highly confident eyewitness.

In addition, witness confidence is malleable. For example, it has been reported that repeatedly questioning eyewitnesses inflates their confidence without affecting the accuracy of memory (Shaw, 1996). Also, if, after making an identification (correct or incorrect), eyewitnesses are provided feedback that they are good witnesses, their subsequent confidence is inflated (Wells & Bradfield, 1999). By the time witnesses testify in court, they have typically been questioned multiple times, and it would not be surprising to learn that along the way, they have either inadvertently or directly received feedback that they "picked the right guy." The high confidence expressed in their trial testimony might simply reflect the effect of these factors that were experienced after the crime.

Estimator Variables

Once an eyewitness expert has convinced the jury that even highly confident eyewitnesses can be wrong, it is then appropriate to discuss the estimator variables associated with accurate and inaccurate identifications. The estimator variables can be divided into the characteristics of the witness and the characteristics of the observed event itself.

Characteristics of the Witness. The strongest witness characteristic associated with identification accuracy is whether the eyewitness and the perpetrator are of the same or different race or ethnicity. In a recent meta-analysis of the cross-race face-identification research, Meissner and Brigham (2001) reported a robust effect of this factor such that same-race faces are identified more accurately than cross-race faces. The age of the witness also affects witness accuracy. Elderly adults and very young children are less reliable eyewitnesses than young adults. There are also a few personality factors associated with the accuracy of eyewitness memory (see Shapiro & Penrod, 1986, for a review). However, the research on these personality factors is not likely to be presented in eyewitness expert testimony because eyewitness experts do not test or interview the actual eyewitnesses in a case, and are not permitted to comment directly on the reliability of any witness.

Characteristics of the Observed Event. Characteristics of the observed event play a more important role than witness characteristics in determining eyewitness accuracy. At the most basic level, the issue is simply, how carefully did the eyewitness observe the perpetrator to begin with? If the eyewitness never saw the perpetrator clearly to begin with, regardless of what occurs afterward, the reliability of the identification will be in doubt: garbage in, garbage out. Some of the relevant factors here are: (a) the duration of the observation (perpetrators observed only briefly are less likely to be correctly recognized afterward); (b) the type of attention given to the perpetrator (was the attention of the eyewitness drawn to the perpetrator or did the eyewitness not know the importance of the event until after the perpetrator had left the scene); (c) the distance and available lighting; (d) the presence or absence of a weapon (weapon focus reduces eyewitness identification accuracy); (e) the presence of multiple suspects or other sources of distraction; (f) whether the perpetrator was wearing a hat, sunglasses, or other disguise; (g) the distinctiveness of the perpetrator's appearance (distinctive-looking individuals are less likely to be misidentified); and (h) the stress that the eyewitness may have experienced while observing the perpetrator (the details of traumatic events are less accurately retained in memory).

In presenting this information to jurors, it is often useful to suggest that the defendant surely looks like the perpetrator; that, after all, is why the eyewitness selected the defendant from the lineup. But the question is, did the eyewitness ever see the perpetrator clearly enough to know that it is the defendant? Having an eyewitness expert systematically unpack the specific conditions under which the perpetrator was observed makes it more likely that the jurors can answer this question accurately.

Systems Variables

Systems variables are factors related to eyewitness identification that can be under the control of the criminal justice system, basically, how and when the identification ability of each eyewitness was tested. Jurors are rarely familiar with how the identification test procedures affect the reliability of eyewitness identification. The testimony of an eyewitness expert regarding systems variables can be especially useful for educating jurors regarding potential fallacies in eyewitness identification. The research on the role of specific systems variables has been reviewed in detail elsewhere (Wells et al., 1998; Wells & Olson, 2003). A summary of these findings is presented here with an emphasis on how this information can be convincingly presented to jurors by an eyewitness expert.

It is important for jurors to understand that just because an eyewitness has selected the defendant from a photographic lineup or a live lineup, it does not necessarily mean that the eyewitness actually remembers the defendant from the scene of the crime. Why is this? This is because a lineup is simply a multiple-choice test, and like all multiple-choice tests, the test can be fair and unbiased or unfair and biased. For example, if I want to assess whether you know which endocrine gland produces the hormone insulin, I might give you a test in which the options are: (a) the parathyroid glands, (b) the adrenal glands, (c) the pancreas, (d) the pituitary gland, (e) the thyroid. Alternatively, I might give you a test in which the options are: (a)the lungs, (b) the heart, (c) the pancreas, (d) the brain, (e) the intestines. If you had selected the answer, the pancreas, from the first set of options, I should be more impressed that you really know that the pancreas is the endocrine gland that produces insulin, because all five options are actually endocrine glands. In the second set of options, all you need to know to get the right answer is that the lungs, heart, brain, and intestines are not endocrine glands. This is quite different from actually knowing that the pancreas is the specific endocrine gland that produces the hormone insulin.

Giving an example like this is likely to change the way jurors think about eyewitness evidence and convince them that they should not be too impressed that an eyewitness has selected the defendant from a lineup until they actually hear the eyewitness' original description of the perpetrator and then see what the lineup looks like. Drawing a parallel to a photographic lineup procedure, all faces in the lineup should match the description given by the eyewitness (Luus & Wells, 1991) and be presented in photographs of similar quality and style such that extra attention is not drawn to the suspect (Buckhout, 1974).

In an attempt to optimize systems variables that impact eyewitness identifications, Wells et al. (1998) suggested three other rules for conducting lineups. First: "The person who conducts the lineup or photospread should not be aware of which member of the lineup or photospread is the suspect" (p. 627). In other words, a double-blind procedure should be used in conducting identifications. There is a large body of research on experimenter expectancy effects, demonstrating that individuals who have expectations about the performance of others (e.g., teachers, researchers, judges, police officers) communicate these expectations to their subordinates (e.g., students, subjects, jurors, witnesses) using a host of nonverbal cues, and actually affect the performance of these individuals (Rosenthal, 1976).

An example that communicates this point to jurors is the story of Clever Hans the horse (cf. Wozniak, 1999). Clever Hans and his trainer traveled around Germany in the early 20th century impressing people with Hans's ability to do mental arithmetic. People from the audience would pose arithmetic questions, and Clever Hans would answer each question by scratching the dirt with his hoof the correct number of times. Systematic research studies concluded that in fact, Clever Hans was not doing mental arithmetic; he was simply picking up nonverbal cues from the audience as to when he should stop scratching the dirt. The audience members had expectancies, and Clever Hans learned to read these expectancies and respond accordingly. If Clever Hans the horse can read nonverbal cues sufficiently accurately to produce correct answers to arithmetic questions, surely an eyewitness can read the nonverbal cues expressed by an investigating officer administering a lineup and respond accordingly. How can this prejudicial systems variable be resolved? The answer is simple. The officer asked to present the lineup or showup to the eyewitness should be one who does not know who the suspect is.

The second rule suggested by Wells et al. (1998) to optimize systems variables that impact eyewitness identifications is: "Eyewitnesses should be told explicitly that the person in question might not be in the lineup or photospread and therefore should not feel that they must make an identification. They should also be told that the person administering the lineup does not know which person is the suspect in the case" (p. 629). This rule follows from the research findings that eyewitnesses are less likely to false alarm and identify an innocent suspect if they are told that the perpetrator may not be in the lineup (Parker & Ryan, 1993). Prior to attempting an identification, most witnesses are read an admonition in which they are told, "You should not conclude or guess that these photographs contain a picture of the person or persons who committed the crime. You are not obligated to identify anyone. It is just as important to exonerate the innocent as it is to identify the suspect." However, this information is often nullified by the fact that officers phone the eyewitnesses after having had no contact with them for weeks or even months. The officer may tell the eyewitness or simply imply that a suspect has been apprehended, and that their appearance at a lineup or showup is requested. If eyewitnesses expect that the police "have the guy," they approach the lineup with the intention to pick someone. Consequently, eyewitnesses are likely to select from the lineup the individual who looks most like the perpetrator, even if they do not actually recognize that individual from the scene of the crime. Under these conditions, a misidentification is likely to occur. Without the testimony of an eyewitness expert, jurors are not likely to realize the potential harm caused when eyewitnesses approach a lineup with the expectation that they are going to pick the closest match.

The third rule suggested by Wells et al. (1998) to optimize systems variables that impact eyewitness identifications is: "A clear statement should be taken from the eyewitness at the time of the identification and prior to any feedback as to his or her confidence that the identified person is the actual culprit" (p. 635). As mentioned before, although the correlation between eyewitness accuracy and confidence is modest, the confidence expressed by eyewitnesses during testimony is the single strongest determinant of whether their identification will be perceived to be accurate. However, eyewitness confidence is malleable and can easily be affected by feedback received after an identification has been made. To minimize the potential for postidentification inflation of confidence, eyewitness feedback should be obtained at the time that a lineup selection is made, before the eyewitnesses perceive any feedback from the officer in attendance. In discussing the accuracy-confidence relationship, an eyewitness expert can help the jury understand how to interpret eyewitness confidence appropriately and identify potential sources that may have influenced confidence malleability.

JURORS' RESPONSE TO EXPERT TESTIMONY ON EYEWITNESS MEMORY AND IDENTIFICATION

Those of us who testify as eyewitness experts want to know how real jurors' perceptions of eyewitness evidence are affected by the testimony of an eyewitness expert witness. But, as one could imagine, it is difficult to have access to real jurors to assess their perceptions. I have a study in process in which jurors, after they have delivered their verdict in a real trial, are asked to assess their opinion of the eyewitness evidence before and after the testimony of an eyewitness expert witness. They are also asked to assess which of the factors that the eyewitness expert discussed influenced their opinion of the eyewitness evidence the most. This is a very slow-moving study, because judges are reluctant to grant access to jurors, and jurors are reluctant to reveal much about their thinking in real trials.

Alternative methods have been used to assess mock jurors' responses to eyewitness expert testimony, but it is difficult to know how well these results are likely to generalize to real jurors in a real trial. Trials typically take multiple days and the testimony of an eyewitness expert typically takes 3 to 5 hours. Any procedure intended to simulate the testimony of an eyewitness expert in a real trial is not likely to deliver the dosage typical of real eyewitness testimony if it involves a condensed version of the testimony or does not avail the full audiovisual presentation of the expert. Unfortunately, most of the mock trial research used to assess the impact of eyewitness expert testimony suffers from this shortcoming in dosage.

In the early studies assessing the impact of eyewitness expert testimony (see e.g., Blonstein & Geiselman, 1990; Loftus, 1980; Maass, Brigham, & West, 1985), mock jurors read a brief (only several pages) description of a criminal case, including a summary of the prosecution's case and the defense case. They then read a brief summary of the testimony of an eyewitness expert (experimental condition) or not (control condition). Although it was generally reported that providing a summary of the testimony of an eyewitness expert decreased guilty verdicts, it is difficult to generalize this finding to real courtroom testimony in light of the mundane realism of this methodology. As discussed earlier, a successful expert witness tries to persuade the jurors and engage them in more accurately evaluating eyewitness evidence. Expert testimony involves not just dishing out information, but actually transforming the way people think about eyewitness evidence. It would be naive to expect that teachers could be assessed by evaluating a one-page verbal summary of one of their lectures, and no one would do this. Similarly, it is naive to expect that the effectiveness of eyewitness experts could be assessed by evaluating a one-page verbal summary of their testimony.

More recently, there have been some better-executed assessments of the effectiveness of eyewitness expert testimony. This work was thoroughly reviewed by Leippe (1995). Rather than reviewing this work here, I will simply focus on two of these studies (Cutler, Dexter, & Penrod, 1989; Cutler, Penrod, & Dexter, 1989). In these studies, over 500 college students and 100 experienced jurors viewed a videotape of an armed robbery trial that included the testimony of an eyewitness to the robbery. The eyewitness evidence was strong or weak, and the confidence expressed by the eyewitness was 80% or 100%. In the experimental condition, an eyewitness expert presented elaborate testimony about factors that affect the accuracy of eyewitness memory and was cross-examined about limitations of the relevant research. The findings were that in the absence of eyewitness expert testimony, jurors' verdicts and ratings of the eyewitness's accuracy were insensitive to correlates of eyewitness accuracy. However, this was not the case when jurors heard eyewitness expert testimony. Following eyewitness expert testimony, jurors' verdicts and ratings of the eyewitness's accuracy were significantly higher under eyewitness conditions associated with higher accuracy. Presence of the expert testimony, however, did not have a significant main effect on either verdicts or ratings of eyewitness accuracy.

Together, these results suggest that eyewitness expert testimony increases jurors' sensitivity to, but not their general skepticism of, eyewitness evidence. This is an important distinction. Certainly, under some conditions eyewitnesses are likely to make accurate identifications and under other conditions they are not likely to make accurate identifications. The goal of eyewitness expert testimony is not to make jurors dubious or skeptical of all eyewitness evidence, but rather to increase jurors' sensitivity to the conditions under which eyewitness identification is reliable or not. However, it is too early to conclude whether eyewitness expert testimony in general is more likely to increase skepticism, sensitivity, or neither. Across the various studies investigating this issue, the results have been mixed, and the methods have varied widely in degree of realism.

In the absence of eyewitness expert testimony, the primary vehicle available to attorneys to educate the jury about the reliability of eyewitness evidence is the instructions from judges, known as the Telfaire instructions. These are instructions read to the jury before they deliberate, delineating some of the factors associated with eyewitness accuracy. Several studies concluded that jurors often misunderstand or ignore judges' instructions (Glassman, Deckelbaum, & Cutler, 1989). Furthermore, Greene (1988) reported that the Telfaire instructions increased jurors' skepticism but not their sensitivity to eyewitness evidence, and Cutler, Dexter, and Penrod (1990) found that the Telfaire instructions had no effect on either jurors' skepticism or sensitivity.

In light of the fact that jurors often overrely on eyewitness evidence, yet are insensitive to whether eyewitnesses are accurate, it is important to consider some way to educate jurors about the reliability of eyewitness evidence. The Telfaire instructions, the most common vehicle for educating jurors about the reliability of eyewitness evidence, are apparently ineffective in this regard. Providing an eyewitness expert at the time of trial appears more promising, but the mundane realism of the research to date on this topic seriously constrains the generalizability of the findings to real trials.

SUGGESTIONS FOR MODIFYING THE LEGAL SYSTEM IN LIGHT OF THE PSYCHOLOGICAL RESEARCH ON EYEWITNESS MEMORY AND IDENTIFICATION

Several specific suggestions for revising the legal system follow from the research reviewed earlier. The first of these concerns how eyewitness evidence is collected, recorded, and used. Photographic and live lineups should be administered in a fair and unbiased manner following the guidelines of the Technical Working Group for Eyewitness Evidence (1999). Every time officers testify about an "identification" that they gleaned from an eyewitness in a showup or lineup, they should be questioned about the procedures followed to obtain this identification. These procedures should then be compared to those recommended in the U.S. Department of Justice (DOJ) guidelines for law enforcement on eyewitness evidence (1999), which can be downloaded from the Internet (http://www.ojp.usdoj.gov/nij/pubs-sum/178240.htm). Although the DOJ guidelines are not as extensive as those available in places such as New Jersey, Massachusetts, Minnesota, and North Carolina, they are better than the procedures followed in most places. However, because these guidelines are rarely followed, an audio-video recording should be made of each eyewitness at each lineup so that the jury can see exactly what transpired.

Another safeguard is important in light of the finding from several studies that misidentifications are especially likely when witnesses are shown a lineup that does not contain the actual perpetrator. A suspect should not be placed in a lineup unless there is compelling evidence that that individual may actually be the perpetrator. Wells (1993) suggested a "probable cause" criterion before placing a person in what he called "lineup jeopardy." This would prevent the police from placing a suspect's picture in a lineup on a whim, or with weak evidence linking him to the crime.

Encouragingly, several states have advanced legislative solutions to reform eyewitness identification procedures. In Hawaii, Maryland, Missouri, Rhode Island, and Virginia, bills have already been introduced to the state legislature for reforms in eyewitness identification procedures. More recently, eyewitness-related legislation has been introduced in California, the District of Columbia, Georgia, Louisiana, Massachusetts, Oregon, Tennessee, Texas, and Wisconsin (Ehlers, 2005).

A second suggestion for revising the legal system follows from the research reviewed earlier. Given the general insensitivity of jurors to eyewitnesses accuracy, it is important to educate jurors about the reliability of eyewitness evidence. This is typically done with the Telfaire instructions read to jurors by judges prior to their deliberation or by eyewitness expert testimony. One suggestion for the legal system is to revise the Telfaire instructions so that they: (a) more accurately reflect the research findings; (b) convey the magnitude and the direction of the effects of the eyewitness factors described; and (c) present the factors in a more elaborated manner, perhaps with examples, to educate the jurors rather than simply conveying information. CALJIC[1] Instruction 2.92, for example, instructs jurors regarding the effect of stress on memory, that they should consider "the stress, if any, to which the eyewitness was subjected at the time of the observation." This instruction conveys neither how stress affects memory (i.e., does stress make memory better or worse?) nor how strong the effect of stress on memory is. This single sentence alone is unlikely to help jurors understand how it is that stress affects eyewitness identification accuracy. Surely more instructive jury instructions could be developed.

---

[1]California Jury Instructions—Criminal (California, USA).

Finally, in appropriate cases, eyewitness expert testimony should be admitted in court as it has proven to be effective in educating jurors about the reliability of eyewitness evidence. But some innovations might improve the effectiveness of eyewitness expert testimony. One of these might be establishing eyewitness experts as court-appointed rather than defense-appointed expert witnesses. Expert witnesses are more likely to be perceived as impartial if not appointed by the prosecution or the defense. Jurors are also more likely to find the expert witness trustworthy and persuasive if appointed by a higher authority, the judge, rather than either attorney. Judges have the discretion to call court-appointed witnesses at any time during a trial. It might also be helpful to have eyewitness experts testify at the beginning of a trial rather than toward the end of the trial during the defense case. Jurors might be less inclined to overrely on eyewitness evidence if they are instructed about the fallacies of eyewitness identification and memory prior to hearing the eyewitness evidence itself.

In conclusion, the recent finding that eyewitness evidence is the major source of evidence used to convict innocent people who were later exonerated based on forensic DNA has served as a call to action. This call to action has motivated both psychologists who study eyewitness memory and testify as eyewitness experts and legal professionals eager to remediate the high rate of eyewitness misidentifications. It is clear that "the need for eyewitness expert testimony is meaningful and large" (Leippe, 1995, p. 947), and the legal community today has a relatively favorable view of psychological research on eyewitness identification. Although some judges and attorneys still harbor ill will toward psychologists who "butt in" to appraise the testimony of an eyewitness, eyewitness expert witnesses are increasingly more likely to consult with legal professionals and testify in courts of law. Viewed in a historic context, the courts are moving in the right direction, especially for defendants facing dubious eyewitness evidence in trial.

REFERENCES

Blonstein, R., & Geiselman, R. E. (1990). Effects of witnessing conditions and expert witness testimony on credibility of an eyewitness. *American Journal of Forensic Psychology*, 8, 11–19.

Buckhout, R. (1974). Eyewitness testimony. *Scientific American*, *231*, 23–31.

CALJIC 2.92 (1984 New).

Criglow v. State, 36 S.W.2d 400 (1931).

Cutler, B. L., Dexter, H. R., & Penrod, S. D. (1989). Expert testimony and jury decision making: An empirical analysis. *Behavioral Sciences and the Law*, *7*, 215–225.

Cutler, B. L., Dexter, H. R., & Penrod, S. D. (1990). Nonadversarial methods for sensitizing jurors to eyewitness evidence. *Journal of Applied Social Psychology, 20,* 1197–1207.

Cutler, B. L., & Penrod, S. D. (1995). *Mistaken identification: The eyewitness, psychology and the law.* New York: Cambridge University Press.

Cutler, B. L., Penrod, S. D., & Dexter, H. R. (1989). The eyewitness, the expert psychologist, and the jury. *Law and Human Behavior, 13,* 311–332.

Ehlers, S. (2005, April). Eyewitness identification: State law reform. *The Champion,* 34–36.

Federal Rules of Evidence for United States Courts and Magistrates. (1975). St. Paul, MN: West Group.

Frye v. United States, 293 F. 1013 (D.C. Cir. 1923).

Fulero, S. M. (1993). *Eyewitness expert testimony: An overview and annotated bibliography, 1931–1988.* Unpublished manuscript, Sinclair College, Dayton, Ohio.

Glassman, I. P., Deckelbaum, J., & Cutler, B. L. (1989). Improving juror understanding for intervening causation instructions. *Forensic Reports, 2,* 173–189.

Greene, E. (1988). Judge's instructions on eyewitness testimony: Evaluation and revision. *Journal of Applied Social Psychology, 18,* 151–276.

Huff, C. R. (1987). Wrongful conviction: Societal tolerance of injustice. *Research in Social Problems and Public Policy, 4,* 99–115.

Huff, C. R., Rattner, A., & Sagarin, E. (1996). *Convicted but innocent: Wrongful conviction and public policy.* Thousand Oaks, CA: Sage.

Kassin, S. M., Tubb, V. A., Hosch, H. M., & Memon, A. (2001). On the "general acceptance" of eyewitness testimony research. *American Psychologist, 56,* 405–416.

Leippe, M. R. (1995). The case for expert testimony about eyewitness memory. *Psychology, Public Policy, and Law, 1,* 909–959.

Lindsay, R. C. L., Wells, G. L., & O'Connor, F. (1989). Mock juror belief of accurate and inaccurate eyewitnesses: A replication. *Law and Human Behavior, 13,* 333–340.

Loftus, E. F. (1980). Impact of expert psychological testimony on the unreliability of eyewitness identification. *Journal of Applied Psychology, 65,* 9–15.

Loh, W. D. (1981). Psychological research: Past and present. *Michigan Law Review, 79,* 659–707.

Luus, C. A. E., & Wells, G. L. (1991). Eyewitness identification and the selection of distracters for lineups. *Law and Human Behavior, 15,* 43–57.

Maass, A., Brigham, J. C., & West, S. G. (1985). Testifying on eyewitness reliability: Expert advice is not always persuasive. *Journal of Applied Social Psychology, 15,* 207–229.

Meissner, C., & Brigham, J. C. (2001). Twenty years of investigating the own-race bias in memory for faces: A meta-analytic review. *Psychology, Public Policy, and Law, 7,* 3–35.

Monahan, J., & Walker, L. (1988). Social science research in law: A new paradigm. *American Psychologist, 43,* 465–472.

Moore, C. (1907). Yellow psychology. *Law Notes, 11,* 125–127.

Munsterberg, H. (1908). *On the witness stand: Essays on psychology and crime.* Garden City, NJ: Doubleday.

O'Toole, T., Cox, T. A., Easterly, C. F., & Schmechel, R. S. (2005, April). District of Columbia Public Defender survey. *The Champion,* 20–32.

Parker, J. F., & Ryan, V. (1993). An attempt to reduce guessing behavior in children's and adults' eyewitness identifications. *Law and Human Behavior, 17*, 11–26.

People v. Collier, 249 P.2d 72 (Cal. 1952).

People v. McDonald, 37 Cal.3d 351, 690 P.2d 709, 716, 208 Cal.Rptr. 236, 245 (1984).

Penrod, S. D., & Cutler, B. (1999). Preventing mistaken convictions in eyewitness identification trials. In R. Roesch, S. D. Hart, & J. R. P. Ogloff (Eds.), *Psychology and law: The state of the discipline* (pp. 89–118). New York: Kluwer.

Rosenthal, R. (1976). *Experimenter effects in behavioral research*. New York: Irvington Press.

Scheck, B., Neufeld, P., & Dwyer, J. (2000). *Actual innocence*. New York: Random House.

Shapiro, P. N., & Penrod, S. (1986). Meta-analysis of facial identification studies. *Psychological Bulletin, 100*, 139–156.

Shaw, J. S., III (1996). Increases in eyewitness confidence resulting from postevent questioning. *Journal of Experimental Psychology: Applied, 2*, 126–146.

Sporer, S. L., Penrod, S. D., Read, J. D., & Cutler, B. L. (1995). Choosing, confidence, and accuracy: A meta-analysis of the confidence-accuracy relation in eyewitness identification studies. *Psychological Bulletin, 118*, 315–327.

State v. Chapple, 135 Ariz. 281, 660 P.2d 1208, 1221 (1983).

State v. Moon, 45 Wash. App. 692, 726 P.2d 1263 (1986).

Technical Working Group for Eyewitness Evidence. (1999). *Eyewitness evidence: A guide for law enforcement*. Washington, DC: U.S. Department of Justice, Office of Justice Programs.

United States v. Amaral, 488 F.2d 1148 (9th Cir. 1993).

U.S. National Institute of Justice (1999). *Eyewitness evidence: A guide for law enforcement*. Washington, DC: NCJ 178240.

Wells, G. L. (1993). What do we know about eyewitness identification? *American Psychologist, 48*, 553–571.

Wells, G. L. (2001). Police lineups: Data, theory and policy. *Psychology, Public Policy, and Law, 7*, 791–801.

Wells, G. L., & Bradfield, A. L. (1999). Distortions in eyewitnesses' recollections: Can the postidentification-feedback effect be moderated? *Psychological Science, 10*, 138–144.

Wells, G. L., Malpass, R. S., Lindsay, R. C. L., Fisher, R. P., Turtle, J. W., & Fulero, S. M. (2000). From the lab to the police station: A successful application of eyewitness research. *American Psychologist, 55*, 581–598.

Wells, G. L., & Olson, E. A. (2003). Eyewitness testimony. *Annual Review of Psychology, 54*, 277–295.

Wells, G. L., Olson, E. A., & Charman, S. D. (2002). The confidence of eyewitnesses in their identifications from lineups. *Current Directions in Psychological Science, 11*, 151–154.

Wells, G. L., Small, M., Penrod, S. D., Malpass, R. S., Fulero, S. M., & Brimacombe, C. A. E. (1998). Eyewitness identification procedures: Recommendations for lineups and photospreads. *Law and Human Behavior, 22*, 603–647.

Wozniak, R. H. (1999). *Classics in psychology, 1855–1914: Historical essays*. Dorset, England: Thoemmes Continuum.

6

Expert Testimony in Sexual Harassment Cases: Its Scope, Limits, and Effectiveness

Maureen O'Connor
John Jay College of Criminal Justice, CUNY

The juxtaposition of law, psychology, and policy is drawn starkly in the domain of sexual harassment. The legal parameters for sexual harassment cases depend on behavioral assumptions and practices, whereas the psychological reality of sexual harassment in the 21st century is much determined by how it transpires in the legal and policy context.

Looking back at the now historic Thomas-Hill controversy for a moment is instructive. During Clarence Thomas's Supreme Court confirmation hearings, Law Professor Anita Hill came forward with allegations of sexual harassment against Judge Thomas stemming from their work together at the Equal Employment Opportunity Commission (EEOC) and Justice Department many years before. Significant attention was paid to Professor Hill's failure to complain until the confirmation hearings. When asked why she did not complain at the time of the alleged sexual harassment, she responded that she was sure she could not answer that question satisfactorily. She cited fear of retaliation, damage to her professional life, and ultimately said, "I can't explain. It takes an expert in psychology to explain how that can happen" (Thomas Hearings, 1991).

Can a psychological expert explain Professor Hill's behavior? What role can and should psychologists play in sexual harassment litigation?

Psychologists are actively involved in sexual harassment cases, with roles for clinicians, clinical scientists, social psychologists, human resource or I-O psychologists, and others. A psychologist might serve as the mental health professional helping to identify and treat any trauma or psychological consequences that might have resulted from the alleged harassment or as the social framework expert discussing the social and organizational climate in which sexual harassment is most likely to occur; or, as Anita Hill hoped, as the expert explaining why a target might or might not complain about it or why an environment might lead someone to sexually harass another. And, of course, given the nature of the adversary system, psychologists testify on both sides of sexual harassment cases, leading to a battle of the experts that might call into question the utility of the psychological information for those tasked with deciding the case. Some of these battles have been quite heated and raise interesting questions about the role of expert witnesses in the legal system.

This chapter examines the scope of the psychological knowledge that experts have brought to bear in sexual harassment cases. It explores the limits of that knowledge, some of the primary battles that have occurred in these cases, and the extent to which we know whether such testimony affects decision making in these cases. It draws on the extensive legal and psychological literature in the field, especially important work by Barbara Gutek, Louise Fitzgerald, Peggy Stockdale, and other scholars; a recent chapter I published with a colleague (O'Connor & Vallabhajosula, 2004); an informal discussion with a number of leading psychologists working as experts in these cases; and a timely and helpful new text edited by Foote and Goodman-Delahunty (2005a) entitled *Evaluating Sexual Harassment: Psychological, Social, and Legal Considerations in Forensic Examinations*.

It is organized to address four overarching questions:

1. What is typically the content of expert psychological testimony on sexual harassment?
2. How strong is the scientific foundation for expert testimony on sexual harassment?
3. Is there research on how jurors respond to expert testimony on sexual harassment?
4. How might the legal system (e.g., procedures, standards, instructions) be modified in light of psychological research on sexual harassment?

Additionally, the chapter touches on a fifth related topic that is applicable beyond sexual harassment, but that is magnified in that context because of the gendered nature of the topic: the effect of gender of the expert.

WHAT IS THE TYPICAL CONTENT OF EXPERT TESTIMONY ON SEXUAL HARASSMENT?

The content of expert testimony provided by psychologists in sexual harassment cases is shaped by the demands of the legal standards and legal framework provided by statutory and case law. Although sexually harassing behavior has been around since time immemorial, it was not considered unlawful until a quarter of a century ago. In 1979, Professor Catherine MacKinnon articulated an argument that such behavior violated the law (MacKinnon, 1979). A ready vehicle at the time was federal antidiscrimination law and, for better or for worse (see, e.g., Franke, 1997; Schultz, 1998), that has shaped and constrained the legal claim of sexual harassment since that time.

Title VII of the Civil Rights Act of 1964 (1994) itself contains no specific language prohibiting sexual "harassment." Instead, it prohibits "discriminat[ion] against any individual with respect to ... compensation, terms, conditions, or privileges of employment, because of such individual's ... sex"[1] (Title VII, 1994, §2000e-2(a) (1)). A narrow reading of Title VII might have restricted it to an equal treatment analysis. Instead, however, through a series of important legal decisions beginning in 1976, the Supreme Court has interpreted the statute to include sexual harassment, slowly recognizing its scope as discrimination on the basis of sex within the meaning of Title VII. Five or six major cases give us much of this legal framework.

The legal parameters begin with the EEOC's definition of sexual harassment:

> [u]nwelcome sexual advances, requests for sexual favors, and other verbal or physical conduct of a sexual nature constitute sexual harassment when (1) submission to such conduct is made either explicitly or implicitly a term or condition of an individual's employment, (2) submission to or rejection of such conduct by an individual is used as the basis for employment decisions affecting such individual, or (3) such conduct has the purpose or effect of unreasonably interfering with an individual's work performance or creating an

[1]Most states now follow Title VII's standards when analyzing sexual harassment claims under their state antidiscrimination statute (see O'Connor & Vallabhajosula, 2004).

> intimidating, hostile, or offensive working environment. (EEOC Guidelines on Discrimination Because of Sex, 1992, §1604.11 (a))

The guidelines envision two basic scenarios that have led to unlawful sexual harassment: quid pro quo and "hostile work environment" sexual harassment. Classic quid pro quo harassment occurs when a supervisor grants or withholds a job benefit based on a subordinate's (un)willingness to comply with sexual advances (*Burlington Industries, Inc. v. Ellerth*, 1998). Hostile work environment harassment occurs when an employee is subjected to unwelcome sexual conduct that is sufficiently severe or pervasive as to alter the conditions of the victim's employment and create an abusive working environment. In its most recent cases, particularly in *Burlington Industries, Inc. v. Ellerth*, the Supreme Court has downplayed this distinction for legal liability purposes, focusing more directly on whether the plaintiff has suffered a tangible employment action of any kind. But the distinction remains descriptively useful to express the breadth of behavior that can be at issue.

In practice, to establish liability for a sexual harassment claim, the plaintiff must establish three basic elements: (a) that she (or he, as the number of claims filed by males has increased in the last several years) was subjected to "unwelcome conduct"; (b) that the conduct was discrimination based upon sex; and, (c) that it caused harm. Each of these challenging elements contains significant psychological content that can be fodder for expert testimony. If plaintiffs succeed in establishing liability, they must then present evidence in support of their damages claim as well. These four components of a typical case, then, will provide the framework for presenting the predominant categories of potential expert testimony in sexual harassment cases.[2]

One further preliminary point should be made. Gutek and Stockdale (2005) recently described the differences in the manner in which plaintiffs and defendants in sexual harassment cases use social science evidence. According to these scholars, plaintiffs tend to borrow more heavily from the extant literature. Plaintiffs' experts generalize the findings from a relevant body of literature to the case at hand. Defendants'

[2]For a book-length treatise on the topic, with a helpful conceptualization and thorough discussion of issues related to conducting an evidence-based forensic consultation in a sexual harassment case, see Foote and Goodman-Delahunty (2005a). Foote and Goodman-Delahunty helpfully reduced the expert witness issues to two: credibility and causation, though within each, many areas of expertise are implicated. For an especially concise overview of the issues on which expert psychologists might be called to testify, see the list provided on pages 66 to 69 of chapter 3 of that volume.

experts, conversely, are likely to assume that the existing literature is too narrow and not applicable to their case. They may insist that only data collected from the defendant work site would be useful. With these important distinctions in mind, the following discussion focuses primarily on the relevance of existing social science findings to sexual harassment cases.

Unwelcome Conduct

The concept of the unwelcomeness of the alleged sexual advances, which was called the "gravamen of any sexual harassment claim" by the late Chief Justice William Rehnquist (*Meritor Savings Bank v. Vinson*, 1986, p. 68), was designed to provide a legal distinction between consensual relationships at the workplace and unlawful sexual harassment. In practice, it often operates to the detriment of the plaintiff because it has the effect of putting the victim on trial. It focuses attention on the victim's behavior before and during the harassment rather than on the accused harasser's conduct (Burns, 1995, p. 196; Fitzgerald, 2004). It also opens the door to inquiry into the plaintiff's prior sexual conduct, abuse, and even mental health history: what Louise Fitzgerald (2003, p. 919) facetiously called the "doctrine of perpetual consent"—once abused, raped, harassed, adulterous, even adopted in one case, always willing to consent to sexual encounters at work. Finally, it places a premium on the plaintiff's postharassment behavior, particularly whether the plaintiff formally complained about the offending behavior.

Psychological expert testimony is highly relevant to each of these inquiries. It can be highly contentious as well. So much of a successful sexual harassment claim turns on whether the plaintiff can tell a credible story. Plaintiff credibility has been shown to be an important predictor of sexual harassment judgments (see, e.g., O'Connor, Gutek, Stockdale, Geer, & Melançon, 2004). Huntley and Costanzo (2003) identified several elements of persuasive plaintiff stories that could be linked to favorable judgments. These include that the victim was a good employee of good character, that the company knew about the harassment but failed to intervene, that the harassment was systemic, that the company retaliated against the victim in some way, and that she feared for her job and suffered because of the harassment. Implicitly recognizing the importance of such factors, the Supreme Court made the complainant's behavior, speech, and dress relevant as a matter of law in determining whether the conduct was unwelcome (*Meritor*, 1986; see also Stockdale, O'Connor,

Gutek, & Geer, 2002). As such, the social framework testimony of a psychologist can be essential to explaining the literature on victim blaming and stereotyping that might influence the judgment regardless of whether harassment occurred (see, e.g., Burgess & Borgida, 1999; see also *Jenson v. Eveleth Taconite*, 1993).[3] In one of the most prominent sex discrimination examples, Susan Fiske testified that Ann Hopkins' lack of conformity to traditional female stereotypes (of being feminine, nurturing, nice) led those in power to make adverse decisions about her employment status based on stereotype rather than on her performance (*Price-Waterhouse v. Hopkins*, 1989; see also Fiske, Bersoff, Borgida, Deaux, & Heilman, 1991).

To provide a specific example of social framework testimony on this point, Fitzgerald (2004, p. 98) observed that a long line of studies "show that men are prone to read sexuality into objectively friendly interactions and incidental interchanges," that they find "implied consent" in many aspects of women's behavior, even in the face of disinterest or even overt discouragement (see also Abbey, 1987; Stockdale, 1998). Such information provides a context for explaining how the plaintiff might perceive the behavior as unwelcome when the alleged harasser would not.

It is possible to discredit the plaintiff's claim of unwelcomeness of the harassment from a more clinical perspective. An expert might claim that the plaintiff's prior sexual life, mental status, or personality sheds light on the interaction between the alleged harasser and the plaintiff (see, e.g., Feldman-Schorrig & McDonald, 1992). Fitzgerald (2004, p. 102) called this "character as evidence of welcomeness."

A 1994 federal shield law is supposed to bar admission of evidence offered to prove that the victim engaged in other sexual behavior or to prove the victim's sexual predisposition or hypersensitivity to these behaviors (Federal Rules of Evidence 412(a)(1)–(2)). Yet, this protection is not foolproof (Fitzgerald, 2003). A court need only find that the testimony's probative value outweighs its prejudicial effect. At least one forensic psychiatric expert called for more not less on this score, asserting that a forensic clinical expert in a sexual harassment case "should explore whether the plaintiff's own emotional condition contributed to the alleged harassment" (Feldman-Schorrig, 1994, p. 342). Under such a view, complainants' prior sexual experiences (unwanted or otherwise) or mental health could be

[3]Monahan and Walker (1986) coined the term social framework evidence to describe the use of general research results, so-called off-the-shelf research, to provide a frame of reference or context for deciding fact issues in a particular case. This is a common form of expert testimony in sexual harassment cases as is described later.

relevant to determining whether a current workplace interaction constitutes consensual social relations or unwanted sexual advances (see Feldman-Schorrig & McDonald, 1992). In a thorough review of the empirical literature on trauma, however, Foote and Goodman-Delahunty (2005b) found no credible support for this approach (see also Fitzgerald, Buchanan, Collinsworth, Magley, & Ramos, 1999). Moreover, although it is impossible to rule out the existence of significant personality disorder as leading to the occasional false or unsubstantiated claim of sexual harassment, it was their informed view that it is "extremely rare" to find such behavior (Foote & Goodman-Delahunty, p. 110). Furthermore, a number of studies have shown that prior exposure to unwanted sexual attention does not produce hypersensitivity to sexual harassment (Fitzgerald, et al.; Reilly, Lott, Caldwell, & DeLuca, 1992; Stockdale et al., 2002). In contrast, clinical expertise can be used to explain that the very conditions that might undermine the plaintiff's credibility (e.g., paranoia, instability, histrionics) can just as readily be the result of the harassment as an indication of lack of credibility (Binder, 1992).

The courts are, of course, focused on process. Both the EEOC and the Supreme Court have placed significant emphasis on process. Under the law, the primary sign of unwelcomeness is the most overt rejection of any unwanted overtures—the filing of a formal complaint. Although it is not an essential element of the claim, its absence must be addressed. And, it is of direct concern in terms of determining who is liable if sexual harassment is established. In talking with experts and reviewing the literature, this issue appears to be one of the most common topics of expert testimony in sexual harassment cases. Professor Hill had it at least partially correct—psychologists do have some demonstrated expertise on this topic, and to a great extent, it runs counter to the legal philosophy.

It is well accepted that overtly complaining is not necessarily a typical reaction to sexual harassment (Brooks & Perot, 1991; DuBois, Knapp, Faley, & Kustis, 1998; Gutek, 1985; Gutek & Koss, 1993; Schneider, Swan, & Fitzgerald, 1997). In a thorough review of the data on complaint prevalence, Fitzgerald (2004) concluded that filing a formal complaint is the least prevalent response to sexually harassing behavior. In one large study, for example, only 3% of those who were harassed reported the harasser (Fitzgerald et al., 1988). The majority of people try to avoid contact with the harasser, whereas a significant proportion say they are uninterested. The empirical reality seems to be that some people complain, others stay silent until they leave, and still others engage the sexual banter and try to fit in (Fitzgerald, Swan, & Fischer, 1995). These responses, though perhaps typical psychologically, pose serious challenges legally because they seriously undermine the targets' claims that they did not "welcome" the behavior. In describing her experiences, one forensic psychiatrist reports that she is often asked about the typicality of the target's behavior, and why there might be discrepancies in the plaintiff's reactions from what others might expect (Binder, 1992). Expert testimony can be essential here to explain the failure of a target of harassment to complain (see, e.g., *Robinson v. Jacksonville Shipyards, Inc.*, 1991; *Stockett v. Tolin*, 1992).

Discrimination "Because of ... Sex"

The second element in a plaintiff's proof relates to the "sex" discrimination aspect of the claim. As the law of sexual harassment developed, some defendants argued that general sexualized environments were not discrimination based on sex because they were not aimed at individual women (see, e.g., *Robinson v. Jacksonville Shipyards, Inc.*, 1991). This line of argument was defeated by social psychological expert testimony on sex stereotyping from Susan Fiske, Barbara Gutek, and others (Burns, 1995). These experts described conditions that would make it more likely than not that stereotyping would occur. The relevant factors can include the male-to-female ratio in the workforce, features in the environment that make sex stereotypes more salient (such as pinups or degrading language), an unprofessional ambience, the absence of clear company norms that would make such conduct unprofessional, and sex-role spillover (wherein traditional sex roles are imposed on women in male-dominated occupations, resulting in an environment more conducive to sexual harassment: see Burgess & Borgida, 1999; Burns, 1995, p. 199; see generally Gutek, 1985).

More recent case law has confirmed that a sexualized or hostile work environment falls within Title VII's antidiscrimination, "because of ... sex" parameters (see generally O'Connor & Vallabhajosula, 2004; see also *Oncale v. Sundowner Offshore Services, Inc.*, 1998). What took a bit longer to resolve was whether that was also true for harassment that occurred between members of the same sex. The Supreme Court resolved the technical, legal question in *Oncale v. Sundowner Offshore Services*—same-sex harassment can be the basis for a cause of action under Title VII. Nevertheless, the jurisprudence in same-sex cases is far from clear or uniform. Significant theoretical critique has ensued (see, e.g., Franke, 2004; Halley, 2004; Spindelman, 2004), suggesting that the U.S. Supreme Court has not sufficiently clarified the meaning of "sex" so as to guide lower courts on when discrimination has actually occurred in this context. And the courts are struggling to translate the guidance in *Oncale* to individual cases before them (see, e.g., *Pedroza v. Cintas Corp.*, 2005, in which the court required evidence to suggest motivation by homosexual desire as part of the legal proof). Expert psychological testimony could elucidate these issues, particularly on stereotyping, reminiscent of the contextual tests provided in the early cases (e.g., *Price Waterhouse v. Hopkins*, (1985); *Robinson v. Jacksonville Shipyards, Inc.*, 1991) to educate the judge or jury about the use and consequences of stereotypes in a same-sex claim. Recent empirical work on same-sex harassment is beginning to illuminate the pertinent issues (see, e.g., Magley, Waldo, Drasgow, & Fitzgerald, 1999; Stockdale, Visio, & Batra, 1999; Waldo, Berdahl, & Fitzgerald, 1998). Although men make up a smaller proportion of sexual harassment targets than women, for those men who are harassed, a much larger proportion of that harassment appears to be same-sex harassment than for women (Foote & Goodman-Delahunty, 2005a; citing DuBois et al., 1998; Magley et al.; Waldo et al.). In general, much less empirical work has focused on male targets and virtually "no systematic research" on same-sex harassment of women is available (Foote & Goodman-Delahunty, 2005a, p. 35).

Harm

If we assume that a complainant has satisfied the first two steps discussed previously, that the complainant was subjected to unwelcome conduct and that it was because of "sex" within the meaning of the law, then the question becomes, was that particular conduct illegal—is it harmful enough to warrant legal protection?

Two aspects of the issue arise: the level of harm required and from whose perspective we should evaluate that harm (O'Connor & Vallabhajosula, 2004). In 1993, the U.S. Supreme Court dealt most directly with these questions, taking "a middle path between making actionable any conduct that is merely offensive and requiring the conduct to cause a tangible psychological injury" (*Harris v. Forklift Systems, Inc.*, 1993, p. 21). To be actionable, the Court reaffirmed the standard set forth in *Meritor Savings Bank v. Vinson* (1986), that the conduct must be "sufficiently severe or pervasive" as to "alter the conditions of the victim's employment and create an abusive working environment." As the Court recognized, this is not a precise formula (see, e.g., *Eich v. Board of Regents for Central Missouri State University*, 2003, in which a dissenting judge reanalyzed alleged abusive acts and found they did cross the "sufficiently severe or pervasive" line; *Smith v. Sheahan*, 1999). What is clear, though, is that the plaintiff must subjectively experience the behavior as "sufficiently severe or pervasive" and that a reasonable person or reasonable woman (depending on the jurisdiction) would also find it to be so.

In this regard, psychologists have been called on to testify about the work environment and how it might affect workers. They may testify on gender differences in reaction to harassing behavior, for example. Where resources are available, they may testify based on original surveys done in the workplace itself to measure the severity and pervasiveness of the behavior or to test the particulars of the case at hand to determine how a reasonable person (man or woman) reacts (see Goodman-Delahunty, 1998; Gutek & Stockdale, 2005; see generally O'Connor & Vallabhajosula, 2004).

Is the Employer Liable?

Before leaving the subject of liability, it is necessary to ask who is liable for the harassing conduct. More specifically, can the employer be held liable for the harassing acts of its employee(s)? Recent Supreme Court decisions have set out rules based on agency principles that have provided significant fodder for expert testimony from psychologists and human resource specialists. In *Faragher v. City of Boca Raton* (1998) and *Burlington Industries, Inc. v. Ellerth* (1998), the Supreme Court developed a two-prong affirmative defense to liability for an employer when the targeted employee was not demoted, fired, or otherwise adversely affected in terms of employment benefits. In that circumstance, an employer can escape liability if it exercised reasonable care in preventing or promptly correcting any sexually harassing behavior; and if the employee unreasonably failed to take advantage of the preventive or corrective opportunities offered by the employer, or otherwise failed to avoid the harm.

This approach has been a "full employment act" for everyone calling themselves an expert on sexual harassment, and on its prevention and remediation (O'Connor & Vallabhajosula, 2004). Such testimony requires a thorough review of the company's policies and procedures, both on paper and in practice. Does the existence of a zero-tolerance policy, for example, guarantee an effective response to sexual harassment? Not necessarily (see Stockdale, Bisom-Rapp, O'Connor, & Gutek, 2004). Was the policy amply advertised so that employees knew how to complain? Did the procedures discourage complaining in some way? Experts now routinely review all of the company's materials, advertising, training manuals, in addition to the formal policy (Gutek & Stockdale, 2005). Recall the empirical findings cited earlier about the reluctance of employees to complain in light of the court's insistence that liability hinge in part on an employee's following the formal complaint procedures. Experts can enlighten the courts on both the safeguards in the policy that should facilitate employee complaints and, in contrast, the reality of the barriers to doing so no matter how the policy is framed.

Damages

Once liability is established, the need for an expert shifts to the question of monetary damages. Although a plaintiff need not show psychological harm to justify damages (*Harris v. Forklift Systems, Inc.*, 1993), it is often part of the claim. Clearly, psychological and somatic symptoms in sexual harassment targets are not uncommon and have been found to be similar to those of sexual assault victims (Kilpatrick, Dansky, & Saunders, 1994). Psychological expertise is often used to support such a claim when made, though not always.[4] In one recent New Jersey case, a male corrections officer alleging sexual harassment was awarded $750,000 even though he did not present any evidence of psychological counseling or treatment for his injuries, nor any expert testimony in support thereof (*Lockley v. N.J. Dep't of Corr.*, 2003). Nevertheless, expert testimony when proffered has been shown to anchor damage awards in discrimination cases. Raitz, Greene, Goodman, and Loftus (1990) found nearly half of their mock jurors selected a damage award that exactly matched the amounts suggested by the expert witness. In sexual harassment claims in particular, forensic psychologists and psychiatrists are often needed to explain a number of serious issues relating to harm. Social and/or I/O psychologists, when testifying about the environment or the psychosocial interactions, may also be asked to comment on the damages.

[4]Several issues that may arise in this context are beyond the scope of this chapter. One controversial issue that arises when the plaintiff claims psychological damages arises from Federal Rule of Criminal Procedure 35, which compels the plaintiffs to submit to a mental examination at the request of the other side if they have placed their mental health in issue. For a thorough discussion of the issue, see Kovera and Cass (2002); see also Foote and Goodman-Delahunty (2005a). Another issue that may well arise in a sensitive area such as sexual harassment is a psychologist being asked to serve in multiple roles, as both consulting or even treating psychologist and expert witness.

The inquiry about damages is complicated. The standard is whether the sexual harassment contributed to distress that the plaintiff would not have otherwise suffered, not whether it was a "substantial factor" in that distress (Foote & Goodman-Delahunty, 2005b, p. 62). For the expert asked to assist in this determination or counter it, the issues raised include: (a) how to measure or quantify the severity of the psychological distress exhibited by the plaintiff, (b) how to determine whether the distress is caused by the harassment, and (c) how to distinguish the emotional or psychological distress stemming from the harassment as opposed to that being experienced because of: (a) emotional or psychological difficulties that might have preceded the harassment, (b) retaliation at work, (c) economic loss or other hardships of daily life caused by the harassment, or (d) the litigation experience itself (Binder, 1992; Goodman-Delahunty & Foote, 1995). This level of scrutiny is necessary because even where liability has been established there is currently no presumption of emotional distress, though some have called for such an approach (Fitzgerald, 2003). Of course, additional factors may need to be considered in support or refutation of punitive damages.

HOW STRONG IS THE SCIENTIFIC FOUNDATION FOR EXPERT TESTIMONY ON SEXUAL HARASSMENT?

As a scholar working in this field, I would like to be able to assign an A+ grade to the scientific foundation for expert psychological testimony in sexual harassment cases, to claim that it would easily survive a general-acceptance analysis in *Frye* jurisdictions and a sound scientific foundation in a *Daubert* analysis. Although I cannot quite do that, I believe the courts can have confidence in a number of key findings, but should have concerns about a number of others.

A long history of work in relevant areas, several meta-analyses, and some very strong theoretical and methodological work in recent years have produced a number of strong and consistent findings. Nevertheless, given the nature of the adversarial process, experts for the opposing sides often take quite different approaches to the issue (see Gutek & Stockdale, 2005) and different views on both the quality and meaning of those findings. Of course from a legal standpoint, there are always both relevance and reliability concerns that must be addressed in each circumstance (*Daubert v. Merrell Dow Pharmaceuticals, Inc.*, 1993). One of the primary relevance battles occurs when an expert relies on off-the-shelf research (as is common with social framework testimony) and the opposing expert points out myriad ways that the research differs from the particular case at hand (see Gutek & Stockdale; for a more detailed discussion of social framework testimony in light of *Daubert*, see Faigman & Monahan, 2005). Reliability concerns generally focus on theoretical and methodological weaknesses and on the inappropriateness of drawing a particular conclusion based on the studies reviewed when an alternative conclusion is possible or when other studies have been ignored or discrepant findings downplayed (see, e.g., Copus, Ugelow, & Sohn, 2005).

A discussion of the legal rules governing the admissibility of expert testimony in general and analysis of specific admissibility decisions in sexual harassment cases in particular are beyond the scope of this chapter. Few cases have specifically addressed the issue (Harris, 2002). Faigman, Kaye, Saks, and Sanders (2002) provided an overview including specific discussion of admissibility issues relevant to sex stereotyping research (see also Borgida, Hunt, & Kim, 2005, p. 1). The most famous example that sets the backdrop for the discussion is *Price-Waterhouse v. Hopkins* (1989), in which Dr. Susan Fiske testified (pre-*Daubert*) on sex stereotyping as context. In its decision favorable to Ms. Hopkins, the plaintiff, the U.S. Supreme Court stated:

> Dr. Fiske's expert testimony was merely icing on Hopkins' case. It takes no special training to discern sex stereotyping in a description of an aggressive female as requiring "a course at charm school." Nor ... does it require expertise in psychology to know that ... if flawed interpersonal skills can be corrected by a soft-hued suit or a new shade of lipstick, perhaps it is the employee's sex and not her interpersonal skills that has drawn the criticism. (Price Waterhouse v. Hopkins, p. 256)

This latter critique is a common one—that sex stereotyping is within the common knowledge of the lay trier of fact and therefore it is not necessary to have a psychology expert on these points (see Borgida et al., 2005, discussing a recent Minnesota case in which the judge excluded such testimony and said that all adults in our society know about gender stereotypes; see also *EEOC v. Dial Corp.*, 2002, precluding expert testimony on sex stereotypes and practices based on a survey of Dial employees, essentially finding the survey unreliable). In *Butler v. Home Depot, Inc.* (1997), however, Dr. Susan Fiske was allowed to testify about gender stereotyping post-*Daubert* despite the Supreme Court's rather dismissive attitude toward it. Because few cases have addressed the admissibility of expert testimony in sex discrimination cases directly , what follows is a brief and nonexhaustive overview of some of the findings that have been well studied and that should satisfy the strictures of the *Daubert* standard:[5]

1. The deleterious effects of pervasive or subtle sex stereotyping in the workplace: From groundbreaking research in the late 1970s and early 1980s (see, e.g., Gutek, 1985; for a summary, see Fiske et al., 1991) to more recent work on the measurement of sexism (see, e.g., Glick et al., 2000; Glick & Fiske, 1996), to the influence of the power dynamic on workplace interactions (Bargh & Raymond, 1995) and an empirical reexamination of the effects of sex-role spillover phenomenon (Burgess & Borgida, 1997), psychologists have documented both the existence and influence of gender stereotypes in the workplace (see generally Borgida et al., 2005). Such social framework testimony (see Wiener, Watts, Goldkamp, & Gasper, 1995) illuminates the hostile or abusive nature of the work environment. It can also illustrate management or environmental conditions that made it more likely that harassment would occur. It can provide content for stereotypes that might have been operating at the workplace that made it more or less likely that a target would complain or trust a sexual harassment policy and procedure. This literature is certainly not without critics or those who are willing to challenge it on the stand (see, e.g., Copus, Ugelow, & Sohn, 2005). And although consensus has not been reached (nor could such be expected, see Borgida et al., 2005), this is an area of expertise that can be exceptionally useful in explaining the reasons for sexually harassing behavior and people's response to it. It is not, as some courts have found, simply common sense that any juror would understand (see Shestowsky, 1999; see generally Faigman et al., 2002).
2. The gender difference findings—that women are more likely to perceive behavior as sexual harassment than men: Men and women perceive sexual harassment differently such that women have a more expansive definition of what constitutes harassment. This stable normative difference has been demonstrated consistently, especially in the spectrum of cases falling between a mild

annoyance and seriously egregious conduct (Blumenthal, 1998; Foote & Goodman-Delahunty, 2005b; Frazier, Cochran, & Olson, 1995; Gutek & O'Connor, 1995; Rotundo, Nguyen, & Sackett, 2001; Wiener et al., 2002). Early findings on this sex difference (see, e.g., Gutek, 1985) suggested that what a man might find harmless, a woman might find highly offensive (see Gutek). Social scientists and legal scholars became especially interested in this issue after certain courts relied on it to justify the necessity for an alternative objective legal standard, the "reasonable woman" standard. For some courts, that standard replaced the purportedly male-valenced, "reasonable person" standard to assess whether the conduct was sufficiently severe or pervasive to justify legal liability (see Ellison v. Brady, 1991; Gutek & O'Connor, 1995; Wiener, Hurt, Russell, Mannen, & Gasper, 1997; Wiener et al., 1995). Over the years, researchers have refined the assessment of this gender difference. They have examined the position or role of the harasser relative to the harassed (e.g., supervisor, peer, subordinate; Rotundo, Nguyen, & Sackett, 2001), the nature of the workplace and the target's response to the harassment (O'Connor et al., 2004), and harasser or target characteristics (e.g., attractiveness and age). In addition, a number of scholars have examined the efficacy of the reasonable woman standard in deciding sexual harassment cases (see, e.g., Gutek et al., 1999; Wiener et al., 1997). In one set of studies, for example, Wiener et al. (2002) found that the reasonable woman standard had less effect on sexual harassment judgments in a less serious case than when more egregious behavior was alleged. Explaining the range and complexity of these findings as backdrop to a plaintiff's claim can assist the judge or jury in understanding the different reactions that people at the workplace might have had to the behavior as well as their own reaction to it.

3. That not everyone complains—the varying pattern of responses to sexual harassment: Most people never report the sexual harassment they experience to anyone (Gutek & Koss, 1993). And people respond in various ways from doing nothing to telling friends or family to actively complaining (Fitzgerald, Swan, & Fischer, 1995). Magley (2002) demonstrated four types of coping strategies that range from passive to active and from taking action to disengaging. The response can also be fluid, evolving over time (Foote & Goodman-Delahunty, 2005a). Some evidence suggests

that those who most actively complain have more negative outcomes (see, e.g., Bergman, Langhout, Palmieri, Cortina, & Fitzgerald, 2002). What is constant is that there is no one consistent response and that formal complaining is an infrequent choice.

4. That trauma often, but not always, results from experiencing sexual harassment: In an excellent and comprehensive review of what we know about the impact of sexual harassment on its targets, Foote and Goodman-Delahunty (2005a, see chap. 6) presented in table format the "Negative Outcomes Observed in Victims of Sexual Harassment," numbering nearly 40 (p. 133, Table 6.1). The effects are categorized as "psychological," "physiological," and "work-related." When the first comprehensive review of this literature was published (Gutek & Koss, 1993), many of the same symptoms were identified, but the work at that stage was largely anecdotal, case study, or nonrepresentative samples (Foote & Goodman-Delahunty, 2005a). Now, this early work has been supplemented by more systematic and longer term studies that confirm significant consequences from exposure to sexual harassment.

   More specifically, the psychological reactions can range from mild distress to serious mental distress, such as depression, decreased life satisfaction, or social withdrawal (Foote & Goodman-Delahunty, 2005a). The more severe or prolonged the harassment, the more severe the symptomatology appears to be. Work-related problems are the "most widely and consistently reported form of injury related to sexual harassment" (Foote & Goodman-Delahunty, p. 131). Negative job attitudes, withdrawal, and a decline in productivity are among the demonstrated outcomes (see, e.g., Gutek, Cohen, & Tsui, 1996; Schneider et al., 1997; U.S. Merit System Protection Board, 1994). Goodman-Delahunty and Foote (1995) provided a more explicit discussion of the effect of the *Daubert* standards on expert testimony for psychological damages in sexual harassment cases.

For a number of topics important to understanding sexual harassment, however, some debate, doubt, or uncertainty about the research foundations exists. Several of these are briefly highlighted here:

1. Problems with measurement: Reviews of sexual harassment research reveal a lack of both careful and consistent measurement and definition of the term sexual harassment, making cross-comparisons difficult. Many scholars either develop their own

definition, or adhere to a more psychological definition ("Have you been sexually harassed?") rather than relying on the more stringent legal definitions outlined by the U.S. Supreme Court in its decisions (but see Gutek, Murphy, & Douma, 2004; Wiener et al., 2002; Wiener & Hurt, 2000). One measurement instrument that has been widely used is the Sexual Experiences Questionnaire (SEQ; Fitzgerald, Gelfand, & Drasgow, 1995; Fitzgerald, Swan, & Magley, 1997). More recently, it has come under criticism on reliability and validity grounds, as well as its failure to track the legal definition of sexual harassment (Gutek et al., 2004; see also Gutek & Stockdale, 2005). Additional work is needed to clarify definitions and to improve existing measures.

2. Concerns about external validity: This problem is certainly not unique to sexual harassment. Some particularly heated exchanges on this point have occurred in both recent scholarship and in expert battles in the courtroom. There are at least two primary issues. First is the inevitable concern about undergraduate research participants generating our knowledge on the topic. Although some excellent work by Brian Bornstein and others has neutralized this line of argument to some extent, in the area of sexual harassment, differences in perspective and judgment between those who have spent time in the workplace and those who have not have been found. This makes reliance on a typical undergraduate sample potentially more problematic. Second, even in some of the more sophisticated experimental work, with realistic trial stimuli, actors and lawyers playing roles, and solid legal instruction coming from a judge, no stimulus material can really simulate the complexity of most workplaces (see Copus, Ugelow, & Sohn, 2005; Gutek & Stockdale, 2005). More recent research has come much closer. It has used contested trial evidence, invoking the he said, she said nature of the dispute, and real workplace contexts (see, e.g., Kovera, McAuliff, & Hebert, 1999; O'Connor et al, 2004; Wiener et al., 1997; Wiener & Hurt, 2000). It is important that the field responds to these points with creativity and thoughtful methodology.
3. Problems with our ability to assess mental health consequences and sequelae of trauma: Goodman-Delahunty and Foote (2005) provided an excellent discussion of the scientific bases for expert testimony on psychological injuries. The challenge for the psychological expert here, of course, is to discern whether any psychological symptoms exhibited by the plaintiffs are, in fact, due to

the sexual harassment or to other stressors in their lives. Although Goodman-Delahunty and Foote conceded that this is not an easy task, they identified a number of empirical studies that can guide this assessment. They noted the relevance of studies that explore sources of stress in everyday life, especially for working women, negative consequences of dysfunctional work environments, and some evidence for how various stressors might interact. A fairly solid body of evidence supports the value of work psychologically, and the effect that loss of employment as a result of the harassment might have. At the same time, it is difficult to disentangle posttraumatic stress disorder (PTSD), for example, that might have resulted from any number of traumatic events from a stress reaction from the harassment itself. No single assessment tool can reliably make these distinctions. Yet, a solid body of foundational evidence can guide such judgments.

4. Lack of solid empirical work on the efficacy of sexual harassment policies, training, and employer procedures designed to curb the behavior in the workplace: What are the elements of an effective policy? When are the procedures sufficiently safe that targets will feel they can follow the procedures without retaliation? How can retaliation be curbed? What types of training will actually change behavior, educate supervisors, and lead to greatly reduced harassment in a workplace? Companies are spending millions of dollars every year to pay psychologists and others to help themselves become liability-proof by writing and implementing policies that the courts will deem sufficient (see generally Gutek & Stockdale, 2005). How much money would need to be spent to write policies and procedures that would actually eradicate harassment? Important theoretical and analytical work on the tendency for employers and defense attorneys to focus on "bulletproofing" their legal liability rather than on eradicating the offensive conduct was done by Bisom-Rapp (1999, 2002). In her latest article, Bisom-Rapp (2002) explores the efficacy of training programs, and recounted that despite their rampant proliferation throughout the country, very little empirical evidence of their efficacy exists (see also Pryor & McKinney, 1995).
5. Insufficient attention to people who have experienced harassment: Outside of the litigation context, there has been little systematic research on the people involved in real-world sexual harassment. Few systematic interviews, surveys, or other documentation of those involved in the legal system—the parties, the

lawyers, the judges trying to manage these cases on both sides—have been done.

IS THERE RESEARCH ON HOW JURORS RESPOND TO EXPERT TESTIMONY ON SEXUAL HARASSMENT?

Systematic study of real jurors' experiences in sexual harassment cases is limited. Anecdotally, however, there is evidence that real jurors can get it wrong (see, e.g., Gutek et al., 1999). In the case discussed by Gutek et al., Dr. Gutek presented social framework expert testimony on the workplace conditions that produced an environment prone to harassment; nevertheless, the jury voted against the plaintiff, concluding (in a direct misunderstanding of the law) that a particular plaintiff was not a reasonable woman and therefore failed to find in her favor. That wayward jury prompted a line of research examining the efficacy of the reasonable woman standard in sexual harassment cases and led to multiple studies and publications on our part. But, what, if anything, do we know more systematically about juror response to expert testimony in sexual harassment cases?

There are a number of ways to consider expert effects on jurors: Does having an expert versus not having one affect judgments overall?, does the content of the expert testimony affect judgments and, if so, how?, and do the personal characteristics of the expert affect juror reaction to the expert's testimony?

In a series of studies providing the most comprehensive exploration of the effect of expert testimony on mock jurors in sexual harassment cases, Kovera et al. (1999) presented participants with expert testimony on conditions that make it more likely for sexual harassment to occur (e.g., rarity of women, paucity of objective evaluation information, sexualized work environment). In addition to their interest in the effects of expert testimony generally, Kovera et al. examined participants' responses to variations in the expert's testimony (whether the study was generally accepted, whether the dependent measures had construct validity, the level of ecological validity of the study, and the presence of cross-examination). The researchers found a main effect for expert testimony such that the presence of expert testimony increased the likelihood that jurors would find that a hostile work environment existed. This effect was, however, more pronounced for male jurors than for female jurors (though, as discussed earlier, in general, women were more likely than men to find sexual harassment overall). Yet, the gender difference was less pronounced in the expert condition, suggesting that the knowledge gained by men from listening to the expert discuss how gender stereotyping can influence the workplace brought their decisions more in line with their female counterparts. Kovera, Russano, and McAuliff (2002) also reported that expert testimony on the factors that influence gender stereotyping increased the likelihood that mock jurors would find a hostile work environment. These studies also highlight the difficulties that mock jurors have in distinguishing quality from junk social science, a finding that mirrored the result for judges as well (see Kovera & McAuliff, 2000).

Similarly, Cassar (2000) presented mock jurors with a lengthy videotaped sexual harassment trial that either did or did not contain a videotape of an industrial or organizational psychologist's deposition in the case. In the expert deposition, the expert discussed gender stereotyping, work environment, and sex-role spillover issues. Mock jurors then answered the question, "Was the plaintiff sexually harassed?" Those who saw the trial with the expert deposition were more likely to find that sexual harassment had occurred. Similar differences were also found on the question, "If the things that happen to [the plaintiff] happened to you, would you consider it sexual harassment?," with those in the expert condition more likely to respond "yes." One possible explanation for this effect is that jurors perceived the expert to be highly credible, and this source credibility may have influenced the persuasiveness of the expert's testimony. This effect disappeared, however, once jurors were given legal instructions explaining in detail the required elements for quid pro quo or hostile work environment harassment.

One particular aspect of this issue directly affects expert testimony on topics such as sexual harassment in ways that might not be true for a non-gender-valenced topic—the sex of the expert witness. A number of studies have examined overall effects for sex of the expert. At least three studies involving gender-neutral subject matter found no differences overall in the perception or effect of female versus male experts, though these studies suffered from methodological limitations, particularly in the strength of the stimulus effect (i.e., manipulating gender merely by pronoun; Couch & Sigler, 2002; Memon & Shuman, 1998; Vondergeest, Honts, & Devitt, 1993).

In a more gender-valenced example, Swenson, Nash, and Roos (1984) found female experts were perceived as having greater expertise than male experts in a simulated child custody case. Schuller and her colleagues directly investigated how the gender of the expert and gender orientation of the case influenced verdicts. In an earlier study, Schuller and Cripps (1998) argued that gender effects would follow the lines of gender-role stereotypes. To test this, Schuller, Terry, and McKimmie (2001) varied the gender of the expert and the domain in which the case occurred (e.g., the supply of crushed rock to a road construction company in the male-dominated industry and the supply of fine cotton to a women's clothing company in the female domain). Although they demonstrated stronger effects for the male expert testimony in the male-oriented domain, they found only weak effects in the female congruence condition. They speculated that because the female expert was described as a statistician, the gender incongruence actually persisted in both conditions. To test further, McKimmie, Newton, Terry, and Schuller (2004) manipulated gender of the expert in a price-fixing case in an either male- (automotive) or female- (cosmetics) dominated industry. As hypothesized, they found that mock jurors awarded more damages when the gender of the expert and the gender domain of the case were congruent. This effect was mediated through participants' evaluations of the expert. According to the researchers, their findings suggest that gender-role stereotypes come into play and differentially affect verdict and other case outcomes. Their dual manipulation of gender of the expert and case domain provide support for the influence of stereotype as opposed to what others have suggested might be at play, beliefs about status and respect. They also found that group discussion enhanced the effect, suggesting that the deliberation process may be an important component in this work.

In one study that systematically manipulated sex of the expert in a sexual harassment context, Cassar (2000) found mixed results. A female expert was not more influential on verdict or credibility ratings, but was more effective than her male counterpart in persuading jurors that the plaintiff's behavior did not contribute to sexual harassment; that the degree of sexual images, sexual language, and sexualized atmosphere at the company characterized in the study was high; and that female employees in work settings are frequently exposed to sexually harassing behaviors. Furthermore, the testimony of a female expert was judged to be clearer than that of a male expert.

As Huntley and Costanzo (2003) observed, attorneys cannot alter the facts as presented to them, but they can control the contextualization of those facts. One future research direction suggested by the work of Huntley and Costanzo and others is to examine the effectiveness of expert testimony to provide that contextualization reinforced by attorney closing arguments. Doing so with considerations of gender of the expert is a promising future direction.

HOW MIGHT THE LEGAL SYSTEM (E.G., PROCEDURES, STANDARDS, INSTRUCTIONS) BE MODIFIED IN LIGHT OF PSYCHOLOGICAL RESEARCH ON SEXUAL HARASSMENT?

A number of areas of possible modification emerge from a close examination of the linkages between the state of the art in psychological research and the existing legal policy and procedure. These can be divided into several overarching themes.

The first theme is a general one that might apply to most issues raised in this volume—that social science research has value-added effect above common sense (see Faigman et al., 2002, p. 374; explaining that "one significant value of much social science research is that it makes clearer what we only dimly perceive, if we perceive it at all"). What the extensive body of research on sexual harassment makes clear is that it is not a one-dimensional construct as often displayed in the media. We know a great deal about the circumstances in which it is most likely to occur. We know the relevance of the gendered nature of an environment and people's complex reactions to it. When a judge declares that most of what a psychology expert would tell a jury is within the commonsense knowledge of that jury, that judge is misrepresenting the phenomenon and underestimating the value of 25 years of social science scrutiny. This is highly reminiscent of the pedagogical challenge of engaging students in critical thinking that pushes them to be accountable for how they know what they know. If judges and lawyers particularly could become better consumers generally of social science, their decisions, questions, and preparation would reflect a more sophisticated understanding of the strengths and weaknesses of the empirical evidence being presented.

This point, though, has a quid pro quo, so to speak. Social scientists are still relatively unsophisticated about the legal system. Much of the research on sexual harassment was not undertaken with the legal framework in mind. Several ongoing debates reflect this concern, especially with respect to defining the construct. Of course, a number of psycholegal scholars have done sophisticated work on the topic. But, there is nevertheless some basis for the courts' criticism that some of the work is not relevant to real cases in the real world. Moreover, the lack of sophistication about the legal framework can lead to mistaken application of the social science evidence. The more stereotyping is described as an unconscious process, for example, the less likely it is to be helpful to the trier in supporting a disparate treatment claim that requires a showing of intent to discriminate. (Bisom-Rapp, 2005)

The second theme is the courts' naive assumptions about the efficacy of sexual harassment policies and procedures. No doubt the clearest example of this is the U.S. Supreme Court and EEOC's preference for "filing a formal complaint" as the preferred response to sexually harassing conduct. The courts need to recognize that complaining is not a talisman for proving sexual harassment because it is simply not possible for everyone to do it in every circumstance. Also, the courts need more sophistication in understanding that zero tolerance (Stockdale et al., 2004) training and policies are not all cut from the same cloth (Bisom-Rapp, 2002).

Judges, it seems, would rather assume that all sorts of measures do work (any kind of antidiscrimination policies, complaint procedures, multistep performance review processes) and then use the presence of those interventions as evidence of nondiscrimination (Bisom-Rapp, 2005). Although this might make their jobs easier (it is certainly easier to determine whether a sexual harassment policy exists than to parse the meaning of veiled threats, innuendos, sexual horseplay, etc., that might exist at a discriminatory workplace). But clearly, from a psychological perspective, the presence of procedural niceties on the one hand do not on the other guarantee a discrimination-free workplace. Although ideally an employer is immediately put on notice by a formal complaint the minute any untoward conduct occurs, that bright-line, zero-tolerance approach simply does not meld with the psychological realities that social scientists have tried to describe and explain (Stockdale et al., 2004).

The third theme is that well-meaning reforms do not always have their intended consequences, and follow-up work by social scientists should inform subsequent changes. When the 9th Circuit concluded that a reasonable woman standard would solve the problem of male judges and jurors being unable to take the perspective of the woman targeted by sexual harassment, that court's assumption may have been important symbolically, but not as effective practically (see Gutek & O'Connor, 1995; O'Connor et al., 2004; Wiener et al., 1997).

A final theme relates generally to the problems faced by lawyers, judges, and the parties themselves in dealing with assessment and proof of psychological harm and distress caused by sexual harassment. Because of the uncertainty here and the large, potential damages claimed if significant psychological injury is shown, lawyers are permitted broad discovery on these questions and, often, can compel mental health examination of the complainant. On the forensic evaluation side, better assessment tools and more carefully refined instruments are needed to assist in teasing out the source and/or sources of psychological distress (see Fitzgerald, 2003; Foote & Goodman-Delahunty, 2005a). Rule 412 of the Federal Rules of Evidence and Rule 35 of the Federal Rules of Criminal Procedure need to be reinforced and interpreted so as to protect against unnecessary disclosure of private, nonrelevant information. Proper implementation of these rules depends on the legal system's willingness to incorporate empirical findings that argue against the necessity for releasing some information relating to a complainant's childhood and prior abuse. Research findings are consistent here that prior exposure to sexualized violence does not, by itself, create hypersensitive plaintiffs who see harassment everywhere.

CONCLUSION

Nearly 15 years ago, Michael Saks, the author of this volume's closing chapter, posed an important challenge to psychologists working in the legal system—that, as expert witnesses, they should be unbiased educators and not advocates (Saks, 1990). In an area such as sexual harassment with its strong gender valence; its he said, she said quality; its victim-blaming and harasser-demonizing potential; and its consequences (material and emotional) for people's lives and careers; this challenge is especially daunting. The high-stakes, adversary context in which sexual harassment litigation occurs places inordinate pressure on psychologists to move toward the advocacy side of Saks' challenge. This review, and the recent extensive analysis provided by Goodman-Delahunty and Foote (2005a), demonstrate that important, evidence-based psychological testimony can be brought to bear in sexual harassment cases. What is also clear, however, is that gaps in our empirically derived knowledge remain. A number of leading scholars, such as Susan Fiske, Louise Fitzgerald, Bill Foote, Barbara Gutek, Jane Goodman-Delahunty, and John Pryor, have greatly advanced our knowledge by creating a bridge between their direct experience with sexual harassment cases as experts in the legal system and relevant research agendas directed toward filling those gaps. This work can lead toward the goal of evidence-based education of all parties in the legal system for sexual harassment and for all topics for which experts are called.

ACKNOWLEDGMENT

Thanks to Rachel Kahn for her invaluable assistance in preparing this chapter.

REFERENCES

Abbey, A. (1987). Misperceptions of friendly behavior as sexual interest: A survey of naturally occurring incidents. *Psychology of Women Quarterly, 11*, 173–194.

Bargh, J. A., & Raymond, P. (1995). The naïve misuse of power: Non-conscious sources of sexual harassment. *Journal of Social Issues, 51*, 85–96.

Bergman, M. E., Langhout, R. D., Palmieri, P. A., Cortina, L. M., & Fitzgerald, L. F. (2002). The (un)reasonableness of reporting antecedents and consequences of reporting sexual harassment. *Journal of Applied Psychology, 87*, 230–242.

Binder, R. L. (1992). Sexual harassment: Issues for forensic psychiatrists. *Bulletin of the American Academy of Psychiatry and the Law, 20*, 409–418.

Bisom-Rapp, S. (Personal communication, March 28, 2005).

Bisom-Rapp, S. (1999). Bulletproofing the workplace: Symbol and substance in employment discrimination law practice. *Florida State University Law Review, 26*, 959–1041.

Bisom-Rapp, S. (2002). Fixing watches with sledgehammers: The questionable embrace of employee sexual harassment training by the legal profession. *Thomas Jefferson Law Review, 24*, 125–148.

Blumenthal, J. A. (1998). The reasonable woman standard: A meta-analytic review of gender differences in perceptions of sexual harassment. *Law and Human Behavior, 22*, 33–57.

Borgida, E., Hunt, C., & Kim, A. (2005). On the use of gender stereotyping research in sex discrimination litigation. *Journal of Law and Policy, 13*, 613–628.

Brooks, L., & Perot, A. R. (1991). Reporting sexual harassment: Exploring a predictive model. *Psychology of Women Quarterly, 15*, 31–47.

Burgess, D., & Borgida, E. (1997). Sexual harassment: An experimental test of sex-role spillover theory. *Personality and Social Psychology Bulletin, 23*, 63–75.

Burgess, D., & Borgida, E. (1999). Who women are, who women should be: Descriptive and prescriptive gender stereotyping in sex discrimination. *Psychology, Public Policy and Law, 3*, 665–692.

Burlington Industries, Inc. v. Ellerth, 524 U.S. 742 (1998).

Burns, S. E. (1995). Issues in workplace sexual harassment law and related social science research. *Journal of Social Issues, 51*, 193–207.

Butler v. Home Depot, Inc., 984 F. Supp. 1257 (N.D. Cal. 1997).

Cassar, D. (2000). *Sex of the expert effects on jurors' sexual harassment judgments.* Unpublished master's thesis, John Jay College of Criminal Justice, City University of New York.

Nomination of Judge Clarence Thomas to be Associate Justice of the Supreme Court of the United States: Hearings before the Senate Judiciary Committee. 102nd Cong. 36-48 (1991; testimony of Anita Hill). Found at: http://www.people.virginia.edu/nybf2u/Thomas-Hill/1011a04d.html (page 16)

Copus, D., Ugelow, R. S., & Sohn, J. (2005). A lawyer's view. In F. J. Landy (Ed.), *Employment discrimination litigation: Behavioral, quantitative, and legal perspectives* (pp. 450–502). San Francisco: Jossey-Bass.

Couch, J. V., & Sigler, J. N. (2002). Gender of an expert witness and the jury verdict. *Psychological Record, 52*, 281–287.

Daubert v. Merrell Dow Pharmaceuticals, Inc., 509 U.S. 579 (1993).

DuBois, C. L. Z., Knapp, D. E., Faley, R. H., & Kustis, G. A. (1998). An empirical examination of same- and other-gender sexual harassment in the workplace. *Sex Roles*, *39*, 731–749.

EEOC Guidelines on Discrimination Because of Sex, 29 C.F.R. §1604.11 (a) (1992).

EEOC v. Dial Corp., 2002 WL 31061088 (N.D. Ill. Sept. 17, 2002).

Eich v. Board of Regents for Central Missouri State University, 350 F.3d 752 (8th Cir. 2003).

Ellison v. Brady, 924 F.2d 872 (9th Cir. 1991).

Faigman, D. L., Kaye, D. H., Saks, M. J., & Sanders, J. (Eds.). (2002). *Modern scientific evidence: The law and science of expert testimony* (Vol. 2). St. Paul, MN: West Group.

Faigman, D. L., & Monahan, J. (2005). Psychological evidence at the dawn of the law's scientific age. *Annual Review of Psychology*, *56*, 631–659.

Faragher v. City of Boca Raton, 524 U.S. 775 (1998).

Feldman-Schorrig, S. P. (1994). Special issues in sexual harassment litigation. In J. J. McDonald & F. B. Kulick (Eds.), *Mental and emotional injuries in employment litigation* (pp. 332–390). Washington, DC: Bureau of National Affairs.

Feldman-Schorrig, S. P., & McDonald, J. J. (1992). The role of forensic psychiatry in the defense of sexual harassment cases. *Journal of Psychiatry and Law*, *20*, 5–33.

Fiske, S. T., Bersoff, D. N., Borgida, E., Deaux, K., & Heilman, M. E. (1991). Social science research on trial: Use of sex stereotyping research in *Price Waterhouse v. Hopkins*. *American Psychologist*, *46*, 1049–1060.

Fitzgerald, L. F. (2003). Sexual harassment and social justice: Reflections on the distance yet to go. *American Psychologist*, *58*, 915–924.

Fitzgerald, L. F. (2004). Who says? Legal and psychological constructions of women's resistance to sexual harassment. In C. A. MacKinnon & R. B. Siegel (Eds.), *Directions in sexual harassment law* (pp. 94–110). New Haven, CT: Yale University Press.

Fitzgerald, L. F., Buchanan, N. T., Collinsworth, L. L., Magley, V. J., & Ramos, A. M. (1999). Junk logic: The abuse defense in sexual harassment litigation. *Psychology, Public Policy, and Law*, *5*, 730–759.

Fitzgerald, L. F., Gelfand, M. J., & Drasgow, F. (1995). Measuring sexual harassment: Theoretical and psychometric advances. *Basic and Applied Social Psychology*, *17*, 425–455.

Fitzgerald, L. F., Shullman, S. L., Bailey, N., Richards, M., Swecker, J., Gold, Y. et al. (1988). The incidence and dimensions of sexual harassment in Academia and the workplace. *Journal of Vocational Behavior*, *32*, 152–175.

Fitzgerald, L. F., Swan, S., & Fischer, K. (1995). Why didn't she just report him? The psychological and legal implications of women's responses to sexual harassment. *Journal of Social Issues*, *51*, 117–138.

Fitzgerald, L. F., Swan, S., & Magley, V. J. (1997). But was it really sexual harassment? Legal, behavioral, and psychological definitions of the workplace victimization of women. In W. O'Donohue (Ed.), *Sexual harassment: Theory, research, and treatment* (pp. 5–28). Needham Heights, MA: Allyn & Bacon.

Foote, W. E., & Goodman-Delahunty, J. (2005a). *Evaluating sexual harassment: Psychological, social, and legal considerations in forensic examinations*. Washington, DC: American Psychological Association.

Foote, W. E., & Goodman-Delahunty, J. (2005b). The legal framework in sexual harassment cases. In *Evaluating sexual harassment: Psychological, social, and legal considerations in forensic examinations* (pp. 47–71). Washington, DC: American Psychological Association.

Franke, K. M. (1997). What's wrong with sexual harassment? *Stanford University Law Review, 49*, 691–772.

Franke, K. M. (2004). What's wrong with sexual harassment. In C. A. MacKinnon & R. B. Siegel (Eds.), *Directions in sexual harassment law* (pp. 169–181). New Haven, CT: Yale University Press.

Frazier, P. A., Cochran, C. C., & Olson, A. M. (1995). Social science research on lay definitions of sexual harassment. *Journal of Social Issues, 51*, 21–37.

Glick, P., & Fiske, S. T. (1996). The ambivalent sexism inventory: Differentiating hostile and benevolent sexism. *Journal of Personality and Social Psychology, 70*, 491–512.

Glick, P., Fiske, S. T., Mladinic, A., Saiz, J., Abrams, D., Masser, B., et al. (2000). Beyond prejudice as simple antipathy: Hostile and benevolent sexism across cultures. *Journal of Personality and Social Psychology, 79*, 763–775.

Goodman-Delahunty, J. (1998). Approaches to gender and the law: Research and applications. *Law and Human Behavior, 22*, 129–143.

Goodman-Delahunty, J., & Foote, W. E. (1995). Compensation for pain, suffering, and other psychological injuries: The impact of *Daubert* on employment discrimination claims. *Behavioral Sciences and the Law, 13*, 183–206.

Gutek, B. A. (1985). *Sex and the workplace: The impact of sexual behavior and harassment on women, men, and organization*. San Francisco: Jossey-Bass.

Gutek, B. A., Cohen, A. G., & Tsui, A. (1996). Reactions to perceived sex discrimination. *Human Relations*, 49, 791–813.

Gutek, B. A. &, Koss, M. P. (1993). Changed women and changed organizations: Consequences of and coping with sexual harassment. *Journal of Vocational Behavior, 42*, 28–48.

Gutek, B. A., & Murphy, R. O., & Douma, B. (2004). A review and critique of the sexual experiences questionnaire (SEQ). *Law and Human Behavior, 28*, 457– 482.

Gutek, B. A., & O'Connor, M. (1995). The empirical basis for the reasonable woman standard. *Journal of Social Issues, 51*, 151–166.

Gutek, B. A., O'Connor, M., Melançon, R., Stockdale, M. S., Geer, T. M., & Done, R. S. (1999). The utility of the reasonable women legal standard in hostile environment sexual harassment cases: A multimethod, multistudy examination. *Psychology, Public Policy and Law, 5*, 596–629.

Gutek, B. A., & Stockdale, M. (2005). Sex discrimination in employment. In F. Landy (Ed.), *I/O psychology and employment discrimination litigation* (pp. 229–255). San Francisco: Jossey-Bass.

Halley, J. (2004). Sexuality harassment. In C. A. MacKinnon & R. B. Siegel (Eds.), *Directions in sexual harassment law* (pp. 182–200). New Haven, CT: Yale University Press.

Harris, J. E. (2002). Evidentiary issues in employment litigation. *American Law Institute-American Bar Association Continuing Legal Education, December 5–7, 2002 (SH039)*, 475–499.

Harris v. Forklift Systems, Inc., 510 U.S. 17 (1993).
Huntley, J. E., & Costanzo, M. (2003). Sexual harassment stories: Testing a story-mediated model of juror decision-making in civil litigation. *Law and Human Behavior, 27*, 29–51.
Jenson v. Eveleth Taconite, 824 F. Supp. 847 (D. Min.1993).
Kilpatrick, D. G., Dansky, B. S., & Saunders, B. E. (1994). *Sexual harassment in the workplace: Results from the National Women's Study*. Charleston: Crime Victims Research and Treatment Center, Department of Psychiatry and Behavioral Sciences, Medical University of South Carolina.
Kovera, M. B., & Cass, S. A. (2002). Compelled mental health examinations, liability decisions, and damage awards in sexual harassment cases: Issues for jury research. *Psychology, Public Policy and Law, 8*, 96–114.
Kovera, M. B., & McAuliff, B. D. (2000). The effects of peer review and evidence quality on judge evaluations of psychological science: Are judges effective gatekeepers? *Journal of Applied Psychology, 85*, 574–586.
Kovera, M. B., McAuliff, B. D., & Hebert, K. S. (1999). Reasoning about scientific evidence: Effects of juror gender and evidence quality on juror decisions in a hostile work environment case. *Journal of Applied Psychology, 84*, 362–375.
Kovera, M. B., Russano, M. B., & McAuliff, B. D. (2002). Assessment of the commonsense psychology underlying Daubert: Legal decision makers' abilities to evaluate expert evidence in hostile work environment cases. *Psychology, Public Policy and Law, 8*, 180–200.
Lockley v. N.J. Dep't of Corr., 779 A.2d 1092 (N.J. Sup. Ct. App. Div. 2001), *aff'd*, 828 A.2d 869 (N.J. 2003).
MacKinnon, C.A. (1979). *Sexual harassment of working women*. New Haven, CT: Yale University Press.
Magley, V. J. (2002). Coping with sexual harassment: Reconceptualizing women's resistance. *Journal of Personality and Social Psychology, 83*, 930–946.
Magley, V. J., Waldo, C. R., Drasgow, F., & Fitzgerald, L. F. (1999). The impact of sexual harassment on military personnel: Is it the same for men and women? *Military Psychology, 11*, 283–302.
McKimmie, B. M., Newton, C. J., Terry, D. J., & Schuller, R. A. (2004). Jurors' responses to expert witness testimony: The effects of gender stereotypes. *Group Processes and Intergroup Relations, 7*, 131–143.
Memon, A., & Shuman, D. W. (1998). Juror perception of experts in civil disputes: The role of race and gender. *Law and Psychology Review, 22*, 179–197.
Meritor Savings Bank v. Vinson, 477 U.S. 57 (1986).
Monahan, J., & Walker, L. (1986). Social authority: Obtaining, evaluating, and establishing social science in law. *University of Pennsylvania Law Review, 134*, 477–517.
O'Connor, M., Gutek, B. A., Stockdale, M. S., Geer, T., & Melançon, R. (2004). Predictors of sexual harassment judgments: More than sex of the rater. *Law and Human Behavior, 28*, 69–95.
O'Connor, M., & Vallabhajosula, B. (2004). Sexual harassment in the workplace: A legal and psychological framework. In B. J. Cling (Ed.), *Sex, violence and women: A psychology and law perspective* (pp. 115–147). New York: Guilford Press.
Oncale v. Sundowner Offshore Services, Inc., 523 U.S. 75 (1998).

Pedroza v. Cintas Corp., 397 F.3d 1063 (8th Cir. 2005).

Pryor, J. B., & McKinney, K. (1995). Research on sexual harassment: Lingering issues and future directions, *Basic and Applied Social Psychology, 17*, 605–609.

Price-Waterhouse v. Hopkins, 490 U.S. 228 (1989).

Raitz, A., Greene, E., Goodman, J., & Loftus, E. (1990). Determining damages: The influence of expert testimony on jurors' decision making. *Law and Human Behavior, 14*, 385–395.

Reilly, M. E., Lott, B., Caldwell, D., & DeLuca, L. (1992). Tolerance for sexual harassment related to self-reported sexual victimization. *Gender and Society, 6*, 122–138.

Robinson v. Jacksonville Shipyards, Inc., 760 F. Supp. 1486 (M.D. Fl. 1991).

Rotundo, M., Nguyen, D.-H., & Sackett, P. R. (2001). A meta-analytic review of gender differences in perceptions of sexual harassment. *Journal of Applied Psychology, 86*, 914–922.

Saks, M. J. (1990). Expert witnesses, nonexpert witnesses, and nonwitness experts. *Law and Human Behavior, 14*, 291–313.

Schneider, K. T., Swan, S., & Fitzgerald, L. F. (1997). Job-related and psychological effects of sexual harassment in the workplace: Empirical evidence from two organizations. *Journal of Applied Psychology, 82*, 401–415.

Schuller, R. A., & Cripps, J. (1998). Expert evidence pertaining to battered women: The impact of gender of expert and timing of testimony. *Law and Human Behavior, 22*, 17–31.

Schuller, R. A., Terry, D. J., & McKimmie, B. M. (2001). The impact of an expert's gender on jurors' decisions. *Law and Psychology Review, 25*, 59–79.

Schultz, V. (1998). Reconceptualizing sexual harassment. *Yale Law Journal, 107*, 1683–1732.

Shestowsky, D. (1999). Where is the common knowledge? Empirical support for requiring expert testimony in sexual harassment trials. *Stanford Law Review, 51*, 357–386.

Smith v. Sheahan, 189 F.3d 529, 534 (7th Cir. 1999).

Spindelman, M. (2004). Discriminating pleasures. In C. A. MacKinnon & R. B. Siegel (Eds.), *Directions in sexual harassment law* (pp. 201–220). New Haven, CT: Yale University Press.

Stockdale, M. S. (1998). The direct and moderating influences of sexual-harassment pervasiveness, coping strategies, and gender on work-related outcomes. *Psychology of Women Quarterly, 22*, 521–535.

Stockdale, M. S., Bisom-Rapp, S., O'Connor, M., & Gutek, B. A. (2004). Coming to terms with zero tolerance sexual harassment policies. *Journal of Forensic Psychology Practice, 4*, 65–78.

Stockdale, M. S., O'Connor, M., Gutek, B. A., & Geer, T. (2002). The relationship between prior sexual victimization and sensitivity to social sexual behavior in workplaces and education: Literature review and empirical study. *Psychology, Public Policy, and Law, 8*, 64–95.

Stockdale, M. S., Visio, M., & Batra, L. (1999). The sexual harassment of men: Evidence for a broader theory of sexual harassment and sexual discrimination. *Psychology, Public Policy and Law, 5*, 630–664.

Stockett v. Tolin, 791 F. Supp. 1536 (S.D. Fla. 1992).

Swenson, R. A., Nash, D. L., & Ross, D. C. (1984). Source credibility and perceived expertness of testimony in a simulated child-custody case. *Professional Psychology: Research and Practice, 15*, 891–898.

Thomas Hearings. (1991). Retrieved March 22, 2006, from http://www.people.virginia.edu/nybf2u/Thomas-Hill/1011a04d.html

Title VII of the Civil Rights Act of 1964, 42 U.S.C. §2000e et seq. (1994).

U.S. Merit System Protection Board. (1994). *Working for America: An update*. Washington, DC: U.S. Government Printing Office.

Vondergeest, L., Honts, C., & Devitt, M. K. (1993). Effects of juror and expert witness gender on jurors' perceptions of an expert witness. *Modern Psychological Studies, 1*, 6.

Waldo, C. R., Berdahl, J. L., & Fitzgerald, L. F. (1998). Are men sexually harassed? If so, by whom? *Law and Human Behavior, 22*, 59–79.

Wiener, R. L., Hackney, A., Kadela, K., Rauch, S., Seib, H., Warren, L., et al. (2002). The fit and implementation of sexual harassment law to workplace evaluations. *Journal of Applied Psychology, 87*, 747–764.

Wiener, R. L., & Hurt, L. E. (2000). How do people evaluate social-sexual conduct: A psycholegal model. *Journal of Applied Psychology, 85*, 75–85.

Wiener, R. L., Hurt, L., Russell, B., Mannen, K., & Gasper, C. (1997). Perceptions of sexual harassment: The effects of gender, legal standard, and ambivalent sexism. *Law and Human Behavior, 21*, 71–93.

Wiener, R. L., Watts, B. A., Goldkamp, K. H., & Gasper, C. (1995). Social analytic investigation of hostile work environments: A test of the reasonable woman standard. *Law and Human Behavior, 19*, 263–281.

7

Capital Mitigation From a Developmental Perspective: The Importance of Risk Factors, Protective Factors, and the Construct of Resilience

Karen L. Salekin
University of Alabama

Recently, the United States Supreme Court has made critical decisions regarding the appropriateness of the application of the death penalty to two cognizable groups. In 2002, the Court held that the execution of offenders with mental retardation represented "cruel and unusual punishment" and was therefore prohibited by the Eighth Amendment of the United States constitution (*Atkins v. Virginia*, 2002). In their 6-3 decision, the Court opined that the standards of decency had evolved to the point that neither the goal of retribution, nor that of deterrence, can be met with the application of the death penalty to mentally retarded offenders. Specifically, the cognitive, emotional, and behavioral impairments associated with mental retardation lessened the individuals' culpability for their criminal behavior.

In 2005, the United States Supreme Court held that the Eighth and Fourteenth Amendments forbid the execution of offenders who were under the age of 18 when their crimes were committed (*Roper v. Simmons*,

2005). Using *Atkins* (2002) as a backdrop, the Court opined that due to immaturity, impulsivity, and vulnerability to external influence, the imposition of the death penalty on juvenile offenders can no longer be justified. In effect, their developmental status reduces their culpability such that neither the goal of retribution, nor that of deterrence, can be met by such a sanction.

The decisions in *Atkins* (2002) and *Roper* (2005) suggest that there is an emerging national consensus that the application of the death penalty must be reserved for only those offenders whose culpability is unquestionable, and for crimes that are so heinous that the sanction is considered deserved. Barring status as a juvenile or having been found by the court to have mental retardation, the capital defendant remains eligible for the death penalty. With that in mind, it becomes clear that the evaluation of culpability of the capital defendant is of utmost importance.

In a capital case, it is the mandate of the defense team to present any aspect of the case or personal attribute or life circumstance that, in the eyes of the jurors, would decrease a defendant's culpability to the level at which the death penalty is considered undeserved. In its decision in *Wiggins v. Smith* (2003) the United States Supreme Court recognized this mandate and ruled that the failure to investigate and present mitigating evidence during the sentencing phase of a capital trial can constitute ineffective assistance of counsel, and therefore violated the defendant's Sixth Amendment right to effective assistance of counsel. In *Wiggins* the defense uncovered numerous potential mitigating circumstances including, but not limited to, severe neglect and physical abuse, sexual abuse, and borderline mental retardation, but chose not to present mitigating evidence to the jury. In the majority opinion, Justice Sandra Day O'Connor stated that the decision of trial counsel had resulted in practices that had fallen below the standard of reasonableness under prevailing professional norms and had prejudiced the defense. She further opined, "Had the jury been able to place [Wiggins'] excruciating life history on the mitigating side of the scale, there is a reasonable probability that at least one juror would have struck a different balance" (p. 536).

In *Wiggins* (2003), Janet Reno, former United States Attorney General, filed an amicus brief in support of the petitioner (Reno, 2003). In that brief she made the following statement:

> Effective representation in and presentation of a capital case requires extensive preparation for both the guilt and the sentencing phases, and can only be accomplished after defense counsel has conducted a thorough investigation into

> whether death is an appropriate sanction under the law in light of the defendant's background. Condoning imposition of a death sentence where the defendant has not had the benefit of such an investigation will, in the long run, undermine public confidence in the criminal justice system as a whole. (p. 2)

Despite having a clear mandate for the investigation and presentation of information regarding potential mitigators, the law has been silent with regard to who should present evidence and how it should be done. Though not exhaustive, the potential list of defense experts includes one or more of the following professionals: clinical psychologists, social workers, neuropsychologists, neurologists, psychiatrists, developmental psychologists, counselors, clinical caseworkers, pharmacologists, and addictions specialists. If appropriately used in this role, each of these experts can offer unique information relevant to mitigation.

With recognition that not all defense attorneys choose to put forth mental health expert testimony during the sentencing phase of a capital trial, the focus of this chapter relates to the more typical mitigation strategy that includes presentation of a defendant's troubled life history. Specifically, the chapter concentrates on the role of the mental health expert whose job it is to relate the life story of the defendant and effectively communicate potentially mitigating information to the trier of fact. It is argued that expert testimony regarding life history, regardless of who presents the data, must be firmly grounded in the research findings of developmental psychopathology. This is not to say that other disciplines do not have anything to offer, but simply that the fruits borne from other research (e.g., psychopathology, cycles of violence, drug addiction, and the ontogeny of antisocial behavior) can often be better explained from within a developmental framework (Luthar, 2003; Luthar, Burack, Cicchetti, & Weisz, 1997). With that in mind, the emphasis of this chapter is on how to portray the capital defendant's life story against the empirical backdrop of science, in particular, in the developmental concepts of risk factors, protective factors, and resiliency.

WHAT IS THE TYPICAL CONTENT OF MENTAL HEALTH EXPERT TESTIMONY ON MITIGATION?

If one were to look to the legal field for guidance on how to present mitigating circumstances to the trier of fact, one would quickly become disheartened. Although it is true that the majority of states have delineated statutory and nonstatutory mitigating factors, and the American Bar

Association (ABA, 2003) developed guidelines for the performance of counsel in death penalty litigation, the bottom line is that there are no guidelines regarding how to conduct an evaluation or how best to present information during the sentencing phase. In an attempt to illustrate the complexity of statutes pertaining to mitigation, an excerpt taken directly from the Criminal Code of Alabama is provided for the reader.

According to the Criminal Code of Alabama, mitigating circumstances shall include but not be limited to the following:

> (1) The defendant has no significant history of prior criminal activity;
> (2) The capital offense was committed while the defendant was under the influence of extreme mental or emotional disturbance;
> (3) The victim was a participant in the defendant's conduct or consented to it;
> (4) The defendant was an accomplice in the capital offense committed by another person and his participation was relatively minor;
> (5) The defendant acted under extreme duress or under the substantial domination of another person;
> (6) The capacity of the defendant to appreciate the criminality of his conduct or to conform his conduct to the requirements of law was substantially impaired; and
> (7) The age of the defendant at the time of the crime. (Alabama Criminal Code, §13A-5-51, Acts 1981, No. 81-178, §13)

Similar to other states, Alabama included a catch-all category for potential mitigating circumstances. As specified in section 13A-5-51:

> Mitigating circumstances shall include any aspect of a defendant's character or record and any of the circumstances of the offense that the defendant offers as a basis for a sentence of life imprisonment without parole instead of death, and any other relevant mitigating circumstance which the defendant offers as a basis for a sentence of life imprisonment without parole instead of death.

In order to seek the death penalty in Alabama, the prosecution must demonstrate the presence of an aggravating circumstance beyond a reasonable doubt (e.g., the offense was especially heinous, atrocious, or cruel compared to other capital offenses), and once this has been done the defense must develop their mitigation. In the end, jurors are required to weigh the mitigating circumstances against the aggravating circumstances to come to a decision on sentencing. It is important to note that the weighing of aggravating against mitigating circumstances is not a simple tallying of factors. Instead, the process requires that jurors consider each factor separately, assign that factor a valence, and then consider each factor in combination with all others. To recommend the death penalty in

Alabama a minimum of 10 jurors must agree on this verdict; the verdict of life without parole need only be a majority vote (Alabama Criminal Code, §13A-5-46, No. 81-178, p. 203, §8).

As evident from the preceding list, there are almost unlimited ways that mitigation could come together in any one case. If one looks only at the combinations possible using the seven statutory mitigating circumstances listed, there are 127 possible presentations.[1] Add one non-statutory mitigating factor to this list of seven (e.g., physical abuse, sexual abuse, neglect, or cognitive deficits, among others) and the total possible presentations increases to 255. Not surprisingly, the process of identifying potential mitigators and then creating an effective presentation of these factors can be a daunting task. It is not a laundry list of negative life events that matters; instead it is the interpretation, integration, and presentation of a life story that will ultimately make a difference.

Developmental Psychopathology: Risk Factors, Protective Factors, and Resiliency.

Perhaps the first question that must be answered is the question of why mitigation research and practice should be guided by the research findings from developmental psychopathology. The answer is quite simple; a person who commits a capital crime is similar to any other person in that he or she has a developmental history. The capital defendant was born, raised, and in the process of growing up, responded to forces that guided and manipulated his or her development. These forces are unique to the individual and can be traced to his or her community, family, and society at large, as well as to his or her biological make-up.

Though not always the case, the most typical capital defendant is a person who has failed to reach success in multiple areas of life and who has experienced tragedy. In other words, these are people who have failed to effectively adapt to societal demands. From the developmental perspective, "Maladaption is viewed as evolving through the successive adaptations of persons in their environments. It is not something a person 'has' or an ineluctable expression of an endogenous pathogen. It is the complex result of a myriad of risk and protective factors operating

[1]Combination: An arrangement of r objects without regard to order and without repetition, selected from n distinct objects is called a combination of n objects taken r at a time. The number of such combinations is denoted by: ${}_nC_r = \frac{n!}{(n-r)!\,r!}$ (Retrieved July 30, 2005 from http://www.wtamu.edu/academic/anns/mps/math/mathlab/col_algebra/col_alg_tut57_comb.htm).

The formula for calculating the number of combinations of seven mitigators would be the sum of: 7C7+7C6+7C5+7C4+7C3+7C2+7C1.

over time" (Sroufe, 1997, p. 251). In other words, maladaptive behavior originates and develops according to a complex system of interactions over a lifetime. In order to understand human development from a systems perspective one must first understand the constructs of risk and protective factors.

Risk Factors. The study of risk factors and their role in the developmental process is one of the central goals of developmental psychopathology. At the most basic level, a risk factor is a predictor that has been scientifically demonstrated to have a strong link to adverse outcomes (e.g., delinquency, adult antisocial behavior, substance abuse, unemployment, limited education, violence). In other words, a risk factor can be any life event or biological factor that, when triggered, negatively impacts the individual.

One of the most well-studied areas of environmental risk factors is the development of conduct disorder. Factors that influence the development of conduct disorder in children and adolescents are many and include child factors (e.g., temperament, low intellectual functioning), parent and family factors (e.g., poor parenting practices, impaired quality of relationships), school-related factors (e.g., limited emphasis on learning, low expectancies for success), and community factors (e.g., negative peer groups, poverty). (See Kazdin, 1997, p. 254 for a comprehensive review; Maughan, 2001; Stoff, Breiling, & Maser, 1997.) Research has demonstrated that there is not any one risk factor, or set of risk factors, that is necessary or sufficient to produce an adverse outcome. Instead, decades of research have clearly demonstrated that outcomes worsen as the number of risk factors increases (see, e.g., Coie et al., 1993; Deater-Deckard, Dodge, & Bates, 1998; Egeland, Carlson, & Sroufe, 1993; Garmezy & Masten, 1994; Masten & Wright, 1997).

With respect to long-term prognosis, individuals who are exposed to multiple risk factors during the developmental period (i.e., childhood and adolescence) are at greater risk of displaying dysfunction as an adult. For example, longitudinal studies have shown that children and adolescents diagnosed with conduct disorder demonstrate broad-based dysfunction over multiple domains. In his review of the literature, Kazdin (1997) linked seven categories of dysfunction in adulthood to a prior diagnosis of conduct disorder. Specifically, data from multiple studies have found that individuals who have been previously diagnosed with conduct disorder are more likely to experience psychiatric disturbances, engage in criminal behavior, have limited occupational success, function poorly in school, have impaired marital relationships, isolate from others, and experience poor physical health. Not surprisingly, these areas of dysfunction are common among death row inmates (Cunningham & Vigen, 2002).

Of import is the notion that early intervention at the individual, familial, and community levels can positively impact the developmental trajectory (e.g., Ricciuti, 1991; Zigler & Styfco, 2001a, 2001b; Zigler & Valentine, 1997). Although treatment for conduct disorder has been studied and demonstrated to be of some success (e.g., Chamberlain & Smith, 2005; Kazdin, 2002; Lochman & Wells, 2004), contextual factors such as single-parent status, financial problems, social isolation, lack of transportation, and caregiver skepticism regarding potential for treatment success influence whether families remain in treatment and succeed in treatment (e.g., Dadds & McHugh, 1992; Dumas & Wahler, 1983; Kazdin, 1995; McKay, Harrison, & Gonzales, 2002).

As evidenced by their support for programs that provide treatment for children and families exposed to violence, the value of intervention has been recognized at both the state and federal governmental levels. For example, on August 12, 2005, the Department of Justice, Office of Justice Programs (OJP) announced the release of 6.2 million dollars to 10 states and 15 sites under OJP's Safe Start Program. Using the California Safe from the Start Initiative as an example, the goal of the program is "to assure that California children grow up in safe, healthy environments." As written on their web site, the main concern leading to the need for intervention is as follows:

> Children exposed to violence and maltreatment suffer increased depression, anxiety, post-traumatic stress, anger, alcohol and drug abuse and lower academic achievement. New scientific research is uncovering the physiological impact of violence on the developing human brain and the long-term consequences of this exposure. Studies show that children exposed to violence, either as victims or witnesses, are more likely to become juvenile and adult offenders. (California Safe From the Start, n.d.)

With respect to expert testimony on mitigation, it is imperative that the mental health practitioner be knowledgeable of the risk factors experienced by the defendant and be able to discuss the impact of these risk factors in relation to interventions that were or were not implemented. Of course, individual risk factors would need to be evaluated over the life course, and be discussed with respect to cumulative stress and the interaction among factors. With regard to diagnostic criteria, it is critical that the mental health professional recognize that symptoms associated with trauma and the need to protect oneself often resemble symptoms of conduct disorder (CD) and later antisocial personality disorder (APD). The concern in capital cases is that defendants will be misdiagnosed as having CD or APD, when in fact the symptoms are reflective of an individual's attempt to remain safe, and at some level succeed, within a highly dysfunctional and often dangerous life context (Cunningham & Reidy, 1998).

Protective Factors. Although the lives of capital murder defendants tend to be riddled with risk factors such as poverty, early exposure to illicit drugs and violence, physical abuse, and ineffective parenting (Cunningham & Vigen, 2002), in even the most disadvantaged of ecological systems, an individual is typically exposed to one or more protective factors (e.g., a teacher or coach who takes an interest in the child, an opportunity to engage in community recreation, a family member who notices danger in the home and takes the child in). For the past 30 years, researchers, practitioners, and policy-makers have recognized the importance of prevention and have been dedicated to finding ways to increase access to various protective factors; the goal of such intervention is to foster resilience in at-risk children and adolescents.

The National Youth Violence Prevention Resource Center (2001) created a fact sheet that summarizes the findings of decades of research on risk and protective factors and their relation to youth violence. In this bulletin, risk and protective factors are placed within an ecological framework, and this framework provides an overview of the mechanisms of influence. Table 7.1 provides a distillation of the information pertaining to protective factors categorized by level of influence.

Another example of the push toward prevention is that of a National Institute on Drug Abuse funded study that has identified protective factors that can help prevent high-risk youths from engaging in delinquency and drug use (Smith, Lizotte, Thornberry, & Krohn, 1995). The authors of this study found that resistance to both drug use and delinquency was directly related to the accumulation of protective factors across multiple domains of an adolescent's life. Some of the protective factors identified in the study are listed in Table 7.2.

Searching for and understanding the role of protective factors has dual purposes in mitigation. First, like most people, the capital defendant will have had exposure to one or more protective factors over the course of his or her life. This may be the influence of a teacher, involvement in a coping skills program, or perhaps the presence of supportive parents. The usefulness of the identification of protective factors lies not in their

TABLE 7.1
Protective Factors for Youth Violence

Environmental-level factors	National, state, and local policies that support child and youth oriented programs Caring, supportive adult relationships
Community-level factors	Strong community infrastructure Access to activities where children and youth have choices, decision making power, and shared responsibility Strong nonkin support network.
Family-level factors	Parents who emphasize the importance of education Parents who offer support and affection Frequent, in depth conversations and communication between parents and children or youth Clear boundaries for behavior Enforcement of rules with reasonable disciplinary actions when rules are violated
Individual-level factors	Sense of purpose and belief in a positive future Commitment to education and learning Ability to act independently and feel a sense of control over one's environment Ability to be adaptable and flexible to changing circumstances Empathy and caring for others Problem solving ability Ability to plan for the future Resourceful in seeking out sources of support Conflict resolution and critical thinking skills

presence, but in their impact on the life course of the defendant. It may be that there were opportunities for change via counseling or involvement in extra-curricular activities, but that these protective factors were not powerful enough to negate the impact of the risk factors. Second, there are cases in which protective factors are absent from the life of the defendant, and this fact must be made apparent to the jury. Furthermore, the court must be made aware that the defendant's life trajectory may have been different had someone come forward and intervened on behalf of the individual, or had his or her contextual life experience included positive influences such as access to prosocial peer groups, financial stability, or a safe living environment. During the presentation of mitigation, it is

TABLE 7.2
Protective Factors for Delinquency and Drug Abuse

Family factors	Parental supervision
	Child's attachment to parent
	Parent's attachment to child
Educational factors	Reading percentile
	Mathematics percentile
	Commitment to school
	Attachment to teachers
	Parent's expectation for child to go to college
	Parent's values about college
Peer factors	Peers have conventional values
	Parent's positive evaluation of peers

Note. Adapted from Mathais (1996).

important to clearly delineate what could have been done to change the defendant's life course, what was done to assist in the process of change, and what tools were readily available yet not implemented.

The constructs of risk and protective factors are components of systems models of human development, also referred to as ecological models of human development. These models are based on the theory that development arises from reciprocal interactions between the person and environment over the course of time. One example of an ecological model is that proposed by Urie Bronfenbrenner in the 1970s (Bronfenbrenner, 1979, 2004); though not the only systems-based model of development, it is a theory that can aid in the transmission of mitigation testimony to the sentencing body.[2]

Bronfenbrenner's ecological model of human development includes four levels of influence: (a) the microsystem (the immediate environment in which the individual functions, e.g., family, day care, school, and community recreation); (b) the mesosystem (interrelationships between two or more of the individual's microsystems, e.g., the mutual influence of parents and teacher with respect to learning); (c) the exosystem (systems of influence that indirectly impact the individual, e.g., governmental systems such as unemployment benefits or welfare, parental experiences in the work setting, and social relationships of the parents); and (d) the macrosystem (dominant ideologies and cultural patterns of influence,

[2]Bronfenbrenner's model was chosen as an example of a systems models that can be applied within this context; other models that are similar in structure would work equally well.

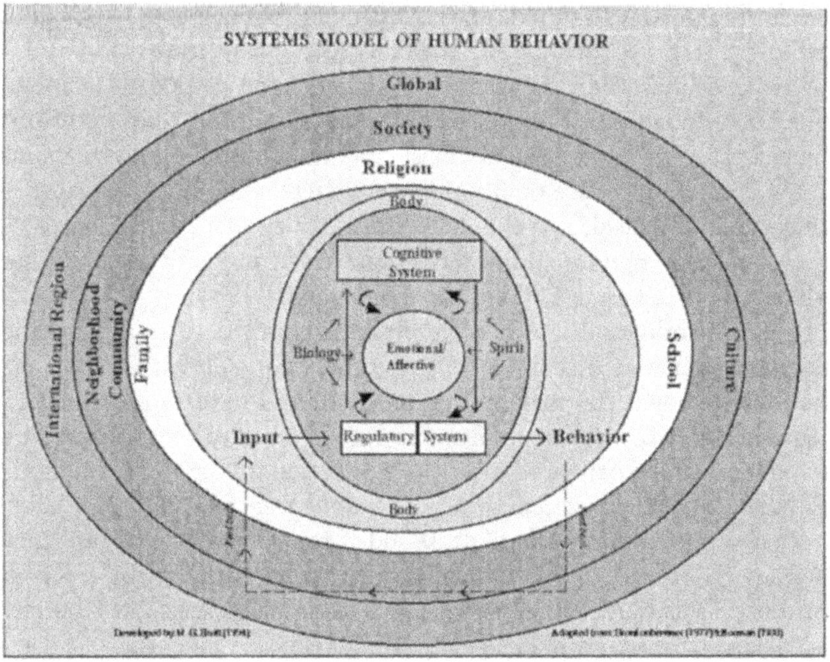

FIG. 7.1. Bronfenbrenner's systems model of human development. Retrieved May 31, 2005, from http://www.psy.pdx.edu/PsiCafeoverheads/SysModBeh.htm

e.g., government-sponsored programs to assist at-risk families, the legal system, and the dominant beliefs of child rearing at the community level), see Fig. 7.1. The four levels of influence do not exist independently of time, but instead exert their influence within a chronosystem. In other words, development occurs gradually over the course of time, and does so in patterns that are unique to the individual (see Sigelman & Rider, 2006, pp. 22–23). The ecological model brings to light the importance of individual differences, and the awareness that overcoming adversity is the result of the interaction of factors at the individual, family, community, and environmental levels.

Resilience and Vulnerability. What has yet to be discussed is the fact that not all people who experience traumatic upbringings or who suffer from a debilitating disease or disorder commit a capital offense. In fact, the majority of these individuals do not engage in crime, but instead find ways to overcome adversity. Judges and jurors are aware of this fact and the problem for the mental health expert is how to provide an explanation for criminal behavior and not have it sound like an excuse.

Perhaps the answer lies in another construct associated with the field of developmental psychopathology, the construct of resilience.

Resilience has been defined as a "dynamic developmental process reflecting evidence of adaptation despite significant life adversity" (Cicchetti, 2003, p. xx). As previously mentioned, studies have demonstrated that the presence of any single risk factor does not cause antisocial behavior; instead, it is the convergence of risk factors that leads to widespread dysfunction, and it is the presence of protective factors that fosters resilience (see, e.g., Garmezy, 1985; Rutter, 1985).

Seminal work in the area of resilience began 50 years ago on the Hawaiian island of Kauai (see Werner & Smith, 1992, 2001). The researchers studied 700 infants born on the island in 1955 and followed them for four decades. The results of the study revealed that the majority of children who experienced extreme deprivation during their childhood and adolescent years successfully negotiated the transition into adulthood; in other words, the majority of these individuals demonstrated resiliency (Werner & Smith, 2001). Individuals who demonstrated resilience in adulthood had a number of shared characteristics, including more resources and fewer adversities early in life, exposure to effective parenting, a greater number of positive relationships with positive adult role models, a longer time between the birth of siblings, easy temperaments, and better cognitive skills than individuals who did not demonstrate resilience (e.g., Masten, 2001; Masten, Hubbard, et al., 1999; Masten & Powell, 2003; Werner & Smith, 2001). These findings, among others, highlight the important role of protective factors in the developmental process.

Although perhaps not obvious, the issue of resiliency is of great import in capital mitigation. Clearly, millions of people experience adverse life events, but it is only the rare few who engage in capital crime. In order for mitigation to be successful, the trier of fact must be convinced that the defendant's experience of similar life events was unique, and that it was the uniqueness of the defendant's response that provides an explanation for the violent behavior. Perhaps the most common way for the issue of resilience to arise in a capital case is when the prosecution makes a relative comparison between the defendant and his or her siblings. Since it is very likely that the siblings grew up under very similar adverse circumstances, and it is unlikely that these siblings have been charged and convicted of capital murder, such a comparison can be quite powerful in the courtroom. As such, it is imperative that the clinician be able to explain why the defendant was not resilient under stress. What is it that makes him or her different from their resilient siblings? Again, a mental health professional involved in capital mitigation is encouraged to look to the developmental literature for answers. It may be that the siblings were raised by grandparents or had access to interventions that the defendant did not. Other influences may be less obvious and relate more to defendant characteristics (e.g., dependency, intellect, gullibility, and lack of coping strategies) than environmental influences. Of course, each would interact with the other, and it is the study of the interaction that will likely provide the greatest understanding of the defendant.

In short, the goal of mitigation is to provide the trier of fact with insight into the defendant; to allow them to appreciate life as it was experienced by the defendant and to understand the interplay between normal and atypical development over the course of time. The desired outcome, a sentence less than death, may be more likely if the mental health professional provides an accurate and easily understood life history of the defendant. Within the framework of the ecological model of human development, the capital defendant becomes more than just a person with a horrendous upbringing who committed a heinous crime; the capital defendant becomes a human being.

HOW STRONG IS THE SCIENTIFIC FOUNDATION FOR EXPERT TESTIMONY ON MITIGATION?

The strength of the scientific foundation for psychological expert testimony on mitigation is a direct function of the information proffered by the mental health professional. Research in developmental psychopathology has been, and continues to be, integral to the understanding of the processes by which normal and pathological development arises. Research in the area of child development, in particular developmental psychopathology, is extensive and spans over 30 years. For the most part, the research in this area has been long term and programmatic. As a result of this methodology, the research findings have widespread applicability and provide a strong basis from which to interpret individual functioning on the basis of group data. In other words, the research provides the mental health professional with a sound base from which to develop theories regarding the developmental trajectory of the person, and provides an empirical backdrop to support interpretive statements.

If one were to take the position that opinion statements are at least strengthened by the presence of empirical data that support that opinion, and that the majority of capital defendants have suffered multiple adversities over the course of their lives, then it would be difficult to envision a case in which the application of research gleaned from developmental psychopathology would be counter to the goals of the defendant. As already described, the literature base from which to develop effective mitigation is extremely broad, and has substantial empirical grounding. Scholars such as Cunningham and Reidy (2001), Haney (1995), and Stetler (1999), among many others, underscored the importance of conducting evaluations that are comprehensive and that reveal the biopsychosocial factors pertinent to the developmental trajectory of the defendant. Haney emphasized the need to tell the life story of the capital defendant, and the mental health professional's obligation to highlight forces that came together to create a person capable of a capital crime. Empirical research that postdates Haney continues to support findings of severe deprivation, abuse, and neglect in capital defendants; what has yet to be addressed, however, is the mechanics of how best to tell the defendant's story. Clearly, telling the defendant's story is a key component in the process of mitigation but the process of telling the story may be as important at the elements that comprise it.

IS THERE RESEARCH ON HOW JURORS RESPOND TO EXPERT TESTIMONY ON MITIGATION?

On the surface, the concepts of mitigating and aggravating circumstances are easily understood: A mitigating circumstance lessens a defendant's moral culpability and militates against a sentence of death, and an aggravating circumstance increases a defendant's moral culpability and may be used to support the imposition of a sentence of death. However, research has consistently demonstrated that jurors' ability to understand and apply the concepts of mitigating and aggravating circumstances to sentencing decisions is limited (e.g., Bentele & Bowers, 2002; Costanzo, 1997; Costanzo & Costanzo, 1992; Diamond, 1993; Haney, Sontag, & Costanzo, 1994; Lynch & Haney, 2000). In their evaluation of comprehension of capital sentencing instructions in California, Haney and Lynch (1994) identified significant problems in this area. Of particular import was the finding that a large percentage of participants had difficulty providing definitions for the core concepts of aggravation and mitigation. In their sample of college-educated individuals, only 15% were able to provide a legally correct definition of aggravation, 12% could provide a correct definition of mitigation, and a mere 8% provided correct definitions of both concepts. Even more concerning was the finding that 30% of the sample provided completely incorrect definitions of mitigation and, despite being read jury instructions three times, 11% of the sample were unable to provide a definition of mitigation. Shortly after completion of this project, California revised its capital sentencing instructions to include explicit legal definitions of the terms *aggravation* and *mitigation*. In response, Haney and Lynch (1997) again evaluated the comprehension of the jury instructions. The results of this study demonstrated that the inclusion of explicit definitions did nothing to improve overall comprehension, and actually reduced comprehension of the term *mitigation*.

Impaired understanding of core concepts that are required for carrying out a task, regardless of what they are, will almost always result in impaired ability to execute that task. For example, if one were to provide driving instructions using the cardinal directions of north, south, east, and west, it would be necessary for the recipient not only to have a clear understanding of front, back, right, and left, but also to understand the concept of a fixed point of reference. Without these skills, the individual would be unable to reach their destination. Along the same lines, in order to participate fully in the sentencing process, it is necessary for the capital juror to understand the concepts of mitigation and aggravation.

To discuss the next point it may be helpful to suspend one's awareness that people simply do not understand the basic constructs required for capital sentencing. Let us assume for a moment that people do have adequate understanding of the terms *mitigating* and *aggravating* and with this knowledge can enter into the process of deliberation. The question now becomes one of application; can the capital juror make a sentencing determination based on the rules of law? Not surprisingly, research using mock jurors has revealed impaired understanding of how to apply the decision rules set forth by the courts (e.g., Bentele & Bowers, 2002; Haney & Lynch, 1997). For example, in the previously described 1997 study by Haney and Lynch, the following decision rule was provided to mock jurors:

> The weighing of aggravating and mitigating circumstances does not mean a mere mechanical counting of factors on each side of an imaginary scale, or the arbitrary assignment of weights to any of them. You are free to assign whatever moral or sympathetic value you deem appropriate to each and all of the various circumstances you are permitted to consider. In weighing the various circumstances you determine under the relevant evidence which penalty is justified and appropriate by considering the totality of the aggravating circumstances with the totality of the mitigating circumstances. To return a judgment of death, each of you must be persuaded that the aggravating circumstances are so substantial in comparison to the mitigating circumstances that it warrants death instead of life without parole. (p. 594)

In this study, a mere 15% of the sample understood that a life sentence was legally required if mitigators and aggravators are given equal weight, only 50% understood that a life sentence was legally required if mitigators outweighed aggravators, and an unacceptably large percentage (i.e., 41%) were under the misconception that in cases in which aggravators outweighed mitigators they had no choice but to impose a sentence of death.

In addition to the misunderstanding of jury instructions, Bentele and Bowers (2002) pointed out that there may be other factors that interact with such misunderstandings and further impair decision making. For example, it may be that jurors tend to focus on evidence of aggravation, and because of this they do not take seriously any of the themes presented by the defense. Another possibility is that two misconceptions are in operation during jury deliberations: (a) In order to give any weight to mitigating evidence there must be unanimous agreement among the jurors and (b) the presence of any mitigator must be proven beyond a reasonable doubt.

Had they truly understood the process, they would have known that each juror must evaluate the evidence for themselves and if a juror believes a mitigating circumstance exists, he or she must consider it in the weighing process, even if all other jurors disagree (see *McKoy v. North Carolina*, 1990; *Mills v. Maryland*, 1988;). In addition, the existence of a mitigating circumstance does not require proof beyond a reasonable doubt. A mitigating circumstance exists if there is undisputed evidence to support its existence or if the evidence of its existence outweighs any conflicting evidence (see *Eddings v. Oklahoma*, 1982; *State v. Thompson*, 1990; *Lockett v. Ohio*, 1978;). These findings strongly indicate that juror instructions, in combination with lack of understanding of the relevance of mitigating factors, significantly impede the ability of jurors to even consider an alternative to the death penalty.

Although there is no research on juror response to expert testimony as presented from the developmental perspective, research has been conducted on jurors' perceptions of expert testimony in capital sentencing hearings. For the most part, experimental studies appear to have been limited to jurors' responses to clinical versus actuarial testimony regarding predictions of future dangerousness (Krauss & Lee, 2003; Krauss, Lieberman, & Olson, 2004; Krauss & Sales, 2001), with the notable exception of Sundby (1997) that will be discussed in detail below. In contrast, however, there have been numerous publications that discuss a variety of topics including, but not limited to: the practical aspects of mitigation (e.g., Connell, 2003; Halleck, 2001; Marczyk, Heilbrun, & DeMatteo, 2003), the implications of expert testimony (e.g., Chamberlain, 2004), and the ethics surrounding mental health professionals' involvement in capital litigation (Foot, 1990; Miller, 2001; Mossman, 1994).

In addition to the previously mentioned studies, information produced from the Capital Jury Project (CJP, n.d.)[3] has illuminated the process by which jurors consider mitigating and aggravating factors during the sentencing phase of the trial. Using data from the CJP, Garvey (1998) evaluated how capital jurors may respond to various aggravating and mitigating circumstances—the overarching question being whether a juror would be more likely, less likely, or just as likely to impose the death penalty after considering each factor. The findings indicate that brutal murders, murders of children, a defendant's lack of remorse, and a defendant's future dangerousness were strong aggravators. In contrast, residual doubt regarding a defendant's guilt, a defendant's youthfulness, the presence of mental retardation, or a defendant's diminished responsibility due to factors beyond the individual's control (e.g., mental illness or extreme emotional distress) were found to be strong mitigators. Of import were that jurors assigned little to no weight to developmental factors such as child abuse or a background of extreme poverty.

Though untested, it is possible that the limited value jurors placed on developmental risk factors is related to lack of knowledge regarding the long-term impact of adverse life events. The importance of expressing a clear message and imparting knowledge of the long-term impact of adversity to the jury was captured in a study by Scott Sundby (1997). In his review of data collected by the CJP, Sundby found that the majority of the jurors held a negative view of expert testimony, particularly defense experts. Review of the qualitative data revealed three overarching problems for defense experts who provide mitigation testimony: (A) jurors believed that such experts lack objectivity (i.e., a hired gun), (b) jurors doubt that experts have the ability to explain human behavior, and (c) the experts that do present mitigating circumstances fail to make a connection between the psychological principles and the

[3]The CJP is an ongoing program of research on the decision making of capital jurors. The project was begun in 1991 by a consortium of university-based researchers and is supported with funds from the National Science Foundation.

defendant's behavior at issue in the case. Without minimizing the importance of the first two problems, it is the third problem that is the focus of this section.

Clearly, it is simply not enough to say that the defendant experienced trauma or grew up in a bad neighborhood. In order to understand how to use this information, jurors must be provided with an explanation of how adversity impacted the development of the defendant and how such adversity can be linked to his or her status as a capital defendant. The following excerpt provides one example of a defense expert's failure to connect the critical components of adversity to actual behavior during mitigation testimony (Sundby, 1997, p. 1141):

Juror: I think they were trying to paint a picture of getting our sympathy for this defendant because he had this traumatic experience in his life. But it was sort of like, okay, well, what do we do with that? It was very hard hard for us to hear that. All the other jurors had great empathy for this 13-year-old boy who lost his brother, and we had a lot of feeling for it, but we didn't know what to do with it!

Interviewer: So you would say the other jurors did feel empathy for the brother's death, but they didn't know where to go with it?

Juror: Very much. It wasn't enough to make sense. Like, if we could somehow tie it in, and say it was so damaging psychologically, you know, in some way make us realize that that could permanently affect a person.

Interviewer: So he basically testified to the trauma of the incident, but not as to what was ongoing? And did the defense attorney take that thread?

Juror: No, it ended.

Interviewer: So basically you ended up with this traumatic experience that everybody agreed was traumatic....

Juror: And then the rest [of the jurors] kind of just disregarded it because, you know, "So what?" You know that's real sad, but it wasn't enough to erase the long string of crime. You couldn't make sense of why, why wasn't he able to overcome that. You had a traumatic experience, you know, you lost a baby when your wife had a miscarriage, you know it didn't ruin your life. So why, how come he didn't get over it?

As apparent from the preceding transcript, jurors are listening to expert testimony, but it is the job of the mental health professional and the attorney to make them hear it.

Finally, it is important for the mental health professional to understand that the presentation of mitigating evidence is set against a backdrop of factors that are highly influential and relate to schemas that are in place long before the jurors enter the courtroom. For example, empirical studies have shown that verdicts are influenced by a variety of factors, such as perceived worth of the victim (e.g., Sundby, 2003), race of the defendant (e.g., Abwender & Hough, 2001), race of the juror (e.g., Eisenberg Garvey, Wells, 2001), juror religion (e.g., Eisenberg, et al., 2001), and juror attitude toward the death penalty (e.g., Sandys & McClelland, 2003). Similar to decision-making in other realms, individuals who are asked to make decisions in the legal arena are doing so, at least in part, on the basis of schemas. In other words, the knowledge that they have accumulated from previous interactions over many years has a direct influence on how jurors think and respond (e.g., Fiske & Taylor, 1984). As such, the strength of mitigation evidence is at least in part related to the relationship between the defendant, the crime, and the preexisting schemata of each juror. In situations in which jurors' schemata are based on biased or inaccurate information that is detrimental to the defendant, the power of mitigation testimony is likely to be greatly reduced. As such, mental health professionals must enter the courtroom ready to discuss stereotypes and to present information that challenges the myths that may surround the character and life history of the defendant.

HOW MIGHT THE LEGAL SYSTEM BE MODIFIED IN LIGHT OF PSYCHOLOGICAL RESEARCH ON MITIGATION?

The question of how the legal system can be modified in light of psychological research on mitigation is difficult to answer. First, there is a vast amount of variability in the quality of mitigation evaluations. Perhaps some variability can be attributed to training, some to experience, and some to other factors such as size of remuneration, work ethic, and access to necessary information. Regardless of the origin, the disparity in work product is of great concern. All work products produced by experts in capital mitigation must be of high quality. With stakes as high as those in death penalty litigation, there is no room for careless error, less than thorough evaluations, or lack of knowledge regarding readily available research on potential mitigating factors.

This chapter has focused on the application of theory and research from the field of developmental psychopathology to that of mitigation. Ecological theories of development are not new, and neither is the application of the theory and the research findings in the legal realm. For a published example of the use of such research in the legal domain, the reader is directed to the 2003 article written by Philip H. Witt. In this article Witt directly stated that he utilized the "generally accepted" findings of research that were pertinent to the legal issue of juvenile waiver to adult court. He further stated that he organized the "Integration of Findings and Recommendations" section, as well as his testimony, around these research findings. Of import in this case was that the judge not only accepted the opinion of Dr. Witt, but openly acknowledged the value of objective, data-driven evaluations and testimony.

Along these lines, it is argued that research from developmental psychopathology can be applied to the process of mitigation and can provide information that would be helpful to the court. First, the use of research in developmental psychopathology can provide the scaffolding for the development of mitigation. For example, the research findings can guide the legal team in their search for information relevant to their case and perhaps can assist them in developing their legal strategy. For example, a member of the legal team may review school records and find a brief reference to a family meeting in the third grade. On further review it becomes apparent that during the second grade there were periods of impaired scholastic functioning, behavioral acting out, and repeated absences from school. This pattern was observed to have continued until the defendant was in the 5th grade and then functioning in the school environment improved. In a situation such as this, knowledge of the field of developmental psychopathology would immediately alert the legal team to investigate multiple aspects of family functioning, including, but not limited to, physical abuse, exposure to violence, experiences with losses or trauma, and what, if anything, happened to change the developmental trajectory. Thus, one recommendation would be for a capital defense team to have an in-house mental health professional to assist them in developing their strategy for mitigation. If this were not possible, it would be of great benefit for attorneys, investigators, and other individuals involved in capital litigation to receive training in the area of developmental psychopathology, specifically in the area of risk and protective factors and resiliency.

Second, mental health professionals would be negligent in their role if they were not well versed in the findings of developmental psychopathology. As previously mentioned, an expert does not have to be formally trained as a developmental psychologist to play a role in mitigation. However, if the role of the expert requires an investigation into the life history of the defendant, the expert must at least have the specialized knowledge in developmental psychopathology to do so. The American Bar Association (ABA, 2003) made clear that the investigation of developmental factors is central to the process of mitigation and, as such, it is imperative that experts have the training, experience, and expertise to be able to interpret the information provided to them from counsel. The following excerpt from the ABA guidelines is illustrative of the weight that they have given to developmental factors:

> It is necessary to locate and interview the client's family members (who may suffer from some of the same impairments as the client), and virtually everyone else who knew the client and his family, including neighbors, teachers, clergy, case workers, doctors, correctional, probation or parole officers, and others. Records—from courts, government agencies, the military, employers, etc.—can contain a wealth of mitigating evidence, documenting or providing clues to childhood abuse, retardation, brain damage, and/or mental illness, and corroborating witnesses' recollections. Records should be requested concerning not only the client, but also his parents, grandparents, siblings, and children. A multi-generational investigation frequently discloses significant patterns of family dysfunction and may help establish or strengthen a diagnosis or underscore the hereditary nature of a particular impairment. The collection of corroborating information from multiple sources—a time-consuming task—is important wherever possible to ensure the reliability and thus the persuasiveness of the evidence. (p. 84)

Clearly, the developmental perspective is integral to the process of mitigation, but the question of how best to communicate the information to the court remains unanswered. Although not yet studied empirically, it is argued that the developmental framework may provide a useful vehicle for communicating to the court the life histories of capital defendants.

Third, the issue of standard of practice is always important. As previously mentioned, the American Bar Association has published guidelines for capital litigation. The first draft of the guidelines was published in 1989, with the most recent version being published in 2003. The goal of the guidelines is to provide attorneys with information pertaining to effective assistance of counsel at all stages of the capital case. These guidelines are not aspirational in nature but instead "embody the current consensus about what is required to provide effective defense representation in capital cases" (ABA, 2003, p. 2), and they have been used by the United States Supreme Court to support findings of ineffective assistance of counsel in capital cases (e.g., *Wiggins v. Smith*, 2003).

Though detailed with respect to legal procedures, the guidelines say nothing about the procedures that must be followed by penalty-phase defense experts. Without some control over the conduct of the expert, even the most comprehensive initial investigation can be found ineffective in the hands of an incompetent or less-than-thorough expert (for a general discussion of the issue, see Nicholson & Norwood, 2000). It is not that mental health professionals are completely without guidance (see Committee on Ethical Guidelines for Forensic Psychologists, 1991), but these guidelines are very general and do not provide direction that is specific to the role of a psychologist in the process of mitigation.

That said, perhaps it is not the role of psychology to dictate how mental health professionals must function in the legal arena. Instead, as it is now, it may be best to leave the responsibility of monitoring the behavior of the mental health professional to the legal team. This places the burden on the legal team to be familiar with the general field of psychology and specifically to many subdisciplines of psychology, one of which would be psychopathology and another would be developmental psychopathology. With this knowledge they would have the freedom to pick and choose their experts and to present only that information that is of assistance to their client. This, of course, fits in with the mandate of the defense attorney.

On the flip side of the coin is, once again, the need for quality control. Although possible, it is unlikely that many attorneys have an intimate knowledge of the field of psychology or know what is required to conduct a thorough biopsychosocial evaluation from a mental health perspective. Psychologists, social workers, and other mental health professionals are trained to provide thorough evaluations and are ethically required to function to the best of their ability in every situation. Unfortunately, it is simply not the case that capital defendants get the benefit of well-trained experts, and because of this, the imposition of some guidelines could provide minimum standards for experts who are conducting evaluations for the purpose of mitigation. Such guidelines would be in line with those put forth by the ABA (2003) and would require such things as mandatory contacts with multiple collateral sources (e.g., parents, siblings, grandparents, aunts, uncles, teachers, employers), mandatory review of records provided from counsel (e.g., school, medical, employment, department of human resources, legal), and mandatory completion of a biopsychosocial interview with the defendant (preferably semistructured with adequate coverage of risk and protective factors). Relatedly, expert opinion testimony based on the evaluation should be accompanied by a citation list with research to support the statements made by the clinician. These suggestions are not new, but making them mandatory would be.

Fourth, there is no quality control regarding what information is admitted during the sentencing phase or who it is that can present the information. At the time of writing, expert testimony presented during the sentencing phase for the purpose of mitigation is not subject to formal evidentiary rules. The testimony of an expert can be based on hearsay (e.g., *Green v. Georgia*, 1979; *Lockett v. Ohio*, 1978;) and cannot be excluded on the basis that the subject matter has not been subject to peer review and publication (as required under *Daubert v. Merrell Dow Pharmaceuticals, Inc.*, 1993), or that it is not generally accepted in the field with which it belongs (as required under *Frye v. United States*, 1923). An excerpt taken from the Alabama Rules of Criminal Procedures provides an example of the degree to which the evidentiary rules are relaxed during the capital sentencing phase:

> Evidence can be presented by defendant and State on any issue the court deems probative on the issue of sentence, i.e., nature and circumstances of offense; defendant's character, background, mental and physical condition, or history; financial gain to the defendant; loss suffered by the victim(s), or any aggravating or mitigating factor. The court determines the probative value of evidence and admissibility; Rules of Evidence do not govern. (Alabama Rules of Criminal Procedure, 1999, 26.6(b)(2))

That said, recent events indicate that the tides may be changing in relation to the application of evidentiary rules to expert testimony during capital sentencing. For example, some jurisdictions have applied a modified *Daubert* standard to mental health expert testimony on dangerousness (see *Nenno v. State*, 1998), and it is not hard to imagine the rules being extended to include all expert testimony presented during this phase. In addition, the American Psychological Association recently submitted an amicus brief urging federal courts to apply *Daubert* to mental health expert testimony in capital sentencing.

Finally, and unrelated to developmental psychopathology, any improvement in the quality of mitigation testimony will likely have little impact unless juror instructions are altered in a way that improves clarity and juror comprehension. Research has clearly demonstrated that juror instructions provide limited guidance, and may in fact provide misleading information as to how to proceed during the sentencing phase of a capital trial. It would be prudent for the judiciary to use the findings of this research to guide the development of new, revised jury instructions. The goal, of course, would be to eliminate the misconceptions that have been documented in the literature.

REFERENCES

American Bar Association. (2003). *Guidelines for the appointment and performance of defense counsel in death penalty cases*. Washington, DC: Author.

Abwender, D. A., & Hough, K. (2001). Interactive effects of characteristics of defendant and mock juror on U.S. participants' judgment and sentencing recommendations. *Journal of Social Psychology, 141*, 603–615.

Alabama Rules of Criminal Procedure, 26.6 (b)(2) (1999).

Atkins v. Virginia, 536 U.S. 304 (2002).

Bentele, U., & Bowers, W. J. (2002). How jurors decide on death: Guilt is overwhelming; aggravation requires death; and mitigation is no excuse. *Brooklyn Law Review*, 66, 1013–1080.

Bronfenbrenner, U. (1979). *The ecology of human development*. Cambridge, MA: Harvard University Press.

Bronfenbrenner, U. (2004). *Making human beings human: Bioecological perspectives on human development*. Thousand Oaks, CA: Sage.

California Safe From the Start. (n.d.). Retrieved August 18, 2005 from http://www.safefromthestart.org/aboutus/psummary.aspx

Capital Jury Project (CJP). (n.d.). Retrieved March 11, 2005 from http://www.cjp.neu.edu

Chamberlain, J. R. (2004). The use of a psychiatric expert who might offer both damaging and mitigating testimony does not constitute ineffective assistance of counsel. *Journal of the American Academy of Psychiatry and the Law, 32*, 329–331.

Chamberlain, P., & Smith, D. K. (2005). Multidimensional treatment foster care: A community solution for boys and girls referred from juvenile justice. In E. D. Hibbs & P. S. Jenson (Eds.), *Psychosocial treatments for child and adolescent disorders: Empirically based strategies for clinical practice* (2nd ed., pp. 557–573). Washington, DC: American Psychological Association.

Cicchetti, D. (2003). Forward. In S. S. Luthar (Ed.), *Resilience and vulnerability: Adaptation in the context of childhood adversities* (pp. XX). New York: Cambridge University Press.

Coie, J. D., Watt, N. F., West, S., Hawkins, J. D., Asarnow, J. R., Markman, H. J., et al. (1993). The science of prevention. *American Psychologist, 48*, 1013–1022.

Committee on Ethical Guidelines for Forensic Psychologists (1991). Specialty guidelines for forensic psychologists. *Law and Human Behavior, 15*, 655–665.

Connell, M. A. (2003). A psychobiographical approach to the evaluation for sentence mitigation. *Journal of Psychiatry and Law, 31*, 319–354.

Costanzo, M. (1997). *Just revenge: Costs and consequences of the death penalty*. New York: St. Martin's Press.

Costanzo, M., & Costanzo, S. (1992). Jury decision making in the capital penalty phase: Legal assumptions, empirical findings, and a research agenda. *Law and Human Behavior, 16*, 185–201.

Criminal Code of Alabama, §§13A-5-51–5-52 (1975).

Cunningham, M. D., & Reidy, T. J. (1998). Antisocial personality disorder and psychopathy: Diagnostic dilemmas in classifying patterns of antisocial behavior in sentencing evaluations. *Behavioral Sciences and the Law, 16*, 333–351.

Cunningham, M. D., & Reidy, T. J. (2001). A matter of life or death: Special considerations and heightened practice standards in capital sentencing evaluations. *Behavioral Sciences and the Law, 19*, 473–490.

Cunningham, M. D., & Vigen, M. P. (2002). Death row inmate characteristics, adjustment, and confinement: A critical review of the literature. *Behavioral Sciences and the Law, 20*, 191–210.

Dadds, M. R., & McHugh, T. A. (1992). Social support and treatment outcome in behavioral family therapy for child conduct problems. *Journal of Consulting and Clinical Psychology, 60*, 252–259.

Daubert v. Merrell Dow Pharmaceuticals, Inc., 113 S. Ct. 2786 (1993).

Deater-Deckard, K., Dodge, K., & Bates, J. E. (1998). Multiple risk factors in the development of externalizing behavior problems: Group and individual differences. *Development and Psychopathology, 10*, 469–493.

Diamond, S. S. (1993). Instructing on death: Psychologists, juries, and judges. *American Psychologist, 48*, 423–434.

Dumas, J. E., & Wahler, R. G. (1983). Predictors of treatment outcome in parent training: Mother insularity and socioeconomic disadvantage. *Behavioral Assessment, 5*, 301–313.

Eddings v. Oklahoma, 455 U.S. 104 (1982).

Egeland, B., Carlson, E., & Sroufe, L. A. (1993). Resilience as process. *Development and Psychopathology, 5*, 517–528.

Eisenberg, T., Garveg, S.P., & Wells, M. T. (2001). Forecasting life and death: Juror race, religion, and attitude toward the death penalty. *Journal of Legal Studies, 30*, 277–311.

Fiske, S. T., & Taylor, S. E. (1984). *Social cognition*. Reading, MA: Addision-Wesley.

Foot, P. (1990). Ethics and the death penalty: Participation by forensic psychiatrists in capital trials. In R. Rosner & R. Weinstock (Eds.), *Ethical practice in psychiatry and the law* (pp. 207–217). New York: Plenum Press.

Frye v. United States, 293 F.1013, 34 A.L.R. 145 (D.C. Cir. 1923).

Garmezy, N. (1985). Stress-resistant children: The search for protective factors. In J. E. Stevenson (Ed.), *Recent research in developmental psychopathology: Journal of Child Psychology and Psychiatry Book Supplement No. 4* (pp. 213–233). Oxford, England: Pergamon Press.

Garmezy, N., & Masten, A. S. (1994). Chronic adversities. In M. Rutter, L. Hersov, & E. Taylor (Eds.), *Child and adolescent psychiatry* (3rd ed., pp. 191–208). Oxford, England: Blackwell.

Garvey, S. P. (1998). Aggravation and mitigation in capital cases: What do jurors think? *Columbia Law Review, 1538*.

Green v. Georgia, 442 US95 (1979).

Halleck, S. (2001). Psychiatry and the death penalty: A view from the front lines. In L. E. Frost & R. J. Bonnie (Eds.), *Evolution of mental health law* (pp. 181–192). Washington, DC: American Psychological Association.

Haney, C. (1995). The social context of capital murder: Social histories and the logic of mitigation. *Santa Clara Law Review, 35*, 547–609.

Haney, C., & Lynch, M. (1994). Comprehending life and death matters: A preliminary study of California's capital penalty instructions. *Law and Human Behavior, 18*, 411–436.

Haney, C., & Lynch, M. (1997). Clarifying life and death matters: An analysis of instructional comprehension and penalty phase arguments. *Law and Human Behavior, 21*, 575–595.

Haney, C., Sontag, L., & Costanzo, S. (1994). Deciding to take a life: Capital juries, sentencing instructions, and the jurisprudence of death. *Journal of Social Issues, 50*, 149–176.

Kazdin, A. E. (1995). Child, parent, and family dysfunction as predictors of outcome in cognitive-behavioral treatment of antisocial children. *Behaviour Research and Therapy, 33*, 271–281.

Kazdin, A. E. (1997). Conduct disorder across the lifespan. In S. S. Luthar, J. A. Burack, D. Cicchetti, & J. R. Weisz (Eds.), *Developmental psychopathology: Perspectives on adjustment, risk, and disorder* (pp. 248–272). New York: Cambridge University Press.

Kazdin, A. E. (2002). Psychosocial treatments for conduct disorder in children and adolescents. In P. E. Nathan & J. M. Gorman (Eds.), *A guide to treatments that work* (2nd ed., pp. 57–85). New York: Oxford University Press.

Krauss, D. A., & Lee, D. H. (2003). Deliberating on dangerousness and death: Jurors' ability to differentiate between expert actuarial and clinical predictions of dangerousness. *International Journal of Law and Psychiatry, 26*, 113–137.

Krauss, D. A., Lieberman, J. D., & Olson, J. (2004). The effects of rational and experiential information processing of expert testimony in death penalty cases. *Behavioral Sciences and the Law, 22*, 801–822.

Krauss, D. A., & Sales, B. D. (2001). The effects of clinical and scientific expert testimony on juror decision making in capital sentencing. *Psychology, Public Policy, and Law, 7*, 267–310.

Lochman, J. E., & Wells, K. C. (2004). The Coping Power Program for preadolescent aggressive boys and their parents: Outcome effects at the 1-year follow-up. *Journal of Consulting and Clinical Psychology, 72*, 571–578.

Lockett v. Ohio, 438 U.S. 586 (1978).

Luthar, S. S. (Ed.). (2003). *Resilience and vulnerability: Adaptation in the context of childhood adversities*. New York: Cambridge University Press.

Luthar, S. S., Burack, J. A., Cicchetti, D., & Weisz, J. R. (Eds.). (1997). *Developmental psychopathology: Perspectives on adjustment, risk, and disorder*. New York: Cambridge University Press.

Lynch, M., & Haney, C. (2000). Discrimination and instructional comprehension: Guided discretion, racial bias, and the death penalty. *Law and Human Behavior, 24*, 337–358.

Marczyk, G., Heilbrun, K., & DeMatteo, D. (2003). Using a model to guide data gathering, interpretation, and communication in capital mitigation evaluations. *Journal of Forensic Psychology Practice, 3*, 89–103.

Masten, A. S. (2001). Ordinary magic: Resilience processes in development. *American Psychologist, 56*, 227–238.

Masten, A. S., Hubbard, J. J., Gest, S. D., Tellegren, A., Garmezy, N., & Ramirez, M. (1999). Competence in the context of adversity: Pathways to resilience and maladaption from childhood to late adolescence. *Development and Psychopathology, 11*, 143–169.

Masten, A. S., & Powell, J. L. (2003). A resilience framework for research, policy, and practice. In S. S. Luthar (Ed.), *Resilience and vulnerability: Adaptation in the context of childhood adversities* (pp. 1–25). New York: Cambridge University Press.

Masten, A. S., & Wright, M. O. (1997). Cumulative risk and protection models of child maltreatment. In B. B. R. Rossman & M. S. Rosenberg (Eds.), *Multiple victimization of children: Conceptual, developmental, research and treatment issues* (pp. 7–30). Binghampton, NY: Haworth Press.

Mathias, R. (1996). Protective factors can buffer high-risk youths from drug use [electronic version]. *NIDA Notes, 11*(3).

Maughan, B. (2001). Conduct disorder in context. In J. Hill & B. Maughan (Eds.), *Conduct disorders in childhood and adolescence* (pp. 169–201). New York: Cambridge University Press.

McKay, M. M., Harrison, M. E., & Gonzales, J. (2002). Multiple-family groups for urban children with conduct difficulties and their families. *Psychiatric Services, 53*, 1467–1468.

McKoy v. North Carolina, 494 U.S. 433, 110 S.Ct. 1227, 108 L.Ed.2d 369 (1990).

Miller, R. D. (2001). The D.A. made me do it: Compulsory capital sentencing evaluations. *Journal of Psychiatry and Law, 29*, 409–431.

Mills v. Maryland, 486 U.S. 367, 108 S. Ct. 1860, 100 L.Ed.2d 384 (1988).

Mossman, D. (1994). Is expert psychiatric testimony fundamentally immoral? *International Journal of Law and Psychiatry, 17*, 347–368.

National Youth Violence Prevention Resource Center. (2001). *Risk and protective factors for youth violence fact sheet*, NYVPRC. Retrieved August 18, 2005, from www.safeyouth.org/scripts/facts/risk.asp

Nenno v. State, 970 SW.2d 549 (1998).

Nicholson, R. A., & Norwood, S. (2000). The quality of forensic psychological assessments, reports, and testimony: Acknowledging the gap between promise and practice. *Law and Human Behavior, 24*, 9–44.

Reno, J. F. (2003). *Amici Curiae* in support of petitioner. *Wiggins V. Corcoran [2002]*.

Ricciuti, H. N. (1991). Malnutrition and cognitive development: Research-policy linkages and current research directions. In L. Okagaki & R. Sternberg (Eds.), *Directors of development: Influences on the development of children's thinking* (pp. 59–80). Hillsdale, NJ: Lawrence Erlbaum Associates.

Roper v. Simmons, 543 U.S., 125 S.Ct. 1183 (2005).

Rutter, M. (1985). Resilience in the face of adversity: Protective factors and resistance to psychiatric disorder. *British Journal of Psychiatry, 147*, 598–611.

Sandys, M., & McClelland, S. (2003). Stacking the deck for guilt and death: The failure of death qualification to ensure impartiality. In J. R. Acker, R. M. Bohm, & C. S. Lanier (Eds.), *America's experiment with capital punishment: Reflections on the past, present, and future of the ultimate penal sanction* (2nd ed., pp. 385–412). Durham, NC: Carolina Academic Press.

Sigelman, C. K., & Rider, E. A. (2006). *Life-span human development*. Belmont, CA: Thompson/Wadsworth.

Smith, C., Lizotte, A. J., Thornberry, T. P., & Krohn, M. D. (1995). Resilient youth: Identifying factors that prevent high-risk youth from engaging in delinquency and drug use. In J. Hagan (Ed.), *Delinquency and disrepute in the life course* (pp. 217–247). Greenwich, CT: JAI Press.

Sroufe, L. A. (1997). Psychopathology as an outcome of development. *Development and Psychopathology*, 9, 251–268.

State v. Thompson, 76 S.W.2d 239 (Tenn. 1989), *cert. denied*, 110 S. Ct. 3288 (1990).

Stetler, R. (1999). Capital cases: Mental disabilities and mitigation. *The Champion Magazine*, *23*, 35–39.

Stoff, D. M., Breiling, J., & Maser, J. D. (1997). *Handbook of antisocial behavior*. New York: Wiley.

Sundby, S. E. (1997). The jury as critic: An empirical look at how capital juries perceive expert and lay testimony. *Virginia Law Review*, 83, 1109–1188.

Sundby, S. E. (2003). The capital jury and empathy: The problem of worthy and unworthy victims. *Cornell Law Review*, 88, 343–381.

Werner, E., & Smith, R. (1992). *Overcoming the odds: High risk children from birth to adulthood*. New York: Cornell University Press.

Werner, E., & Smith, R. (2001). *Journey from childhood to midlife: Risk, resiliency, and recovery*. New York: Cornell University Press.

Wiggins v. Smith, 539 U.S. 510 (2003).

Witt, P. H. (2003). Transfer of juveniles to adult court: The case of H. H. *Psychology, Public Policy, and the Law*, 9, 361–380.

Zigler, E., & Styfco, S. J. (2001a). Can early childhood intervention prevent delinquency? A real possibility. In A. C. Bohart & D. J. Stipek (Eds.), *Constructive and destructive behavior: Implications for family, school, and society* (pp. 231–248). Washington, DC: American Psychological Association.

Zigler, E., & Styfco, S. J. (2001b). Extended childhood intervention prepares children for school and beyond. *Journal of the American Medical Association, 285*, 2378–2380.

Zigler, E., & Valentine, J. (1997). *Project Head Start: A legacy of the war on poverty* (2nd ed.). Alexandria, VA: National Head Start Association.

8

Insanity's Disconnect, the Law's Madness, and the Irresistible Impulses of Experts

Norman J. Finkel
Georgetown University

In this chapter, I connect three topical areas to explain why psychological experts may sometimes overstep, proffering what appears to be illegitimate inferences and conclusions in courts in insanity cases. Nearing chapter's end, I examine expert psychological testimony in two recent high-profile insanity cases: that of Andrea Pia Yates (found guilty of murder for drowning her five children) and that of Lee Boyd Malvo (found guilty of capital murder and violating Virginia's antiterrorism law for 13 "random shootings" involving 10 deaths). In both cases multiple experts testified, drawing not only divergent but suspect inferences and conclusions, from a scientific perspective, about the defendants' state of mind and whether they knew right from wrong.

However, expert psychological opinions occur within a legal context that places constraints—some new, some quite old—on the story experts may tell, and thus what may appear to be the irresistible impulses of experts to cross scientific boundaries and legal constraints may not be the whole story. The older constraint results from "insanity's disconnect," which the lawyer Erskine identified 200 years ago in *Hadfield's Case* (1800): This is the problem of a delusional defendant who knows right from wrong in the abstract legal sense, but where a *mens rea* or symptom test does not reflect the essence of insanity in the deeper psychological sense. This disconnect between the disciplines of psychology and law (which is detailed later) over the fundamental concept of insanity has been a long-standing contention, one that continues to date. Here I ask whether the law's historic test definitions, when put under psychological scrutiny, have captured the essence of insanity; my labeling of this area as "insanity's disconnect" anticipates my answer.

The newer constraint (detailed in later) focuses on: (a) recent legislative changes made to insanity laws following the landmark *Hinckley* decision (*United States v. Hinckley*, 1981), where the aim was to limit the defense and restrain the experts from undue influence over the jurors' ultimate opinion, and (b) a prosecutorial trend (illustrated in my two focal cases) to turn insanity cases into capital cases, where the specter of the death penalty may color expert testimony. Here I ask whether the new statutory laws are theoretically coherent and move us closer to (or further from) the essence of insanity, and whether raising the dispositional stakes (i.e., the death penalty specter) muddles culpability adjudication and pushes expert testimony beyond legal and scientific bounds; labeling this area "law's madness" anticipates my answer.

Then I move to psychological experts testifying, where some proffers appear illegitimate and mistaken, but, here, the fact that I label this topical area "the irresistible impulses of experts" does not anticipate my whole answer. I begin with a distinction between mistakes that may be legitimate and those that appear illegitimate. In *Commonwealth of Virginia v. Lee Boyd Malvo* (2003), I focus on the testimony of the defense experts, all of whom testified that Malvo suffered from a "dissociative disorder," testimony that provided support for the defense's "brainwashing insanity" claim—before that claim was undercut by the prosecution and toppled by the jury. This diagnosis, I maintain, was off the mark, for it fit neither with the defining criteria of dissociative disorder, nor with the common pattern of dissociation in documented cases, nor with the facts in Malvo's case. But this is a minor point, because an erroneous diagnosis may result from a legitimate mistake, which may well have occurred in this case, given that Malvo, like Hamlet (Shakespeare, 1938, I, v. 175), was alleged to have "put an antic disposition on." When a defendant feigns a disorder the experts may be fooled, and thus this may have been a legitimate mistake. My main point involves mistakes that appear to result from illegitimate reasons, and to analyze some of these to see whether they are truly illegitimate, or whether they reveal added complexity to this maddening story of insanity.

In the 2002 trial of Andrea Pia Yates (*Texas v. Yates*, 2005), I focus on the testimony of the prosecution's expert, because a number of trial commentators (e.g., Colb, 2003; Denno, 2003; O'Malley, 2004) held that his inferences and conclusion tipped the balance in favor of the guilty verdict, despite the fact that only he testified that Yates knew right from wrong, whereas five other experts testified that Yates "did not know right from wrong, was incapable of knowing right from wrong, or believed that her acts were right" (*Yates v. Texas*, 2005, p. 5). Another distinction is made here. My specific focus is not on the factual mistake he made, which the Court of Appeals for the First District of Texas ruled was not intentional, but rather on mistakes involving: (a) certain inferences that, I argue, were not legitimate psychiatric inferences, but highly suspect moral or religious inferences having no scientific basis, and (b) his use of an objective or rational perspective to analyze Yates' delusion, which was inconsistent with the subjective perspective that a sound clinical approach requires and with what the M'Naghten test requires.

In connecting these three topical areas—where the disciplines of psychology and law meet at the empirical-normative nexus—I am guided by Rousseau's (1950, p. 3) opening sentence in *The Social Contract*, where he advised that we take men and women "as they are," in order to see "laws as they might be." Put another way, normative culpability judgments ought to rest on an empirically grounded theory about the nature of human nature. In my conclusion, I offer some thoughts on illegitimate testimony, given these old and new constraining contexts, and what this augurs for future insanity cases, experts testifying, and the law. When certain mistaken opinions are examined within these contexts, bad science (and even good science) and bad law appear as both antagonistic and conspiratorial bedfellows in a bad marriage, each pushing the other beyond sanity's bounds.

INSANITY'S DISCONNECT

Thomas Erskine, said to have been the ablest attorney in England at that millennium time of 1800 (e.g., Finkel, 1988; Walker, 1968), successfully defended his delusional client, James Hadfield, by bringing about a not guilty by reason of insanity (NGRI) verdict. This outcome was not easy to effect, for Hadfield was no wild beast, and the wild beast test (*Rex v. Arnold*, 1723) was the legal test then. This case was significant, not only because Erskine effectively slew the wild beast test (i.e., though the beast, dead on its feet, staggered on for 43 years until it was replaced by the

M'Naghten test in 1843), but primarily because Erskine pinpointed the central problem that would plague legal insanity tests to date, and because he offered arguments for new criteria, which he believed were at the essence of insanity, and which would eventually find their way into subsequent legal tests.

Erskine's Psychological Theory of a Disconnect Within and Between

Erskine began his defense by ridiculing the law's wild beast test, a stratagem that allowed him to then offer a new psychological theory and test of insanity, and then to embed his psychological theory within a substantively grounded organic theory and test, where the psychological delusion and motives irresistible that followed were anchored to underlying brain damage. First, Erskine (*Hadfield*, 1800, p. 1312) argued:

> If a TOTAL deprivation of memory was intended by these great lawyers to be taken in the literal sense of the words:—if it was meant, that, to protect a man from punishment, he must be in such a state of prostrated intellect, as not to know his name, nor his condition, nor his relation towards others—that if a husband, he should not know he was married; or, if a father, could not remember that he had children; nor know the road to his house, nor his property in it—then no such madness ever existed in the world.

Hyperbole aside, Erskine's pragmatic point was that the number of totally impaired was far too small to account for all the true cases of insanity that medical men, alienists, and citizens saw, and his psychological point was that such totally deranged, out-of-contact-with-reality individuals were probably unable to commit crimes like murder and treason, which required not only planning, but the down-to-earth ability to execute the plan in reality.

In the psychological theory he proposed, Erskine (*Hadfield*, 1800) claimed that the essence of insanity was delusion, a partial insanity, such that a truly insane individual could be deluded at one moment but lucid at another. Hadfield's delusional beliefs were that Christ's Second Coming was at hand, but that Christ would not step foot in England as long as that mad monarch, George III, was on the throne; in addition, Hadfield came to believe that he had a special role and mission to play in paving the way for the higher moral good, Christ's reappearance—by making King George III disappear—so he attempted to kill the king, though his aim, like his beliefs, proved untrue. Erskine thus presented the law with what I called "the Hadfield problem" (Finkel, 1988, 1995)—the core problem of insanity that the law has yet to solve—for a delusional defendant like Hadfield knows right from wrong in the abstract legal sense, yet disconnects his concrete actions from the shared background nexus and sees his act as right, in a higher, moral sense. One realizes, with a bit of reflection, that this problem cannot be solved by a simple *mens rea* analysis.

Specifically, what Erskine offered the jury was this: "Reason is not driven from her seat, but distraction sits down upon it along with her, holds her, trembling upon it, and frightens her from her propriety. 'The madman ... reasons from false premises,' because a delusive image, the inseparable companion of real insanity, is thrust upon the subjugated understanding, incapable of resistance because of unconscious attack" (Walker, 1968, p. 77). Here we have the imagery of a seduction, with the siren's call coming from within the psyche, as unreason seduces reason with false thoughts and distracting emotions, coming at her by stealthy unconscious attack. This delusional complex (of images, emotions, false thoughts, and premises) embraces, envelopes, subjugates, and finally topples reason and her virtuous volitions. Erskine's picture of delusion is far more substantial than a symptom—for it is the self that is torn and divided.

Although Erskine's evocative words, imagery, and story played well with the jurors, a critical unraveling of his theory reveals two knotty and entangled problems: first, the problem of two selves inhabiting one and the same person (i.e., how, when, and why did this split come about in the first place?), and second, the problem of self-deception. To make these entwining problems clearer, let us examine Erskine's theory more closely. Erskine's story already begins with two selves within that psyche, reason and distraction, with the latter having its own thoughts and passions, and possessing motives clearly in opposition to those of reason. In

Erskine's portrayal, this distraction self turns out to be quite the seducer, or in the language of that time, a cad, for he possesses no gentlemanly instincts. For example, distraction deviously frightens reason, yet appears instantly as her comforter, sitting down beside the now trembling reason as she shakes with fright; then, while she is in this vulnerable state, this siren sings a "Killing Me Softly" song that mixes gossamer images and false premises, as distraction subjugates reason through this unconscious attack. Oh, what villainy, what treachery! Although distraction clearly deceives reason, our second problem emerges, because as these two are parts of the whole psyche, there must be a self-deception occurring.

But wait a minute! We must wake up, lest our reason slumber to Erskine's soft song. In Erskine's drama, reason is played not as a wise Athena, but as if she were some 13-year-old ingenue who is positively slow on the uptake, because this easily frightened maiden remains oblivious to all of distraction's ploys, unconscious to all his thinking, and blind to his deception aimed at her upending. One might ask, "Has this 'reason' grown up in a nunnery where she never experienced a cad or sociopath before?" But as she shares the same psychic space with this character and, more importantly, is reason, why does she not see through the self-deception? So the second problem, of self-deception, is not adequately explicated in Erskine's account. And we still have the first problematic question: How, when, and why did this disconnect take place in the first place that produced this distraction self? This has not been answered at all.

Why Erskine's Psychological Theory Fails, Yet Self-Deception Stubbornly Stands

The philosopher Herbert Fingarette (1974, p. 80) started his article, "Self-Deception and the 'Splitting of the Ego,'" with these two questions: "Who can doubt that we do deceive ourselves? Yet who can explain coherently and explicitly how we do so?" The problem with Erskine's account is that it commits us to a process of self-deception that should not deceive at all—because in hiding something from oneself (Fingarette, p. 89) there appears to be "no inner 'victim' of this secretiveness," as the hider knows the truth. A similar argument is found in Sartre's (1974, p. 74) "Mauvaise Foi [bad faith] and the Unconscious," where he too criticized accounts like Erskine's, which cuts the psychic whole into two (I am the ego but I am not the id), and creates the possibility "of a lie without a liar" (p. 75). As Sartre (pp. 72–73) stated, "I must know in my capacity as deceiver the truth which is hidden from me in my capacity as the one deceived … [and thus] the lie falls back and collapses beneath my look; it is ruined *from behind* by the very consciousness of lying to myself which pitilessly constitutes itself well within my project as its very condition." These two philosophers argued that Erskine's distraction self has to know the truth in order to fashion the delusional lie it foists on reason, so if one self knows, then a claim that *mens rea* was negated is apparently false.

Still, the philosopher Fingarette (1974) asked, "Who can doubt that we do deceive ourselves?" In answering the philosopher's question, we do not doubt that we deceive ourselves because we know that the phenomenon is real. We recognize it when we see it in others (e.g., our children, spouses, students, colleagues), though we may be slow to recognize it in ourselves, because the process of acknowledging it likely involves embarrassment, pain, and shame. Moreover, therapists know that there is a stubbornness (i.e., resistance) to self-deceptions, particularly delusions, for they do not collapse easily, contrary to what Sartre (1974) predicted.

An Ego Nuclear Complex, Split off by the Ego, in the Process of Defense

Fingarette (1974, p. 83) took a position, consistent with an older view put forth by Isaac Ray (1983) and with recent social constructionist theorists (e.g., Harré, 1998; Harré & Gillett, 1994; Harré & van Langenhove, 1999; Sabat, 2001), that the self is "a synthesis, an achievement by the individual"—that it is something we make. But self-deceivers, who are engaged in the world in some way, refuse to avow certain engagements as theirs, and thus these actions are not synthesized into the personal identity they claim. "Having disavowed the engagement, the self-deceiver is then forced into protective, defensive tactics to account for the inconsistencies in his engagement in the world as acknowledged by him" (Fingarette, p. 81). If one continues to disavow certain engagements then "a nuclear, dynamic complex" is likely to be "split off from the more rational system (i.e., the system which is defended)" because "the incompatibility between the ego-nucleus and the current Ego are so great, relative to the integrative capacities of that Ego, that the latter gives up any attempt to integrate the ego-nucleus itself," said Fingarette (p. 93), and this nuclear entity that forms is "a complex of motive, purpose, feeling, perception, and drive towards action."

If Fingarette (1974) was right in his origins account, then he was reversing Erskine's story: It is the ego (reason) that creates the "counter-ego nucleus" (distraction) by giving up on any attempt to integrate it into the self; thus it is reason that gives distraction its life, so to speak, by turning its back on it, disavowing it, and making it not me. And by isolating this counter-ego nuclei "from the civilizing influence of the Ego" (p. 96), the consequence is that this nucleus is less concerned with "strict logical, causal, temporal, and other rational relationships," and "much cruder," more "primitive," "closer" to "the id," with its "uncivilized, highly unspecific basic drives." It is no wonder, then, that this counter-ego nucleus can develop into a delusion. And if avowing our engagements is a "necessary condition of moral action," then unlawful and immoral actions may follow. Thus this counter-ego nucleus becomes disconnected from the shared background nexus, where our legal *dos* and *don'ts* reside.

A Fundamental Incapacity in the Mens: Isaac Ray's Theory of a Defect of Reason

Such a disconnect, I believe, was what Isaac Ray (1983, pp. 33–34) had in mind when he said that in madmen their "abstract conceptions of crime" are not "perverted by the influence of disease," but the "*particular* criminal act, however, becomes divorced in their minds from its relations to crime in the *abstract*." Ray was highlighting the disconnect between the morality of what they are doing and the legality of the criminal act in the abstract.

Isaac Ray's *A Treatise on the Medical Jurisprudence of Insanity* (1983), originally published 5 years before the M'Naghten Rules were formulated, was highly influential on the justices who formulated those rules (Walker, 1968). Unfortunately, those justices grabbed hold of Ray's "defect of reason" phrase only to lose its deeper import when they fastened on mere surface symptoms of the defect—the cognitive symptoms of knowing the nature of the act, and whether it was right or wrong. But it is the fundamental disconnect-incapacity-defect of reason that is the essence of insanity, Fingarette and Hasse (1979, p. 218) argued, for it connotes the splitting of the ego, disavowing of the counter-ego nucleus, and developing of a delusion unchecked, which leaves the individual with a "lack of capacity for rational conduct in regard to the criminal significance of the conduct," such that the person is not "response-able." When defendants are not able to connect their actions, beliefs, thoughts, feelings, and motives to the shared background nexus, which "is central to what we wish to express when we speak of someone as 'out of his mind,' 'out of touch with reality,' 'mentally incompetent,' 'crazy,' or 'mad'" (Fingarette & Hasse, p. 218). When we understand nonculpability this way, the insane person is not someone whose *mens rea* is simply negated (i.e., for Hadfield knew that what he was doing was legally wrong); rather, the defect of reason points to a defect at the level of *mens*, revealing a more fundamental incapacity.

Social Constructionist Theory, and Disconnects Among Self 1, Self 2, and Self 3

Modern social constructionist theory (e.g., Harré, 1998; Harré & Gillett, 1994; Harré & van Langenhove, 1999; Sabat, 2001), which makes a tripartite division (e.g., Self 1, Self 2, and Self 3), provides support and added nuance to this emerging picture. Self 1 (Sabat, p. 17) is "the self of personal identity which is experienced as the continuity of one's own singular point of view from which one perceives, and acts in, the world," though psychopathology, and delusion in particular, can rent this Self 1. For example, when the once-upon-a-time high-functioning Andrea Yates (e.g., a National Merit winner, high school valedictorian, and successful nurse) finds herself sliding into psychiatric hospitals again and again, being told repeatedly by doctors that she needs medication to control her depression, hallucinations, suicidal ideation, and most of all believes that Satan has lodged within her, then her personal identity is thrown into doubt.

Self 2 (Sabat, 2001, p. 17) covers "a unique set of mental and physical attributes [along with beliefs about those attributes] that render us different to some extent from any other person," with some of those attributes "being relatively stable or constant over time," whereas "others may change." In the Yates case, her abilities and competencies, which once seemed solid, sure, and defining of her Self 2—are no longer so. Self 3 requires "the cooperation of others" (Sabat, p. 18), for it emphasizes the different social personae a person may manifest. In Yates, being a good Christian wife and mother, a good home-school teacher of her children, and a good caregiver to her ailing father (who died), all start to shatter. Each of these constructed selves may be constant and consistent, or one or more may show instability and fractionation, and there may be inconsistency among the three selves.

A Growing Disconnect Between Psychology and Law

Roger Smith (1981), in *Trial by Medicine: Insanity and Responsibility in Victorian Trials*, detailed the consequences of this growing disconnect between psychology and the law. More and more, the alienists and medicopsychological experts who came into Victorian courts to testify believed that the M'Naghten rules "presupposed an outdated psychology by choosing the presence of knowledge as the criterion of responsibility" (Smith, p. 42). Moreover, to the likes of Pritchard, Winslow, and Maudsley, the "irresistible impulse" notion was already dated and superficial. Winslow, for example, expressing his frustration with the law's standards for insanity, exclaimed, "The act itself bears insanity on its face!" (1854, p. 617). That courts and justices would not yield to this manifest evidence was indication to Winslow and others that medicine ought to decide this maddening matter of insanity, rather than leave this scientific decision up to an out-of-touch and out-of-date law. No wonder, then, that these experts pushed at the law through their testimony, and went beyond the legal tests' criteria in their inferences and conclusions, for, from their scientific, psychological perspective, the law's limited and erroneous perspective would doom a truly insane person with a guilty verdict.

Erskine's Organic, Origins Theory of Insanity

In this final subsection, I return to Erskine's second theory of insanity, which is an organic theory that embraces the psychological within it, and provides an account of insanity's origin. In *Hadfield* (1800), Erskine called a number of witnesses whose factual testimony focused not on the moment of the act, which, shortsightedly, continues to be the key moment of time under de jure law. An officer from Hadfield's former regiment testified that Hadfield been an excellent soldier before he suffered a saber wound to the head, but afterward he had been incoherent, with "manifest symptoms of derangement." This wound that produced organic brain damage, however, occurred 6 years prior to Hadfield's alleged insanity act, which may thus appear irrelevant to the legal question at bar. The most impressive witness (Walker, 1968, p. 76) was probably Dr. Creighton from Bethlem, "who testified that in his medical opinion Hadfield's madness was probably the result of his wounds, and although in law it did not matter what the cause was ... we can guess that this must have made a favorable impression on a war-time jury." It may not have mattered under de jure law, but I believe it mattered greatly under the jurors' de facto law (e.g., Finkel, 1990, 1996), in terms of the jurors' prototypes of insanity (e.g., Finkel, 1997; Finkel & Groscup, 1997) and the commonsense justice and fairness notions (e.g., Finkel, 1995, 2001) they bring to the jury box. But why?

This type of testimony, which is typically offered by the defense, addresses a cluster of issues relating to the origin, source, cause, nature, reality, and legitimacy of the defendant's mental disorder. To note, quite a bit of this sort of testimony was presented by the defense at Malvo's and Yates's trials. Yet, from the prosecution's vantage point under de jure law, they must show that the defendants either: (a) did not suffer from a serious mental disorder at the moment of the act or, (b) if they did have such a disorder, that it did not negate either the *actus reus* or the *mens rea* at the moment of the act. But the defense's burden is not just to show the inverse of (a) and (b), I submit, because jurors are likely predisposed against the notion that insanity negates our responsibility, given that most citizens and the law assume that people are responsible for their actions. If jurors have a suspicion that the delusion is one that Erskine is conjuring whole cloth from his mind and inserting into his client's mind, then what evidence can legitimate the disorder in the jurors' minds? What better way to legitimate Hadfield's mental disorder than to root it in an organic brain disorder, over which Hadfield had no control?

Erskine's physiological theory attempted to etiologically ground Hadfield's delusions, motives irresistible, and criminal actions on brain damage. Erskine claimed that the organic brain damage caused the mental defect of reason (the delusion), and the delusion caused motives irresistible, and the motives irresistible caused the criminal act (that obviously could not have been controlled), as Erskine created a brain®mind®motive® behavior causal chain for the jurors. For his chain to hold, however, his if-then linkages had to be steely. Unfortunately, though, there were gaps. For example, between brain and mind, we could no doubt find many soldiers on the battlefield with brain damage similar to Hadfield's, yet most of these soldiers would not develop delusions, and probably none developed Hadfield's delusion of Christ's Second Coming; and between mind and motive and between motive and behavior, we can go into any psychiatric hospital with a sizable schizophrenic population and find many patients with grandiose delusions, yet very few of these individuals feel compelled to kill (or do harm) on the basis of their delusions. With the correlations between delusions and compulsion to kill and between delusions and attempts to kill falling far short of 1.00, there is no credible scientific proof for delusions causing motives irresistible, which in turn cause criminal acts.

Nonetheless, Erskine's theory, dramatized by his invitation to the jurors to inspect the visible membranes of Hadfield's brain, and by his rubbing of Hadfield's head during his closing summation to the jury, concretely solidified his point: Hadfield's capacity was shot. As a strategy aimed at countering the jurors' scepticism, it was effective, and there are reasons, derived from modern research, why this strategy paid verdict dividends. It is harder to hold someone responsible if the delusion resulted from brain damage over which the defendant had no control or, in Malvo's case, if his actions were the result of dissociation caused by a powerful external brainwasher. Mounting a successful insanity defense, as criminal attorneys know, is an uphill battle and a long-shot proposition. The psychological literature points to reasons for this. Most people hold attitudes hostile to the insanity defense (Hans, 1986; Hans & Slater, 1983; Perlin, 1989–1990, 1994), and hold prototypes of insanity (Finkel & Groscup, 1997; Skeem & Golding, 2001) that reveal that they are more likely to believe in the legitimacy of the insanity defense when the disorder is rooted in the brain and beyond one's control.

Still, the uphill climb is steeper when the insanity case is also a death penalty case, because death-qualified (DQ) jurors are more antagonistic to the insanity defense than non-DQ jurors (Ellsworth, Bukaty, Cowan, & Thompson, 1984; Roberts & Golding, 1991). What we see later on is a second strategy emerging, which not only adds complexity to our story, but increases the likelihood of a confounding judgment and illegitimate mistakes. This second strategy involves developing a mitigation argument (i.e., for life rather than death) in the culpability phase, when the first strategy (i.e., for exculpation) is likely to fail.

THE LAW'S MADNESS

The sentiment, aim, and direction at the federal level was unmistakably revealed in the title that the U.S. Senate Subcommittee on Criminal Law of the Committee of the Judiciary (1983) gave to its report, *Limiting the Insanity Defense*. In accord with that aim, Congress lopped off the volitional prong (i.e., Erskine's motives irresistible), the irresistible impulse criterion of the American Law Institute's (ALI, 1962) Model Penal Code test, the prong that many critics blamed for Hinckley's NGRI verdict, though these critics failed to cite sound empirical evidence to support their claim. Nonetheless, Congress' amputation of the volitional prong left its new Insanity Defense Reform Act (IDRA, 1984) test as but a semantic dust-off of the M'Naghten test (1843)—a cognitive-symptom test focusing on impairments in knowledge and understanding—that had been failing, according to Erskine and the science of psychology, for nearly two centuries. In addition, Congress shifted the burden of proof from the prosecution to the defense, presumably making an NGRI verdict harder to obtain, and limited experts to penultimate opinion only, as the intent was to restrain these experts from unduly influencing the jurors' ultimate opinion. Though consistent with the underlying sentiment, empirical evaluations (Finkel, 1989, 1995; Fulero & Finkel, 1991; Ogloff, 1991) of these changes have shown that they were not likely to work as intended—or at all (Finkel & Fulero, 1992).

But when we move to the state level, the states, like ships fleeing the *Hinckley* (1981) storm, scattered in all directions—toward M'Naghten, toward even more restrictive versions of M'Naghten, toward the Guilty But Mentally Ill (GBMI) test, toward abolition of the defense entirely, or to holding pat with the ALI. When this scatteration is analyzed for underlying patterns, two emerge: These varied courses either embrace mere surface symptoms of insanity or try to make insanity disappear, by legal magic, into the old *mens rea* hat. Still, uniting the consistent federal course and the disparate state directions was the fact that these changes were guided without any pretext of theory, being propelled by expedient, political, pragmatic, or poll-reading quick-fix concerns, with none getting us closer to the essence of insanity, I submit, and most moving us further from that goal.

Now I narrow the focus to the insanity laws in Virginia and Texas, where the cases of Malvo and Yates were tried. Malvo's case could have landed in any one of a number of states that initially claimed jurisdiction and wanted first crack at him. The jurisdictional dispute was settled by the Attorney General of the United States, John Ashcroft, who selected the Commonwealth of Virginia, where sympathy for the insanity defense was low, where the death penalty was more likely to be given, and more likely to be given to a 17-year-old, given Virginia's track record. Virginia had used the M'Naghten test of insanity since 1871, though in 1984, after *Hinckley* (1981), it shifted the burden of proof to the defense (*Price v. Commonwealth*, 1984), making it harder to obtain an NGRI verdict.

Texas, as Denno (2003, p. 9) pointed out, "consistently executes more individuals than any other state," accounting "for one-third of all executions in the country," and Harris County, where Yates was tried, "is responsible for over one-third of the state's death row inmates, making it the harshest death penalty jurisdiction in the country." Texas also changed its law following *Hinckley* (1981), creating a much stricter version of the M'Naghten test than the 1843 original. In the original, Yates would be found insane if, because of disease of mind at the time of her act, she (a) did not know the "nature and quality of the act" that she was performing or, (b) if she was aware of the act, she did not know that what she "was doing was wrong," and under the original formulation, the justices' amplification about delusions was typically added to the rule, which states that "where a person labors under partial delusions only and is not in other respects insane, and commits an offense in consequence thereof, she must be considered in the same situation as to responsibility as if the facts with respect to which the delusion exists were real" (*United States v. Currens*, 1961, fn. 5). In contrast with the original M'Naghten instructions, Texas's stricter version omits the amplification requiring jurors to see the facts through the subjective perspective of the defendant before objectively judging whether those facts would warrant a mistaken or delusional self-defense or defense of another claim. Furthermore, it omits (a), about the nature and quality of the act, which thereby makes the test hinge only on (b), knowledge about right versus wrong. And finally, Texas's statute did not clarify an old ambiguity as to whether wrong meant a legal or moral wrong, though at trial the prosecution argued forcefully that guilt must result if Yates knew that what she had done was legally wrong, an interpretation the court seemed to accept.

The severe narrowing of Texas's insanity law and the shifting of the burden of proof in Virginia reflect, to some degree, legislators' poll readings of perceived community sentiment regarding insanity, which may comport, to some degree, with empirical findings (e.g., Skeem & Golding, 2001) regarding citizens' narrow prototypes of what constitutes legitimate insanity. A result of such a confluence of commonsense justice sentiments and the sentiments behind recent legislative enactments translates into a widening disconnect between the legal view of insanity and the psychological view. Moreover, the ability of psychologists to challenge the legal view and tell the full story of insanity in court has been constrained by the limitations of these new tests, as expert proffers must be tailored to a legal test that fewer defendants could pass. With guilty verdicts more likely—which, from a psychological perspective, may appear as wrongful verdicts for some defendants—experts may push their proffers over the law's line for reasons the experts believe are legitimate, on scientific grounds. Yet, with the death penalty being a possible consequence of a guilty verdict, experts may push their proffers over the law's line for reasons illegitimate.

THE IMPULSES, INFERENCES, AND CONCLUSIONS OF EXPERTS IN MALVO

Dissociation or Delusion as the Proper Diagnosis?

The case of *Commonwealth of Virginia v. Lee Boyd Malvo* (2003) was indeed a high-profile case. The 13 random shootings, involving 14 victims and 10 deaths, that Malvo and John Allen Mohammad perpetrated, brought a reign of terror down on the region, for the safety of citizens in Maryland, Virginia, and the District of Columbia was threatened by the randomness of these killings. But the case involving Malvo was significant in yet another way, when newspapers reported that the defense was going to employ a novel defense, a brainwashing insanity defense. The insanity defense, per se, is an extreme, but a brainwashing insanity defense seemed to be the extreme of the extreme.

In *Malvo* (2003), four defense experts (psychologists Dewey Cornell, Steve Eichel, and Diane Schetky, and psychiatrist Neil Blumberg) testified that Malvo suffered from a "dissociative disorder," and their inferences supported the defense's brainwashing insanity claim that the powerful external agent and father figure, John Allen Mohammad, caused Malvo's dissociation and obliterated his moral conscience. Put another way, the indoctrination produced the dissociative disorder, which turned Malvo into an automaton-victim, who could neither resist nor sanely understand the nature of his acts. This alleged disorder is a potent one, for it nullifies the cognitive knowledge prong of the M'Naghten test and undermines the volitional prong, which may have been in the jurors' minds, even though this prong was not part of Virginia's insanity law. As a minor point, I claim that their diagnosis is off base, for it fits neither with the defining criteria of dissociative disorder, nor with the common pattern of dissociation in documented cases, nor with the facts in Malvo's situation; the diagnosis that fits the etiology, symptoms, and actions of Malvo is delusion.

To explicate, we must first understand the key causal factors of brainwashing accounts—be they of American POWs held in Red China during the Korean War (Hunter, 1951), of Cardinal Mindszenty in Hungary by Russian captors (Oldenburg, 2003), and "thought reform" (Lifton, 1963) and "coercive persuasion" (Schein, Schneier, & Barker, 1961) in cults (Singer & Lalich, 1995)—to appreciate the difference from Malvo's situation. The preceding brainwashing accounts all stress the extreme physical control that the captor has over the captive. In such a controlled environment, physical abuse (e.g., solitary confinement, drugs, and gun-to-the-head coercion) and psychological methods (e.g., hypnosis, Pavlovian and operant conditioning) are employed, where the goal is to first create a sense of powerlessness, fear, and dependency; second, to break down the self; and third, to instill new attitudes and behavior.

As an illustration, "total physical control" was what court-appointed clinical psychologist Margaret Thaler Singer (Singer & Lalich, 1995, p. 56) stated was present in the Patty Hearst case, where a version of the brainwashing defense (creating diminished capacity) was argued: "The Symbionese Liberation Army (SLA) ... kidnapped newspaper heiress Patricia Hearst and abused her psychologically and otherwise. The SLA used mind manipulations as well as gun-at-the-head methods to coerce Patty into compliance." And when we move from fact to fiction, we see the same etiological depiction in the 1962 movie *The Manchurian Candidate* (Frankenheimer, 1962): a POW who was physically controlled and then psychologically "conditioned" to enter a dissociative state when a conditioned stimulus cue appears (e.g., seeing the queen of diamonds), whereupon he obediently and unconsciously follows the next command (e.g., to kill), without memory for the act.

In contrast with the previous depictions, Malvo's situation does not fit in several ways. First, the external agent Mohammad did not have total physical control of Malvo's environment: The two were physically separated on many occasions, and even when they were together, the father figure did fall asleep, so the son could have walked away on many occasions from a control that was only psychological. Second, the alleged indoctrination and dissociation had to take time to develop (i.e., because it was not some instantaneous spell that was cast), and this meant that Malvo had the time to make moral judgments, reject the indoctrination, and walk away. However, the evidence that best contradicts the dissociative diagnosis comes straight from Malvo's lips to defense experts' ears. Malvo told defense expert witnesses that Mohammad's plan was to create a utopia in Canada, cultivate "child soldiers," kill as a way of improving the lives of Black people, and eventually demand $10 million in exchange for an end to the shootings; yet Malvo admitted to these experts that he had doubts about the sniper plan, that he believed that killing was wrong, and that he "tried to shoot himself" (Jackman, 2003a), revealing an independent self, moral judgment, and guilt. And in preparation for the mission, Mohammad wanted Malvo to perform a "test killing" of 21-year-old Keenya Cook, in Tacoma, Washington, on February 16, 2002, and Malvo reported that he was in conflict about this beforehand, and "was a mess afterward," one expert testified (Jackman, 2003c). These facts contradict the Manchurian Candidate portrayal, for they reveal conflicting emotions and some sense of right and wrong.

From these facts, the prosecution would argue that Malvo made conscious choices and fateful decisions to join with Mohammad and embrace Mohammad's delusion, despite what his choices were doing to him. If he chose to disregard his mental deterioration, his "disability of mind" (DOM), as Fingarette and Hasse (1979) called it, then he bears culpability for what follows, because he causes the condition of his own defense, to paraphrase the words of Law Professor Paul Robinson (1985, p. 1). However, under historic and existing insanity law, where the focus is on culpability at the moment of the act, jurors are not asked to make this type of culpability judgment, yet empirical evidence shows that they do make this judgment (e.g., Finkel, 1988; Finkel & Handel, 1989; Finkel & Slobogin, 1995).

In examining his actions, symptoms, and mentation, Malvo again does not look like the Manchurian Candidate (Frankenheimer, 1962). In one scene from the film, when this "conditioned assassin" is playing solitaire and turns over the queen of diamonds (the cue), he just happens to hear a bartender telling a customer a story where the bartender's next words (which become the command) are "go jump in the lake in Central Park," whereon the assassin suddenly, unconsciously, and somnambulistically leaves the bar and travels (in this fugue state) to the lake and jumps in; and he is amnesiac to the entire episode, his consciousness returning only when he is wet in the water, but he has no memory of how or why he got there. This scene captures the amnesia, fugue, and somnambulism-automatism that have been characteristic of clinical cases of dissociation historically. Malvo, by contrast, neither showed nor claimed these characteristics—nor could he—for his actions (be they shooting, spotting, planning, executing, or eluding police roadblocks and helicopter searches) required so much awareness, vigilance, and contact with reality that a claim that he was unconscious is far-fetched.

Finally, Malvo's actions were nothing like the dissociative act of Esther Griggs, an automatism case that went before a British grand jury in 1859 (Walker, 1968, p. 168), where Esther, in a sleepwalking nightmare (somnambulism), threw her baby through a glass window to save the child from a burning house (her dream), and where the grand jury found no "true bill against her," holding her not responsible because in this sleepwalking, unconscious, dissociative state she did not commit an "act" in the legal sense, something that Malvo's defense never claimed regarding his acts, nor could it claim from the facts. Nor does Malvo's condition look like the Multiple Personality Disorder (MPD) variety of dissociation that one of the Los Angeles Hillside Stranglers, Kenneth Bianci (*State v. Bianci*, 1979), alleged, claiming that another personality did the killings unbeknownst to him (e.g., Allison, 1984; Orne, Dinges, & Orne, 1984; Watkins, 1984). Malvo's experts did not claim that there was another personality, only that Malvo's sense of right and wrong had been completely replaced by Mohammad's vision of right and wrong.

So the question becomes: What does his condition look most like? With his awareness and vigilance heightened at the time of the acts, and with his lack of amnesia, it appears that Malvo came to believe and embrace Mohammad's delusion as his own.

Legitimate Versus Illegitimate Mistakes

Still, evidence pointing to a mistaken diagnosis is a minor point, for reasons legal and psychological. On legal grounds, diagnosis testimony has been accepted by courts for some two centuries, and diagnostic and penultimate testimony were sanctioned in the Insanity Defense Reform Act (IDRA) of 1984; moreover, such testimony, according to most judges, is acceptable under *Daubert v. Merrell Dow Pharmaceuticals, Inc.*, (1993), *Kumho Tire Co., Ltd. v. Carmichael* (1999), or an opinion rule (Faigman & Monahan, 2005). On empirical grounds, diagnostic mistakes can occur for legitimate reasons, particularly where malingering (i.e., as was alleged about Malvo) arises, where feigned responses can understandably negate diagnostic accuracy. Put another way, these defense experts may simply have been fooled. The prosecution thought so, and countered the defense's claim with letters Malvo wrote to a fellow inmate about his manipulations, in which he stated (Jackman, 2003b, p. B4): "I play the stupid fool" and

"Look at how I act and speak, everybody underestimates me.... It gives me the edge I need to study, conquer and overcome."

The main point I wish to make follows from a consideration of why diagnostic testimony may be in error for seemingly illegitimate reasons. Here, I wish to question whether some of these reasons may be both illegitimate and legitimate, once we situate them in the contexts of the old and new constraints, and from the perspectives of psychology and law. I start with a simple case and an easy conclusion: It would clearly be illegitimate to purposely proffer a wrong diagnosis (which is not what I believe happened in Malvo), for such testimony would overstep ethical bounds of honest and objective scientific testimony, as well as violating the legal oath of witnesses regarding truth telling.

But consider a more interesting case, where the defense's strategy, like Erskine's in the *Hadfield* (1800) case, is not to play to the existing law—which is seen as substantively off base and restrictive—but to play to the jurors' commonsense justice and fairness (Finkel, 1995, 2001). This strategy hopes that jurors will either disregard or reconstrue the law in ways that embrace the more complex psychological view of insanity. If jurors dilate their view to embrace mitigation for a partial insanity, and consider treatment rather than prison for a 17-year-old defendant, then they may render an NGRI verdict as their best de jure option. Now, defense attorneys may believe that this strategy and its supportive testimony are legitimate, given the obligation of attorneys to zealously defend clients to the best of their ability. Furthermore, the defense experts may believe that this testimony is legitimate because it more accurately reflects the science of insanity. Prosecutors, however, from a strict adherence to the written law (i.e., black-letter law), may view this as illegitimate.

Now imagine a still more interesting case, where the line distinguishing legitimate from illegitimate strategies and testimony blurs even further. This hypothetical arises from the trend to try high-profile insanity cases as death penalty cases. In this version, imagine that the diagnosis offered is not a bona fide exculpatory insanity strategy at all, but a mitigating death penalty strategy played out in the culpability phase. Within a strict legal context of a bifurcated trial, where insanity is defined as a yes-no decision with only the two traditional verdicts (Guilty and NGRI) available, it would appear that mitigating testimony—in the culpability phase—would be irrelevant and illegitimate. But getting this detailed testimony in early sets up a culpability contrast between Malvo and Mohammad: For even if the two defendants are judged by their respective juries as having premeditated and deliberated, the adult Mohammad is cast as either the felony-murderer planner or as the perpetrator by means, whereas the juvenile Malvo is seen as the underling, accomplice, or dupe (e.g., Finkel, 1995). In this sleight-of-hand strategy, mitigating arguments are presented in the wrong phase of the trial. But is this testimony illegitimate, and has the expert crossed the line?

THE IMPULSES, INFERENCES, AND CONCLUSIONS OF EXPERTS IN YATES

In *Yates* (*Texas v. Yates*, 2005), I focus on the testimony of the prosecution's expert, Park Deitz, because a number of trial commentators (e.g., Colb, 2003; Denno, 2003; O'Malley, 2004) believed his inferences and conclusion tipped the balance in favor of the guilty verdict, despite the fact that only he testified that Yates knew right from wrong, whereas five other experts testified that Yates "did not know right from wrong, was incapable of knowing right from wrong, or believed that her acts were right" (*Yates v. Texas*, 2005, p. 5). My specific focus is not on the factual mistake that Deitz made, where he alleged that Yates may have watched an episode of the TV series *Law & Order* about a woman who kills her children, and gotten the idea for the killings from that episode. Although Deitz serves as a consultant to that TV series, the executive producer, Dick Wolf, said that no such episode ever occurred, and there was never a script for such an episode. The Court of Appeals for the First District of Texas ruled that this mistake was not intentional but was material—in the way the prosecutor used the false testimony to undercut Yates's delusional claim, which the court held required a new trial. But memory being what it is, this sort of mistake, though unfortunate, does occur. However, it is the type of mistake that the law calls "honest but reasonable" or "honest but unreasonable," and thus it does not raise my question of whether it is illegitimate and goes over the line of good science, as it does not involve conscious choice. Rather, I focus on mistakes that involve: (a) certain inferences Deitz drew, which I argue were not legitimate psychiatric inferences but highly suspect moral or religious inferences having no scientific basis; and (b) his choice to use an objective-rational perspective to analyze Yates' delusion, which is inconsistent with the subjective perspective that a sound clinical approach and the M'Naghten test requires first.

Under questioning (Denno, 2003, p. 114), Deitz acknowledged that Yates's taped confession statements pointed in both directions, toward her knowing right from wrong (and a guilty verdict), and pointed toward believing that the act was morally right (an NGRI verdict): "On the one hand, she knows that it's sinful and that, and she attributes the idea to Satan, and she knows it's illegal, and she knows it will be judged as bad by society and by God, but on the other hand she believes that this saves the children from torment or from having their souls go to Satan. And that therefore it's the right thing for the children." But Deitz (p. 114) went on to say that he was skeptical of the beliefs that pointed toward insanity "because her behavior, as she kills them, doesn't do the things I would expect a mother with that belief to do." When asked, "And what would that be, Doctor?," he answered, "I would expect her to try to comfort the children, telling them they are going to be with Jesus or be with God, but she does not offer words of comfort to the children."

Now, even for a woman like Yates (who was captain of her high school swim team), someone with strong swimmer's arms, it would take considerable force, exerted for 2 minutes or more, to drown each of the children, who would be reflexively thrashing and fighting for breath and life. To perform that act while voicing soothing and comforting words that "you're going to be with Jesus or God" seems—to me—to be not only "crazy" but cruel. Still, in reaching my judgment I am employing an objective, outsider's perspective, as Deitz did. But what about the inverse—not speaking while performing the act? From the subjective vantage point that the M'Naghten test directs us to take—from inside her delusional leap of faith that God was ordering and supporting this act—could I (or any clinician or forensic expert) scientifically conclude that her silence reveals knowledge of wrongfulness, making this not an insane act, but a murderous one? I think not.

In contrast to the subjective analysis, Dietz attempted an objective, rational analysis of Yates' actions. In doing such an objective analysis, though, key questions arise. For example, what story model (e.g., Bennett & Feldman, 1981; Pennington & Hastie, 1992), prototype (e.g., Finkel, 2003; Smith, 1991), or standard guided him in reaching his conclusion? Is this standard one that is grounded in science? Or, as one legal critic (Denno, 2003, p. 20) asked in response to Dietz's comments, "Is one to infer that it is somehow more loving to invoke the name of Jesus while you drown your children than to drown them without any religious commentary?" In contrast with the objectivity of science, "Dietz appears to be stressing religion, not facts, a focus more aligned with Southern Bible belt culture rather than medical assessment of Andrea's mental state" (Denno, p. 20). Dietz's standard, when examined, is not scientifically grounded, and his inference is not a scientific inference at all; rather, his inference and conclusion go quite beyond what the facts and the science permit. In effect, Dietz is delivering his own sermon from the stand.

But even as a sermon, Dietz fails to reference Genesis 22:4, for when Abraham and Isaac get to Moriah, Abraham speaks no soothing and comforting words to Isaac, as "Abraham built an altar there, and arranged the wood, and bound his son Isaac, and laid him on the altar, on top of the wood. And Abraham reached out and picked up the knife to slaughter his son" (Mitchell, 1996, p. 43). Of course, Abraham's leap of faith has Biblical imprimatur behind it, where the Voice that earlier says, "Take your son, your darling, whom you love, Isaac, and go to the land of Moriah, and burn him there as a sacrifice on one of the hills that I will show you" (Mitchell, p. 42) is identified as God's. But what happens if we extract this story from the Bible, turn Abraham into a woman who has had hallucinations and hospitalizations on many occasions, and where there is no authoritative authentication of the voice? Would Dietz judge this woman's silence indicative of knowledge of wrongfulness and guilt? Again, I submit that there is no scientific grounds for concluding either way without a further investigation of her subjectivity.

CONCLUSION

Sometimes it is easy to judge when a psychological expert crosses over scientific and legal lines to proffer illegitimate inferences and conclusions, but sometimes not. In making a case-by-case judgment of a particular expert's testimony, though, we must appreciate the disconnect between psychology's perspective regarding the essence of insanity, and the law's position. From the vantage point of psychology, the law's context has been simplistically narrowed, and its historic tests of insanity have been built on surface symptoms, which led to an erroneous picture of insanity, which has reigned for nearly 300 years, despite repeated revisions and changes of the law. This basic inadequacy is coupled, now, with the new restraints enacted following *Hinckley* (1981), which have moved the substantive legal definition further from insanity's essence and have further constrained the experts from bringing scientific light and legitimate inferences to the triers of fact. Finally, the trend of having the death penalty hang over allegedly insane defendants has added confound and compromise to the maddening matter of insanity. When taken together—the alleged illegitimate inferences of experts, the new constraining limits of the law, the increased appearance of the death penalty at trial, and the old but unsolved Hadfield problem of delusions and the disconnect between psychology and law over the essence of insanity—we find that we are no closer to clarity and consistency, let alone validity. If *Malvo* (2003) and *Yates* (2005) are illustrative regarding legal strategies and the so-called irresistible impulses of experts, then today's situation may be a sign that sanity and science are losing ground.

There are multiple dramas at an insanity trial, with the defendant's drama being but one. Psychological experts are involved in their own drama, where their scientific objectivity and ethical obligations of honest truth seeking may collide with a legal oath and bad law. The law is also involved in a culpability drama of its own making, where its theories, legal tests, and procedures have masked and mocked its truth-seeking function. This normative law seems less informed by empirical facts in recent times, becoming more inconsistent and incoherent, rather than the reverse, which makes it more subject to disrespect. If good law (the normative ground) and good science (the empirical ground) ought to work hand in hand in a sane and sound world, where we take men and women "as they are," in Rousseau's (1950) words, then we are clearly not there yet, for insanity, on multiple levels, once again reigns.

REFERENCES

Allison, R. B. (1984). Difficulties diagnosing the multiple personality syndrome in a death penalty case. *International Journal of Clinical and Experimental Hypnosis, 32,* 102–117.

American Law Institute. (1962). *Model penal code*. Philadelphia: Author.

Bennett, W. L., & Feldman, M. S. (1981). *Reconstructing reality in the Courtroom: Justice and judgment in American culture*. New Brunswick, NJ: Rutgers University Press.

Colb, S. F. (2003). The conviction of Andrea Yates: A narrative of denial. *Duke Journal of Gender Law and Policy, 10,* 141–147.

Commonwealth of Virginia v. Lee Boyd Malvo, aka John Lee Malvo, K102888 (2003).

Daubert v. Merrell Dow Pharmaceuticals, Inc., 509 U.S. 579 (1993).

Denno, D. W. (2003). Who is Andrea Yates? A short story about insanity. *Duke Journal of Gender Law and Policy, 10,* 1–139.

Ellsworth, P. C., Bukatay, R. M., Cowan, C. L., & Thompson, W. C. (1984). The death-qualified jury and the defense of insanity. *Law and Human Behavior, 8,* 45–54.

Faigman, D. L., & Monahan, J. (2005). Psychological evidence at the dawn of the law's scientific age. *Annual Review of Psychology, 56,* 631–659.

Fingarette, H. (1974). Self-deception and the "splitting of the ego." In R. Wollheim (Ed.), *Freud: A collection of critical essays* (pp. 80–96). Garden City, NY: Anchor Books.

Fingarette, H., & Hasse, A. F. (1979). *Mental disabilities and criminal responsibility*. Berkeley: University of California Press.

Finkel, N. J. (1988). *Insanity on trial*. New York: Plenum Press.

Finkel, N. J. (1989). The Insanity Defense Reform Act of 1984: Much ado about nothing. *Behavioral Sciences and the Law, 7*, 403–419.

Finkel, N. J. (1990). De facto departures from insanity instructions: Toward the remaking of common law. *Law and Human Behavior, 14*, 105–122.

Finkel, N. J. (1995). *Commonsense justice: Jurors' notions of the law*. Cambridge, MA: Harvard University Press.

Finkel, N. J. (1996). Culpability and commonsense justice: Lessons learned betwixt murder and madness. *Notre Dame Journal of Law Ethics and Public Policy, 10*, 101–154.

Finkel, N. J. (1997). Commonsense justice, psychology, and the law: Prototypes common, senseful, and not. *Psychology, Public Policy, and Law, 3*, 461–489.

Finkel, N. J. (2001). *Not fair! The typology of commonsense unfairness*. Washington, DC: American Psychological Association.

Finkel, N. J. (2003). Haute couture, poorly tailored crimes, and ill-fitting verdicts. *Duke Journal of Gender Law and Policy, 10*, 173–223.

Finkel, N. J., & Fulero, S. M. (1992). Insanity: Making law in the absence of evidence. *International Journal of Medicine and Law, 11*, 383–404.

Finkel, N. J., & Groscup, J. L. (1997). Crime prototypes, objective vs. subjective culpability, and a commonsense balance. *Law and Human Behavior, 21*, 209–230.

Finkel, N. J., & Handel, S. F. (1989). How jurors construe "insanity." *Law and Human Behavior, 13*, 41–59.

Finkel, N. J., & Slobogin, C. (1995). Insanity, justification, and culpability: Toward a unifying schema. *Law and Human Behavior, 19*, 447–464.

Frankenheimer, J. (Producer and Director). (1962). *The Manchurian Candidate* [motion picture].

United States: MGM/UA.

Fulero, S. M., & Finkel, N. J. (1991). Barring ultimate issue testimony: An insane rule? *Law and Human Behavior, 15*, 495–507.

Hadfield's Case, 27 Howell's State Trials 1281 (1800).

Hans, V. P. (1986). An analysis of public attitudes toward the insanity defense. *Criminology, 24*, 393–414.

Hans, V. P., & Slater, D. (1983). John Hinckley, Jr., and the insanity defense: The public's verdict. *Public Opinion Quarterly, 47*, 202–212.

Harré, R. (1998). *The singular self: An introduction to the psychology of personhood*. London: Sage.

Harré, R., & Gillett, G. (1994). *The discursive mind*. London: Sage.

Harré, R., & van Langenhove, L. (Eds.). (1999). *Positioning theory: Moral contexts of intentional action*. Malden, MA: Blackwell.

Hunter, E. (1951). *Brain-washing in Red China*. New York: Vanguard Press.

Insanity Defense Reform Act of 1984, Pub. L. No. 98-473, §§ 401, 402, 20 (1984).

Jackman, T. (2003a, December 10). Malvo killed to please Mohammad, court told. *The Washington Post*, pp. B1, B4.

Jackman, T. (2003b, December 16). Prosecution psychologists say Malvo was not insane. *The Washington Post*, pp. B1, B4.

Jackman, T. (2003c, December 11). 2 psychiatrists testify that Malvo was insane. *The Washington Post*, pp. B1, B8.
Kumho Tire Co., Ltd. v. Carmichael, 526 U.S. 137 (1999).
Lifton, R. J. (1963). *Thought reform and the psychology of totalism: A study of "brainwashing" in China*. New York: Norton.
Mitchell, S. (1996). *Genesis: A new translation of the classic biblical stories*. New York: HarperCollins.
M'Naghten's Case, 10 Cl. & Fin. 200, 8 Eng. Rep. 718 (1843).
Ogloff, J. R. P. (1991). A comparison of insanity defense standards on juror decision making. *Law and Human Behavior, 15*, 509–531.
Oldenburg, D. (2003, November 21). Stressed to kill: The defense of brainwashing. *The Washington Post*, pp. C1, C2.
O'Malley, S. (2004). *Are you there alone? The unspeakable crime of Andrea Yates*. New York: Simon & Schuster.
Orne, M. T., Dinges, F. D., & Orne, E. C. (1984). On the differential diagnosis of multiple personality in the forensic context. *International Journal of Clinical and Experimental Hypnosis, 32*, 118–169.
Pennington, N., & Hastie, R. (1992). Explaining the evidence: Tests of the story model for juror decision making. *Journal of Personality and Social Psychology, 62*, 189–206.
Perlin, M. L. (1989–1990). Unpacking the myths: The symbolism mythology of insanity defense jurisprudence. *Case Western Reserve Law Review, 40*, 599–731.
Perlin, M. L. (1994). *The jurisprudence of the insanity defense*. Durham, NC: Carolina Academic Press.
Price v. Commonwealth, 228 Va., 452, 469, 323 S.E.2d 106, 110 (1984).
Ray, I. (1983). *A treatise on the medical jurisprudence of insanity*. New York: Da Capo Press.
Rex v. Arnold, 16 Howell's State Trials, 684 (1723).
Roberts, C. F., & Golding, S. L. (1991). The social construction of criminal responsibility and insanity. *Law and Human Behavior, 15*, 349–376.
Robinson, P. H. (1985). Causing the conditions of one's own defense: A study in the limits of theory in criminal law doctrine. *Virginia Law Review, 71*, 1–63.
Rousseau, J. J. (1950). *The social contract and discourses* (G. D. N. Cole, Trans.). New York: Dutton. (Original work published 1762)
Sabat, S. R. (2001). *The experience of Alzheimer's disease: Life through a tangled veil*. Oxford, England: Blackwell.
Sartre, J. P. (1974). *Mauvaise foi* and the unconscious. In R. Wollheim (Ed.), *Freud: A collection of critical essays* (pp. 70–79). Garden City, NJ: Anchor Books.
Schein, E. H., Schneier, I., & Barker, C. H. (1961). *A socio-psychological analysis of the "brainwashing" of American civilian prisoners by the Chinese Communists*. New York: Norton.
Shakespeare, W. (1938). *Hamlet, Prince of Denmark. In the works of William Shakespeare, gathered in one volume* (prepared by Arthur Henry Bullen), 670–713. The Shakespeare Head Edition, Oxford: Oxford University Press.
Singer, M. T., & Lalich, J. (1995). *Cults in our midst*. San Francisco: Jossey-Bass.

Skeem, J. L., & Golding, S. L. (2001). Describing jurors' personal conceptions of insanity and their relationship to case judgments. *Psychology, Public Policy, and Law, 7*, 561–621.

Smith, R. (1981). *Trial by medicine: Insanity and responsibility in Victorian trials.* Edinburgh, Scotland: Edinburgh University Press.

Smith, V. L. (1991). Prototypes in the courtroom: Lay representations of legal concepts. *Journal of Personality and Social Psychology, 61*, 857–872.

State v. Bianci, Wash. Sup. Ct. 79-10116 (1979).

Subcommittee on Criminal Law of the Committee of the Judiciary, U.S. Senate (1983). *Limiting the insanity defense* (Serial No. J-97-122). Washington, DC: U.S. Government Printing Office.

Texas v. Andrea Pia Yates, 171 S.W.3d 215 (2005).

United States v. Currens, 290 F.2d (3d Cir. 1961).

United States v. Hinckley, 525 F. Supp. 1342 (D.C. 1981).

U.S. Senate, Subcommittee on Criminal Law of the Committee of the Judiciary (1983). *Limiting the insanity defense* (Serial No. J-97-122), Washington, DC: U.S.

Walker, N. (1968). *Crime and insanity in England: Vol. 1: The historical perspective.* Edinburgh, Scotland: Edinburgh University Press.

Watkins, J. G. (1984). The Bianchi (L.A. Hillside Strangler) case: Sociopath or multiple personality? *International Journal of Clinical and Experimental Hypnosis, 32*, 67–101.

Winslow, F. (1854). Recent trials in lunacy, *JPM, 7*, 572–625.

Yates v. Texas, Ct. App., TX. 1st (2005).

9

Expert Evidence Pertaining to Battered Women: Limitations and Reconceptualizations

Regina A. Schuller
Gwen Jenkins
York University

A comprehensive report prepared in the mid-1990s by the National Clearinghouse for the Defense of Battered Women (NCDBW), undertaken at the request of Congress, analyzed the use of expert testimony on battering in over 250 state and federal court decisions. Expert testimony on battering and its effects was found to be admissible, "at least to some degree ... in each of the 50 states and the District of Columbia"; 12 states had enacted statutes specifically providing for the admissibility of the testimony (Parrish, 1996, p. 83). It must be noted, however, that although the majority of these 12 states placed no limitations on the types of case in which the expert testimony may be admitted into evidence (e.g., self-defense, duress, civil litigation), several of the states restricted the admissibility of the testimony to self-defense cases only. Following its introduction in the United States (*Ibn-Tamas v. United States*, 1979), expert evidence pertaining to battered women, in particular "battered woman syndrome" evidence, has now been admitted with some frequency not only in U.S. courtrooms across the country but in courtrooms across Canada (Schuller, 2003), Great Britain (Edwards, 1997), Australia (Stubbs & Tolmie, 1999), and New Zealand (Robertson, 1998).

The impact of *Daubert v. Merrell Dow Pharmaceuticals, Inc.* (1993) on the continued admissibility of battered woman syndrome evidence is not yet fully understood (see Sales & Schuman, chap. 2, this vol.). It has been argued that battered woman syndrome is a "poorly unsubstantiated hypothesis," which has been found to lack sufficient validity to survive the test in Texas, one of the Daubert states (Faigman, Kaye, Saks, & Sanders, 2002, p. 36). Daubert, however, is "binding only on federal courts" (Bernstein & Jackson, 2004, p. 355), not state courts, and few states have adopted the Daubert trilogy (see Sales & Schuman, chap. 2, this vol.); the remainder of the states preferring to adopt one or two, but not all, of the standards (Bernstein & Jackson, 2004). As such, the inconsistency and infrequency of the application of the test to date render it difficult to speculate about its impact on battered woman syndrome evidence.

In contrast to its current reception in the courts, within the legal community the admissibility of this form of expert testimony sparked much debate and controversy almost from its inception (Crocker, 1985; Schneider, 1986). In particular, the testimony, which describes the common patterns found in battering relationships and the impact of battering on a woman, has been criticized by numerous scholars (e.g., Dutton, 1993; Schneider; Rothenberg, 2003) on the grounds that its focus on the woman's passivity, as well as its portrayal of a singular profile of battered women, fails to capture the varied reactions and responses of battered women. It is against this backdrop that the present chapter examines the use of expert evidence pertaining to battered women in trials of battered women who have killed.[1] We first outline the rationale underlying its admission and then consider its content, with particular attention given to the scientific foundation of the evidence. The validity of the concerns that have been raised regarding its use are also examined. Following this, we review the body of research that examines the impact of expert evidence pertaining to battered women on mock jurors' evaluations and verdict decisions in trials of battered women who have killed their abusers. Examination of this literature offers some insights into how the testimony may alter jurors' perceptions of both the battered woman defendant and her actions. The chapter concludes with a reformulation of expert testimony

[1]The testimony has been offered in a "sizable minority" of states in criminal and noncriminal cases involving charges other than a claim of self-defense (20% of states have admitted the testimony in civil actions, 16% in duress defenses or charges involving a crime committed against a third party; Parrish, 1996). As the research on the topic has been limited to its application in defense cases, the focus of the current chapter is on its application in this domain.

pertaining to battered women that focuses on the social reality of the battered woman's situation as opposed to her psychological reactions to the abuse.

TRADITIONAL NOTIONS OF SELF-DEFENSE AND ITS INCONGRUENCE WITH BATTERED WOMEN'S ACTIONS

The laws of self-defense, in and of themselves, present a significant challenge to the battered woman defendant (see Gillespie, 1989). It is for this reason that the defense counsel in *Ibn-Tamas v. United States* (1979) first sought to introduce battered woman syndrome evidence. This case, like those that followed in its wake, involved a battered woman charged with the murder of her violent partner. The defendant did not deny the killing, but argued that the act was committed in self-defense. Although the precise definition of self-defense varies somewhat from jurisdiction to jurisdiction, perceived or real imminence of danger of death or bodily harm at the time of the killing is uniformly required for a finding of self-defense. Moreover, the laws of self-defense stipulate that only a necessary and proportionate use of force can be used to preserve oneself from this danger. And in some jurisdictions, the defendant is required to have exhausted other avenues of escape (Gillespie).

The difficulties for the battered woman defendant stem largely from the male-based notions of violence inherent in the laws of self-defense. That is, the laws, as they developed historically, were founded on violent situations that typically involved men and typically involved a one-time altercation (e.g., barroom brawl, fending off an intruder). As numerous scholars have repeatedly noted (Gillespie, 1989; Littleton, 1989; Schneider, 1980, 1986), these circumstances fail to adequately capture the battered woman's situation. For instance, in terms of size and brute force, women are typically not the equals of their abusers. As such, it is not uncommon for a battered woman to utilize a weapon such as a gun or knife to fend off her abuser. Yet such force can be difficult to equate with a beating, and may be viewed as excessive. Moreover, although for the most part battered women do kill their abusers in the midst of a direct confrontation (Parrish, 1996), a small proportion either kill during a lull in the violence or during a period of relative calm, such as while the abuser is sleeping (e.g., *State v. Martin*, 1984). In the landmark Canadian case, *Lavallee v. Regina* (1990), the defendant fatally shot her common law husband in the back of the head as he turned to leave the room.

Without consideration of the ongoing nature of the abuse and its impact on a woman, however, it may be especially difficult for the jurors to view such actions as a reasonable and proportionate use of force. Compounding the problem in some jurisdictions is the requirement that the victim of the assault (i.e., the battered woman) attempt to flee, where possible, from the aggressor (Gillespie, 1989). Yet, even for those jurisdictions where retreat is not required, the woman's failure to do so may foster doubts in a juror's mind as to why the battered woman did not attempt to escape. Indeed, questions such as why a battered woman would remain in an abusive relationship and why she would endure such abuse are particularly troubling for the jurors and reflect the skepticism with which they perceive the battered woman's claim to self-defense (Dodge & Greene, 1991). Myths and misconceptions about battered women and battering relationships abound (Walker, Thyfault, & Browne, 1982), with some research indicating that the general public's (hence jurors') knowledge base with regard to the nature and impact of battering relationships is somewhat at odds with that of experts in the field (Dodge & Greene; Ewing & Aubrey, 1987; Gentemann, 1984; Greene, Raitz, & Lindblad, 1989; Saunders, Lynch, Grayson, & Linz, 1987).

In summary, then, the battered woman's claim of self-defense is not only difficult to reconcile with the requirements of self-defense, but is also inconsistent with beliefs (misconceptions) held by the jurors. It is in recognition of these difficulties that the courts acknowledged the importance of expert testimony pertaining to battered women in trials of battered women who have killed. In essence, the information it conveys provides the jurors with a conceptual or "social framework" (Walker & Monahan, 1987) that attempts to dispel preexisting misconceptions they may harbor about battered women, replacing them with a framework that takes account of these women's unique circumstances and perspective. It is not necessarily a defense in and of itself, although it has, at times, been erroneously conceptualized as such (i.e., the battered woman syndrome defense). Rather, the intended import of the testimony is to provide a framework for interpreting a battered woman's actions within the confines of the existing laws of self-defense. We turn now to the content of the testimony itself.

BATTERED WOMAN SYNDROME EVIDENCE

The term battered woman syndrome was first coined in the late 1970s by Dr. Lenore Walker, who pioneered much of the research on the topic.

The syndrome, as developed by Walker (1979, 1984), describes the pattern of violence found in abusive relationships and the psychological impact that this violence can have on a woman. Two theoretical constructs comprise the syndrome: the cycle theory of violence and the theory of learned helplessness. Drawing on her clinical work, as well as on interviews she conducted with hundreds of battered women, Walker identified a repetitive three-phase cycle that characterizes the battering relationship (Walker, 1984, 1993). The first phase, referred to as the tension-building phase, is characterized by "minor" abusive incidents (e.g., outbursts, verbal threats). These more minor incidents of abuse, however, eventually build up to the second or acute battering phase, which is posited to be the shortest of the three and is the period during which the most harm is likely to occur to the battered woman (Walker, 1984, 1993). Battered women may even provoke a beating during this period, not for masochistic tendencies, but rather to control the environment in which the beating occurs (Walker, 1993). For example, it may be safer for a woman to be beaten in the company of family than at home alone with her abuser. This second phase in the cycle is then followed by the third or final phase, which is referred to as the period of loving contrition. It is in this final phase that the abuser professes his love, promising never to harm the woman again. Believing his promises, the woman is provided some hope that the violence will cease. Eventually, however, the cycle repeats itself.[2] It is this repetitive, yet unpredictable, nature of the violence, and the impending imminence of harm it presents, that eventually reduce the woman to a perpetual state of fear.

Alongside the cycle of violence theory, Walker proposed a "psychological rationale" for why battered women remain in abusive relationships (Walker, 1984). Drawing on Seligman's (1975) classic research on learned helplessness in which the helpless responses of dogs exposed to inescapable electrical shocks were observed, Walker employed the theory of learned helplessness to explain how battered women can become psychologically trapped in an abusive relationship. That is, given the cyclical, repetitive nature of the violence and the woman's experience with

[2]In response to early criticisms of the three-phase cycle (Walker, 1993), Walker modified her theory slightly to incorporate various thresholds of battering through which the three phases may or may not pass. For example, the most common pattern of violence observed by Walker adheres to the three-phase cycle but does not reach a lethal threshold. In contrast, Walker noted that the lethal threshold occurs within the cyclical pattern characterizing battering relationships in which a woman kills her abuser.

the "noncontingent nature of [her] attempts to control the violence," she is eventually reduced to a state of "psychological helplessness," perceiving that there is little she can do to alter the situation (Walker, 1984, p. 87). The cycle of violence and increased severity of beatings reinforce the battered woman's feelings of helplessness and she learns to accept the inevitability of the beatings. Walker (1977–1978) further proposed that traditional sex-role norms teach women that their life situation is beyond their control, and that this is particularly true for battered women.

More recently, the term battered woman syndrome has taken on a more specific and clinical meaning and a number of courts have adopted this concept of the syndrome (Faigman et al., 2002). Although not specifically listed in the Diagnostic and Statistical Manual of Mental Disorders (American Psychiatric Association, 2000), Walker (1988), in her later work, noted that "the literature supports the acceptance of an identifiable pattern of symptoms called Battered Woman Syndrome" (p. 142) that comprise a subcategory of Post Traumatic Stress Disorder (PTSD). Thus, the expert may describe the syndrome from the perspective of PTSD. Although it must be noted that not all battered women exhibit all, or indeed any, of the symptoms that comprise PTSD, according to the description of the disorder a battered woman would be expected to exhibit symptoms from three clusters comprising the diagnosis: arousal symptoms (activation of autonomic nervous system, hypervigilance), intrusive symptoms (e.g., nightmares, flashbacks, intrusive memories), and avoidance symptoms (e.g., denial, minimization, repression). Arousal symptoms prepare the battered woman for fight-or-flight reactions to danger (Walker, 2000), whereas the intrusive symptoms or reliving of the battering contribute to the battered woman's perceptions of imminent danger, even when none may be apparent to an outside observer (Dutton & Goodman, 1994). Finally, avoidance symptoms provide a means by which the battered woman may avoid the gravity of the battering relationship (Walker, 1992). According to Dutton and Goodman, the battered woman suffering from PTSD alternates between the phases of the intrusive and avoidance symptoms, explaining what appears on the surface to be contradictory behaviors.

As the content of the testimony suggests, battered woman syndrome testimony speaks to the woman's mental state and provides a context for understanding why she perceived herself to be in danger at the time of the killing. More than 50% of U.S. states have found testimony on battering and its effects relevant to the jurors' assessment of the reasonableness of the woman's belief that she was in imminent danger and 37% have found it relevant to the woman's perception of the "temporal proximity of the perceived danger" (Parrish, 1996, p. 121). The testimony can also provide an explanation for why she felt that there was no option other than to resort to violence to avoid this danger. On this basis, two thirds of the states have found testimony on battering and its effects to be relevant for the determination of why the woman did not leave the relationship or to explain other conduct (e.g., actions committed under duress; Parrish). Finally, and more generally, the testimony provides an educative function by dispelling any misconceptions jurors may harbor about battered women. In short, by providing a contextual framework that presumably normalizes her behavior, the jurors can now "fairly apply the same legal standards" to her actions as they would to any defendant (Schneider, 1986, p. 214).

VALIDITY AND LIMITATIONS OF BATTERED WOMAN SYNDROME EVIDENCE

Since its introduction into the courtroom, numerous scholars and battered women's advocates (e.g., Crocker, 1985; Dutton, 1993; Ferraro, 2003; Rothenberg, 2003; Schneider, 1986, 1996) have challenged the validity and applicability of the syndrome evidence to battered women's claims of self-defense. These objections neither diminish the role of the abuse nor eliminate justification for the act, but rather focus on the portrayal of battered women that is conveyed via the testimony (e.g., Crocker; Schneider, 1986, 2000). As early as the mid-1980s, critics of the testimony voiced the concern that the syndrome terminology, although merely descriptive, was likely to be interpreted as an illness or clinical disorder. Thus, as opposed to providing a framework that normalizes the battered woman and her actions, she is characterized as an "irrational and emotionally damaged" woman (Schneider, 1986). Coupled with this concern were fundamental problems regarding the content of the testimony itself. That is, with its focus on the woman's learned helplessness and passivity, its characterization of the battered woman appeared more suggestive of loss of control and incapacity. Along these lines, Schneider (1986) argued that battered woman syndrome evidence conjures up "images of a psychological defense—a separate defense and/or an impaired mental state defense" (Schneider, 1986, p. 199) and, as such, is more likely to be associated with explanations of excuse (i.e., what she did was wrong, albeit understandable) rather than justification (i.e., what she did was right). As our later review of the empirical research examining the impact of battered woman syndrome evidence on jurors' judgments, suggests, there may be some validity to these concerns.

In addition to these interpretational concerns associated with the testimony, various components of the battered woman syndrome have been critiqued. For instance, in the face of considerable variability in the battered woman's experiences of the cycle of violence in both Walker's (1979) data and the data of others (Browne, 1987; Dobash & Dobash, 1984), the generalizability of the cycle theory of violence has been questioned (Faigman, 1986; McMahon, 1999). Similarly, Dutton (1992) concluded that not all violent relationships follow the cyclical pattern and would be better conceptualized as a "single and continuing entity" (p. 29).

Perhaps one of the most problematic aspects of the testimony, however, has been the application of the theory of learned helplessness to the battered woman's experiences. Not only is the focus on learned helplessness and the woman's passivity incongruent with her reactive and fatal response to the batterer, but this portrayal of battered women is inconsistent with the behavioral responses of battered women identified in the research. That is, researchers have consistently documented a wide range of strategies and help-seeking behaviors employed by battered women in their attempts to end the violence (Bowker, 1986; Dobash & Dobash, 1984; Gelles & Straus, 1988; Gondolf & Fisher, 1988), with these behaviors increasing rather than decreasing over time (Gondolf & Fisher). Furthermore, in addition to the batterer's domination and control (Mahoney, 1991), researchers consistently cite a range of external and social barriers women face when trying to end the abuse (Bowker, 1986; Nichols & Feltey, 2003; Rhodes & McKenzie, 1998). Stark (1992), using the term entrapment to characterize the battering experience, argued that the woman's failure to leave has less to do with learned helplessness than the "actual level of control enforced through violence, cultural restraints, and institutional collusion with the batterer" (p. 280).

Finally, Dutton (1993), one of the authors of the review of battered woman syndrome evidence undertaken at the direction of Congress, noted that the syndrome testimony, as it has developed, fails to adequately capture the diverse "psychological realities" of battered women. Indeed, she recommended that the testimony should "incorporate the diverse range of traumatic reactions described in the psychological literature, and should not be limited to an examination of learned helplessness, PTSD, or any other single reaction or 'profile'" (Dutton, 1993, p. 1201). Noting that the "notion of a syndrome does not represent the recognized variation in battered women's experience nor the corpus of scientific knowledge in the field," Dutton recommended that the term itself battered woman syndrome, should be dropped from the testimony.

In its place reference should be made to expert testimony on "battering and its effects" (Dutton, 1993, p. 1201), a recommendation adopted by the authors of the report (Dutton, 1996).

In summary, as researchers have noted, the singular portrayal of the battered woman as a passive and helpless victim conveyed via expert testimony fails to take into account both the uniqueness of each woman's battering experience, and the variability in the woman's responses to the battering relationship (Briere & Jordan, 2004; Dutton, 1993). As such, the actions of some battered women may cast doubt on the applicability of the syndrome to the particular defendant on trial (Ferraro, 2003; Jenkins & Davidson, 1990; Schneider, 2000). Indeed, unless the syndrome evidence fits the battered woman defendant, it may never even reach the ears of the trier of fact. For example, in the case of Buhrle v. State (1981), the Wyoming Supreme Court refused the introduction of expert testimony pertaining to battered woman syndrome because, in its opinion, the defendant had failed to act like a typical battered woman. Examination of Canadian cases similarly suggests that the testimony may benefit only those women who conform to all aspects of the syndrome (Shaffer, 1997). The dangers of adopting such a restrictive conceptualization of the testimony were aptly articulated by Madame Justice Claire L'Heureux-Dube in R. v. Malott (1998): "It is possible that those women who are unable to fit themselves within the stereotype of a victimized, passive, helpless, dependent, battered woman will not have their claims to self-defense fairly decided" (p. 40).

Given these limitations of the testimony, numerous researchers (e.g., Bowker, 1986; Dutton, 1996; Ferraro, 2003; Mahoney, 1991; Sheehy, Stubbs, & Tolmie, 1992) offered various recommendations for redefining the testimony. In addition to dropping the term battered woman syndrome, proponents for reform of the testimony contended that the scope of expert testimony pertaining to battered women should place greater emphasis on women's circumstances and social realities. For instance, Martinson, MacCrimmon, Grant, and Boyle (1991), argued that the expert evidence provided in these cases needs to focus more on the contextual factors that prevent a battered woman from leaving the relationship, such as the batterer's domination and control, the risks of leaving, the woman's economic dependence on the abuser, isolation from family and friends, and the inadequacy of police and other interventions (see also Mahoney). In this vein, Dutton (1993) argued that it is imperative that the testimony convey the "overall social context necessary to adequately understand the responses of battered women to violence" (p. 1242).

Given that the question of how expert testimony pertaining to battered women influences the adjudication of these cases may ultimately rest on the jurors' use of the testimony, it is essential that we determine how such evidence is actually utilized by the jurors. That is, what impact does battered woman syndrome testimony have on the jurors? How might alternative forms of the testimony be received? What impact does it have on their evaluations of the woman's actions? What impact does it have on their verdicts? According to Walker (1992), the introduction of battered woman syndrome evidence has resulted in "more not guilty jury verdicts or convictions of a lesser crime than first degree murder" (p. 322). Results of a trend analysis conducted by the National Clearninghouse for the Defense of Battered Women (NCDBW; Parrish, 1996) are less clear about the beneficial effects of the testimony. Examining primarily appellate court cases of battered women who were convicted at trial, Parrish compiled a database that incorporated and updated an earlier database (Maguigan, 1991) in which expert testimony had been introduced at trial. Examining the cases over time, her analysis revealed a 20% increase in the odds that the conviction would be affirmed. Such results, in addition to the controversy surrounding the application and admissibility of battered woman syndrome evidence, have presented social psychologists with a timely opportunity to explore the impact of this type of evidence on jurors' judgments and evaluations in trials of battered women who have killed their abusers. It is to the results of empirical research into the impact of battered woman syndrome evidence, as well as to alternative forms of testimony, that we now turn.

RESEARCH EXAMINING THE IMPACT OF EXPERT TESTIMONY PERTAINING TO BATTERED WOMEN

Research on the impact of battered woman syndrome evidence began in the late 1980s, with much of this work employing juror/jury simulation techniques. Using this methodology, mock jurors are presented with a simulated or mock trial and are asked to render a verdict and various judgments about the defendant and case. In one of the earliest of these studies, Follingstad et al. (1989) attempted to identify the influence of three different variables, one of which was battered woman syndrome evidence, on jurors' decisions in a homicide trial involving a battered woman accused of killing her husband. To this end, participants read a transcript of a criminal case that included the defendant's case history and a summary of the case facts. Within the transcript, the level of threat posed by the batterer was systematically varied to produce three versions of the case. In one version, the wife shot her husband as he advanced on her with a weapon; in another, she shot him as he advanced on her without a weapon; in the third, she shot him while he lay sleeping after he had beaten her and verbally threatened to harm her when he awoke. In addition, half of the participants received battered woman syndrome evidence, whereas for the other half this evidence was omitted. Finally, the researchers also varied the verdict options that were available; in addition to the verdicts of guilt (murder and manslaughter), some were provided with a not guilty by reason of insanity (NGRI) option, whereas for others the option of not guilty by reason of self-defense (NGRSD) was available.

After reading the case, participants were initially asked to render a verdict; 60% chose either NGRSD or NGRI. Next, participants were presented with a full range of verdict options and were permitted to either change or retain their initial verdict choice. Almost half of the participants, primarily those not provided with the verdict choice of self-defense, changed their verdicts. In total, 80% now rendered a not guilty verdict. Follingstad et al. (1989) found that the batterer's level of threat influenced final verdict decisions such that when the husband advanced on his wife with a weapon, compared to the other two conditions, participants were more likely to find her not guilty. The presence of the expert testimony, however, was not found to directly impact jurors' judgments or verdict decisions. Similarly, simulation research conducted by Finkel, Meister, and Lightfoot (1991) also found no direct effects for the presence of battered woman syndrome evidence on mock jurors' verdict decisions.

In contrast to this research, studies conducted by Schuller and colleagues suggest that exposure to battered woman syndrome evidence does result in more favorable evaluations of a defendant accused of killing her abuser, and more lenient verdicts. For example, compared to jurors who were not exposed to battered woman syndrome evidence, mock jurors to whom expert testimony was provided tended to find the defendant less responsible, and the deceased more responsible, for the killing (Schuller, Smith, & Olson, 1994). They were also more likely to believe the defendant's claim that the killing was committed in self-defense. Moreover, research conducted by Schuller (1992) suggests that the influence of expert testimony on jurors' verdicts may be mediated by jurors' interpretations of the trial testimony. That is, battered woman syndrome evidence primarily influenced jurors' evaluations of the defendant and her actions, and it was these evaluations that ultimately determined the verdicts that jurors rendered.

Contrary to the notion that the impact of battered woman syndrome evidence on jurors' decisions might operate by informing jurors about the general dynamics and impact of abuse, as of yet, there is little research to suggest that it performs this function. Schuller et al. (1994) investigated the issue specifically by measuring participants' beliefs about battered women both before and after their participation in a juror simulation study involving a battered woman who killed her abuser. Approximately 6 weeks prior to participating in the study, participants' beliefs about battering relationships were collected in an unrelated study. These beliefs were found to be strong predictors of the mock jurors' judgments in the case. For instance, compared to mock jurors who were more informed about battering and its impact, participants who were less informed about battering were less believing of the defendant's claim and assigned greater responsibility for the events to the defendant and less responsibility to the batterer. In terms of the expert testimony, its presence led to more lenient verdict decisions. That is, although it had no impact on the number of not guilty verdicts rendered, the mock jurors (women in particular) who selected a guilty verdict were more likely to render a verdict of manslaughter when the expert testimony was present, whereas, when the expert testimony was omitted, the guilty verdicts were more evenly distributed between murder and manslaughter. As little change was evidenced in mock jurors' pre- and post-beliefs about abuse, support for the notion that the battered woman syndrome evidence performed an educative function was not found.

Although the educative function of battered woman syndrome evidence, thus far, has not been demonstrated, evidence that the testimony alters mock jurors' perceptions of the defendant and her actions has been found. Schuller (1992) conducted a series of two studies investigating the influence of battered woman syndrome evidence on jurors' evaluations and verdict decisions. The first study examined individual case judgments and verdicts, whereas the second study examined case judgments and group verdicts following deliberation. To this end, jurors were exposed to one of three versions of a homicide trial in which the presence of expert evidence pertaining to battered woman syndrome was systematically varied. One third of the jurors received expert testimony that described the research findings with regard to the syndrome as well as the expert's opinion that the defendant on trial was suffering from battered woman syndrome. The expert's opinion regarding the consistency of the defendant's behavior with respect to the syndrome is a primary reason for the introduction of the evidence (Walker, 1993); however, 20% of states preclude the admission of expert opinion for this purpose, preferring instead a more general form of the testimony only (Parrish, 1996). In order to explore the impact of this more general form of testimony, one third of the jurors received expert testimony in which only the research findings pertaining to the battered woman syndrome were described (as in the first condition) and no opinion about the defendant on trial was offered. The remaining jurors received no expert testimony (control).

Results of individual verdicts and judgments in the first study by Schuller (1992) indicated that the mock jurors provided with the expert testimony that included an opinion that the defendant suffered from battered woman syndrome, compared to those in the expert testimony condition that omitted the opinion or the no-expert control condition, found the defendant more credible and were more likely to believe that the defendant feared for her life, that her life was in danger, and that the killing was not intended. Overall, the specific form of expert testimony resulted in predominantly manslaughter or not guilty verdicts, and very few murder verdicts, whereas the no-expert and the more general form of expert testimony resulted in verdicts evenly split between murder, manslaughter, and not guilty.

In contrast, the results of group judgments and verdicts following deliberation (Schuller, 1992, Study 2) indicated that, when jurors deliberated, the general form of testimony was found to be as effective as the specific form of testimony, both of which produced greater verdict leniency compared to the no-expert control condition. The impact of general versus specific forms of expert testimony has also been investigated in a criminal case of child sexual assault in which the congruency of the complainant's behavior with the expert testimony was systematically varied (Kovera, Borgida, Gresham, Gray, & Regan, 1997). Kovera et al. found that, following deliberation, the specific form of expert testimony produced more convictions of the abuser when the complainant's behavior was congruent, as opposed to incongruent, with the expert's testimony. The more general form of testimony, however, tended to produce more convictions of the abuser when the complainant's behavior was incongruent with the expert's testimony. That is, in the absence of other probative factors, the more general form of testimony appeared to bolster the credibility of the complainant. Thus, in this domain of expert testimony, the form of testimony, general or specific, interacted with the fit of the target to the testimony.

The potentially detrimental impact that expert testimony may have when the battered woman's behavior is viewed as inconsistent with the conceptualization of battered women conveyed by the testimony has been examined in simulation studies by varying the defendants' behavior (Schuller & Hastings, 1996; Schuller & Rzepa, 2002; Terrance & Matheson, 2003). In one of these studies (Terrance & Matheson), the expert testimony provided was only general in nature, whereas in the other two studies (Schuller & Hastings; Schuller & Rzepa) participants were provided with expert testimony that was specifically tied to the woman on trial. In terms of verdicts rendered, across all three studies, the presence of the expert evidence did not interact with the woman's degree of stereotype fit with the testimony. It should be noted, however, that in only one of these studies (Schuller & Rzepa) was the manipulation of the defendant's degree of passivity strong enough to provoke differential perceptions of the woman's behavior, thus leaving the issue of defendant-stereotype fit somewhat unclear.

In addition to exploring the degree of stereotype fit, one of the main goals of the research conducted by Terrance and Matheson (2003) was to examine whether expert testimony that presented battered woman syndrome evidence in terms of a DSM–IV–TR (2000) clinical diagnosis of PTSD would be associated with interpretations of psychological dysfunction. To this end, participants were exposed to battered woman syndrome evidence that either included or omitted references to PTSD, comparing these two conditions to a no-expert testimony control condition. In terms of the expert testimony, prior to deliberation, those provided with battered woman syndrome testimony that included PTSD were less likely to rate the defendant guilty than those provided with the battered woman syndrome evidence that omitted the PTSD diagnosis. Surprisingly, ratings of guilt in the control condition fell midway between the two expert testimony conditions and differed from neither—the reason for this outcome remains uncertain. Following deliberation, however, the differential impact of the expert testimony on verdicts disappeared.

In terms of the defendant's mental stability, presentation of the battered woman syndrome evidence framed as PTSD, as opposed to no expert testimony, resulted in increased perceptions that the defendant had been "driven insane," was "out of her mind at the time of the killing," and was "more mentally unstable" (Terrance & Matheson, 2003, p. 43). Ratings in the condition in which the battered woman syndrome evidence omitted PTSD fell between these two conditions such that it did not differ from either. Moreover, compared to the battered woman syndrome evidence that omitted reference to PTSD, when the testimony was framed within the context of PTSD, participants' perceptions regarding the legitimacy of the clinical diagnosis were enhanced. Thus, although it appears that the inclusion of PTSD increases the legitimacy of the battered woman syndrome as a valid psychological disorder, consistent with the concerns that have been raised, it would also appear to be associated with interpretations of mental instability. Similar to these findings, the results of the juror simulation conducted by Finkel et al. (1991) found that the presence of expert evidence that provided a diagnosis of battered woman syndrome, compared to the no-expert control condition, led the mock jurors to view the woman as more distorted in her thinking, less capable of making responsible choices, and less culpable for her actions.

Results of a recent study suggest that, rather than providing a framework for evaluating the battered woman's actions as reasonable, battered woman syndrome evidence may operate by evoking feelings of sympathy for the defendant (Schuller & Rzepa, 2002). Using a nullification manipulation, Schuller and Rzepa assessed the extent to which the testimony allows the mock jurors to conceptualize the woman's actions as falling within the legal requirements of self-defense. Within the United States, jurors, though not always informed of their right to do so, may disregard or nullify the law. Research examining the impact of informing jurors of this right suggests that the presence of nullification instructions encourages jurors to render a verdict consistent with their own moral convictions if they feel that following the law in the particular case at hand would lead to an unjust outcome (Horowitz, 1985, 1988; Wiener, Habert, Shkodriani, & Staebler, 1991). Schuller and Rzepa reasoned that because the battered woman's lethal actions are in response to the batterer's violent and abusive treatment, this situation would likely invoke feelings of injustice. Thus, the presence of nullification instructions would release the jurors from following the letter of the law and would allow them to more readily follow their conscience. If the battered woman syndrome evidence provides the jurors with a framework for understanding her actions as reasonable, however, a nullification instruction should have little impact (i.e., verdict leniency can now be achieved by applying the laws of self-defense to the case).

Schuller and Rzepa's (2002) results indicated, however, that this was not the case. Although greater verdict leniency was demonstrated when mock jurors were provided with battered woman syndrome evidence, compared to the control condition, the interaction of this variable with the nullification manipulation was not in the expected direction. That is, the greater verdict leniency displayed in the expert testimony condition was only present when the nullification instruction was present (i.e., when the mock jurors were released from a strict application of the law). Furthermore, under these circumstances, the mock jurors expressed more sympathy for the defendant, and perceived her options to be more limited (with this effect more pronounced for women than men). Thus, Schuller and Rzepa concluded that the process by which the evidence influenced jurors' decisions appeared to have more to do with evoking sympathy for the defendant than with providing jurors with a better fit between her actions and the requirements of self-defense.

In response to the criticism that battered woman syndrome evidence characterizes battered women as psychologically damaged (Crocker, 1985; Schneider, 1986), Schuller and colleagues conducted a series of studies to explore the impact of an alternative form of expert evidence that incorporated some of the suggested proposals for its reform (Schuller & Hastings, 1996; Schuller, McKimmie, & Janz, 2004; Schuller, Wells, Rzepa, & Klippenstine, 2004). Specifically, Schuller and colleagues explored the impact of a reformation of the evidence that, although retaining the core element of the cycle theory of violence, eliminated references to battered woman syndrome, learned helplessness, and PTSD, substituting this information with information pertaining to the actions battered women might take and the obstacles they face. Thus, as opposed to psychopathologizing the defendant's reaction to the batterer's domination, the alternative form of evidence placed greater emphasis on the battered woman's agency (i.e., effortful and active rather than passive and helpless) and social realities (e.g., lack of social support). As such, the researchers labelled the testimony "social agency" evidence.

The first of these studies (Schuller & Hastings, 1996) drew participants from a large university campus as well as from the community. Within the trial transcript, the presence and form of expert testimony was manipulated such that participants received the battered woman syndrome evidence, the alternative form of evidence, or no expert evidence. Results indicated that, compared to no expert testimony, the inclusion of expert evidence, regardless of the form, resulted in fewer guilty verdicts. Moreover, the presence of expert testimony (again, in either form), compared to the no expert testimony control condition, led to more favorable evaluations of the defendant's claim (e.g., "plausibility of claim," "she was trapped in the relationship"), although it must be noted that this finding was more pronounced for the student sample. Specifically, only ratings of the availability of the woman's "other options" were affected by expert testimony for the nonstudent sample, whereas for the student sample the impact of the evidence was found on other case judgments as well. Finally, lending some support to the concern that battered woman syndrome evidence may lead to interpretations of dysfunction, participants provided with traditional battered woman syndrome evidence, as opposed to those provided with no expert testimony, were more likely to view the success of a plea of insanity to be greater (Schuller & Hastings). In contrast, the alternative form of the testimony garnered similar ratings to the no-expert condition on this measure.

A comparable study (Schuller, McKimmie, & Janz, 2004) conducted on student samples drawn from Australia and Canada yielded similar results to those found by Schuller and Hastings (1996), that is, fewer guilty verdicts were rendered when expert testimony was presented compared to a no expert testimony condition. Few differences were observed between the two samples. Of note, however, is that Canadian participants provided with expert testimony, compared to those provided with no expert testimony, were more likely to indicate that the defendant's actions were justified, whereas no such difference was observed for Australian participants. Also, Canadian participants rendered more guilty verdicts than Australian participants when expert testimony was not provided, but no difference was observed between the two groups when the expert testimony was provided. In terms of the two forms of expert testimony, participants provided with the alternative form of testimony, compared to the traditional form, perceived the defendant to be more fearful. In contrast to earlier research (Schuller & Hastings), however, no difference was observed on participants' ratings of the defendant's psychological stability for the two forms of testimony.

In another study, Schuller, Wells, et al. (2004) investigated the impact of the alternative compared to the traditional form of expert testimony in a simulation that systematically varied the perceived imminence of the batterer's threat (i.e., the killing was committed in the midst of an attack vs. the killing was committed while he lay sleeping). Because a delay between the batterer's violence and the woman's fatal response poses one of the most serious problems for the woman's claim of self-defense (Finkel et al., 1991; Follingstad et al., 1989; Follingstad, Shillinglaw, DeHart, & Kleinfelter, 1997; Terrance, Matheson, & Spanos, 2000), the inclusion of this variable offered an assessment of the expert testimony under the most difficult of circumstances. Overall, results indicated that when the alternative form of the expert testimony was provided, the imminence manipulation had little impact (no differences observed between the conditions that varied the circumstances in which the killing occurred). In contrast, the traditional form of testimony was found to be less effective when the killing occurred outside of a direct confrontation (i.e., batterer was sleeping). And, consistent with the other studies conducted, compared to the alternative form of the testimony, mock jurors who received the traditional form of testimony tended to perceive the defendant as more psychologically unstable.

Taken in their entirety, these findings suggest that an alternative form of testimony that emphasizes the social aspects of the battering relationship and omits references to the term battered woman syndrome, learned helplessness, and PTSD may be as successful as the traditional form of testimony in terms of verdict decisions. Furthermore, it appears to avoid some of the pitfalls typically associated with the syndrome evidence (McDonald, 1997).

CONCLUSION

Prior to the introduction of battered woman syndrome evidence, battered women who killed their abusers had little choice but to "plead guilty to murder" (Walker, 1992). In order to meet the legal standard for a claim to self-defense, justification for the killing was dependent on the view that the battered woman was, and perceived herself to be, in imminent danger at the time of the killing (Raitt & Zeedyk, 2000). The courts' failure to acknowledge the implications of the circumstances surrounding the woman's fatal response (the cumulative nature of the abuse) rendered it difficult for the battered woman to advance the claim that her actions were in fact a reasonable response to her situation (Raitt & Zeedyk). The introduction of battered woman syndrome evidence (*Ibn-Tamas v. United States*, 1979) was instrumental in bringing to the courts' attention the problems confronting a battered woman claim of self-defense, and it is clear that important advances to the defense of battered women have been achieved with its introduction. Coupled with the significant success that the syndrome evidence has been met with in the courtroom (Raitt & Zeedyk, 2000; Schneider, 1986; Walker, 1992), however, significant concerns have been raised regarding its use (e.g., Crocker, 1985; Ferraro, 2003; Schneider, 1986). The body of empirical work reviewed herein suggests that there may be some validity to these concerns. Although the research suggests that the introduction of battered woman syndrome evidence is associated with positive effects for a battered woman on trial, the findings also point to some shortcomings of its use. That is, although verdict decisions were more favorable to the defendant when battered woman syndrome evidence was presented, concordant with the concerns raised by some of its critics (e.g., Crocker; Ferraro; Schneider), there was also evidence consistent with the notion that battered woman syndrome evidence is likely to be associated with interpretations of psychological dysfunction.

As this review of the research also highlights, the treatment of expert testimony need not remain static (Sheehy et al., 1992). Along these lines, various scholars and legal activists have proposed adoption of a broader, more contextualized form of testimony about battering and its effects (Dutton, 1993). The research exploring the impact of such testimony on mock jurors' decisions, although still in its infancy, suggests that omitting the potentially psychopathologizing aspects of battered woman syndrome evidence (i.e., syndrome terminology, learned helplessness, PTSD) does not appear to alter the beneficial impact of the expert testimony, and under some conditions (i.e., when the killing was committed outside of a direct confrontation) it was rendered more effective than the traditional form of the testimony. These results are encouraging and very timely. Some experts have adopted this more contextualized form of the testimony (Ferraro, 2003). For example, Ferraro, who has provided expert testimony on battering and its effects since the mid-1980s and, since the mid-1990s, has adopted this broader conceptualization of battering and its effects in the evidence she provided, noted that she has met with considerable resistance on the part of attorneys and judges. Although considerable work still remains to be done, the research exploring the impact of a more generalized form of testimony pertaining to battering and its effects suggests that their resistance may be unwarranted.

REFERENCES

American Psychiatric Association. (2000). *Diagnostic and Statistical Manual of Mental Disorders: DSM–IV–TR*. Washington, DC: Author.

Bernstein, D. E., & Jackson, J. D. (2004). *The Daubert trilogy in the sates. Jurimetrics*, *44*, 351–366.

Bowker, L. H. (1986). *Ending the violence: A guidebook based on the experiences of 1,000 battered wives*. Holmes Beach, FL: Learning.

Briere, J., & Jordan, C. E. (2004). Violence against women: Outcome complexity and implications for assessment and treatment. *Journal of Interpersonal Violence*, *19*, 1252–1276.

Browne, A. (1987). *When battered women kill*. New York: The Free Press.

Buhrle v. State, 627 P.2d 1374 (Wyo. 1981).

Crocker, P. L. (1985). The meaning of equality for battered women who kill men in self-defense. *Harvard Women's Law Journal*, *8*, 121–153.

Daubert v. Merrell Dow Pharmaceuticals, Inc., 509 U.S. 579 (1993).

Dobash, R. E., & Dobash, R. P. (1984). The nature and antecedents of violent events. *British Journal of Criminology, 24*, 269–288.

Dodge, M., & Greene, E. (1991). Jurors and expert conceptions of battered women. *Violence and Victims*, 6, 271–282.

Dutton, M. A. (1992). *Empowering and healing the battered woman: A model for assessment and intervention*. New York: Springer.

Dutton, M. A. (1993). Understanding women's responses to domestic violence: A redefinition of battered woman syndrome. *Hofstra Law Review, 21*, 1194–1201.

Dutton, M. A. (1996). *Impact of evidence concerning battering and its effects in criminal trials involving battered women*. Retrieved September 30, 2004 from www.ncjrs.org/pdffiles/batter.pdf

Dutton, M. A., & Goodman, L. A. (1994). Posttraumatic stress disorder among battered women: Analysis of legal implications. *Behavioral Sciences and the Law, 12*, 215–234.

Edwards, S. (1997). Battered women: In fear of Luc's shadow. *Denning Law Journal, 1997*, 75–105.

Ewing, C. P., & Aubrey, M. (1987). Battered women and public opinion: Some realities about the myths. *Journal of Family Violence, 2*,257–264.

Faigman, D. L. (1986). The battered woman syndrome and self-defense: A legal and empirical dissent. *Virginia Law Review, 72*,619–647.

Faigman, D. L., Kaye, D. H., Saks, M. J., & Sanders, J. (2002). The legal relevance of research on domestic violence against women. In D. Faigman, D. Kaye, M. Saks, & J. Sanders (Eds.), *Modern scientific evidence: The law and science of expert testimony*, (2nd ed., Volume 2, pp. 2–37). St. Paul, MN: West Group.

Ferraro, K. J. (2003). The words change but the melody lingers: The persistence of the battered woman syndrome in criminal cases involving battered women. *Violence Against Women*, 9, 110–129.

Finkel, N. J., Meister, K. H., & Lightfoot, D. M. (1991). The self-defense and community sentiment. *Law and Human Behavior, 15*, 585–602.

Follingstad, D. R., Polek, D. S., Hause, E. S., Deaton, L. H., Bulger, M. W., & Conway, Z. D. (1989). Factors predicting verdicts in cases where battered women kill their husbands. *Law and Human Behavior, 13*, 253–269.

Follingstad, D. R., Shillinglaw, R. D., DeHart, D. D., & Kleinfelter, K. J. (1997). The impact of elements of self-defense and objective versus subjective instructions on jurors' verdicts for battered women defendants. *Journal of Interpersonal Violence, 12*, 729–747.

Gelles, R. J., & Straus, M. A. (1988). *Intimate violence: The causes and consequences of abuse in the American family*. New York: Simon & Schuster.

Gentemann, K. M. (1984). Wife beating: Attitudes of a non-clinical population. *Victimology*, 9, 109–119.

Gillespie, C. K. (1989). *Justifiable homicide*. Columbus: Ohio State University Press.

Gondolf, E. W., & Fisher, E. R. (1988). *Battered women as survivors: An alternative to treating learned helplessness*. Lexington, MA: Lexington Books.

Greene, E., Raitz, A., & Lindblad, H. (1989). Jurors' knowledge of battered women. *Journal of Family Violence*, 4, 105–125.

Horowitz, I. A. (1985). The effect of jury nullification instructions on verdicts and jury functioning in criminal trials. *Law and Human Behavior*, 9, 25–36.

Horowitz, I. A. (1988). Jury nullification: The impact of judicial instructions, arguments, and challenges on jury decision making. *Law and Human Behavior, 12*, 439–454.

Ibn-Tamas v. United States, 407 A.2d 626 (1979).

Jenkins, P., & Davidson, B. (1990). Battered women in the criminal justice system: An analysis of gender stereotypes. *Behavioral Sciences and the Law*, 8, 171–180.

Kovera, L. W., Borgida, E., Gresham, A. W., Gray, E., & Regan, P. C. (1997). Does expert psychological testimony inform or influence juror decision making? A social cognitive analysis. *Journal of Applied Psychology, 82*, 178–191.

Lavallee v. Regina, 55 C.C.C.3d 97 (1990).

Littleton, C. A. (1989). Women's experience and the problem of transition. *University of Chicago Legal Forum, 1989*, 23–57.

Maguigan, H. (1991). Battered women and self-defense: Myths and misconceptions in current reform proposals. *University of Pennsylvania Law Review, 140*, 379–486.

Mahoney, M. R. (1991). Legal images of battered women: Redefining the issue of separation. *Michigan Law Review*, 90, 1–94.

Martinson, D., MacCrimmon, M., Grant, I., & Boyle, C. (1991). A forum on Lavallee v. R: Women and self-defense. *University of British Columbia Law Review, 25*, 23–68.

McDonald, E. (1997, December). Battered woman syndrome. *New Zealand Law Journal*, 436–438.

McMahon, M. (1999). Battered women and bad science: The limited validity and utility of battered woman syndrome. *Psychiatry, Psychology, and Law*, 6, 23–49.

Nichols, L., & Feltey, K. M. (2003). "The woman is not always the bad guy." *Violence Against Women*, 9, 784–806.

Parrish, J. (1996). Trend analysis: Expert testimony on battering and its effects in criminal cases. *Wisconsin Women's Law Journal, 11*, 75–173.

R. v. Malott, 1 S.C.R. 123 (1998).

Raitt, F. E., & Zeedyk, M. S. (2000). *The implicit relation of psychology and law: Women and syndrome evidence*. London: Routledge.

Rhodes, N. R., & McKenzie, E. B. (1998). Why do battered women stay? Three decades of research. *Aggression and Violent Behavior, 3*, 391–406.

Robertson, J. B. (1998). Battered woman syndrome: Expert evidence in action. *Otago Law Review*, 9, 277–300.

Rothenburg, B. (2003). "We don't have time for social change": Cultural compromise and the battered woman syndrome. *Gender and Society, 17*, 771–787.

Saunders, D. G., Lynch, A. B., Grayson, M., & Linz, D. (1987). The inventory of beliefs about wife beating: The construction and initial validation of a measure of beliefs and attitudes. *Violence and Victims, 2*, 39–57.

Schneider, E. M. (1980). Equal rights to trial for women: Sex bias and the law of self-defense. *Harvard Civil Rights Law Review, 15*, 623–647.

Schneider, E. M. (1986). Describing and changing: Women's self-defense work and the problem of expert testimony on battering. *Women's Rights Law Reporter*, 9, 195–222.

Schneider, E. M. (1996). Resistance to equality. *University of Pittsburgh Law Review, 57*, 477–524.

Schneider, E. M. (2000). *Battered women and feminist lawmaking*. New Haven, CT: Yale University Press.

Schuller, R. A. (1992). The impact of battered woman syndrome evidence on jury decision processes. *Law and Human Behavior, 16*, 597–620.
Schuller, R. A. (2003). Expert evidence and its impact on jurors' decisions in homicide trials involving battered women. *Duke Journal of Gender, Law, & Policy, 10*, 225–246.
Schuller, R. A., & Hastings, P. A. (1996). Trials of battered women who kill: The impact of alternative forms of expert evidence. *Law and Human Behavior, 20*, 167–187.
Schuller, R. A., McKimmie, B. M., & Janz, T. (2004). The impact of expert testimony in trials of battered women who kill. *Psychiatry, Psychology and Law, 11*, 1–12.
Schuller, R. A., & Rzepa, S. (2002). Expert testimony pertaining to battered woman syndrome: Its impact on jurors' decisions. *Law and Human Behavior, 26*, 655–673.
Schuller, R. A., Smith, V. L., & Olson, J. M. (1994). Jurors' decisions in trials of battered women who kill: The role of prior beliefs and expert testimony. *Journal of Applied Social Psychology, 24*, 316–337.
Schuller, R. A., Wells, E., Rzepa, S., & Klippenstine, M. A. (2004). Rethinking battered woman syndrome evidence: The impact of alternative forms of expert testimony on mock jurors' decisions. *Canadian Journal of Behavioural Science, 26*, 127–136.
Seligman, M. (1975). *Helplessness: On depression, development and death*. San Francisco: Freeman.
Shaffer, M. (1997). The battered woman syndrome revisited: Some complicating thoughts five years after R. v. Lavallee. *University of Toronto Law Journal, 47*, 1–33.
Sheehy, E. A., Stubbs, J., & Tolmie, J. (1992). Defending battered women on trial: The battered woman syndrome and its limitations. *Criminal Law Journal, 16*, 369–394.
Stark, E. (1992). Framing and reframing battered women. In E. S. Buzawa & C. G. Buzawa (Eds.), *Domestic violence: The changing criminal justice response* (pp. 271–292). New York: Auburn House.
State v. Martin, 666 S.W.2d 895 (Mo. Ct. App. 1984).
Stubbs, J., & Tolmie, J. (1999). Falling short of the challenge? A comparative assessment of the Australian use of expert evidence on the battered woman syndrome. *Melbourne University Law Review, 23*, 709–748.
Terrance, C., & Matheson, K. (2003). Undermining reasonableness: Expert testimony in a case involving a battered woman who kills. *Psychology of Women Quarterly, 27*, 37–45.
Terrance, C. A., Matheson, K., & Spanos, N. A. (2000). Effects of judicial instructions and case characteristics in a mock jury trial of battered women who kill. *Law and Human Behavior, 24*, 207–229.
Walker, L. E. (1977–1978). Battered women and learned helplessness. *Victimology, 2*, 525–534.
Walker, L. E. (1979). *The battered woman*. New York: Harper & Row.
Walker, L. E. (1984). *The battered woman syndrome*. New York: Springer.
Walker, L. E. (1988). The battered woman syndrome. In G. T. Horaling, D. Finkelhor, J. T. Kirkpatrick, & M. A. Straus (Eds.), *Family abuse and its consequences: New directions in research*. Newbury Park, CA: Sage Publications, Inc.
Walker, L. E. A. (1992). Battered women syndrome and self-defense. *Notre Dame Journal of Law, Ethics and Public Policy, 6*, 321–334.

Walker, L. E. (1993). Symposium: Women and the law. *Pepperdine Law Review, 20*, 1170–1190.

Walker, L. E. (2000). *The battered woman syndrome* (2nd ed.). New York: Springer.

Walker, L. E., & Monahan, J. (1987). Social framework: A new use of social science in law. *Virginia Law Review, 73*, 559–598.

Walker, L. E., Thyfault, R. K., & Browne, A. (1982). Beyond the juror's ken: Battered women. *Vermont Law Review, 7*, 1–14.

Wiener, R. L., Habert, K., Shkodriani, G., & Staebler, C. (1991). The social psychology of jury nullification: Predicting when jurors disobey the law. *Journal of Applied Social Psychology, 21*, 1379–1401.

10

Expert Testimony on Risk and Future Dangerousness

Daniel Krauss
Claremont McKenna College
Joel Lieberman
University of Nevada, Las Vegas

Over the past quarter-century, the prediction of an individual's future dangerousness or risk of seriously reoffending has come to play an increasing role in the United States criminal justice system. This determination is central to several significant legal outcomes, including: pretrial detention of criminal defendants (e.g., *United States v. Salerno*, 1987), civil commitment of the mentally ill (e.g., *O'Connor v. Donaldson*, 1975), sentencing of criminal defendants (e.g., U.S. Sentencing Commission, 1987), the postprison civil commitment of sexual offenders (e.g., *Kansas v. Hendricks*, 1997), and the execution of criminal defendants (e.g., *Barefoot v. Estelle*, 1983). The U.S. legal system relies heavily on experts being able to differentiate those individuals who will commit future crimes or other serious harms from those who will not.

Unfortunately, there is limited evidence to suggest that mental health expert predictions of future dangerousness are likely to be highly accurate. Consequently, expert testimony on future risk has become one of the most hotly debated topics in psychology and law, and highlights many of the problems associated with the intersection of legal standards and psychology expertise. For example, the legal system tends to view future dangerousness as a predictable, dichotomous, stable, characterological trait, whereas psychology favors a more probabilistic and management focus in which alterable contextual and clinical factors combine with historical factors to determine risk (Heilbrun, Dvoskin, Hart, & McNeil, 1999).

Although many mental health professionals have been willing to offer their expertise to the courts in future violence decisions, and the courts have uniformly accepted that expertise (e.g., *Barefoot v. Estelle*, 1983), scholars have criticized the role mental health professionals have played in these proceedings (Melton, Petrila, Poythress, & Slobogin, 1997). More specifically, critics have questioned the ethics (Edens, Buffington-Vollum, Keilin, Roskamp, & Anthony, 2005; Faust & Ziskin, 1988), the validity (Miller, Amenta, & Conroy, 2005; Cunningham & Reidy, 1999, 2002; Edens, Petrila, & Buffington-Vollum, 2001), and the effects that these potentially unreliable expert predictions might have on these important legal determinations (Krauss, Lieberman, & Olson, 2004; Guy & Edens, 2003; Krauss & Lee, 2003; Krauss & Sales, 2001). This chapter first explores psychological research on risk prediction (we use the terms *risk prediction*, *future dangerousness*, and *future violence* interchangeably to refer to the prediction of serious future violent acts) and the advances that have been made in its assessment in the past decades. Subsequently, using capital sentencing future dangerousness evaluations as an exemplar, the problems inherent in typical expert testimony on this issue are examined. The scientific foundations of expert testimony in this area are also evaluated with special emphasis placed on whether new standards for the admissibility of expert testimony apply to this testimony (i.e., the *Daubert* standard), and if they do, whether courts have determined that different forms of psychological expert testimony meet this threshold. Additionally, the chapter summarizes the limited research indicating how jurors are likely to react to divergent content in psychological expert testimony on dangerousness; finally, the chapter offers suggestions for how the legal system might modify existing standards to better utilize available psychological knowledge.

HISTORICAL DEVELOPMENT OF CLINICAL PREDICTION

A number of early empirical studies indicated that mental health professionals' predictions of future violence were exceedingly inaccurate—in fact, that they were wrong two out of three times (Monahan, 1981). All of these initial studies examined clinicians' ability to predict violence based solely on intuitive methods of combining information, commonly referred to as unstructured clinical judgment. There are a number of reasons why such unstructured judgments are likely to be incorrect, including a variety of cognitive biases or heuristics that individuals engage in when making these types of decisions, such as: (a) ignoring base-rate information (not knowing or not using the rate at which the predicted event occurs in the population of interest); (b) assigning nonoptimal weights to factors (combining and weighing factors based on intuitive judgments rather than on empirical research); and (c) employing the representativeness heuristic (the tendency to make decisions or judge information in a manner that fits preconceived categories or stereotypes of a situation; Krauss & Sales, 2001; see Grove & Meehl, 1996, and Tversky & Kahneman, 1982, for extensive discussion of these issues). For example, a mental health professional might incorrectly place excessive weight on the heinousness of the defendant's most recent act (a factor not commonly associated with future violence) in arriving at a conclusion that the defendant will be dangerous in the future.

Given the unreliability of such testimony, it is surprising how willing the court system has been to accept this testimony for decisions that affect the most important liberty interests—those of life and imprisonment. The admissibility during capital sentencing of several mental health professionals' unstructured clinical predictions of a defendant's future dangerousness was the central constitutional question considered by the U.S. Supreme Court in the landmark case *Barefoot v. Estelle* (1983).

In *Barefoot* (1983), the defendant was convicted of murder in state court and sentenced to death. In Texas, in order for a defendant to receive the death penalty, the sentencing jury is required to find by beyond a reasonable doubt that "there is a probability that the defendant would commit criminal acts of violence that would constitute a continuing threat to society" (Texas Criminal Code, 2004). This special sentencing question is often referred to as the future dangerousness standard. In *Barefoot*'s case, two prosecution psychiatrists who did not interview the defendant opined that there was a "100% and absolute chance" that the defendant would continue to be dangerous. Based on this testimony, the jury sentenced Barefoot to death. Barefoot appealed his death sentence based largely on the admission of this inaccurate expert testimony, and used a brief submitted by the American Psychiatric Association (APA) to help substantiate his claim. The APA brief summarized the five existing studies on such predictions highlighting their 65 to 85% error rate, and concluded that expert psychiatric testimony on future dangerousness was well recognized as unreliable (Monahan, 1981). The U.S. Supreme Court nevertheless upheld the death sentence of the defendant. Justice White, writing for the majority, argued, "The suggestion that no psychiatric testimony may be presented with respect to the defendant's dangerousness is somewhat like asking us to disinvent the wheel" (*Barefoot v. Estelle*, 3396). In essence, the Court reasoned that regardless of how inaccurate the psychiatric expert testimony is, it would represent a veritable overhaul of the legal system to prohibit expert testimony on future dangerousness or remove it as a legal standard. Furthermore, the Court suggested that adversary procedures (i.e., cross-examination and competing experts) would be competent to undo any unfair prejudice caused to the jury by this potentially inaccurate expert testimony. This latter assumption is dubious, given the existing research on jury decision making (this contention is explored later in the section entitled "Research on Jurors' Reactions to Expert Testimony on Future Dangerousness").

Since *Barefoot* (1983), courts have willingly accepted mental health professionals' potentially unreliable testimony on future dangerousness. Yet psychological researchers have strived to develop better methods of predicting future violent behavior and better methods of evaluating predictive accuracy in this domain. Subsequent research has demonstrated that, in fact, unstructured clinical judgments are not as inaccurate as originally believed (see Mossman, 1994, whose meta-analysis found above-chance accuracy for unstructured clinical judgments of future violence), and may even be fairly accurate for some short-term, contextual predictions of violent behavior (McNeil, Sanders, & Binder, 1998). Perhaps most importantly, researchers have developed a number of new prediction techniques that demonstrate superiority to unstructured clinical judgment in forecasting dangerousness.

FORMAL RISK-PREDICTION TECHNIQUES

A variety of methods exist for predicting risk of future dangerousness. As we previously discussed, expert witnesses often use unstructured clinical evaluations as the basis of their dangerousness judgments. Although many experts continue to rely on clinical evaluations, a number of promising alternative techniques that allow for more formal and structured judgments (known as actuarial approaches and guided professional judgments) have been developed.

Actuarial Techniques

Actuarial-based risk predictions of future dangerousness are created from empirically verified risk factors (e.g., past history of violence, psychopathic personality, prior arrests) that have demonstrated the ability to predict the outcome of interest for the population being studied (Monahan et al., 2001). Once risk factors are established, often through longitudinal studies, they are statistically combined in a manner that maximizes their predictive ability. The Violence Risk Appraisal Guide (VRAG) is an actuarial instrument that has garnered substantial empirical support for its accuracy in predicting future violence (Borum, 1996; Harris, Rice, & Cormier, 2002). The VRAG consists of twelve variables: The Hare Psychopathy Checklist (PCL–R), elementary school maladjustment, age of present offense, diagnosis of personality disorder (American Psychiatric Association, *Diagnostic and Statistical Manual of Mental Disorders*, 1980), separation from parents under the age of 16, failure in prior conditional release, criminal history for property offenses, marital status, diagnosis of schizophrenia (DSM–III, 1980), victim injury in present offense, history of alcohol abuse, and female victim in present offense. The VRAG was normed on 618 Canadian mentally ill individuals who had committed at least one serious violent offense. This cohort was followed for 7 to 10 years, with 31% committing a violent act over that time period, and risk factors were subsequently selected and combined in a manner that maximally predicted this group's violent recidivism. A number of studies have found the VRAG's classification accuracy to be high in predicting serious future violent acts, at approximately 75% (e.g., Harris et al.).

Besides the VRAG, a number of other actuarial instruments were developed that are designed to predict individuals' future dangerousness in legal domains ranging from sexual offending (e.g., Static-99, Hanson & Thorton, 2000) to civil commitment. For example, Monahan et al. (2001) used an iterative classification tree (ICT) approach to construct a risk assessment measure for dangerousness among a civilly committed population. The ICT approach allows many different types of risk factors to be combined by asking respondents a series of questions that are dependent on the answers provided to a prior question. Thus, all respondents are asked an initial question. Depending on the answer the given, one of two subsequent questions is asked, the response given for the second question allows one of two third questions to be asked, and so on. Thus, responses to a predetermined sequence of questions allow individuals to be classified into groups based on successive factors that best discriminate between recidivators and nonrecidivators. The ICT approach demonstrated exceptional predictive accuracy (classification accuracy greater than 80%) for both its development and validation samples (Monahan et al.).

Actuarial-based risk predictions of future dangerousness have outperformed unstructured clinical judgments in a number of head-to-head comparisons (see, e.g., Gardner, Lidz, Mulvey, & Shaw, 1996; Harris et al., 2002, for two studies supporting their superiority). Critics have, however, questioned actuarial instruments': (a) generalizability (i.e., their ability to accurately predict behavior in a population dissimilar from the one they were derived from); (b) failure to incorporate very rare but important risk factors (i.e., factors that would not be relevant to a large population of offenders but might be especially significant to particular cases, such as a direct threat of violence); (c) failure to include dynamic factors (i.e., factors that allow for change over time indicating whether an individual's level of risk has increased or decreased, such as successful treatment completion), which is especially important for legal instances that require demonstrating that a defendant is nondangerous before release is possible (e.g., sexually violent predator commitments, civil commitments); and (d) failure to include risk-reducing or protective factors, such as a supportive family; (Krauss, 2004; Monahan, 2003).

Perhaps the strongest criticism of actuarial instruments, however, is that they are unlikely to include an especially predictive factor, such as a verbalized direct threat of violence against a victim. Scholars have contended that it would be inappropriate to ignore such direct threats of violence even though they are not contained in the assessment instrument (Monahan, 2003). The counterargument to this contention is that verbalized threats of violence are not always predictive of conduct (see Krauss, 2005, for discussion of this issue with regard to targeted school violence), nor are other factors that an evaluator might think are especially predictive. Thus, individualized adjustment of the instrument allows the evaluator to engage in the intuitive and potentially unreliable decision making that actuarial instruments are designed to limit (Harris et al., 2002).

Guided Professional Judgment

Based on concerns with actuarial instruments, some researchers have developed risk assessment instruments that combine the benefits of actuarial instruments with the flexibility of clinical judgments. These instruments are commonly referred to as guided professional judgments or aide-memoirs (Webster, Douglas, Eaves, & Hart, 1997). Aide-memoirs can be thought of as checklists that remind the user of relevant factors that have predictive power. Risk factors chosen for these instruments were found in the empirical literature, but had not necessarily demonstrated an independent statistical relationship to risk. These tools do not mandate how each of these factors should be combined for a clinician to reach a decision. The HCR-20 is a guided clinical judgment instrument designed to evaluate risk of future violence. It consists of a checklist of 20 items: 10 assess Historical factors related to risk, five assess Clinical risk factors, and five assess future Risk factors. Each item is scored 0 (absent), 1 (possibly or partially present), or 2 (definitely present). After scoring the 20 items and evaluating protective factors, the evaluator is instructed to intuitively combine the items and assign the individual to low, medium, or high risk (Webster et al., 1997). The HCR-20 has demonstrated significantly above-chance accuracy in a number of studies, and has outperformed unstructured clinical judgments in predictions of future dangerousness (Douglas & Webster, 1999; Douglas, Ogloff, Nicholls, & Grant, 1999).

Yet although these assessment tools allow for greater flexibility than actuarial techniques, guided clinical judgments suffer from many of the same problems that plague unstructured clinical judgment. Assigning nonoptimal weights to factors and combining factors in a subjectively appealing but inaccurate manner are issues that present significant problems for this method, and have led some scholars to suggest that guided clinical judgments are unlikely to be the equals of well-validated actuarial predictions of dangerousness (Quinsey, Harris, Rice, & Cormier, 1998). However, regardless of the weaknesses of the newly developed instruments, there is strong support for the contention that they are more accurate in forecasting future violence than unstructured clinical judgments (Harris et al., 2002; cf. Litwack, 2001).

THE CONTENT OF EXPERT TESTIMONY ON FUTURE DANGEROUSNESS

Notwithstanding the superiority of newly emerging risk assessment tools to more generally predict future violence, their usefulness in addressing particular legal standards remains controversial (e.g., Edens et al., 2005; Miller et al., 2005). Many of the newly developed risk assessment tools were not designed with specific legal standards and outcomes in mind and even instruments that purportedly were, fail to recognize jurisdictional differences in the explicit wording and interpretation of future risk. Legal definitions of risk vary based on: (a) the definitional specificity of risk being predicted (serious violent acts v. any criminal behavior vs. sexual violence vs. no definition); (b) the time period of the risk being assessed (imminent vs. long term vs. no time period specified); (c) the likelihood of the risk (high probability vs. likely); and (d) the requirement of a concomitant mental illness (severe mental illness vs. personality disorder vs. no disorder). These differences also exist within the individual legal standards themselves (e.g., sexually violent predator laws vary markedly from jurisdiction to jurisdiction). As a result, the exact statutory language and judicial interpretation of a jurisdiction's legal standard must be addressed when conducting evaluations and choosing an assessment tool, and assessing risk of future dangerousness in a sexual predator hearing requires the evaluator to address different factors than one conducting a civil commitment evaluation.

Future Dangerousness in Capital Sentencing

To more sufficiently examine the controversy surrounding expert predictions of future risk, it is necessary to examine expert testimony on a specific legal standard in detail, and also to examine the typical expert testimony offered to address it. As a result, the capital sentencing future dangerousness standard is first described, and then what is currently known about typical expert testimony in this domain is summarized.

Of the 38 states that currently allow the death penalty, close to two thirds allow a criminal defendant's future dangerousness to be a factor during capital sentencing (Dorland & Krauss, 2005). The use of future dangerousness in capital sentencing, however, has been incorporated by these states in a number of different ways, including: (a) explicitly listing future dangerousness as a statutory aggravating or a primary sentencing criteria (e.g., Oklahoma); (b) explicitly listing the absence of future dangerousness as a statutory mitigating criterion (e.g., Colorado); (c) allowing prosecutors to argue future dangerousness as a nonstatutory aggravating factor or as a factor jurors may consider (e.g., Alabama); and (d) permitting prosecutors to present future dangerousness in rebuttal to mitigating evidence (e.g., Arizona). (For an extensive discussion of these issues and various state policies, see Dorland & Krauss.) For example, Texas and Oregon both require a finding of future dangerousness before a criminal defendant can be executed, whereas most jurisdictions use an aggravating and mitigating framework in which the criminal defendant will be executed only if the aggravating factors are judged to outweigh the mitigating factors in the jury's mind (Salekin, chap. 7, this vol.). Consequently, expert testimony on future dangerousness is necessarily driven by significant jurisdictional differences in procedures, admissibility, and legal rules. Twenty-one states currently use future dangerousness as some form of aggravating factor, and this serves as the focus of our discussion (Cunningham & Reidy, 1999).

Additionally, although the explicit language of the future dangerousness standard varies little from jurisdiction to jurisdiction, judicial interpretations of this standard do differ. Texas's future dangerousness standard, defined as "whether there is a probability that the defendant will commit future acts of violence that constitute a continuing threat to society" (Texas Criminal Code, 2004), serves as a common prototype for these legal rules. Yet, the federal system interprets "threat to society" as exclusively focused on future prison society, largely because there is no possibility of parole for offenders who are not executed, whereas other jurisdictions include both prison and general society in the interpretation of "Threat to society," even though in these jurisdictions (e.g., Virginia, Oklahoma, and Oregon) there is also no possibility of parole (Dorland & Krauss, 2005). Texas and New Mexico are the only two states that do not have life without parole as a sentencing option (Dorland & Krauss).

There are several probable reasons why states include nonprison society in their future dangerousness interpretations. First, although parole is not available to these inmates, they could be released back into society if their sentence is commuted, they are pardoned, or they escape (although such outcomes are extremely rare). Second, the future dangerousness standard might be viewed as a more hypothetically driven inquiry. States may want to only execute the worst of the worst, and their proxy for this determination is whether defendants would commit additional acts if they were released, regardless of whether they could actually be released (for further discussion of this issue, see the section entitled "The Scientific Foundations and Admissibility of Alternative Risk Assessment Measures").

Expert Testimony in Capital Sentencing

Because of these jurisdictional differences, one might expect that the expert testimony proffered by mental health experts in these cases would vary as well. Surprisingly, there is little data available on the accuracy, frequency, or content of mental health professional expert testimony on future dangerousness in capital sentencing (Cunningham & Reidy, 1999; but see Cunningham & Reidy, 2002, for a brief discussion of expert testimony in federal capital sentencing cases).

What is known about mental health professional expert testimony on future dangerousness is that it is largely an inaccurate predictor of one measure of future violence—that is, serious prison misconduct. A series of studies in Texas found that inmates predicted by expert testimony and court decisions to be a future danger are not more likely to be violent than inmates judged not to be a danger, and that they are substantially less likely than other types of inmates to engage in serious violent acts (see Edens et al., 2005, for an extensive discussion of these studies). Similarly, with regard to prison society, the Edens et al. study of 155 Texas death row inmates found expert predictions of future dangerousness were correct only 5% of the time.

In contrast to the question of accuracy, little is known about the frequency or content of expert testimony in these proceedings. A large number of scholars have argued that mental health professional expert testimony is the most common method of proving future dangerousness in capital sentencing (Dorland & Krauss, 2005). Yet, other than anecdotal reports of mental health professionals proffering outrageous unstructured clinical judgment testimony, as in the *Barefoot* (1983) case where the experts claimed "100%" certainty, and characterized the defendant as an "above 10" on a scale or 1 to 10 of sociopathy, there is currently no information on the type of expert testimony most frequently offered by either prosecution or defense experts (Cunningham & Reidy, 1999). Recent reports and court decisions do, however, indicate that expert testimony based on unstructured clinical judgments is still making its way into the courtroom (APA, 2005; Texas Defender Services, 2004).

EVIDENTIARY ADMISSIBILITY AND FUTURE DANGEROUSNESS

Historically, the *Frye* rule governed the admissibility of scientific expert testimony, and it allowed scientific testimony to be admitted if it "was sufficiently established to have gained general acceptance in the pertinent field in which it belongs" (*Frye v. United States*, 1923, p. 1014). However, in a series of federal evidentiary admissibility cases in the 1990s (i.e., *Daubert v. Merrell Dow Pharmaceuticals, Inc.*, 1993; *General Electric v. Joiner*, 1996; *Kumho Tire v. Carmichael*, 1999, hereinafter referred to as the *Daubert* trilogy of cases), the U.S. Supreme Court ushered in a new era for the admissibility of scientific and expert testimony.

In the initial *Daubert* (1993) decision, the Supreme Court outlined a flexible, nonexhaustive list of factors that judges could use in performing the evidentiary determinations required by its rulings, including evaluating: (a) whether the theory or technique being offered is subject to being tested and has been tested, (b) whether the theory or technique being offered has been subjected to peer review and publication, (c) whether there is a known or potential rate of error in applying the particular scientific theory or technique being offered, and (d) whether and to what extent the theory or technique has received general acceptance in the relevant scientific community. More recently, the Court made clear that the factors outlined in *Daubert* are not required for admissibility decisions, but rather that any factor(s) chosen by trial judges that evaluate(s) the scientific validity of proffered expert testimony is acceptable (*Kumho Tire v. Carmichael*, 1999; for further discussion of these issues, see Sales & Shuman, chap. 2, this vol.).

Thus, subsequent to the Supreme Court's decisions in the *Daubert* trilogy of cases, the following issues were clarified: (a) the *Frye* test no longer controls the admissibility of expert testimony in federal courts, (b) judges are required to adjudicate the admissibility of proffered expert testimony based on the evidentiary reliability or scientific validity of the testimony presented, (c) trial judges are primarily responsible for determining the admissibility of expert testimony and scientific evidence presented at trial (i.e., there is limited appellate review of these decisions), and (d) the judicial duty created by these decisions applies to all expert testimony (Krauss, in press; Krauss & Sales, 1999).

The admissibility framework announced in the *Daubert* trilogy of cases would seem to prohibit the admissibility of unstructured expert testimony on future dangerousness in capital sentencing proceedings, because of the lack of scientific validity associated with such testimony and its notable error rate. However, *Daubert* and its progeny were based exclusively on the Court's interpretation of Federal Rule of Evidence 702, and as a result, apply only to the admissibility determinations of expert testimony in federal courts, which are bound by the Federal Rules of Evidence. Although most states have adopted the majority of the elements of Rule 702, not all have explicitly adopted the Supreme Court's interpretation of that rule or all aspects of the trilogy's decisions (Bernstein & Jackson, 2004; Goodman-Delahunty, 1997). Approximately 27 states have held that the *Daubert* standard was either helpful or controlling in their jurisdictions; 11 states have rejected *Daubert* in favor of retaining *Frye* (e.g., New York, Florida, and California); 5 states have rejected *Daubert* in favor of their own unique evidentiary standard; and 7 states have not yet decisively addressed the question (Hamilton, 1998). Even in those jurisdictions that do follow *Daubert*, it is unclear whether its evidentiary admissibility framework applies to sentencing proceedings (APA, 2005; Krauss & Sales, 2001). Additionally, even if *Daubert* were to apply to sentencing, there is strong evidence that judges have had great difficulty understanding and applying the *Daubert* criteria effectively (Sales & Shuman, chap. 2, this vol.). In fact, one recent survey of judges found that state judges have limited comprehension of several of the *Daubert* factors, and that less than 5% of a surveyed sample clearly understood the concepts of error rate and falsifiability (Gatowski et al., 2001).

One jurisdiction, Texas, has already applied *Daubert* to expert testimony using unstructured clinical judgments to predict future dangerousness at capital sentencing, and strangely found that such expert testimony does meet the *Daubert* admissibility threshold (*Nenno v. State*, 1998). It is not clear whether this decision is a result of misunderstanding of the *Daubert* criteria or based on a justification having little to do with scientific validity (for a more detailed discussion of other justifications that may be involved in a court's *Daubert* decision, see Sales & Shuman, chap. 2, this vol.). More recently, the American Psychological Association (APA, 2005) offered an amicus brief, in *United States v. Fields*, in which the application of the *Daubert* standard to expert testimony in a federal capital sentencing case is at issue. In *Fields*, the unstructured clinical judgment of a psychiatrist was proffered in regard to the defendant's likelihood of future violence in prison. The APA (2005) brief argued that *Daubert* should apply to federal capital sentencing cases because of the heightened need for evidentiary reliability in such proceedings, and that if it were to be applied, the expert testimony based on unstructured clinical judgment offered would fail to meet the *Daubert* standard. A decision on this case is still pending in the fifth circuit, and the eventual decision and reasoning is likely to have a substantial impact on other courts grappling with this issue.

SCIENTIFIC FOUNDATIONS AND ADMISSIBILITY OF ALTERNATIVE RISK ASSESSMENT MEASURES

Although generally outperforming unstructured clinical judgment decisions, actuarial and guided professional judgment instruments also suffer from a number of fundamental problems that make their application to future dangerousness predictions in capital sentencing suspect. The scientific validity of existing actuarial and guided professional judgment instruments has been questioned with regard to their ability to predict violence both in prison society and in society more generally. With regard to prison society, actuarial and guided professional judgment instruments have been criticized for a number of reasons. First these instruments' generalizability to the American prison population and context has been questioned. Most notably, the VRAG was developed on a Canadian mentally ill population that was subsequently released, and it is not clear if this population is sufficiently similar to a death-penalty-eligible, American, secured prison population. In addition, research suggests that risk factors central to violent acts in a prison environment may be substantially dissimilar to those in a nonsecure environment (APA, 2005). Perhaps the best example of this problem is the construct of psychopathy, usually measured by the PCL-R (Hare, 2003), which is a central feature of existing predictive instruments and has demonstrated a significant relationship to violence in the community, but has failed to show a significant relationship to future acts of violence in prison (Edens et al., 2005).

Second, the serious violence predicted by many of these instruments involves many acts that most people may feel are not particularly violent or serious. In order to increase their predictive accuracy, many of the predictive instruments broaden their definitions of violence to include more common but less serious acts. This problem is especially true for actuarial instruments that were specifically designed for prison misconduct, such as the Level of Service Inventory-Revised (LSI-R), which includes acts such as spitting and failure to follow orders (Andrews & Bonta, 1999; Edens et al., 2005). Although the VRAG and the HCR-20 suffer from this problem to a lesser degree, their ability to predict more serious violent acts may be outweighed by their lack of validation on a prison sample.

To address both of these problems, there have been several attempts to create actuarial instruments specific to prison society and serious violence (Cunningham, Sorensen, & Reidy, 2005; Sorensen & Pilgrim, 2000). These instruments have been modestly successful in predicting future violent acts, but it is still questionable whether they can generalize beyond the samples on which they were originally developed. Additionally, given the extremely low base rates of serious violence among the death-penalty-eligible incarcerated population (approximately 5%), it is not clear how much predictive ability is added to an individual case by instruments that are only modestly predictive on a large sample of inmates. Amenta, Guy, and Edens (2003) noted that even instruments with high predictive accuracy will likely cause a large number of false positives in individual cases (i.e., wrongly identifying someone as dangerous when they are not) when predicting low-base rate events, such as serious violent acts. Additional research will be necessary before confidence in these tools' ability to predict future violence in capital sentencing is justified, and before they should survive *Daubert* challenges.

In jurisdictions that define "threat to society" as including elements beyond prison society, the scientific foundation of expert testimony based on guided professional judgment and actuarial instruments is somewhat more promising. It should be noted, however, that all jurisdictions using the future dangerousness standard in capital sentencing require that some assessment of future dangerousness in prison also be made, and that it is constitutionally required that the jury be made aware that the defendant would not be parole eligible if not executed in jurisdictions that have a life without parole alternative sentence (*Simmons v. South Carolina*, 1994). As a result, part of the predictive assessment in these jurisdictions could be viewed as a largely hypothetical one—Is this defendant likely to commit future violent acts in society even though the defendant will not be eligible for release? It should be noted that even though death penalty cases have been used as an example in this chapter, many dangerousness decisions are not hypothetical in nature. For example, in civil commitment hearings for sex offenders, a legal decision must be made whether to release sex offenders back into the community (because they have completed their prison sentence) or to continue to confine the offenders because they represent a danger to the community.

The use of dangerous predictions in death penalty cases represents a unique application of future risk testimony, because if defendants are found to have a high likelihood of future dangerous, they are punished for crimes that will never be committed. This distinction can best be understood by contrasting death penalty dangerousness testimony with other uses of expert testimony regarding dangerousness prediction. For example, in a civil commitment of a sex offender, if defendants are found to be dangerous, they will continue to be confined. Confinement then serves a punishment philosophy of incapacitation (i.e., removing individuals from society, so they can do no harm). However, in a death penalty case, when a defendant is found to have a high likelihood of future dangerousness, and a death sentence is rendered, the punishment philosophy of incapacitation is not better met than if a defendant was held under a life imprisonment sentence. Thus, the additional penalty of death does not satisfy the incapacitation philosophy, or any other punishment philosophy, except for retribution. However, retribution is based on making offenders pay for crimes they have committed. But, in the case of using future dangerousness as a factor in death penalty decisions, defendants are given the additional punishment of death (over life imprisonment) because of hypothetical crimes they will never actually be able to commit (Dorland & Krauss, 2005).

The process of rendering a more severe sentence to a defendant because of the likelihood of being dangerous in future hypothetical crimes may seem nonsensical, but there are several legitimate interpretations that make it less so. First, as previously noted, in rare instances defendants can be pardoned, have their sentence commuted, or escape if not executed. As a result, a lack of parole eligibility does not truly mean that a defendant will never return to society. Second, a legal standard can rely on evaluation of what would happen in the abstract. Given that society may only want to execute the worst offenders, they may decide through their legislatures that they only want to execute those who, if released, would be dangerous, regardless of whether they will be released. The fact that most of the jurisdictions that use this broader definition of society will not define what it means for jurors further substantiates the notion that, rather than a singular interpretation, multiple interpretations of society are intended.

Some have argued that a general society-based interpretation is incorrect and that it is illegitimate to offer expert testimony related to this issue (e.g., Edens et al., 2005). However, the law, and not psychology, gets to choose what outcome is of interest to its determination, and psychologists can choose not to participate if they find the outcome too abhorrent or speculative. Although these tools are likely to be more accurate in forecasting serious violence in the community because of both increases in the base rate of violence and greater similarity of context to their derivation samples, it is still questionable whether they are sufficiently accurate for death penalty adjudications. The predictive accuracy of most of these tools has hovered around AUC = .75, which represents a 75% probability that a randomly selected recidivist will have a higher score on the test than a randomly selected nonrecidivist, but the accuracy has demonstrated substantial decreases when applied to divergent populations (Edens et al.). It was argued elsewhere (Dorland & Krauss, 2005) that this level of accuracy does not justify the use of these tools in future dangerousness capital sentencing hearing—that is, their error rate is too high. No courts to date, however, have applied *Daubert* to the admissibility of expert testimony based on these instruments in capital sentencing, nor have courts made any additional determinations concerning their usefulness in these proceedings.

RESEARCH ON JURORS' REACTIONS TO EXPERT TESTIMONY ON FUTURE DANGEROUSNESS

Given that courts have been willing to admit expert testimony of questionable scientific validity on future dangerousness in capital sentencing proceedings, the question becomes whether jurors are influenced by this unreliable testimony. The answer to this question appears to be a qualified "yes." A number of naturalistic studies in which capital sentencing juries were interviewed suggested that juries spend considerable time discussing future dangerousness, even in the large number of jurisdictions that do not mandate its use during capital sentencing (Blume, Garvey, & Johnson, 2001; Sundby, 1997). For example, in Oklahoma over the past 14 years, approximately 70% of cases that led to execution involved a jury finding that the defendant was a "continuing threat to society" (Dorland & Krauss, 2005). Furthermore, Costanzo and Costanzo (1994) found that future dangerousness was an important concern among jurors who had previously served on different capital murder trials in Oregon. An analysis of interviews with 27 jurors found that their decisions regarding imposing a sentence of life imprisonment or the death penalty were strongly guided by sentencing instructions. The instructions asked jurors to consider three specific issues: whether the crime was committed deliberately, whether the defendants' behavior was unreasonable, in response to any provocation by the victim, and whether the defendants would likely commit future violent acts that would pose a continuing threat to society. Although there was only a small amount of disagreement and discussion for the first two issues regarding deliberate behavior and victim provocation, there was considerable attention paid to the future dangerousness element of the instructions: "Nearly all jurors ... offered the observation that the penalty decision hinged on the issue of whether the defendant would pose a continuing threat to society" (Costanzo & Costanzo, p. 160).

The fact that capital sentencing juries appear to be focused on future dangerousness does not necessarily mean that these juries were unfairly influenced by expert testimony on this topic. Research has produced inconsistent results regarding whether jurors will generally use evidence provided by experts in an appropriate manner (Vidmar et al., 2000). However, there has been some limited empirical data that suggests that in particular, juries are inappropriately influenced by expert testimony on future dangerousness. For example, a series of jury simulation experiments suggested that mock jurors in a Texas capital sentencing proceeding were more influenced by unstructured clinical judgment expert testimony on future dangerousness than they were by expert testimony based on an actuarial assessment instrument. The jurors' bias in favor of the less scientifically valid expert testimony remained after adversary procedures (i.e., cross-examination and defense expert testimony) and deliberations (Krauss & Lee, 2003; Krauss & Sales, 2001).

The apparent appeal of clinical over actuarial testimony may be the product of a natural tendency for individuals to process information in an intuitive, experiential manner rather adopting a more rational and analytic approach. This theoretical explanation involves the application of cognitive-experiential self-theory (CEST; Epstein, 1994; Epstein & Pacini, 1999), which maintains that information can be processed in an experiential mode that is emotionally oriented, rapid, and efficient, and that utilizes heuristic judgments (i.e., preexisting beliefs or mental shortcuts). Information can also be processed in a rational mode that is a more deliberate and abstract system, and that is relatively affect-free and more effortful than the experiential system. Krauss et al. (2004) hypothesized that individuals' tendency to use the intuitively oriented experiential mode as a default system might explain why people are more influenced by clinical testimony (which relies on the clinician's intuitions) over actuarial assessments of dangerousness. However, if individuals were motivated to think rationally, they might be more receptive to the more analytic, probabilistically oriented actuarial testimony.

To investigate this possibility, Krauss et al. (2004) conducted a mock jury study in which participants were directed to adopt either a rational or experiential mode of processing information, and were presented with expert testimony regarding defendant dangerousness in a death penalty case. The conclusions in the testimony were based on either a clinical or actuarial assessment of the defendant. The results demonstrated that rational mode jurors were more influenced by actuarial expert testimony in their dangerousness assessments, whereas jurors in the experiential condition were more influenced by clinical expert testimony. These basic findings were replicated in a recent study examining dangerousness assessments of sex offenders (Lieberman, Krauss, Kyger, & Lehoux, 2005). An important feature of the Lieberman et al. and Krauss et al. studies was that processing mode was manipulated by giving participants explicit instructions to think either rationally or experientially, which were embedded among other jury instructions relevant to the case. As we discuss later, the incorporation of specific instructions provides a mechanism for courts to adopt to motivate jurors to give greater weight to the more reliable actuarial assessments.

In addition to the overutilization of clinical assessments (or underutilization of actuarial assessments), another problem that emerges when jurors are presented with future dangerousness testimony is the impact that heuristic cues may have on their judgments. Previous research has shown that individuals rely on heuristic cues to evaluate and weigh testimony (Cooper, Bennett, & Sukel, 1996; Schuller & Vidmar, 1992), which according to CEST may be the result of utilizing an experiential processing mode (Epstein, 1994; Epstein & Pacini, 1999; Lieberman, 2002). If clinically based dangerousness assessments foster experiential processing because of their intuitive nature, then heuristic cues may be more influential when clinical testimony is delivered. This may cause jurors to be unfairly biased by an expert's introduction of the term *psychopath* during testimony (Edens, Colwell, Desforges, & Fernandez, in press; Edens, Desforges, Fernandez, & Palac, 2004). Several studies have determined that jurors appear to be unfairly prejudiced by such a label, which is especially troubling because psychopathy has not been empirically linked to an important aspect of "continuing threat to society"—future prison violence. Future research is necessary to more fully examine the effects of various forms of expert testimony on juror decision making in capital sentencing, and to determine whether procedural remedies based on psychological theory (i.e., CEST-based jury instructions) can be employed to reduce these biases.

MODIFYING EXISTING LEGAL STANDARDS AND CONCLUSIONS

Clearly, expert testimony on future dangerousness and violence has become an integral part of the U.S. legal system. Yet, as our discussion of expert testimony on future dangerousness in capital sentencing hopefully points out, the use of psychological expertise in these proceedings is questionable at best and may be in direct opposition to the purposes of the legal system. Having created a system that inappropriately uses psychological expertise in important legal decisions, it is necessary that the legal system begin to reexamine whether predictions of future dangerousness or violence are useful components of existing legal standards. Several steps could be taken that might lessen the impact of inappropriate expert testimony or lead to more effective utilization of existing psychological knowledge in this area. First, the legal system needs to be more cognizant of empirical research that suggests that a legal standard is not having its intended effect, and take remedial steps if necessary. The fact that expert testimony commonly used in capital sentencing proceedings is often unreliable and appears to unfairly bias jurors in their decision making should be cause for considerable concern. With regard to expert testimony on future dangerousness in capital sentencing, the most appropriate legal reform may be to simply bar expert testimony on this topic. Such draconian measures may be unnecessary with regard to expert testimony addressing future violence in other legal areas where outcomes are more clearly defined and repercussions of poor decisions are less monumental.

Second, if the legal system is unwilling to disinvent the wheel, it must more clearly define what it intends by its terms, such as "threat to society" and "probability that the defendant will commit criminal acts." Without more useful guidance from legislatures on what these terms mean, it is impossible to scientifically develop and evaluate expertise that might be offered to the court by psychologists. For example, if *society* is simply intended to mean prison society, more effective risk prediction instruments that focus on that context could be further developed and tested (e.g., Cunningham et al., 2005; Sorensen & Pilgrim, 2000). Crystallized definitions would also allow judges to do a more adequate job of adjudicating the admissibility of expert testimony in this area. If the outcome of interest were known, then the judge would have more ability to determine if expert testimony offered in a case met the evidentiary admissibility standards in that jurisdiction. This is especially true with regard to jurisdictions that apply the *Daubert* criteria, because it is quite simply impossible to adjudicate the scientific validity of expertise without a defined outcome. Additionally, definitional clarity would lead to greater uniformity in decisions based on the same standard within and between jurisdictions.

Third, if the legal system is unwilling to pursue either of these options, it might consider either remodeling its procedures or using psychological knowledge that might improve jurors' decisions. For example, jurisdictions could adopt jury instructions or cautionary instructions based on CEST that could limit or even reverse the bias caused by less scientific forms of expert testimony by motivating jurors to process information in primarily a rational mode. From a CEST-based perspective, such instructions would involve specifically directing jurors to think rationally and analytically about the testimony. Instructions could be delivered immediately after the presentation of the testimony or at the same time as procedural and substantive pattern instructions presented at the end of the trial. Because CEST research has shown that individuals default to an experiential mode (Epstein, 1994; Epstein & Pacini, 1999), it may be beneficial to deliver the instructions twice in order to reinforce the adoption of a rational processing mode.

Finally, it is incumbent on mental health professionals to be aware of existing legal standards and the psychological research relevant to them. If mental health professionals refused to testify in jurisdictions in which there is limited scientific validity for their expert testimony, it would force courts to reevaluate the areas in which they are asking for psychological expertise. It is also ethically questionable for psychologists to offer expert testimony that is not supported by relevant facts (Edens et al., 2005). In the end, without psychological experts willing to proffer their expertise, there would be little likelihood that jurors would be unfairly biased by their unscientific opinions, and little likelihood that injustice would result.

REFERENCES

Amenta, A., Guy, L., & Edens, J. (2003). Sex offender risk assessment: A cautionary note regarding measures attempting to quantify violence. *Journal of Forensic Psychology Practice, 3*, 39–50.

American Psychiatric Association. (1980). *Diagnostic and statistical manual of mental disorders, third edtion*. Washington, DC: American Psychiatric Association.

American Psychological Association. (2005). *Brief of amicus curiae in United States v. Fields* Case No. 04-50393 (5th Cir.).

Barefoot v. Estelle, 82-6080, 463 U.S. 880 (Sup. Ct. 1983).

Andrews, D. A., & Bonta, J. L. (1999). *LSI-R:SV level of service inventory revised: Screening version user's manual*. Toronto: Multi-Health Systems.

Bernstein, D., & Jackson, H. (2004). The *Daubert* trilogy in the states. *Jurimetrics, 44*, 1–16.

Blume, J., Garvey, S., & Johnson, S. (2001). Future dangerousness in capital sentencing: Always "at issue." *Cornell Law Review, 86*, 397–410.

Borum, R. (1996). Improving the clinical practice of violence risk assessment. *American Psychologist, 51*, 945–956.

Cooper, J., Bennett, E., & Sukel, H. (1996). Complex scientific testimony: How do jurors make decisions? *Law and Human Behavior, 20*, 379–395.

Costanzo, S., & Costanzo, M. (1994). Life or death decisions: An analysis of capital jury decision making under the special issues sentencing framework. *Law and Human Behavior, 18*, 151–170.

Cunningham, M., & Reidy, T. (1999). Don't confuse me with facts: Common errors in violence risk assessment at capital Sentencing. *Criminal Justice and Behavior, 26*, 20–43.

Cunningham, M., & Reidy, T. (2002). Violence risk assessment at federal capital sentencing: Individualization, generalization, relevance, and scientific standards. *Criminal Justice and Behavior, 29*, 512–537.

Cunningham, M., Sorensen, J., & Reidy, T. (2005). An actuarial model for assessment of prison violence risk among maximum security inmates. *Assessment, 12*, 40–49.

Daubert v. Merrell Dow Pharmaceuticals, Inc., 509 U.S. 579 (Sup. Ct. 1993).

Dorland, M., & Krauss, D. (2005). The danger of dangerousness in capital sentencing: Exacerbating the problem of arbitrary and capricious decision-making. *Law and Psychology Review, 29*, 63–104.

Douglas, K., Ogloff, J., Nicholls, T., & Grant, I. (1999). Assessing risk for violence among psychiatric patients: The HCR-20 violence risk assessment scheme and the psychopathic checklist: Screening version. *Journal of Consulting and Clinical Psychology, 67*, 917–930.

Douglas, K., & Webster, C. (1999). The HCR-20 violence risk assessment scheme: Concurrent validity in a sample of incarcerated offenders. *Criminal Justice and Behavior, 26*, 3–19.

Edens, J., Buffington-Vollum, J., Keilin, A., Roskamp, P., & Anthony, C. (2005). Predictions of future dangerousness in capital murder trials: Is it time to "disinvent the wheel?" *Law and Human Behavior, 29*, 55–87.

Edens, J., Colwell, L., Desforges, D., & Fernandez, K. (in press). The impact of mental health evidence on support for capital punishment: Are defendants labeled psychopathic considered more deserving of death? *Behavioral Sciences and the Law.*

Edens, J., Desforges, D., Fernandez, K., & Palac, C. (2004). Effects of psychopathy and violence risk testimony on mock juror perceptions of dangerousness in a capital murder trial. *Psychology, Crime, and Law, 10*, 393–412.

Edens, J., Petrila, J., & Buffington-Vollum, J. (2001). Psychopathy and the death penalty: Can the psychopathic checklist-revised identify offenders who represent "a continuing danger to society?" *Journal of Psychiatry and Law, 29*, 433–482.

Epstein, S. (1994). Integration of the cognitive and the psychodynamic unconscious. *American Psychologist, 49*, 709–724.

Epstein, S., & Pacini, R. (1999). Some basic issues regarding dual-process theories from the perspective of cognitive-experiential self-theory. In S. Chaiken & Y. Trope (Eds.), *Dual process theories in social psychology* (pp. 462–483). New York: Guilford Press.

Faust, D., & Ziskin, J. (1988). The expert witness in psychology and psychiatry. *Science, 241*, 31–35.

Frye v. United States, 292 F. 1013 (D.C. Cir. 1923).

Gardner, W., Lidz, C., Mulvey, E., & Shaw, E. (1996). Clinical versus actuarial predictions of violence in patients with mental illness. *Journal of Consulting and Clinical Psychology, 64*, 602–609.

Gatowski, S., Dobbin, S., Richardson, J., Ginsburg, G., Merlino, M., & Dahir, V. (2001). Asking the gatekeepers: A national survey of judges of judging expert evidence in the post-*Daubert* world. *Law & Human Behavior, 25*, 433–458.

General Electric v. Joiner, 522 U.S. 136 (Sup. Ct. 1996)

Goodman-Delahunty, R. (1997). Forensic psychological expertise in the wake of Daubert. *Law and Human Behavior, 21*, 121–140.

Grove, W., & Meehl, P. (1996). Comparative efficiency of informal (subjective, impressionistic) and formal (mechanical, algorithmic) prediction procedures: The clinical-statistical controversy. *Psychology, Public Policy, and Law, 2*, 293–323.

Guy, L., & Edens, J. (2003). Juror decision-making in a mock sexually violent predator trial: Gender differences in the impact of divergent types of expert testimony. *Behavioral Science and the Law, 21*, 215–237.

Hamilton, H. G. (1998). Note: The movement from *Frye* to *Daubert*: Where do the states stand? *Jurimetrics, 38*, 201–210.

Hanson, R., & Thorton, D. (2000). Improving risk assessment for sex offenders: A comparison of three actuarial scales. *Law and Human Behavior, 24*, 119–126.

Hare, R. (2003). *The Hare psychopathic checklist-revised technical manual* (2nd ed.). Toronto Canada: Multi-Health Systems.

Harris, G., Rice, M., & Cormier, C. (2002). Prospective replication of the Violence Risk Appraisal Guide in predicting violent recidivism among forensic patients. *Law and Human Behavior, 26*, 377–394.

Heilbrun, K., Dvoskin, J., Hart, S., & McNeil, D. (1999). Violence risk communication: Implications for research, policy, and practice. *Health, Risk and Society, 1*, 91–106.

Kansas v. Crane, 534 U.S. 407 (Sup. Ct. 2002).

Kansas v. Hendricks, 521 Sup. Ct. 2072 (1997).

Krauss, D. (in press). Evaluating science outside the trial box: Applying *Daubert* to the Federal Sentencing Guidelines' Criminal History score. *International Journal of Law and Psychiatry*.

Krauss, D. (2004). Adjusting risk of recidivism: Do judicial departures worsen or improve recidivism prediction under the Federal Sentencing Guidelines? *Behavioral Sciences and the Law, 6*, 731–750.

Krauss, D. (2005). Predicting school violence. In F. Denmark, H. Krauss, P. Wesner, U. Gielen, & J. Midlarski (Eds.), *Violence in schools: Cross-national and cross-cultural perspectives* (pp. 253–275). New York: Plenum/Kluwer Academic.

Krauss, D., & Lee, D. (2003). Deliberating on dangerousness and death: Jurors' ability to differentiate between expert actuarial and clinical predictions of dangerousness. *International Journal of Law and Psychiatry, 26*, 113–137.

Krauss, D., Lieberman, J., & Olson, J. (2004). The effects of rational and experiential information processing of expert testimony in death penalty cases. *Behavioral Sciences and the Law, 6*, 801–822.

Krauss, D., & Sales, B. (1999). The problem of helpfulness in applying *Daubert* to expert testimony: Child custody determination in family law as an exemplar. *Psychology, Public Policy, and Law, 5*, 78–100.

Krauss, D., & Sales, B. (2001). The effects of clinical and scientific expert testimony on juror decision-making in capital sentencing. *Psychology, Public Policy, and Law, 7*, 267–310.

Kumho Tire v. Carmichael, 526 U.S. 137 (Sup. Ct. 1999).

Lieberman, J. D. (2002). Head over the heart or heart over the head? Cognitive-experiential self-theory and extra-legal heuristics in juror decision-making. *Journal of Applied Social Psychology, 32*, 2526–2553.

Lieberman, J. D., Krauss, D., Kyger, M., & Lehoux, M. (2005). *Expert testimony in sexually violent predator cases*. Unpublished manuscript.

Litwack, T. (2001). Actuarial versus clinical assessments of dangerousness. *Psychology, Public Policy, and Law, 7*, 409–443.

McNeil, D., Sanders, D., & Binder, R. (1998). The relationship between confidence and accuracy in clinical predictions of psychiatric patients' potential for violence. *Law and Human Behavior, 25*, 655–671.

Melton, G., Petrila, J., Poythress, N., & Slobogin, C. (1997). *Psychological evaluations for the courts: A handbook for mental health professionals and lawyers*. New York: Guildford Press.

Miller, H., Amenta, A., & Conroy, M. (2005). Sexually violent predator evaluations: Empirical evidence, strategies for professionals, and research directions. *Law and Human Behavior, 29*, 29–54.

Monahan, J. (1981). *The clinical prediction of violent behavior*. Beverly Hills, CA: Sage.

Monahan, J. (2003). Violence risk assessment. In I. B. Weiner (Series Ed.) & A. Goldstein (Vol. Ed.), *The handbook of psychology: Vol. 11. Forensic psychology* (pp. 527–542). Hoboken, NJ: Wiley.

Monahan, J., Steadman, H., Silver, E., Appelbaum, P., Robbins, P., Mulvey, E., et al. (2001). *Rethinking risk assessment: The MacArthur study of mental disorders and violence*. New York: Oxford University Press.

Mossman, D. (1994). Assessing predictions of violence: Being accurate about accuracy. *Journal of Consulting and Clinical Psychology, 62*, 783–792.

Nenno v. State, 970 S.W.2d 544 (Tx. Crim. App. 1998).

O'Connor v. Donaldson, 422 U.S. 563 (Sup. Ct. 1975).

Quinsey, V., Harris, G., Rice, M., & Cormier, C. (1998). *Violent offenders: Appraising and managing risk*. Washington, DC: American Psychological Association.

Schuller, R., & Vidmar, N. (1992). Battered wife syndrome evidence in the courtroom: A review of the literature. *Law and Human Behavior, 16*, 273–291.

Simmons v. South Carolina, 512 U.S. 154 (Sup. Ct. 1994).

Sorensen, J., & Pilgrim, R. (2000). An actuarial risk assessment of violence posed by capital murder defendants. *Journal of Criminal Law and Criminology, 90*, 1251–1270.

Sundby, S. (1997). The jury as critic: An empirical look at how capital juries perceive expert and law testimony. *Virginia Law Review, 83*, 1109–1188.

Texas Criminal Code. (2004). *Texas Code Criminal Procedure* (Article 37.071).

Texas Defender Services. (2004). *Deadly speculations: Misleading Texas capital juries with false predictions of future dangerousness*. Retrieved May 27, 2005, from http://www.texasdefender.org/DEADLYSP.PDF

Tversky, A., & Kahneman, D. (1982). Judgments of and by representativeness. In D. Kahneman, P. Slovic, & A. Tversky (Eds.), *Judgment under uncertainty: Heuristics and biases* (pp. 84–100). New York: Cambridge University Press.

United States v. Salerno, 481 U.S. 739 (1987).

U.S. Sentencing Commission. (1987). *Federal sentencing guidelines manual*. Washington, DC: Westlaw.

Vidmar, N., Lempert R., Diamond, S., Hans, V., Landsman, S., MacCoun, R., et al. (2000). Amicus brief: Kuhmo Tire v. Carmichael. *Law and Human Behavior, 24*, 387–400.

Webster, C., Douglas, K., Eaves, D., & Hart, S. (1997). *HCR-20: Assessing risk for violence*. Burnaby, Canada: Simon Fraser University, Mental Health, Law, and Policy Institute.

11

The Law, Process, and Science of Child Custody Evaluation

Randy K. Otto
University of South Florida
David A. Martindale
State University of New York at Stony Brook

Custody is contested in only a minority of divorce proceedings involving children, and mental health professionals conduct evaluations of parents and children in only a small subset of these contested cases (Maccoby & Mnookin, 1992; McIntosh & Prinz, 1993; Wallace & Koerner, 2003; Otto & Edens, 2003). Yet the high rate of divorce in the United States, the increasing rate of childbirth occurring outside of marriage, and the potential for separated and divorced parents to relitigate custody-related issues until their children enter adulthood combine so that family courts are faced with a large number of cases involving matters of custody (Ostrom & Kauder, 1996; Schepard, 2004).

In this chapter, after a brief overview of child custody law in the United States, the practices of child custody evaluators are reviewed and critiqued, the scientific basis and underpinnings for mental health professionals' involvement in these cases is discussed, the judiciary's response to products delivered by examiners is reviewed, and recommendations for practice are offered.

THE LAW OF CHILD CUSTODY

In his model for forensic evaluation, Grisso (1986/2003) opined that the primary responsibility of mental health professionals conducting forensic evaluations is to richly describe the behavior, capacities, or emotional functioning of the examinee that are relevant to the legal issue(s) before the court. Only by becoming familiar with the relevant law, argued Grisso, will the examiner be able to identify the relevant "psycholegal capacities" that should be the focus of the evaluation. Accordingly, it is with a review of the law of child custody that we begin.

Central to understanding the custody decision-making process is the definition of, and distinction between, different types of custody (Melton, Petrila, Poythress, & Slobogin, 1997; Otto, 2000; Schutz et al., 1989). Custody statutes typically distinguish between decision-making authority for the children (referred to as legal custody or parental responsibility in some jurisdictions) and physical placement or residence of the children (referred to as residential or physical custody in some jurisdictions). In cases of custody, therefore, courts not only decide the living arrangements and visitation schedule for the children postdivorce, but also who will be involved in making important life decisions about them (Gunnoe & Braver, 2001).

Questions of custody and parenting fitness were not heard by American courts until the end of the 19th century because children were considered, according to Common Law, to be property, ownership of which—like all property—was granted to the husband-father postdivorce (Jacob, 1988; Wyer, Gaylord, & Grove, 1987). But custody laws began to change in the late 1800s, likely as a result of two factors. First, legal authorities explicitly acknowledged new conceptualizations of the needs of children, and granted them increasing priority with respect to custody decision making. Second, compulsory education laws, and the move from an agrarian economy to an industrial one, transformed children from economic assets to economic liabilities. As a result, the legal system, which was dominated by males, came to see children as less valuable, and the Common Law rights of fathers became less important.

By the end of the 19th century, the "tender years" doctrine, which held that mothers were uniquely qualified to rear children (*Ex Parte Devine*, 1981; Lyman & Roberts, 1985) was in place and controlled child custody decision making in the United States. Thus, the legal presumption was that children were best served by entering their mothers' custody in cases of divorce (Wyer et al., 1987).

TABLE 11.1
Factors Identified as Important to Consider in State Statutes When Making Custody Decisions

Subject	*Domain*
Child	Age and sex
	Adjustment to current and prior environments, including the length of time in each
	History of child abuse or victimization
	Educational needs
	Special mental health or medical needs
	Wishes or desires regarding placement, if of sufficient age
	Effects of separation of siblings
Parents	History of spouse abuse
	Economic status and stability
	Wishes and desires regarding placement and custody
	Mental and physical health
	Substance abuse
	Level of hostility
	Flexibility
	Parenting skills
	Caretaking involvement before and after separation
Other factors	Religion
	Prior custody determinations
	Agreements between parents
	Any other factors considered to be relevant to the case at hand

The tender years doctrine controlled custody decision making until the 1960s. In response to changing conceptualizations of sex roles and the transition to no fault divorce, the tender years doctrine was challenged as sexist and lacking logic (Horne, 1993). Because women were no longer considered to be better parents due to innate abilities, the tender years doctrine was replaced with the "best interests of the child" standard. This standard, which has been adopted by all U.S. jurisdictions (Artis, 2004; Elrod & Spector, 2004; Hall, Pulver, & Cooley, 1996; Rohman, Sales, & Lou, 1987), directs the judge (and in Texas, the jury) to consider the children's interests to be paramount when making custody-related decisions.

In addition to directing the decision maker to place children's interests first when deciding matters of custody, many states have identified factors that the legal decision maker is to consider when trying to reach a decision regarding the children's best interests. Although these factors vary across jurisdictions, Schutz et al. (1989) identified general consistencies (see Table 11.1).

Although the legislatures' attempts to identify factors worthy of consideration when deciding matters of custody are noteworthy, the relative importance of these various factors and the weight they are to be accorded typically goes unstated. Moreover, many state laws allow the decision maker to consider factors that are not identified by statute, but that are determined to be relevant in the case at hand. Finally, and perhaps most importantly, the large majority of states do not specifically define the child's best interests. This void leaves the decision maker with a dilemma that was summarized well by Mnookin (1975) over a quarter of a century ago:

> Deciding what is best for a child poses a question no less ultimate than the purposes and values of life itself. Should the judge be primarily concerned with the child's happiness? Or with the child's spiritual and religious training? Should the judge be concerned with the economic productivity of the child when he grows up? Are the primary values of life in warm interpersonal relationships, or in discipline and self-sacrifice? Is stability and security for a child more desirable than intellectual stimulation? These questions could be elaborated endlessly. And yet, where is the judge to look for the set of values that should inform the choice of what is best for the child? (pp. 260–261)

The preceding conditions are likely to cause both evaluators and decision makers to weight statutory factors differently, rely on different and idiosyncratic nonspecified factors on a case-by-case basis, and define the best interests of the child in inconsistent ways. This, in turn, is likely to result in a number of bad outcomes, including: idiosyncratic and inconsistent decision making; decreased reliability and predictability of evaluators' recommendations and decision makers' judgments; an increased likelihood of litigating, which, in turn, magnifies acrimony between parties as a result of the adversarial litigation process itself; and limited power of appellate review (Artis, 2004; Charlow, 1994; Crosbie-Currie, 1996; Emery, Otto, & O'Donahue, 2005; Garrison, 1996; Mnookin, 1975; Pearson & Luchesi-Ring, 1983; Weinstein, 1997). As a result of this lack of clarity, in combination with the nature of the questions involved, the legal system has sought the assistance of mental health professionals in the decision process (Feller et al., 1992; Wald, 1976).

THE FAMILY BAR'S PERCEPTION OF MENTAL HEALTH PROFESSIONALS' CONTRIBUTIONS

It is reasonable to assume that lawyers and judges, who regularly seek the assistance of psychologists and other mental health professionals when deciding cases of disputed custody, would consider their contributions to be valuable. Yet the professional literature is replete with critical commentary on the contributions of mental health professionals in this arena. Attorneys, judges, and mental health professionals alike have criticized the expert opinions offered by mental health professionals in custody proceedings as too frequently: based on assessment methods that are either invalid or irrelevant to the issues at hand (e.g., Krauss & Sales, 2000; O'Donahue & Bradley, 1999; Otto, Edens, & Barcus, 2000; Shuman, 2002); grounded in assumptions that lack empirical support (e.g., Goldzband, 1982; Melton et al., 1997); and constituting legal-moral judgments that are covered in a veneer of science (e.g., Emery, Otto, & O'Donahue, 2005; Okpaku, 1976; Shuman, 1997).

The preceding criticisms notwithstanding, few investigators have systematically studied the judiciary's perception of mental health contributions in this area, and the existing work suffers from a number of substantial limitations. The literature that does exist indicates that judges and attorneys are wary consumers when it comes to the custody-relevant opinions offered by mental health professionals (Otto, Buffington-Vollum, & Edens, 2003).

Bow and Quinnell (2004) surveyed Michigan family law attorneys and judges with family court experience. Usable surveys were received from 89 of the 300 attorneys, and 32 of the 124 judges. Seventy-one percent of the judges and attorneys rated custody evaluations completed by court-appointed evaluators (as opposed to those completed by an expert retained by one of the parties) as very or extremely helpful. The most common complaint offered by the judiciary was the length of time it took for evaluations to be completed (26% of judges and 22% of attorneys cited this as an issue). Fifteen percent of the judges also expressed concerns about the evaluators' lack of objectivity, ignorance regarding the relevant legal criteria and standards, and the absence of data to support opinions, conclusions, and recommendations that were sometimes offered. Similar concerns were offered by the attorneys regarding these same issues.

Using a similar approach, Settle and Lowery (1982) surveyed 57 judges and special masters with family law experience. Although these respondents identified custody evaluations as valuable with respect to serving as an efficient means of collecting relevant information about the family appearing before them, "professional advice" was ranked 12th on a list of 20 factors on which custody decisions could be based. In their interviews with 13 family law judges presiding in circuit courts on the west coast of Florida, Kuehnle and Weiner (2000) reported that one of the aspects of custody evaluations most valued by these decision makers was the information-gathering function they served.

A sample of Virginia judges who completed a survey compiled by Melton, Weithorn, and Slobogin (1985) reported finding mental health testimony no more than occasionally useful in cases of contested custody. Felner, Rowlison, Farber, Primavera, and Bishop (1987) reported that only 20% of the attorneys ($N = 74$) and 2% of the judges ($N = 44$) they surveyed considered the recommendations of mental health professionals as one of the five most important factors to consider when deciding cases of contested custody. Finally, Reidy, Silver, and Carlson (1989) reported that the 156 family law judges they surveyed, although they rated the opinions and recommendations of court-appointed examiners as valuable, considered them to be less important than the testimony of the parties or their children.

These criticisms and concerns notwithstanding, the little available research to date indicates that there is considerable agreement that the opinions and recommendations offered by custody evaluators have some impact on judicial decision making. Ash and Guyer (1991) reported that mental health professionals' recommendations regarding custody and placement were followed by judges in 85% of the cases in one jurisdiction, whereas Ackerman and Schoendorf (1992) reported an agreement rate of 90% between custody evaluators' recommendations and judges' decisions. In contrast, Horvath, Logan, and Walker (2002) reported an agreement rate of 64% between evaluators' custody recommendations and court decrees in their survey of 102 custody evaluations completed in a Kentucky circuit. Of course, these above-chance rates of agreement do not necessarily indicate that judges are heavily influenced by the input of mental health professionals because such agreement rates could result if the best outcome in a large number of cases before the court were obvious or without question.

CHILD CUSTODY EVALUATION PRACTICES

With increasing frequency, investigators have devoted energy to examining the child custody evaluation practices of psychologists and other mental health professionals. Most research has been limited to practitioners' responses to anonymous surveys, whereas, more recently, content analyses of professionals' reports have been conducted as well.

Surveys of Reported Practice

In the first study of its type, Keilin and Bloom (1986) described the practices reported by 82 custody evaluators who responded to an anonymous survey, the large majority of whom (78%) were psychologists. Examiners reported spending an average of 19 hours per evaluation, and almost always interviewing the litigating parents and their children. The five factors the subjects identified as most persuasive with respect to custody decision making included the preferences of a teenage child, attempts to alienate the children from the other parent, emotional bonding between the parents and children, parents' psychological stability, and the parents' relative parenting skills. Approximately three quarters of the respondents reported conducting psychological testing with the parents (76%) and children (74%), most reported that they observed parent–child interactions (69%), approximately half reported that they observed the two parents interact with each other, approximately one third reported making home or school visits, and about half of the respondents reported interviewing collateral informants (e.g., friends and relatives) in an attempt to better understand the children and parents who were the subjects of their evaluations.

With respect to assessment of the children, no psychological test was used by a majority of the respondents, but almost half of the mental health professionals reported using intelligence tests in their attempts to better understand the children whose custody was the subject of dispute. The next most frequently used instruments were the Thematic Apperception Test or the Children's Apperception Test (39%), followed by various projective drawing tasks, the Rorschach Inkblot Technique, and the Bender-Gestalt Visual Motor Test. The measure most commonly employed when assessing parents was the Minnesota Multiphasic Personality Inventory (MMPI; 70% reported using this measure), followed by the Rorschach Inkblot Technique (42%), and the Thematic Apperception Test (38%).

A decade later, Ackerman and Ackerman (1997) published the results of a survey sent to 800 doctoral-level psychologists who conducted child custody evaluations, with usable responses being obtained from 201 (25%). The psychologists reported devoting, on average, 21 hours to each evaluation, but indicated spending more time writing reports and reviewing collateral materials than did their predecessors who were surveyed by Keilin and Bloom (1986) 10 years earlier. The five factors the psychologists identified as most persuasive with respect to custody decision making included: parents' use of substances, parents' attempts to alienate the children from the other parent, parents' relative parenting skills, emotional bonding between the parents and children, and parents' psychological stability.

Intelligence tests and projective measures continued to be the instruments most frequently employed by examiners in their assessments of children, and the MMPI or MMPI–2 was the assessment instrument most frequently used with parents, followed by the Rorschach Inkblot Technique. Many evaluators also reported use of assessment instruments with children that were developed for use in custody contexts, all of which have been consistently criticized as lacking in theoretical grounding and psychometric rigor (see, e.g., Emery et al., 2005; Heinze & Grisso, 1996; Otto et al., 2003; Otto, Edens, & Barcus, 2000). More specifically, over one third reported use of the Bricklin Perceptual Scales (Bricklin, 1990a), whereas 16% used the Perception of Relationships Test (Bricklin, 1989). Fewer respondents (11%) used the Ackerman–Schoendorf Parent Evaluation for Custody Test (Ackerman & Schoendorf, 1992), a custody assessment battery. Fewer than 10% reported use of other custody assessment tools such as the Parent Awareness of Skills Survey (PASS; Bricklin, 1990b) and the Custody Quotient (Gordon & Peek, 1989).

Findings similar to these were also reported by Bow and Quinnell (2001), who received usable surveys from 198 of 563 psychologists who conducted child custody evaluations on a regular basis. The psychologists reported devoting between 25 and 29 hours to each evaluation, on average. Almost all respondents described interviewing the parents and children and observing parent-child interactions, half indicated that they interviewed third parties (e.g., family physician, pediatrician, friends, relatives) about the family, and essentially all reported relying on collateral documents of some type. Although the investigators did not report data regarding test selection, they indicated that the majority of evaluators reported use of psychological tests with adults (91%) and children (61%). One third of the psychologists indicated use of home visits, and the majority (78%) indicated that they made some contact with the children's teachers.

Also using a survey approach, Gourley and Stolberg (2000) described the evaluation practices of 21 Virginia psychologists who conducted child custody evaluations and were identified as "highly credible" by family law attorneys in the state. The respondents reported devoting an average of 31 hours to each evaluation, and the large majority indicated reliance on interviews with the parents and children, whereas only 24% reported regularly conducting home visits. Three quarters (76%) of the psychologists reported administering the MMPI–2 to adults. The Child Behavior Check List (parent form) was the next most frequently utilized measure, followed by the Thematic Apperception Test, Rorschach Inkblot Technique, intelligence tests, and projective drawings, (utilized by 57%, 48%, 43%, and 43% of the psychologists, respectively). Six of the twenty-one psychologists (29%) indicated use of at least one of Bricklin's measures. Over 90% of this sample reported assessing the parents' mental health, the children's mental health, parent–child conflict, parental conflict, parenting skills, sibling relationships, and the role of extended family members. These psychologists ranked the following factors as most important when considering issues of custody: the parents' mental health, parenting skills, the children's mental health, parent–child conflict, and parental conflict.

Content Analysis of Custody Evaluations

Bow and Quinnell (2002) provided data based on actual custody evaluation reports—as distinguished from surveys in which mental health professionals reported what they did when conducting such evaluations. In response to queries sent to a convenience sample of 265 psychologists who conducted child custody evaluations, requesting that they send copies of reports they had completed, the investigators received reports from 52. The reports ranged in length from 5 to 63 pages (mean = 24, median = 18). All examiners reported interviewing the parents, and most (92%) referenced interviews with the children as well. The large majority of psychologists completed psychological testing with the parents, observed parent–child interactions (83%), reviewed collateral documents (79%), interviewed parents' significant others (75%), and made independent contact with third parties (85%). Fewer reported conducting psychological testing with the children (39%), completing home visits (35%), and interviewing the parents together (15%). Of those psychologists who used testing with adults, the MMPI–2 was the measure most frequently employed (93%) followed by the MCMI–III (44%). The Parenting Stress Index and Parent Child Relationship Inventory were also used by a majority of the psychologists who conducted testing (59% and 55% respectively), and significant numbers relied on child rating scales as well (using the parents as informants). With children, no test was used by a majority of the psychologists, but two child custody evaluation measures (Bricklin Perceptual Scales, Perception of Relationships

Test) and a number of projective personality measures were referenced in 22% of the reports (representing 55% of the psychologists who used measures with children). Ninety-two percent of the reports included explicit recommendations for physical custody and placement, 85% for legal custody, and 80% for visitation. Twenty-nine percent of the reports included recommendations for a guardian *ad litem* or special master and 15% included recommendations for mediation.

The investigators concluded that the reports, taken as a whole, were comprehensive, not overly test focused, and based on multiple sources of information. Concerns noted by the authors included the examiners' failure to: document the informed consent process (50% lacked such discussion); list documents and sources of information considered (36% of the reports included no such reference); or interview third-party collaterals (15% of the reports included no such information). Perhaps most alarming, however, is the finding that many of the examiners failed to comprehensively investigate and describe the children's adjustment and functioning (50% of the reports did not contain a history of the children).

In the only other published study of actual custody evaluation practices, Horvath et al. (2002) examined 102 custody evaluation reports that were submitted to a Kentucky circuit court by doctoral- and masters-level professionals. Interviews with the father, mother, and new partners (when applicable) were referenced in the large majority of evaluations (all in excess of 89%), observations of the parents interacting with the children were reported in approximately two thirds of the cases, and home visits were referenced in one third of the reports. Interviews with a variety of informed third parties were conducted in a fair number of evaluations, including counselors (31%), teachers (25%), day-care providers (10%), and medical personnel (9%). Although psychological testing was referenced in less than 20% of the reports, significant disciplinary differences were reported. Doctoral-level providers employed some type of psychological testing with 72% of the adults assessed and 48% of the children, whereas significantly smaller percentages of masters-level providers collected this type of data.

The majority of evaluators described the parents' parenting skills (87%), the psychological and developmental needs of the children (80%), and the ability of the parents to meet their children's needs (73%). In over 92% (94 out of 102) of the reports a specific custody recommendation was offered by the examiner, with considerable agreement between the examiners' recommendations and the court findings occurring in 64% of the cases.

Conclusions

A number of conclusions can be drawn regarding the custody evaluation approaches of mental health professionals. First, there appears to be considerable variability in assessment approaches across disciplines, with psychologists being much more likely to employ testing of some type. A fair number of psychologists use tests of questionable validity, including both unstructured projective measures, and tools specifically designed for use in custody evaluation contexts. This literature also indicates that reliance on multiple sources of information is common in custody evaluations, with considerable use of collateral sources that include review of relevant records and interviews with a variety of informed third parties. These data suggest that examiners focus their inquiries on a number of factors, including: the psychological functioning and stability of all relevant persons (i.e., the parents, the children, the parents' significant others); the parents' parenting abilities; the nature of the parent–child relationships; and the nature of the relationship between the parents, including the level of hostility between the parents and their ability to work together on behalf of their children. Finally, this body of research indicates that evaluators are not reluctant to offer opinions on specific legal issues including physical placement, legal decision-making authority, and visitation.

In the abstract, these data indicate that psychologists and other mental health professionals who conduct custody evaluations may well conduct inquiries and gather information about factors that could be relevant to the adjudication of custodial disputes. But the question remains as to whether mental health professionals should be permitted to provide expert opinions in custody proceedings.

SHOULD MENTAL HEALTH PROFESSIONALS PROVIDE EXPERT OPINIONS IN CHILD CUSTODY PROCEEDINGS?

Whether there is a place for psychologists seeking to assist legal decision makers when deciding issues of child custody primarily depends on whether the testimony and opinions they offer meet requirements set out by the law and are based in science. We turn to these issues next.

Evidence Law

Although evidence law varies across jurisdictions, consideration of the relevant Federal Rules of Evidence (FREs) as applied to testimony offered by mental health professionals in custody cases is helpful because many states have adopted rules that are similar or identical.

Perhaps the easiest evidentiary hurdle for proffered expert testimony in cases of child custody is that of relevance (FRE 401). That evidence offered by experts about the children, their parents, their needs, and relationships is relevant to issues before the court in custody cases is without question. FRE 702's requirement that expert evidence and testimony assist the decision maker also appears easily met, providing that psychologists and other mental health professionals have expertise and special knowledge about matters that the court must consider when making custody decisions (e.g., the parents' and children's mental health, the nature and quality of the relationships between the parents and the children, the children's parenting needs and the ability of the parents to meet them; see Table 11.1 above for a summary of factors). Provision of such knowledge and opinions that flow from it, then, will presumably result in more accurate legal decisions.

The most challenging issue is whether expert evidence offered by mental health professionals in custody cases is truly expert. Historically, questions concerning the admissibility of proffered expert evidence were decided using a legal test developed by a U.S. district court. In *Frye v. United States* (1923) the court wrote:

> Just when a scientific principle or discovery crosses the line between the experimental and demonstrable stages is difficult to determine. Somewhere in this twilight zone the evidential force of the principle must be recognized, and while courts will go a long way in admitting expert testimony deduced from a well recognized scientific principle for discovery, the thing from which the deduction is made must be sufficiently established to have gained general acceptance in the particular field in which it belongs. (p. 1014)

The *Frye* test, however, has been criticized as both too conservative and too liberal (Shuman, 2000). In describing it as too conservative, some commentators offered that the *Frye* test may result in inappropriate exclusion of expert evidence that is based on novel, yet valid, techniques and approaches. Yet others argued that the test enunciated in *Frye* is too liberal in that it allows for testimony based on invalid techniques that nonetheless have gained "general acceptance" in the "relevant scientific community."

In *Daubert v. Merrell Dow Pharmaceuticals, Inc.* (1993), the U.S. Supreme Court ruled that the general acceptance test developed in *Frye* (1923) "is not a necessary precondition to the admissibility of scientific evidence under the Federal Rules of Evidence" (p. 2799) and directed that it was the responsibility of the trial judge to ensure that expert evidence be based on an "inference or assertion ... derived by the scientific method" and to determine "whether the reasoning or methodology underlying the testimony is scientifically valid and ... whether that reasoning or methodology can be applied to the facts in issue" (p. 2796). The *Daubert* court identified four factors for judges to consider (and supplement) when making such decisions, including: (a) the "testability" of the theoretical basis for the opinion; (b) the error rates associated with the approach, if known; (c) whether the technique or approach on which the opinion is based has been subjected to peer review; and (d) whether the technique or approach is generally accepted in the relevant scientific community. In a follow-up case—*Kumho Tire Co. v. Carmichael* (1999)—the Supreme Court made clear that the test it promulgated in *Daubert* applied to a broad universe of expert testimony, including testimony like that offered by mental health professionals. Although the federal courts have abandoned *Frye* in light of the Supreme Court's ruling in *Daubert*, there is not a consensus regarding the impact of the Supreme Court's ruling on states' evidence laws. For example, whereas Hamilton (1998) reported that 33 states adopted the *Daubert* approach in some important way, Bernstein and Jackson (2004) offered that no more than 27 states had adopted a test consistent with *Daubert*, whereas only 9 "have either explicity or implicitly adopted the full holdings" (p. 8).

There are no empirical data regarding how frequently expert evidence offered in custody proceedings is challenged, or how often trial judges bar experts at the courthouse door. Anecdotal accounts and personal impressions, however, appear to be essentially unanimous in the perspective that evidence offered by experts in such cases is rarely objected to and even less frequently excluded. Consistent with this, a review of appellate cases suggests that the opinions of mental health experts are rarely excluded from custody proceedings on the grounds that they do not meet the requisite legal standards. Shuman (1997, 2002) offered several possible explanations for this lack of scrutiny, including the judiciary's belief that such protections are not needed in proceedings that do not involve juries (Texas notwithstanding), the fact that family lawyers have no "settled constituency" (i.e., what family law attorneys might challenge in one proceeding might be helpful to them in another), and the frequent use of court appointed experts, whose very appointment constitutes an endorsement or imprimatur by the judge.

Evidence Law and Its Implications for Involvement of Psychologists and Other Mental Health Professionals in Cases of Contested Custody

During the 1992 preelection debates, Admiral James Stockdale, candidate for vice president, took the stage and opened with a question: "Who am I and what am I doing here?" The quality of testimony offered by custody evaluators might improve significantly if evaluators periodically asked themselves that question and searched for a meaningful answer.

Both issues raised by Admiral Stockdale—identity and purpose—were discussed in what is best described as an open letter to psychologists, written in the form of an article by a consumer of psychological expertise, the Honorable Stephen Hjelt (2000). The issue of professional identity was addressed quite directly by Judge Hjelt, who observed that psychologists are representatives of a "profession [with] strong roots as a discipline that has a foundation in the scientific method" (Hjelt, p. 12). Noting that the primary role of experts is to assist the trier of fact, Judge Hjelt issued a strong challenge to psychologists: "You know in your collective heart that there is much that masquerades as professional psychology that is quackery and sham. Expose it and renounce it" (Hjelt, p. 13).

Although answering the question of purpose ("What am I doing here?") appears easily answered, it is not. Further examination reveals this to be a two-part question. With respect to part 1, most experts are aware that their purpose, as defined by law, is to assist triers of fact. With regard to part 2—defining assistance—many judges and many experts would assert that assistance is in the eye of the recipient insofar as experts should provide that which triers of fact request. We disagree.

Just as patients sometimes seek to have prescribed medications that their physicians know to be ineffective and possibly harmful, attorneys and judges sometimes seek advisory input that may lead them astray. With increasing frequency, concern has been expressed that evaluators often become de facto triers of fact (Eaton, 2004; Hunter, 2005; Schepard, 2005; Shuman, 2002) and that judges fail to examine the bases for opinions expressed by the experts who appear before them (*Daubert v. Merrell Dow Pharmaceuticals, Inc.*, 1993). Judge Hjelt (2000, p. 9), presenting a perspective with which no one can disagree, reminded experts and judges that "deference paid to poor testimony logically creates poor judicial outcomes."

Any ambiguity that may have previously existed concerning the defining features of helpful advisory input to courts was removed by the U.S. Supreme Court's reasoning in *Daubert* (1993; also see previous discussion).

In *Daubert*, the Supreme Court described FRE 702 as setting forth a "helpfulness standard" (at 2796). FRE 702, as amended in 2000, declared that expert testimony must be "based upon sufficient facts or data," must be "the product of reliable principles and methods," and must be offered by a witness who has "applied the principles and methods reliably to the facts of the case."

The helpfulness of opinions offered by experts to courts cannot be judged by the scope and quality of the experts' education and training: "The defining attributes of an expert opinion relate not to the credentials held by the individual whose fingers type the words or from whose mouth the words flow; rather, the requisite characteristics relate to the procedures that were employed in formulating the opinion and the body of knowledge that forms the foundation upon which those procedures were developed" (Martindale, 2001, p. 503). No matter how well qualified an expert may be, credentials are of little consequence if the information needed by the court is not contained within the knowledge base of the field in which the expert's credentials have been earned (Tippins & Wittmann, 2005). That admissible expertise is defined not by credentials but by methodology was established by the U.S. Supreme Court in *Kumho* (1999). In upholding an Alabama court's rejection of testimony proffered by an expert, the Supreme Court noted that "the District Court did not doubt [the expert's] qualifications.... Rather, it excluded the testimony because, despite these qualifications, it initially doubted, and then found unreliable, 'the methodology employed by the expert'" (at 153).

Psychological Science and Child Custody Decision Making

Kelly and Johnston (2005) wrote that there is an "existing body of empirical literature on divorce, parenting, child development, and children's emotional and social adjustment" that can be used "for purposes of formulating questions to guide the collection of data, and for making inferences and recommendations" in cases of contested child custody (pp. 233–234). These authors, however, lamented that too few evaluators draw on the empirical literature as they make decisions concerning the procedures that they will employ in conducting evaluations. In contrast, some writers (e.g., O'Donahue & Bradley, 1999) opined that not enough is known about the innumerable factors affecting children's best interests to justify mental health professionals offering advisory input that is genuinely helpful, that the assistance offered is illusory, and that we should refrain from conducting evaluations in child custody disputes as a result. Yet others, while expressing considerable concern over the product delivered by mental health professionals who evaluate parents and children in the context of custody disputes, offered a less polemic perspective (cf. Emery et al., 2005; O'Donahue & Bradley). What are we to do? Gould and Martindale (2005) opined: "Knowledge is derived through inquiry and professional activity stimulates inquiry. If mental health professionals stop performing custody evaluations, the interactions that catalyze empirical research will not occur and no progress will be seen. If we are to provide the assistance that the legal system seeks, we must persevere, but as we do so, we must be mindful of our limitations and must respond to the call for clinical humility by articulating those limitations" (p. 258). All seem to agree that there is a place for psychologists and other mental health professionals in custody proceedings, providing the opinions they offer are the product of specialized expertise and are science based. Although the nature and scope of this chapter preclude us from reviewing all that psychological science tells us about matters relevant to custody decision making (see Emery et al., 2005; Kelly & Johnston, 2005; Otto et al., 2003, for such discussion), we offer here a template that mental health and legal professionals alike can employ when considering such testimony.

Mental health professionals can offer expert assistance to the court considering matters of child custody in two primary ways. Using an analysis offered by psychologist and law professor Stephen Morse (Morse, 1978) and elaborated by Melton et al. (1997), mental health professionals can play a useful role in custody proceedings to the degree that they are able to gather information and make available to the decision maker information that it would not otherwise have but that is relevant to the legal issues to be decided. In this way, truly expert mental health professionals have knowledge about parents, children, parent–child relationships, parenting, and family functioning that allows them to gather and present information relevant to custody decision making that laypersons do not. In this capacity the mental health professional serves an expert information-gathering function that, narrowly construed, is free of opinion, but the product of expertise nonetheless.

In addition, truly expert mental health professionals may know something about parents, children, parent–child relationships, parenting, and family functioning that allows them to offer opinions about likely outcomes that may be expected given particular custody arrangements. Here, truly expert opinions are offered, and these expert opinions may or may not be based on observations that result from special expertise as well. But involvement in either of these capacities is only appropriate when there is true expertise and specialized knowledge. For each data-gathering technique to be employed or each opinion to be offered, evaluators, expert witnesses, attorneys, and judges alike should consider the scientific basis. Use of a particular data-gathering information approach (e.g., employing a specific psychological test) or the offering of an opinion (e.g., regarding what kinds of child outcomes a particular parenting style is associated with, regarding the special needs of a child with a specific learning disability, regarding the impact of intense parental conflict on children's emotional adjustment and well-being) is appropriate, providing there is appropriate scientific support for its use.

Some Special Problems

Psychological Testing and the Human Preference for Hard Data. Despite ongoing debates concerning the usefulness of the data obtained through the administration of formal assessment instruments, the considerable survey and report review data cited earlier indicate that psychological tests are used by the vast majority of psychologists who conduct child custody evaluations, and other mental health professionals engaged in this work frequently have psychological tests administered for them by psychologists. How do we and how should we gauge the reliability and validity of our test data?

In those rare cases in which the methods employed by a custody evaluator are challenged by means of motions *in limine*, some states employ the *Frye* (1923) standard (or a variant thereof) and some states employ the *Daubert* (1993) criteria. If we limit our discussion to the more basic *Frye* standard, in *Jones v. United States* (1988), the court pointed out that *Frye*'s general acceptance standard directs the gatekeeper's attention to a simple nose count of professionals and their practice, and does not require that methodological integrity be examined. In considering the assessment devices employed by custody evaluators, this distinction is of critical importance. Frequency of use (an indicator of acceptance) cannot be interpreted as evidence of psychometric integrity. Two common human weaknesses affect mental health professionals as they select assessment instruments. One is the tendency to continue doing that which one has done in the past; the other is the susceptibility to skillful marketing. With regard to the first, the vast majority of mental health professionals conducting evaluations of comparative custodial fitness were initially trained as therapists. Some have brought to forensic matters assessment instruments that they found useful in their therapeutic work without contemplating the many ways in which the evidentiary demands of forensic work make these instruments inappropriate. Although yet unrealized (see previous discussion), *Daubert*, its progeny, and the reasoning underlying them have the potential to make an impact in this area. That is, if mental health professionals fail to meet their professional duties by continuing to offer opinions in custody proceedings that are based on assessment techniques that have an inadequate scientific foundation, then judges and attorneys can meet their professional duties by using the tests and method laid out in *Daubert* to bar these scienceless opinions.

With regard to susceptibility to marketing, two decades ago, Lanyon (1984) opined that "consumer professionals are generally unable to discriminate among [the various available instruments] and are predisposed to believe whatever is printed" (p. 690). There is no indication that, in the last two decades, test purchasers have become more skeptical consumers of measures that are published, and the effects of vigorous marketing can be seen in the popularity of some of the custody assessment instruments, essentially all of which have been the subject of negative reviews and little, if any, convincing research. In a concurring opinion in *People v. Wesley* (1994), New York's Cheif Judge, Judith Kaye, offered a perspective on controversy (and its absence) that is applicable to the selection of assessment instruments by custody evaluators. Kaye observed that an absence of controversy may reflect nothing more than the fact that criticism does not emerge over night. Her observation explains the general acceptance of psychometrically unsound instruments.

Gould-Saltman (2005), an experienced family law attorney, expressed the view that attorneys like tests because they "break things down to numbers, and we understand numbers ... tests give the sense of objectivity to counterbalance the much more subjective clinical portion of a custody evaluation" (p. 71). If only it were this simple.

Ongoing Reliance on Clinical Intuition. Just as problematic as the false reassurance and comfort that the scientific patina created by "tests with numbers" allows some consumers (i.e., judges and attorneys) to enjoy is the skepticism of true scientific rigor offered by some who offer expert testimony. Calloway (2002) declared that "when forensic rigor is overly applied ... clinical intuition, hunches, expertise, methods, and techniques are castigated as inherently inferior" (p. 216). One evaluator's clinical intuition is another's hokum. Clinical insights, hunches, and intuition should not qualify as opinions, or as the basis of opinions, that an expert is expressing with a reasonable degree of professional certainty.

Blurring of Roles. Though survey data referenced earlier shed some light on those components of the custody evaluation process that are deemed most useful by judges, there is no way of knowing what contributes to or detracts from the persuasive power of a testifying witness. There is reason for concern that judges may be swayed by perceived sincerity. Unfortunately, crusaders come cloaked in sincerity and some of the most egregious procedural errors have been made by evaluators describing themselves as passionately concerned about the well-being of children (Bruck & Ceci, 1995; Treacy, 1991). Treating therapists also tend to convey sincerity, but, with only rare exceptions, their advisory input is limited as a function of their role. In explaining these limitations, Shapiro (1988, p. 84) noted, "The skepticism, distance, and objectivity necessary to perform a comprehensive forensic evaluation" are not present in a therapeutic relationship. The desire to blend helping efforts with investigative efforts creates a significant risk that neither task will be handled appropriately (Greenberg & Shuman, 1997), and Ceci and Hembrooke (1998, p. 4) expressed the view that "the uniquely human qualities that compel us to want to help are the very qualities that can make us poor experts."

Although no survey data are available, judges in some jurisdictions accept expert testimony from mental health professionals who, prior to evaluating the litigating parties, have overseen conciliation efforts (Strochak, 2002). Assisting litigating parents in constructing a parenting agreement, thereby obviating the need for further court involvement, is a worthwhile goal but it is a goal that is inconsistent with the goal of conducting an evaluation. Efforts aimed at constructing a parenting plan require that each parent focus on the other's strengths. An evaluator must focus on strengths and deficiencies. Any procedure that encourages a mind-set that will lead to an emphasis either on strengths or on deficiencies creates a risk that not all the needed information will be provided.

Similarly, in some jurisdictions, judges accept expert testimony from evaluators who have taken "the opportunity to do some vital educating during the process" (Trubitt, 2004, p. 9). We cannot simultaneously evaluate people's parenting skills while endeavoring to assist them in improving those skills. The unfortunate irony is that evaluators who do more than that which they were assigned to do are sometimes perceived as being more caring and this perceived quality often enables such evaluators to be quite persuasive.

The Limits of Expertise and the Resulting Importance of Humility in the Courtroom

Gross and Mnookin (2003) opined, "One of the central problems with much expert testimony introduced in court—both scientific and nonscientific alike—is that experts claim as matters of fact or probability opinions that should be couched in more cautious terms, as possibilities or hypotheses" (p. 143). What must be addressed is the unfortunate reality that courts often encourage experts to confidently testify to inferences that go well beyond those that can responsibly be drawn based on available data. Judges seeking answers in the adjudication of custody disputes may be more receptive to hearing from experts who confidently claim that they have the answers than to experts who acknowledge that the answers are elusive. Particularly where the issues are complex, the expert who offers facile solutions may be perceived as most helpful, whereas the expert who declines to speculate may be considered to be uncooperative (Gould & Martindale, 2005).

RECOMMENDED SYSTEM CHANGES

Psychologists and other mental health professionals are ultimately responsible for the product they deliver to the courts. Those offering expert testimony in the context of divorce and custody proceedings would better serve the families they evaluate, attorneys, and judges if they: only employed assessment and data-gathering techniques with demonstrated reliability and validity, limited opinions they offered to those for which there was empirical support, refrained from offering opinions on moral-legal matters that may enter custody decision making, and were wholly candid in representing the scientific basis for the techniques they employed and the opinions they offered. These practice principles could be better embraced and adhered to. In addition, although there is much that we do know about divorce, custody arrangements, and their effects on children (see, e.g., Emery et al., 2005; Kelly & Johnston, 2005; Otto et al., 2003), there remains much that we need to learn more about, including the true impact of varying custody arrangements on children and differential impacts of divorce on children and their families.

Although mental health professionals who participate in the divorce and custody process should meet the requirements set forth earlier, they sometimes do not. In such cases, the consumers of these forensic services—judges and attorneys—must hold their feet to the fire. This requires, of course, that attorneys and judges better understand what experts do and do not know, and what they can and cannot say. It is judges and attorneys that are the ultimate gatekeepers, and when mental health professionals who involve themselves in legal proceedings fail to meet what professional ethics, practice standards, and the law require of them, then the legal system must take appropriate action, both in the interests of justice, and for the families that are to be served.

REFERENCES

Ackerman, M. J., & Ackerman, M. C. (1997). Custody evaluation practice: A survey of experienced professionals (revisited). *Professional Psychology: Research and Practice*, *28*, 137–145.

Ackerman, M. J., & Schoendorf, K. (1992). *Ackerman-Schoendorf Scales for Parent Evaluation of Custody Manual.* Los Angeles: Western Psychological Services.

Artis, J. E. (2004). Judging the best interests of the child: Judges' accounts of the tender years doctrine. *Law and Society Review*, *38*, 769–786.

Ash, P., & Guyer, M. J. (1991). Biased reporting by parents undergoing child custody evaluations. *Journal of The American Academy of Child and Adolescent Psychiatry*, *30*, 835–838.

Bernstein, D. E., & Jackson, J. D. (2004). The *Daubert* trilogy in the states. *Jurimetrics*, *44*, 1–17.

Bow, J. N., & Quinnell, F. A. (2001). Psychologists' current practices and procedures in child custody evaluations: Five years after American psychological association guidelines. *Professional Psychology: Research and Practice*, *132*, 261–268.

Bow, J. N., & Quinnell, F. A. (2002). A critical review of child custody evaluation reports. *Family Court Review*, *40*, 164–176.

Bow, J. N., & Quinnell, F. A. (2004). Critique of child custody evaluations by the legal profession. *Family Court Review*, *42*, 115–127.

Bricklin, B. (1989). *Perception of Relationships Test.* Furlong, PA: Village Publishing.

Bricklin, B. (1990a). *Bricklin Perceptual Scales.* Furlong, PA: Village Publishing.

Bricklin, B. (1990b). *Parent Awareness of Skills Survey.* Furlong, PA: Village Publishing.

Bruck, M., & Ceci, S. J. (1995). Amicus brief for the case of *State of New Jersey v. Michaels* presented by committee of concerned social scientists. *Psychology, Public Policy, and Law*, *1*, 242–322.

Calloway, G. (2002, April). *When forensic rigor is overly applied.* Paper presented at the Fifth International Symposium on Child Custody Evaluations and the Fifth International Congress on Parent Education and Access Programs, Madison, WI.

Ceci, S. J., & Hembrooke, H. (1998). *Expert witnesses in child abuse cases: What can and should be said in court.* Washington, DC: American Psychological Association.

Charlow, A. (1994). Awarding custody: The best interests of the child and other fictions. In S. R. Hummetal (Ed.), *Child, parent, and state: Law and policy reader* (pp. 3–37). Philadelphia: Temple University Press.

Crosby-Currie, C. A. (1996). Children's involvement in contested custody cases: Practices and experiences of legal and mental health professionals. *Law and Human Behavior, 20*, 289–311.

Daubert v. Merrell Dow Pharmaceuticals, Inc., 509 U.S. 579 (1993).

Eaton, L. (2004, May 23). For arbiters in custody battles: Wide power and little scrutiny. *The New York Times*, p. 1.

Elrod, L. D., & Spector, R. G. (2004). A review of the year in family law: Children's issues remain the focus. *Family Law Quarterly, 37*, 527–575.

Emery, R., Otto, R. K., & O'Donahue, W. (2005). A critical assessment of child custody evaluations: Limited science and a flawed system. *Psychological Science in the Public Interest, 6*, 1–29.

Ex Parte Devine, 398 So.2d 686 (ALA, 1981).

Feller, J. N., Davidson, H. A., Hardin, M., & Horowitz, R. M. (1992). *Working with the courts in child protection*. Washington, DC: U.S. Department of Health and Human Services.

Felner, R. D., Rowlison, R. T., Farber, S. S., Primavera, J., & Bishop, T. A. (1987). Child custody resolution: A study of social science involvement and impact. *Professional Psychology: Research and Practice, 5*, 468–474.

Frye v. United States, 293 F. 1013 (D.C. Cir. 1923).

Garrison, M. (1996). How do judges decide divorce cases? An empirical analysis of discretionary decision making. *North Carolina Law Review, 74*, 401–552.

Goldzband, M. (1982). *Consulting in child custody*. Lexington, MA: Lexington Books.

Gordon, R., & Peek, L. A. (1989). The Custody Quotient. *Research Manual*. Dallas, TX: Wilmington Institute.

Gould, J. W., & Martindale, D. A. (2005). A second call for clinical humility and judicial vigilance: Comments on Tippins and Wittmann. *Family Court Review, 43*, 253–259.

Gould-Saltman, D. (2005). Testing, one, two, three, testing: An attorney perspective. *Journal of Child Custody, 2*, 71–82.

Gourley, E. V., & Stolberg, A. L. (2000). An empirical investigation of psychologists' custody evaluation practices. *Journal of Divorce and Remarriage, 33*,1–29.

Greenberg, S. A., & Shuman, D. (1997). Irreconcilable conflict between therapeutic and forensic rules. *Professional psychology: Research and Practice*, 50–63

Grisso, T. (1986). *Evaluating competencies: Forensic assessments and instruments*. New York: Plenum.

Grisso, T. (2003). *Evaluating competencies: Forensic assessments and instruments* (2nd ed.). New York: Kluwer/Plenum.

Gross, S. R., & Mnookin, J. L. (2003). Expert information and expert evidence: A preliminary taxonomy. *Seton Hall Law Review, 34*, 140–185.

Gunnoe, M. L., & Braver, S. L. (2001). The effects of joint legal custody on mothers, fathers, and children controlling for factors that predispose a sole maternal versus joint legal award. *Law and Human Behavior, 25*, 25–43.

Hall, A. S., Pulver, C. A., & Cooley, M. J. (1996). Psychology of the best interests standard: Fifty state statutes and their theoretical antecedents. *American Journal of Family Therapy, 24*, 171–180.

Hamilton, H. G. (1998). The movement from *Frye* to *Daubert*: Is a pattern unfolding? *Jurimetrics, 35*, 191–212.

Heinze, M., & Grisso, T. (1996). Review of instruments assessing parenting competencies used in child custody evaluations. *Behavioral Sciences and the Law, 14*, 293–313.

Hjelt, S. (2000). Professional psychology: A view from the bench. *Register Report, 26*, 8–13.

Horne, J. E. (1993). The Brady Bunch and other fictions: How courts decide child custody disputes involving remarried parents. *Stanford Law Review, 45*, 2074–2142.

Horvath, L. S., Logan, T. K., & Walker, R. (2002). Child custody cases: A content analysis of evaluations in practice. *Professional Psychology: Research and Practice, 33*, 557–565.

Hunter, L. (2005). Introduction to the symposium issue on child custody evaluations. *Family Court Review, 43*, 191–192.

Jacob, H. (1988).*Silent revolution: The transformation of divorce law in the United States*.Chicago: University of Chicago Press.

Jones v. United States, 548 A.2d 35 (D.C. App. 1988).

Keilin, W. G., & Bloom, L. J. (1986). Custody evaluation practice: A survey of experienced professionals. *Professional Psychology: Research and Practice, 17*, 338–346.

Kelly, J. B., & Johnston, J. R. (2005). Commentary on Tippins and Wittmann's "Empirical and ethical problems with custody recommendations: A call for clinical humility and judicial vigilance." *Family Court Review, 43*, 233–241.

Krauss, D. A., & Sales, B. D. (2000). Legal standards, expertise, and experts in the resolution of contested child custody cases. *Psychology, Public Policy, and Law, 6*, 843–879.

Kuehnle, K., & Weiner, I. (2000). *A survey of judges' opinions regarding child custody evaluations*. Unpublished manuscript.

Kumho Tire Co. v. Carmichael, 526 U.S. 137 (1999).

Lanyon, R. I. (1984). Personality assessment. *Annual Review of Psychology, 35*, 689–701.

Lyman, R. D., & Roberts, M. C. (1985). Mental health testimony in child custody litigation. *Law and Psychology Review, 9*, 15–34.

Maccoby, E., & Mnookin, R. (1992). *Dividing the child: Social and legal dilemmas of custody*. Cambridge, MA: Harvard University Press.

McIntosh, J. A., & Prinz, R. J. (1993). The incidence of alleged sexual abuse in 603 family court cases. *Law and Human Behavior, 17*, 95–101.

Martindale, D. A. (2001). Cross-examining mental health experts in child custody litigation. *Journal of Psychiatry and Law, 29*, 483–511.

Melton, G. B., Petrila, J., Poythress, N., & Slobogin, C. (1997). *Psychological evaluations for the courts: A handbook for mental health professionals and attorneys* (2nd ed.). New York: Guilford Press.

Melton, G. B., Weithorn, L. A., & Slobogin, C. (1985). *Community mental health centers and the courts: An evaluation of community-based forensic services*. Lincoln: University of Nebraska Press.

Mnookin, R. (1975). Child custody adjudication: Judicial functions in the face of indeterminacy. *Law and Contemporary Problems, 39*, 226–293.

Morse, S. (1978). Law and mental health professionals: The limits of expertise. *Professional Psychology, 9*, 389–399.

O'Donahue, W., & Bradley, A. (1999). Conceptual and empirical issues in child custody evaluations. *Clinical Psychology: Science and Practice, 6*, 310–322

Okpaku, S. (1976). Psychology: Impediment or aid in child custody cases? *Rutgers Law Review, 29*, 1117–1153.

Ostrom, B. J., & Kauder, N. B. (1996). *Examining the work of state courts, 1995: A national perspective from the court statistics project*. Williamsburg, VA: National Center for State Courts.

Otto, R. K. (2000). *Child custody evaluation: Law, ethics, and practice*. Tampa, FL: Louis De LaParte Florida Mental Health Institute.

Otto, R. K., Buffington-Vollum, J., & Edens, J. F. (2003). Child custody evaluation: Research and practice. In A. Goldstein (Ed.), *Forensic psychology* (pp. 179–208). New York: Wiley.

Otto, R. K., & Edens, J. F. (2003). Parenting capacity. In T. Grisso (Ed.), *Evaluating competencies: Forensic assessments and instruments* (2nd ed., pp. 229–308). New York: Kluwer/Plenum.

Otto, R. K., Edens, J. F., & Barcus, E. (2000). The use of psychological testing in child custody evaluations. *Family and Conciliation Courts Review, 38*, 312–340.

People v. Wesley, 83 N.Y.2d 417, 633 N.E.2d 451, 611 N.Y.S.2d 97 (1994).

Pearson, J., & Luchesi-Ring, M. A. (1983). Judicial decision-making in contested custody cases. *Journal of Family Law, 21*, 703–724.

Reidy, T., Silver, R., & Carlson, A. (1989). Child custody decisions: A survey of judges. *Family Law Quarterly, 23*, 75–87.

Rohman, L., Sales, B., & Lou, M. (1987). The best interests of the child in custody disputes. In L. Weithorn (Ed.), *Psychology and child custody determinations* (pp. 59–105). Lincoln: University of Nebraska Press.

Schepard, A. I. (2004). *Children, courts, and custody: Interdisciplinary models for divorcing families*. New York: Cambridge University Press.

Schepard, A. (2005). Mental health evaluations in child custody disputes. *Family Court Review, 43*, 187–190.

Schutz, B., Dixon, E., Lindenberger, J., & Ruther, N. (1989). *Solomon's sword: A practical guide to conducting child custody evaluations*. San Francisco: Jossey-Bass.

Settle, S. A., & Lowery, C. R. (1982). Child custody decisions: Content analysis of a judicial survey. *Journal of Divorce, 6*, 125–138.

Shapiro, D. L. (1988). Ethical constraints in forensic settings: Understanding the limits of our expertise. *Psychotherapy in Private Practice, 6*, 71–86.

Shuman, D. W. (1997). What should we permit mental health professionals to say about "the best interests of the child?" An essay on common sense, *Daubert*, and the rules of evidence. *Family Law Quarterly, 31*, 551–569.

Shuman, D. W. (2000). *Psychiatric and psychological evidence*. Minneapolis: West Group.

Shuman, D. W. (2002). The role of mental health experts in custody decisions: Science, psychological tests, and clinical judgment. *Family Law Quarterly, 36*, 135–162.

Strochak, R. (2002, January). *A conciliation/evaluation model for child custody determination*. Workshop presented at the workshop of the American Academy of Forensic Psychology, New Orleans, LA.

Tippins, T. M., & Wittmann, J. P. (2005). Empirical and ethical problems with custody recommendations: A call for clinical humility and judicial vigilance. *Family Court Review, 43*, 193–222.

Treacy, E. (1991, October). Untitled presentation at the Conference on Child Sexual Abuse, New York.

Trubitt, A. (2004) *Play therapy goes to court: Implications and applications in contested child custody* (2nd ed.). Kailua, HI: Author.

Wald, M. (1976). State intervention on behalf of "neglected" children: A search for realistic standards. In M. Rosentteim (Ed.), *Pursuing justice for the child* (pp. 246–278). Chicago: University of Chicago Press.

Wallace, S. R., & Koerner, S. S. (2003). Influence of child and family factors on judicial decisions in contested custody cases. *Family Relations*, *52*, 180–188.

Weinstein, J. (1997). And never the twin shall meet: The best interests of children and they adversary system. *University of Miami Law Review*, *52*, 79–175.

Wyer, M., Gaylord, S., & Grove, E. (1987). The legal context of child custody evaluations. In L. Weithorn (Ed.), *Psychology and child custody determinations* (pp. 4–22). Lincoln: University of Nebraska Press.

12

Pitfalls and Ethics of Expert Testimony

Michael J. Saks
Richard I. Lanyon
Arizona State University

A great deal that is illuminating and helpful has already been written about the challenges of being an expert witness and how to try to meet those challenges. (e.g., American Academy of Psychiatry and Law, 2005; American Psychology-Law Society, 1991; Anderten, Staulcup, & Grisso, 1980; Appelbaum, 1987; Brodsky, 1991, 1999; Haddad, 1979; Ogloff, 1999; Saks, 1990; Shuman & Greenberg, 2003; Wrightsman & Fulero, 2005). In one brief chapter we cannot hope to summarize, surpass, or supplant that literature. What we can do is alert the reader to issues, steer the reader to some of the answers, and highlight some of the most vexing problems.

This chapter is organized into two parts. The first focuses on the notion that the role of the expert witness in modern Anglo-American trials is fundamentally paradoxical. To maintain one's ethical posture in the midst of the role conflict into which the expert has been thrown requires an understanding of the dimensions of this conflict and of the impossibility of a complete solution. The second part focuses on the notion that the way to avoid most of the pitfalls awaiting experts is to be well prepared as a professional, for the task in general, and for the task as it presents itself in each individual case.

THE ETHICALLY DEMANDING ROLE OF THE EXPERT WITNESS

The expert witness is caught in a tug-of-war between what the formal rules expect of the role and the dominant messages sent by the structure of the process. Formally, expert witnesses, like all witnesses, serve the fact finder, not the parties. This is implicit in the various procedural and evidentiary rules that govern the trial, but is perhaps made most plain in the rule that all witnesses, including expert witnesses, must take an oath to tell the "the truth, the whole truth, and nothing but the truth." Expert witnesses are required, as they mount the witness stand, to undertake that obligation. Advocates are placed under no similar obligation to affirmatively help the court develop a complete and accurate picture of the relevant facts. (Lawyers have a different obligation: to help the court correctly understand what the applicable law is.) On the other hand, because expert witnesses are selected, prepared, befriended, and paid by counsel for one side, the experts' sense of who they are serving becomes confused and conflicted. In short, experts are placed in a situation of role conflict. The bind they are in today did not always exist, and continues not to exist for court-appointed experts.

Before further exploring this role conflict and its implications, we must say something more general and historical about the rules of evidence and of trial procedure. Our legal system has an exclusionary system of rules of evidence, that is to say, the rules of evidence work mainly by filtering out certain kinds. Examples include: evidence not logically relevant to the law at issue, character evidence, repairs after an accident, settlement discussions, hearsay, and insufficiently well-grounded expert testimony, among many others. For a century the dominant view of the origin of our legal system's extensive evidence rules had been that it is a product of the jury system. This conclusion was based on the observation that complex rules of evidence existed in the Anglo-American system but not in the civil law system that developed in continental Europe. The jury was a prominent feature of the former system but not the latter, so the theory developed that the existence of juries of lay decision makers required more careful screening of evidence, lest the jurors draw incorrect conclusions from evidence. Thus, detailed rules of evidence developed (one might say overdeveloped) where there were juries.

But more recent comparative evidence scholarship has reached a different conclusion. This more recent scholarship noted that the Anglo-American trial system had used juries for centuries before exclusionary evidence rules evolved. Why did such rules of evidence materialize relatively suddenly between 1750 and 1800—more than 400 years after juries became a feature of the trial system? Did something happen around that time period that is the real explanation for the development of detailed rules of evidence? These scholars found that the advent of exclusionary evidence rules coincided with the rise of the adversary process. The power to control the development and presentation of trial evidence shifted from judges to lawyers, and with that shift the rules of evidence emerged (Gallanis, 1999).

Think of the implications: Judges were so worried about the power of lawyers to shape the fact presentation that they felt the need to screen evidence to filter out the excesses of adversarial presentations. Although expert witnesses did not start to become familiar sights in courts until another century passed, such witnesses have become one of the most worrisome parts of that worrisome process.

Here are some of the reasons why. In contrast to ordinary fact witnesses, experts exist in large numbers, the precise content of their testimony is subject to various kinds of influence by the attorney (because a witness whose function is to provide an opinion about the evidence has more degrees of freedom than a witness who only has observations to share), the relationship between the expert and the attorney appears more collaborative, and future opportunities might be contingent on how the expert performs on this occasion. Each of these reasons is now explored in more detail.

Witness Selection

Consider the selection of witnesses. The eyewitnesses to the events surrounding a traffic accident or a murder case are limited in number, are whoever they happen to be, and can testify only to what they recall seeing, hearing, or otherwise sensing. But the range of potential expert witnesses (from a wide array of fields) and the range of potential theories and opinions that could be brought to bear on the (possible) facts of a case are—to rely on a cliché and an overstatement—limited only by the imagination of the attorney.

To give an example: A lawyer acquaintance from the Midwest once phoned one of the authors and said that he had a case and a theory of what caused what happened. But, he said, he had asked every psychologist and psychiatrist he knew and none of them would testify in support of such an idea. The attorney was wondering if I (the author he called) could think of anyone who might. This attorney was in search mode. He was testing the population of experts. What if he found one who did subscribe to a theory that the attorney found useful, and offered that expert to a court? This ability to create a desired spin on evidence can be achieved only with expert witnesses, not with fact witnesses. Moreover, the court might never learn of the 100 experts who had been contacted and who thought no plausible support for the lawyer's theory was available. The result can be an impression of balance where reality consists of extreme skewness.

On the other hand, the court might learn that an expert is the 1 in 100 who subscribes to this particular cockamamie theory. (Not that it is better for the world if 99 of every 100 experts believe the cockamamie theory. But they at least have the illusory advantage of consensus.) There is nothing wrong with holding a minority view, so long as an expert knows that is what it is, has evaluated it carefully and with a clear head, and is prepared to defend it with good science.

Thus, from the earliest moments of the use of expert witnesses, they provide an opportunity for attorneys to create impressions of the case facts that might not fairly and accurately reflect the state of knowledge on a topic.

Influence Over the Formation of Testimony

Advocates can influence the evidence that develops in a case in a variety of ways. They are expected (indeed, professionally and ethically obligated) to conduct a biased search for facts. Their job is to build the best case they can for their client, not to find facts helpful to the other side. The same job description does not apply to the expert witness. But advocates can draw unwitting experts into that task.

As lawyers work their way through several experts in their hunt for the best one, they learn which case facts lead to helpful conclusions and which facts lead to unhelpful conclusions. They can dismiss experts who were consulted early in the case development process, and those hired later can be given selected information on which to form expert opinions. In this way, the experts finally selected for trial can be insulated from contrary information when they form their opinions. These are sometimes known as "clean" versus "dirty" experts. Not only is the expert led to reach a more favorable conclusion than the facts might support, but the unwitting expert might not learn of that incomplete information until the time comes to be cross-examined by the other side. (Q: In reaching your opinion that Mr. Smith would make a fine custodial parent, did you take into account the fact that 6 months ago he was convicted of torturing small animals?)

In contrast to the shielding of experts from information that might lead them in the "wrong" direction, they also can be exposed to information that will lure them in the "correct" direction. This sort of information can come from what the lawyer teaches the expert about a case, from clients, from investigators, or from other experts. Some commentators have elaborated on the problem of observer effects and suggestion, and even suggested that the courts would acquire better opinions by requiring that expert opinions be reached in a blind or double-blind fashion (Risinger, Saks, Rosenthal, & Thompson, 2002).

Quasi-Collaborative Relationship

Sometimes, in preparing for trial, lawyers negotiate with experts over just how far the expert is prepared to go in the lawyer's favored direction, or what language the expert will use to express the point (e.g., the history of prosecutors negotiating with forensic scientists to find the most incriminating sorts of conclusions tolerable to their expert witness; Saks, 1998). In doing so, attorneys are acting in their directorial role of the drama that will be the trial (or the negotiated settlement).

However, such discussions can make it appear to experts that they are part of the prosecution or defense or plaintiff team, and that as a team member their job is to work together to help the team achieve its goals. This, of course, is contrary to the official role of the witness, which is to help the court achieve its goals. Discussions with experts can of course be legitimate provided they do not put words into the experts' mouths. So it is critical that experts should have developed their conclusions as fully as possible before presenting them to the attorney. Having done so serves to inoculate the experts, at least partially, against undue influence.

Experts are too often in an impossible position—needing to know information the lawyer is not sharing with them, being exposed to information it would be better for them to remain blind to. One of the best settings in which the problems of insufficient and biasing information could be tamed would be in an organization, where some persons can undertake to screen the evidence in an optimal way (optimal for getting at the truth) and then manage the flow of information to the experts. Risinger et al. (2002) recommended this sort of regime for crime laboratories.

In these and in other ways, experts can be seduced into a role that is inappropriate and risky—for the attorneys and parties as well as for the experts. To avoid being a pawn of information manipulation or of the experts' own overenthusiasm, experts need to establish a professional working relationship with the litigation team, and to recognize that they are not a member of that team. Experts need to have their own professional and justifiable notion of what is needed to do the job properly, and to do their best to perform that job. Appelbaum (1987) called for the expert to be appropriately viewed as a consultant to the legal team of advocates. Specifically, "the attitude to be conveyed is, 'I am here to be of help by sharing my expertise with you, but I cannot go beyond the bounds of that expertise, even if doing so might be useful to your case'" (p. 22).

Future Contingencies

People can, of course, also be influenced by incentives and contingencies. Experts who hope to be asked to serve in a similar capacity in the future, called either by the same attorney or others in the community with parallel needs (whether those are prosecutors or defense counsel, personal injury plaintiffs or defense, etc.), might be tempted to be more helpful than they have any right to be. This problem might seem most obvious in the case of freelance experts for whom serving as an expert witness is their primary source of income. But other repeat players, such as crime laboratory personnel on fixed salaries, might worry about their futures within their organizations—their raises, promotions, vacation schedules, or the regard in which they are held by colleagues and clients.

The influences just discussed can have consequences for the behavior of experts. One temptation for unwitting experts is to try to be excessively helpful. Experts who by whatever means are seduced into thinking that their role is to help bring about the outcome sought by the side that has engaged them are not only at risk of being embarrassed by the cross-examiner or the court, but are a threat to the integrity of the trial fact-finding process.

Such biases can lead to opinions that are shaded to artificially favor their side or to be less forthcoming with information that will assist the other side. In DNA exoneration cases, expert witnesses (in particular forensic scientists) account for more fabrications and seriously misleading exaggerations than any other type of witnesses—more lies than jailhouse snitches (Saks & Koehler, 2005). According to Moenssens (1993): "All [forensic science] experts are tempted, many times in their careers, to report positive results when their inquiries come up inconclusive, or indeed to report a negative result as positive" (p. 17).

In West Virginia, the head serologist of the State Police crime laboratory, Fred Zain, falsified test results in as many as 134 cases in one decade. Defendants, later exonerated, were sent to prison for long terms based on Zain's testimony. A judicial inquiry concluded that "as a matter of law, any testimonial or documentary evidence offered by Zain at any time in any criminal prosecution should be deemed invalid, unreliable, and inadmissible" (cited in Giannelli, 1997, p. 442). In another example, Texas pathologist Ralph Erdmann was convicted of faking autopsies. For more than a decade, Erdmann worked closely with prosecutors and police, "shad[ing] things to follow along with the police theory of a case." The special prosecutor remarked, "If the prosecution theory was that death was caused by a Martian death ray, then that was what Dr. Erdmann reported." Erdmann consistently testified that he performed over 400 autopsies a year. Cynical law enforcement officers referred to his practice as "drive-by autopsy" (cited in Giannelli, 1997, p. 451).

Other findings suggest that serious expert misbehavior is not limited to a few state laboratories. An investigation by the Office of the Inspector General of the U.S. Department of Justice (1997) found that it was not unusual in at least some sections of the FBI's national crime laboratory for forensic science experts to fudge their results in order to make them better fit the prosecutor's theory of the case and other facts found in the investigation of the case, rather than to straightforwardly do their scientific work and report it.

No one knows how common such dishonest expertise is. But it seems safe to say that it is far too common. And it almost certainly is far more frequent in criminal cases, where the adversarial process is not as effective, so fraud of this kind is less likely to be discovered and exposed.

By contrast, consider this incident from the world of civil litigation. An attorney representing a large pharmaceutical company was contemplating a lawsuit against a competing company for falsely asserting that a product made by the latter company was as effective as a product made by the attorney's client company. The attorney contacted one of the authors to ask a statistical question. The prospective defendant said that it had conducted three studies comparing the efficacy of the two medications, and the studies revealed no significant differences. The attorney's own experts reviewed those studies and concluded that their small sample sizes made it unlikely that real differences could be detected (perhaps a deliberate research strategy by the defendant corporation). The plaintiff's experts carried out a meta-analysis combining the three studies and found a statistically significant difference favoring the plaintiff. The attorney called his psychologist acquaintance to ask if meta-analysis was a recognized statistical procedure appropriate for a situation of this kind. Note, first, that in this potential litigation the (probable) chicanery of one company was scrutinized and detected by attorneys for the other company. That is far more common in civil cases than in criminal cases. Second, note that the attorney was checking up on his own experts, out of fear, he explained, that they might be overly eager to produce findings that would please their client. This incident illustrates an attorney who recognizes that knowing the whole truth will help him to win his case, and is suspicious that some experts are too eager to provide the evidence they think their client wants to hear.

Expert witnesses need to understand that the essence of their role is to educate, not to advocate, not—odd as it may sound—to endeavor to help the side employing the expert to prevail. The job of experts is to teach what they can about their field, or to apply their field's knowledge to the case, and then step down, without concern for what the court ends up deciding. Experts who argue or insist that the judge or jury must accept the correctness of their assertions and reject the contrary position likely are making themselves less persuasive. This is not easy, because we are all human, curious, ego involved, and affiliative.

Expert witnesses are placed in a role conflict, required to serve too many masters with competing expectations. The side calling the expert wants the expert's help in winning the case. The court (which is the audience to whom the expert owes the highest duty) wants the expert to inform, educate, and help the fact finder to reach its correct conclusion. The expert's professional field wants the expert to adhere to the field's substantive knowledge and to its ethical code. The other side has no choice but to adopt the view that the experts called by its adversary are (at best) mistaken and (at worst) incompetent liars. And it is their responsibility to try to demonstrate those failings to the judge or jury.

As we earlier noted, expert witnesses were not always selected, briefed, nurtured, and presented by the adversaries in a case. Before the rise of the adversary process in Anglo-American courts, the judges had primary responsibility for obtaining experts and their expertise as it applied to the case. That was a far more comfortable position for experts, and it led to much more trust in them by the judges who worked with them. The difference between court-appointed experts and adversary-selected experts is perhaps most easily illustrated by a study in which researchers surveyed judges about their experiences with court-appointed experts (which is permitted by Federal Rule of Evidence 706, but rarely used by judges).

Cecil and Willging (1993) found that judges usually adored the experts who became their court-appointed witnesses. These could be the very same people who might come before the court as an expert called by a party, but in the court-appointed role the judges had far more confidence in them. This is how it must have been before the late 18th century. The expert's role is far less conflicted, if indeed there is any conflict at all. The expert is called by the judge and paid by the judge. Loyalty to the court is not just formal (as it is now), loyalty to the court is the social-psychological reality of the situation. Faithfulness to the expert's field is entirely compatible with loyalty to the court. And, though attorneys for one or both sides might distrust the court's expert, they are hesitant to attack too vigorously, lest they alienate the judge, because the expert is identified with the judge.

One further point needs to be made. Expert witnesses are in general not highly thought of by judges, and often not by juries either. An additional burden is therefore placed on the expert, who is not only subject to the conflicts discussed earlier but tends to be viewed with some degree of suspicion by the very people that the attorney wants to impress. This problem was well illustrated in the results of a study by Kassin, Williams, and Saunders (1990) entitled "Dirty Tricks of Cross-Examination." The purpose of the study was to demonstrate how the cross-examining attorney can affect the credibility of the witness in the jury's mind. Kassin et al.'s research was essentially a study of the use of innuendo. Two kinds of witnesses were studied: a victim and an expert for the defense. Six different versions of a transcript of a rape trial were prepared: Three involved the victim witness and three involved an expert for the defense. College student judges read one of the six versions. In each version, the cross-examining attorney asked the witness a question that implied something negative about the reputation of the witness. In other words, the attorney smeared the witness.

For example, the victim witness was asked, "Isn't it true that you have accused men of rape before?" The expert witness was asked, "Isn't it true that your work is poorly regarded by your colleagues?" Three kinds of responses were offered: denial that the innuendo was true, admission that the innuendo was true, or an objection from the defense attorney. There were also control groups in which there were no smears. Then the college student judges rated the credibility of the witness. The study found that, compared with no-smear control groups, the credibility of the victim witness was not affected by the smear. But the credibility of the expert witness was diminished in all three conditions. Kassin et al. (1990)

concluded that "from a practical standpoint, this study suggests that the use of presumptuous questions is a dirty trick that can be used to distort jurors' evaluations of a witness's credibility" (p. 382). Worse, cross-examiners are known to regularly employ such tactics (e.g., Underwood & Fortune, 1988), although they must believe that evidence exists to support the smear.

AVOIDING PITFALLS

The overarching thought that expert witnesses should bear in mind as they approach the task of serving as an expert witness is that they will be scrutinized like they have never been scrutinized before. If the attorneys conducting the preparation, depositions, and direct and cross-examinations are knowledgeable, competent, and well prepared, experts should feel as though they are back in graduate school, undergoing their oral comprehensive examination or dissertation defense at the hands of someone who seeks to understand the concepts of the field and the findings and conclusions of the witness—or to expose them as unsound or even fraudulent.

This is not to say that the attorneys on the offering and the opposing sides are likely to conduct their examinations in this way. Often they will not be knowledgeable or especially well prepared for the close examination of a scientific expert witness, especially on the criminal side of the courthouse. But witnesses must assume they will be and prepare as if they will be. Anything less is to expose oneself to potential expert witness disaster. But witnesses must also be prepared for examinations by attorneys who—either because of their own lack of preparation or because it is their considered tactic—will try to undermine them more with sophistry than with substance. To respond to such tactics, witnesses must not only be prepared with substantive answers but also with a manner of responding that will bring the focus back to the substance (see Brodsky, 1991, 1999, for many ideas on how to do this). In other words, witnesses might be asked brilliant questions or stupid questions. Even if the lawyers think that all that matters is winning, and aim to accomplish that in any manner not prohibited to them, it remains the experts' job to inform, however difficult that task is made.

Before examining specific topics and issues, it is worth spending some time on a general issue whose appreciation is critical to the comfort and sophistication of the expert witness in psychology. We are referring to the fact that the domain of psychology (and other sciences) differs massively and in fundamental ways from the domain of law. It is no exaggeration to say that psychologists who find themselves on the witness stand for the first time without an understanding of this fact can become confused and dysfunctional, often leading to strong anxiety or anger. They have been invited onto the turf of the law, to play by the rules of the law—rules that are completely different from and sometimes diametrically opposite to, those of psychological science. Here we mention just three of these fundamental differences. A number of authors have addressed this area (e.g., Haney, 1980; Melton, Petrila, Poythress, & Slobogin, 1997; Ogloff & Finkelman, 1999), and their work can be consulted for further information.

The first of the differences involves the nature of legal knowledge versus psychological knowledge, the building blocks of knowledge, the nature of a fact. In psychology, knowledge is built from empirical findings. These empirical findings lead to the discovery of consistencies, and then to general principles. This procedure is the same for all sciences. For legal knowledge, the building blocks are not empirical findings at all, but statutes and appellate case decisions, pronouncements by people with the authority to say what the law is and what it is not. These statutes and judicial opinions ultimately are (or should be) consistent with the highest authority of all, the U.S. Constitution. In other words, the law is what those in authority say it is (provided that they can say it with sufficient persuasiveness not to cause a revolt—legal, political, or armed).

The second fundamental area of difference is in procedures for arriving at the truth in individual cases, the process of fact finding. Lawyers use the adversarial method, whereas scientists use the empirical method (and, whenever possible, the experimental method). In the empirical method, psychologists employ structured methodologies for designing the process of data collection. They then apply statistical procedures that are especially developed for the purpose of fair and unbiased consideration of all aspects of the data, and they weigh as many explanations as possible for the observed findings. This entire procedure is designed to minimize the contribution of personal biases and to maximize the contribution of the data to the conclusions reached.

In the adversarial method, lawyers represent the interests of one side to a dispute and therefore adopt a point of view in advance of knowing all the facts. Then they zealously advocate for that point of view, selecting and assembling facts in whatever way will advance their client's position. They are free to ignore facts that do not fit, and rules limit the availability of some such facts to the other side. (Public prosecutors are supposed to be more attentive to the full array of evidence and to share with the defense what is exculpatory, but they have a hard time shedding the traditional mantle of advocacy.) The key to finding the truth is vigorous debate and argument, during which the truth is believed to gradually unfold. The job of trial lawyers is to advance their client's interests by all legal means, and their failure to do so can constitute malpractice.

The adversarial process often causes problems for experts on the witness stand. The lawyers who have retained the experts will want the experts to state, or overstate, their findings in a crisp, black-and-white manner so that they unequivocally support the case (or, at the least, to try to ignore findings that are not favorable to the case). Now, the experts have sworn to tell the truth, "the whole truth." But the experts are still not at liberty to divulge anything that they are not asked about. So the jury may get a biased version of the experts' findings. Of course, it is then the job of the opposing attorney to expose the unfavorable findings.

Finally, the language and concepts of law often have no counterpart in psychology. This is particularly troublesome when psychologists are asked to answer questions framed in legal terminology, for example, whether the defendant was insane at the time of the offense. *Insane* is a legal concept, not a psychological one, and it has no direct equivalent in psychology. And sometimes the legal definition and psychological definition of a concept are in conflict. An example is "the best interests of the child." The best interests of the child are defined by state statutes. However, empirical research findings as to what are indeed the child's best interests are not entirely consistent with the definitions given in the statutes (e.g., Krauss & Sales, 2000). And studies of what psychologist custody evaluators actually do when assessing the extent to which each parent is likely to meet the child's best interests show still a different conception of best interests (Ackerman & Ackerman, 1997).

Based on all of the foregoing discussion, the following is a list of areas of preparation and understanding that are necessary for a witness to be ready to enter the strange world of litigation:

1. Understand the fundamental differences between the domains of psychology and law. And deal with your likely ambivalence about the use of the adversarial method to arrive at the facts of the case. Interestingly, a version of the adversarial process does occur in science, through debate in scientific journals. Proponents of different theories or different schools of thought about the inferences to be drawn from data engage in similarly adversarial debate, though they feel more of an obligation to account for all of the evidence one way or another, and will be more persuasive to the extent that

they do so successfully. Actually, the same is true of litigators: Dealing ineffectively with contrary evidence undermines one's case. Nevertheless, the goals and trial processes of litigation place advocacy at the center of the truth-finding process.

2. Be as knowledgeable as possible about the aspects of your field that are relevant to the case. Especially in the post-Daubert (*Daubert v. Merrell Dow Pharmaceuticals, Inc.*, 1993) era, the extent of your field's scientific or empirical foundation can become an issue, not only your own qualifications (Dixon & Gill, 2002; Krafka, Dunn, Johnson, Cecil, & Miletich, 2002). In response to these evolving standards, Hom and Denney (2002) recently published a book on the use of several specialized psychological tests to detect response bias in neuropsychological assessment. This volume systematically evaluates each of the tests according to the specific Daubert criteria for admissibility. More literature of this type can be expected, in various areas of psychology, and the expert needs to become familiar with it.
3. Have adequate knowledge of the law relevant to the issues you are testifying about. Unfortunately, your major tutor is the lawyer who is requesting your services, a person whose role is to be an advocate for a position. But introductory textbooks in psychology and law can provide some of the basics, and lawyers should be willing to give you a copy of the relevant statutes or cases. Perhaps most useful for issues related to mental health is the American Psychological Association's series of publications entitled Law and Mental Health Professionals, which systematically document the law relevant to psychology and mental health for a given state. This series is now available for 25 states, with some volumes in their second edition.
4. Learn everything there is to know about the relevant facts of the specific case. It is obvious that the more you know about the situation, the more accurate your evaluation can be. You can and should speak directly with informants who can provide additional parts of the picture. But bear in mind that some of these informants will be biased in favor of the client (or against the client), and so a sampling of sources and appropriate skepticism are needed.
5. Be thorough in your examination of the client. There are two aspects to this point. First, the ideal forensic examination covers everything of possible relevance, regardless of time or cost. This is unrealistic, of course, because there will always be limits on time and cost. But you are going to have to take an examination on the

examination! The lawyer will help by gathering relevant data, such as medical records (office and hospital), police reports present and past, school records, and so on, by subpoena if necessary. And, if relevant to the case, interviewing family members, friends, neighbors, and others often is helpful. This can often be done rapidly by telephone and can yield information not available by other means. In summary, we are referring to the obvious advantages of multimodal assessment (Lanyon & Goodstein, 1997; Ney, 1979). Another advantage of casting the broadest possible net within the bounds of relevance is the likelihood of finding information that you need to know but for one reason or another has not been made available to you.

There was an old tradition in psychological assessment that championed the use of blind testing, that is, the desirability of administering and interpreting a test such as the Rorschach without knowing anything else about the client. The advantage was said to be the ability to avoid any type of bias in the interpretation, based on the belief that the client's responses had an absolute meaning independent of outside influences. Although it remains important to approach the assessment task without having acquired expectations about the client that can influence the examiner (and through the examiner, the client), it is now well known that test responses are subject to a myriad of influences, so it is important to understand what these influences are and to take careful account of them both in interpreting individual tests and in integrating the data from all sources.

An interesting and potentially productive approach might be to have two psychologists work together on a case, with one being aware of all the background information about the client, but filtering any information that is unnecessary to and might bias the examination of the other psychologist. After the examination by the second psychologist, the two would then combine and integrate their findings, resulting in a perspective that is able to utilize the psychological test data both in a pure sense and also as viewed in the full light of the client's background.

6. Educate the attorney who will be calling you to the stand. This process begins with the first contact with any attorney who is interested in purchasing your services. It is often the case that the attorney does not have an accurate picture of what services are most relevant to the client's condition (and that might also best serve the client's interests), or even what services are available.

For example, an attorney with a client who was depressed after being physically injured in an automobile accident was surprised to learn that some of the symptoms strongly suggested the possibility of brain injury, and that the psychologist could utilize a comprehensive test battery to determine whether the client's functioning in areas related to head injury was impaired when compared to relevant norms. After providing the lawyer with the necessary information, the expert should negotiate which specific services will be provided and what the costs will be.

A second aspect of the educational process takes place after the evaluation has been completed and the psychologist has determined what the findings are. It is very important to have engaged in this step, and to be comfortable with the findings, before sharing the findings with the lawyer. The first role of the expert is as a finder of facts for the legal team and the second is as a consultant to the team (Appelbaum, 1987). The expert educates the team about the meaning of the findings, and helps in the process of integrating them into the overall effort.

7. Prepare yourself for direct examination with the attorney who is calling you. If you have structured your overall role as an extended professional-to-professional consultation, the stage should be set for this step. Basically, what the attorney needs to know is what you have to say that will help the case, and how to elicit it from you in a way that best advances the client's case. Because you should already know what the attorney is aiming for, you will also know the extent to which your data support it. What you, the expert, need to do is to share this information without losing sight of the fact that your findings, all of your findings, are to be available to the court if either side of a case, or the judge, asks about them. This is not an easy balancing act. Occasionally an attorney will try to extend the expert on the witness stand, that is, try to get the expert to go a bit further than they have agreed is supported by the data. This can throw the expert off balance, but you should be ready for it. Sometimes attorneys do this out of the general pressure of the occasion or because of less-than-perfect preparation by the attorney.
8. Prepare yourself for cross-examination with the help of the attorney who is calling you. Many experts fear the cross-examination. But preparing for it is straightforward and pays big dividends in greater comfort on the witness stand. The attorney knows, or

should know, what you are likely to be asked; and you as the expert should know about any factual weaknesses or limitations in your presentation. You should also remember that in nearly all routine cases and jurisdictions, the expert knows substantially more than the cross-examining attorney. On the other hand, there is considerable literature available to assist attorneys in preparing the cross-examination, and if you have testified several times in similar circumstances there may be specific information in their files about you. Just keep in mind the one member of your dissertation committee who asked the most difficult questions. You did fine then because you were well prepared, and you can do well again.

We have just addressed the substance of the cross-examination. We should also address the style. An important task of the cross-examining attorney is to make you appear less than convincing, to knock you off balance, to diminish your credibility. There are many, many ways of doing this that are not immediately obvious to a jury. Think of the most annoying people you know, who are always trying to get a rise out of you, to put you down. And now think of how you have learned to deal with them: politely and with dignity. Those skills will work for you here too. As mentioned earlier, the volumes by Brodsky (1991, 1999) are helpful in this regard.

After all of that, it may be that cross-examination of expert witnesses has little impact on the effectiveness of their direct testimony, at least on some topics and under some circumstances. Diamond, Casper, Heiert, and Marshall (1996) conducted an experiment in which a psychiatrist gave direct testimony diagnosing and predicting the future dangerousness of a defendant. The psychiatrist's testimony ought to have been quite vulnerable, because it was based on a review of prison and court records containing little psychiatric content, he had not examined the defendant, and the asserted accuracy of predictions greatly exceeded what was possible for his methods. Nevertheless, even an experimental condition involving "strong" cross-examination failed to reduce the initial impact of the direct testimony. In that condition the cross-examining attorney brought out that the witness usually testified for the government, that the expert's prediction of future dangerousness was inconsistent with research on the subject (which showed much higher error rates), that the expert did not employ standard methods for diagnosing future dangerousness, and that the expert had never published his findings in professional journals.

Whether cross-examination incinerates the witness or has no effect at all, prepare yourself for it anyway.

9. Understand your own motives. This point was well made by Anderten et al. (1980). It is well established that competent psychotherapists should have come to terms with their reasons for choosing their profession, and in doing so they will have learned which kinds of clients they are comfortable working with, which they are not, and why. Other kinds of psychologists will also learn in short order which kinds of cases and clients they are (or are not) comfortable working with. Because of the high degree of stress and conflict inherent in the task of an expert witness, this principle applies even more strongly in that setting.

   As an example, individuals whose motivation for testifying on behalf of abused children is fueled by their own childhood abuse might well have difficulty remaining objective and be subject to dysfunctional anger or anxiety on the witness stand. And strong but unrecognized needs to be impressive and admired might interfere with an expert's dispassionate presentation of the facts. This is not to say that such persons should avoid expert witness work. But they should be thoroughly aware of the possibility that their needs could interfere with their effectiveness, and come to terms with themselves on any such issues.

10. Understand that you will be an object of manipulation by both sides. What you can do about this is limited. You are a part of a process over which you have limited control. And that is as it should be, because the case is not about the expert witness (it is about the parties and the preferences of society expressed through the law), the expert witness does not have primary or ultimate responsibility for marshalling the facts (the lawyers do), and the expert witness is not the decision maker in the case (the judge or jury are). So keep your ego in check, thicken your skin, and do not take what happens in court personally.

CONCLUSION

In this chapter we have tried to illuminate the role of the expert witness in modern American trials, which we argue has come to be fundamentally contradictory and paradoxical, and filled with mixed messages and structures that work at cross-purposes. We briefly describe the historical evolution of the trial process that has led to the present difficult state. In addition to alerting readers to issues expert witnesses need to consider, we suggest some partial solutions and point readers to other literature that explores various aspects of these problems.

In closing, we note that psychologists who serve as expert witnesses are among the more visible representatives of our field to the public, and are viewed as having a significant role in the public legal process. For this reason, among others, it is important that psychologists who undertake this work be among the best qualified, skilled, and mature members of the profession. The importance of offering to the law and to the public the best that psychology can provide also dictates that psychologists should take seriously the need for careful personal and professional preparation for expert witness work.

REFERENCES

Ackerman, M. J., & Ackerman, M. C. (1997). Custody evaluation practices: A survey of experienced professionals (revisited). *Professional Psychology: Research and Practice*, *28*, 137–145.

American Academy of Psychiatry and the Law. (2005). *Ethical guidelines for the practice of forensic psychiatry*. Retrieved May 10, 2006, from http://www.aapl.org/ethics.htm

American Psychology-Law Society, Committee on Ethical Guidelines for Forensic Psychologists. (1991). Specialty guidelines for forensic psychologists. *Law and Human Behavior*, *15*, 655–665.

Anderten, P., Staulcup, V., & Grisso, T. (1980). On being ethical in legal places. *Professional Psychology*, *11*, 764–773.

Appelbaum, P. S. (1987). In the wake of *Ake*: The ethics of expert testimony in an advocate's world. *Bulletin of the American Academy of Psychiatry and the Law*, *15*, 15–25.

Brodsky, S. L. (1991). *Testifying in court: Guidelines and maxims for the expert witness*. Washington, DC: American Psychological Association.

Brodsky, S. L. (1999). *The expert expert witness: More maxims and guidelines for testifying in court*. Washington, DC: American Psychological Association.

Cecil, J., & Willging, T. (1993). *Court-appointed experts: Defining the role of experts appointed under Federal Rule of Evidence 706*. Washington, DC: Federal Judicial Center.

Daubert v. Merrell Dow Pharmaceuticals, Inc., 509 U.S. 579 (1993).

Diamond, S. S., Casper, J. D., Heiert, C. L. & Marshall, A. (1996). Juror reactions to attorneys at trial. *Criminal Law & Criminology*, *87*, 17–47.

Dixon, L., & Gill, B. (2002). Changes in the standards for admitting expert evidence in federal civil cases since the *Daubert* decision. *Psychology, Public Policy, and Law*, *8*, 251–308.

Gallanis, T. P. (1999). The rise of modern evidence law. *Iowa Law Review*, *84*, 499–551.

Giannelli, P. C. (1997). The abuse of scientific evidence in criminal cases: The need for independent crime laboratories. *Virginia Journal of Social Policy and the Law*, *4*, 439–478.

Haddad, F. E. (1979). Cross-examination of the medical expert. *American Journal of Trial Advocacy*, *3*, 239–246.

Haney, C. (1980). Psychology and legal change: On the limits of factual jurisprudence. *Law and Human Behavior*, *4*, 147–200.

Hom, J., & Denney, R. L. (Eds.). (2002). *Detection of response bias in forensic neuropsychology*. New York: Haworth Press.

Kassin, S. M., Williams, L. N., & Saunders, C. L. (1990). Dirty tricks of cross-examination. *Law and Human Behavior*, *14*, 373–384.

Krafka, C., Dunn, M. A., Johnson, M. T., Cecil, J. S., & Miletich, D. (2002). Judge and attorney experiences, practices, and concerns regarding expert testimony in federal civil trials. *Psychology, Public Policy, and Law*, *8*, 309–332.

Krauss, D. A., & Sales, B. D. (2000). Legal standards, expertise, and experts in the resolution of contested child custody cases. *Psychology, Public Policy, and Law*, *6*, 843–879.

Lanyon, R. I., & Goodstein, L. D. (1997). *Personality assessment* (3rd ed.). New York: Wiley.

Melton, G. B., Petrila, J., Poythress, N., & Slobogin, C. (1997). *Psychological evaluations for the courts* (2nd ed.). New York: Guilford Press.

Moenssens, A. A. (1993). Novel scientific evidence in civil and criminal cases: Some words of caution. *Journal of Criminal Law and Criminology*, *84*, 1–21.

Ney, W. R. (1979). *Multimodal clinical assessment*. New York: Gardner.

Office of the Inspector General, U.S. Department of Justice. (1997). *The FBI laboratory: An investigation into laboratory practices and alleged misconduct in explosives-related and other cases*. Washington, DC: Author.

Ogloff, J. R. P. (1999). Ethical and legal contours of forensic psychology. In R. Roesch, S. D. Hart, & J. R. P. Ogloff (Eds.), *Psychology and law: The state of the discipline* (pp. 403–422). New York: Kluwer Academic/Plenum.

Ogloff, J. R. P., & Finkelman, D. (1999). Psychology and law: An overview. In R. Roesch, S. D. Hart, & J. R. P. Ogloff (Eds.), *Psychology and law: The state of the discipline* (pp. 1–20). New York: Kluwer Academic/Plenum.

Risinger, D. M., Saks, M. J., Rosenthal, R., & Thompson, W. (2002). The *Daubert/Kumho* implications of observer effects in forensic science: Hidden problems of expectation and suggestion. *California Law Review*, *90*, 1–58.

Saks, M. J. (1990). Expert witnesses, non-expert witnesses, and non-witness experts. *Law and Human Behavior*, *14*, 291–313.

Saks, M. J. (1998). Merlin and Solomon: Lessons from the law's formative encounters with forensic identification science. *Hastings Law Journal*, *49*, 1069–1141.

Saks, M. J., & Koehler, J. J. (2005). The coming paradigm shift in forensic identification science. *Science*, *309*, 892–895.

Shuman, D. W., & Greenberg, S. A. (2003). The expert witness, the adversary system, and the voice of reason: Reconciling impartiality and advocacy. *Professional Psychology: Research and Practice*, *34*, 219–224.

Underwood, R. H., & Fortune, W. H. (1988). *Trial ethics*. Boston: Little, Brown.

Wrightsman, L. S., & Fulero, S. M. (2005). *Forensic psychology* (2nd ed.). Belmont, CA: Thompson/Wadsworth.

Author Index

A

B

G

H

Subject Index

C

D

About the Authors

Simon A. Cole is Assistant Professor of Criminology, Law, and Society at the University of California, Irvine. He specializes in the historical and sociological study of the interaction between science, technology, law, and criminal justice. Dr. Cole is the author of *Suspect Identities: A History of Fingerprinting and Criminal Identification* (Harvard University Press, 2001), which was awarded the 2003 Rachel Carson Prize by the Society for Social Studies of Science. Dr. Cole has spoken widely on the subjects of fingerprinting, scientific evidence, and science and the law, and he has consulted and testified as an expert witness on the validity of fingerprint evidence. He received his PhD in Science and Technology Studies from Cornell University.

Mark Costanzo is Professor of Psychology and codirector of the Center for Applied Psychological Research at Claremont McKenna College. He has published research on a variety of law-related topics including police interrogations and false confessions, jury decision making, sexual harassment, attorney argumentation, alternative dispute resolution, and the death penalty. He is author of *Psychology Applied to Law* (Wadsworth, 2004) and *Just Revenge: Costs and Consequences of the Death Penalty* (St. Martin's Press, 1997). Professor Costanzo has served as an expert witness and has appeared on national radio and television programs to discuss the applications of psychological science to the legal system. He serves on the editorial board of *Law and Human Behavior* and is co-organizer of the annual Claremont Symposium on Applied Psychology.

Norman J Finkel is Professor of Psychology at Georgetown University. He has published widely in the area of psychology and law, with a particular focus on how jurors' notions of "commonsense justice" (*Commonsense*

Justice: Jurors' Notions of the Law, Harvard University Press, 1995) and "commonsense fairness" (*Not fair! The Typology of Commonsense Unfairness*, American Psychological Association, 2001) may affect, nullify, or perfect black letter law. He recently published an edited volume (with Fathali Moghaddam), *The Psychology of Rights and Duties: Empirical Contributions and Normative Commentaries* (American Psychological Association, 2004), and has also authored *Insanity on Trial* (Plenum Press, 1988), and is coeditor of *Law and Public Policy: Psychology and the Social Sciences*, a book series published by the American Psychological Association. His new book (with W. Gerrod Parrott), *Emotions and Culpability: How the Law is at Odds with Psychology, Jurors, and Itself* (American Psychological Association), will appear in 2006.

Gwen Jenkins received her MA from York University in 2005, and is currently a doctoral candidate in the psychology program at York University. Her research interests intersect psychology and law, with a specific focus on juror and jury decisions in sexual assault trials. Her present area of research explores issues related to drug-facilitated sexual assault.

Daniel Krauss is Associate Professor in the Psychology and Legal Studies departments at Claremont McKenna College. Prior to joining the faculty, Dr. Krauss served as a clinical psychology intern at the Federal Bureau of Prisons and at the University of North Carolina Medical School-Chapel Hill, where he conducted insanity, competency, and treatment evaluations for federal defendants. Dr. Krauss also served as the Supreme Court Fellow to the U.S. Sentencing Commission for 2002–2003. He currently serves on the APA's Committee on Legal Issues (COLI), which recommends to the APA board of directors whether the organization should submit a scientifically based amicus brief in Supreme Court decisions. His research and clinical experience have focused on the intersection of law and psychology, with an emphasis on evidentiary standards of admissibility for expert testimony. Dr. Krauss is a licensed clinical psychologist in the state of California and a member of the American Bar Association, the American Psychological Association, the American Psychological Society, the Arizona Bar, and the U.S. Supreme Court Bar.

Richard I. Lanyon is Professor of Psychology at Arizona State University and a former director of the Clinical Psychology program. His prior appointments have included Chief Psychologist in the Massachusetts General Hospital Psychiatry Department and Associate Professor of Psychology at Harvard Medical School. His published works include books on the Minnesota Multiphasic Personality Inventory, personality and adjustment, behavior therapy, and three editions of a graduate-level textbook on personality assessment. His psychological tests include the Multidimensional Health Profile and the Psychological Screening Inventory. His research interests involve the intersection of psychological assessment and the law, especially in regard to the assessment of personal misrepresentation. He is a fellow of the American Psychological Association and a diplomate in Clinical Psychology and in Forensic Psychology.

Richard A. Leo is Associate Professor of Criminology, Law, and Society, and Psychology and Social Behavior at the University of California, Irvine. He has conducted extensive research and published numerous articles on police interrogation practices, Miranda requirements, false confessions, and miscarriages of justice. He is the recipient of the Ruth Shonle Cavan Young Scholar Award from the American Society of Criminology and the Saleem Shah Career Achievement Award from the American Psychological Association and the American Academy of Forensic Psychology. Since 1996, Dr. Leo has served as a consultant on more than 500 criminal and civil cases involving disputed interrogations and confessions and he has testified as an expert witness more than 100 times in state, federal, and military courts in 18 different states.

Joel D. Lieberman is Associate Professor and Chair of the Criminal Justice Department at the University of Nevada, Las Vegas. He received his PhD in Psychology from the University of Arizona in 1997. His work focuses on the application of social- psychological theories to criminal justice issues. His recent research has been in the areas of jury decision making, aggression, and intergroup conflict. More specifically, his research has focused on identifying social psychological factors that may lead jurors to rely on less reliable expert witness testimony, and to overutilize inadmissible evidence. He has also authored articles and a recent book on the topics of hate crimes, jury instructions, and scientific jury selection.

David A. Martindale is in private practice in New Jersey, offering forensic psychological consulting services to psychologists, attorneys, and psychology licensing boards. He holds a diplomate in forensic psychology from the American Board of Professional Psychology. His clinical work with families led him to develop an interest in the resolution of custody disputes and between 1986 and 2000 he performed evaluations of comparative custodial suitability for the courts in New York. He is an Adjunct Clinical Professor of Psychiatry at the State University of New York at Stony Brook and an Adjunct Clinical Supervisor in the Graduate Program in Psychology at the John Jay College of Criminal Justice of the City University of New York. He has published articles on cross-examining mental health experts in child custody litigation and (with Jonathan Gould) on the forensic model as applied to child custody evaluations. He regularly offers presentations to attorneys and to psychologists on custody-related topics.

Maureen O'Connor is Associate Professor and Chair of the Psychology Department at John Jay College of Criminal Justice and also has appointments on the faculty of the doctoral programs in Forensic Psychology, Social-Personality Psychology, and Criminal Justice at the Graduate Center of the City University of New York. She received her JD and her PhD in law, psychology, and policy, from the University of Arizona. Her research interests are in the intersection of psychology, gender, and law. Current projects include work on stalking and sexual concepts. She is also interested in the use of scientific information and expert testimony in the legal system. Prior to attending graduate school, Dr. O'Connor worked for the National Institute of Justice and served as Research Director of President Reagan's Task Force on Victims of Crime. After receiving her law degree, Dr. O'Connor served as law clerk to the Honorable Patricia M. Wald, then Chief Judge of the U.S. Court of Appeals for the D.C. Circuit. She is a member of the Bar in Arizona and Washington, DC.

Randy K. Otto is Associate Professor in the Department of Mental Health Law and Policy at the University of South Florida. He also serves as adjunct faculty at Stetson University College of Law, and in the Department of Psychology and the Department of Rehabilitation and Mental Health Counseling at the University of South Florida. Dr. Otto obtained an MA and PhD in clinical psychology from Florida State University, he completed a clinical psychology internship at the Medical University of South Carolina, and he was a postdoctoral fellow in the Department of Psychology and College of Law at the University of Nebraska-Lincoln, where he obtained a master's degree in legal studies. Dr. Otto's research, writing, and practice focuses on forensic psychological assessment. He has served as President of the American Academy of Forensic Psychology, the American Psychology-Law Society, and the American Board of Forensic Psychology. He currently serves on the editorial boards of a number of leading psychological assessment and forensic practice journals including *Assessment*, *Law and Human Behavior*, *Criminal Justice and Behavior*, *Behavioral Sciences and the Law*, and the *Journal of Child Custody*.

Kathy Pezdek is Professor of Psychology and Associate Dean at Claremont Graduate University, where she has served on the faculty and directed the PhD program in Applied Cognitive Psychology since 1981. Dr. Pezdek's extensive research has focused on the study of eyewitness memory. Her recent book, *The Recovered Memory/False Memory Debate* has played a critical role in defining the false memory issue among psychologists. She is a Fellow of the American Psychological Society, has served as the editor of the journal *Applied Cognitive Psychology*, and has been on the editorial boards of numerous other journals. Dr. Pezdek frequently testifies as an expert witness in the area of eyewitness identification. She received her PhD in 1975 from the University of Massachusetts, Amherst.

Before joining the College of Law faculty, Professor **Michael Saks** taught at Boston College, Georgetown University, and the University of Iowa, where he was the Edward F. Howrey Professor of Law. He has served as editor of *Law and Human Behavior*, and is coeditor of *Modern Scientific Evidence*. His research focuses on empirical studies of the legal system, especially decision making, the behavior of the litigation system, and the law's use of science. His work has earned several awards and has been cited in a number of judicial opinions, including several by the U.S. Supreme Court. He serves on the advisory boards of the Best Practices Institute of the National Center for State Courts and of the Center for Justice and Democracy.

Karen L. Salekin received her PhD in Clinical Psychology from the University of North Texas in 1997. She completed a postdoctoral fellowship in the Law-Psychiatry Program at the University of Massachusetts Medical Center. She has published journal articles and chapters on assessment in forensic evaluations, and on cognitive- behavioral interventions. Dr. Salekin is currently Assistant Professor at The University of Alabama, serving in the Psychology and the Law concentration within the Clinical Psychology program and conducts forensic evaluations for the courts.

Bruce D. Sales is Professor of Psychology, Sociology, Psychiatry, and Law at the University of Arizona, where he also directs its Psychology, Policy, and Law Program. Among his recent publications are the following books: *Criminal Profiling: Developing and Effective Science and Practice* (with S. Hick, in press), *Scientific Jury Selection* (with J. Lieberman, in press), *Experts in Court: Reconciling Law, Science, and Professional Knowledge* (with D. Shuman, 2005), *More Than the Law: Social and Behavioral Knowledge in Legal Decision-Making* (with P. English, 2005), *Family Mediation: Facts, Myths and Future Prospects* (with C. Beck, 2001), and *Treating Adult and Juvenile Offenders with Special Needs* (coedited with J. Ashford & W. Reid, 2001). Professor Sales, the first editor of the journals *Law and Human Behavior* and *Psychology, Public Policy, and Law,* is a fellow of the American Psychological Association and the American Psychological Society, an elected member of the American Law Institute, and twice served as President of the American Psychology-Law Society. He received the Award for Distinguished Contributions to Psychology and Law from the American Psychology-Law Society, the Award for Distinguished Professional Contributions to Public Service from the American Psychological Association, and an honorary Doctor of Science degree from the City University of New York for being the "founding father of forensic psychology as an academic discipline."

Regina A. Schuller is Professor of Psychology at York University. She completed her PhD at the University of Western Ontario. Prior to joining the faculty at York University she completed a postdoctoral fellowship in the Law and Social Sciences program at Northwestern University. She is currently Director of the Psychology Graduate Programme at York University. Her research interests intersect the areas of psychology, gender, and law. Much of her research focuses on jury decision-making processes, particularly in cases involving violence against women (e.g., battered women, sexual assault). She published an edited volume (with James Ogloff), *Introduction to Psychology and Law: Canadian Perspectives* (2001) and also serves on the editorial boards of *Law and Human Behavior* and Psychology, Pubic Policy, and Law.

Daniel Shuman is Professor of Law at Southern Methodist University School of Law, an Adjunct Professor of Psychiatry at the University of Texas, Southwestern Medical School, and an Adjunct Professor of Psychology at the University of North Texas. He is the author of *Psychiatric and Psychological Evidence* (1986; winner of the 1988 American Psychiatric Association Manfred S. Guttmacher Award and 2nd ed., 1994); *Justice and* *the Prosecution of Old Crimes: Balancing Legal, Psychological, and Moral Considerations* (2000; with McCall Smith); *Conducting Insanity Defense Evaluations* (2nd ed., 2000; with Rogers); *Law, Mental Health, and Mental Disorder* (with Sales, 1996); *Law and Mental Health Professionals: Texas* (1990; and 2nd ed., 1997); *Doing Legal Research: A Guide for Social Scientists and Mental Health Professionals* (1996; with Morris and Sales); and *The Psychotherapist Patient Privilege* (with Weiner, 1987). He has also authored more than 60 articles and book chapters. He is a member of the American Law Institute and former chair of the Association of American Law Schools sections on Law and Mental Disability, and Law and Medicine. Prior to joining the Faculty of the SMU School of Law he served as Assistant Attorney General for the State of Arizona and a legal services attorney in Tucson, Arizona.

William C. Thompson is Professor of Criminology, Law, and Society at the University of California, Irvine. He is also a member of the California Bar. He received a PhD in psychology from Stanford University and a JD from the University of California's Boalt Hall School of Law. His research and publications focus on the development and use of scientific evidence in the courtroom, particularly forensic DNA testing. His law practice has focused on novel and controversial applications of scientific and statistical evidence in criminal trials. He is Associate Director of the University of California, Irvine's Center for Psychology and Law.

For Product Safety Concerns and Information please contact our EU representative GPSR@taylorandfrancis.com
Taylor & Francis Verlag GmbH, Kaufingerstraße 24, 80331 München, Germany

www.ingramcontent.com/pod-product-compliance
Lightning Source LLC
LaVergne TN
LVHW011113300926
849160LV00008B/372

9780805856484